Plane-Strain Slip-Line Fields For Metal-Deformation Processes

A SOURCE BOOK AND BIBLIOGRAPHY

Other Pergamon Titles of Interest

CHRISTIAN: The Theory of Transformations in Metals, 2nd Ed., Part 1

EASTERLING: Mechanisms of Deformation and Fracture

HAASEN et al: Strength of Metals and Alloys (ICSMA 5), 3 Vols.

HEARN: Mechanics of Materials, 2 Vols.

HOPKINS & SEWELL: Mechanics of Solids

KRAGELSKY: Friction and Wear: Calculation Methods

MARSHALL & MARINGER: Dimensional Instability

MASUBUCHI: Analysis of Welded Structures

MILLER & SMITH: Mechanics of Materials (ICM 3), 3 Vols.

REID: Deformation Geometry for Materials Scientists

SMITH: Fracture Mechanics: Current Status, Future Prospects

SMITH: Internal Friction and Ultrasonic Attenuation in Solids

Pergamon Related Journals
Free specimen copy glady sent on request

ACTA METALLURGICA

ENGINEERING FRACTURE MECHANICS

FATIGUE OF ENGINEERING MATERIALS AND STRUCTURES

INTERNATIONAL JOURNAL OF MECHANICAL SCIENCES

JOURNAL OF PHYSICS AND CHEMISTRY OF SOLIDS

JOURNAL OF THE MECHANICS AND PHYSICS OF SOLIDS

MATERIALS RESEARCH BULLETIN

THE PHYSICS OF METALS AND METALLOGRAPHY
PROGRESS IN MATERIALS SCIENCE

SCRIPTA METALLURGICA

SOLID STATE COMMUNICATIONS

Plane-Strain Slip-Line Fields For Metal-Deformation Processes

A SOURCE BOOK AND BIBLIOGRAPHY

By

W. JOHNSON
University Engineering Department
Cambridge, England

R. SOWERBY
Department of Mechanical Engineering
McMaster University, Canada

and

R. D. VENTER
Department of Mechanical Engineering
University of Toronto, Canada

PERGAMON PRESS

OXFORD · NEW YORK · TORONTO · SYDNEY · PARIS · FRANKFURT

U.K.	Pergamon Press Ltd., Headington Hill Hall, Oxford OX3 0BW, England
U.S.A.	Pergamon Press Inc., Maxwell House, Fairview Park, Elmsford, New York 10523, U.S.A.
CANADA	Pergamon Press Canada Ltd., Suite 104, 150 Consumers Rd., Willowdale, Ontario M2J 1P9, Canada
AUSTRALIA	Pergamon Press (Aust.) Pty. Ltd., P.O. Box 544, Potts Point, N.S.W. 2011, Australia
FRANCE	Pergamon Press SARL, 24 rue des Ecoles, 75240 Paris, Cedex 05, France
FEDERAL REPUBLIC OF GERMANY	Pergamon Press GmbH, 6242 Kronberg-Taunus, Hammerweg 6, Federal Republic of Germany

First edition 1982

British Library Cataloguing in Publication Data

Johnson, W.
Plane strain slip line fields for metal
deformation processes.
1. Dislocations in metals
2. Deformations (Mechanics)
I. Title II. Sowerby, R.
III. Venter, R.
620.1'1233   TA418.4
ISBN 0-08-025452-7

Library of Congress Catalog Card no: 81-81220

In order to make this volume available as economically and as rapidly as possible the typescript has been reproduced in its original form. This method unfortunately has its typographical limitations but it is hoped that they in no way distract the reader.

Printed in Great Britain by A. Wheaton & Co. Ltd., Exeter

Preface

The last thirty years has seen the emergence, establishment and consolidation of a body of well-defined knowledge, the theory of metal plasticity. It has tended to be composed of two principal parts, one concerned with structural elements, the other with metal processing. Within the scope of the latter there has appeared a fairly well-defined set of techniques for analysing and predicting loads, pressures and deformations using what is known as Slip Line Field Theory (s.l.f.t.). The situations for which this field theory may be applied are ones in which there is either plane strain, plane stress or axial symmetry. It is applied to isotropic materials, anisotropic materials and to materials such as soils to which a Coulomb-type criterion belongs. However, for metals, the plane-strain category is the one which has been very intensively exploited and very successfully cultivated. It is in the subject of plane-strain metal deformation that s.l.f.t. has been extremely valuable, especially as a tool for students of engineering and solid mechanics in helping them to appreciate the mechanics of metal processing. Axial symmetry, though of enormous industrial importance and despite the fact that the computer can facilitate iterative numerical procedures for resolving problems, seems still to present theoretical difficulties which render it hard to develop solutions that can be of great practical use. The number of practical problems for which useful solutions have been given is small. This is not so for plane-strain, where there now exist solutions for very complex situations. It is, however, still a subject in which there is much scope for theoretical development, witness the matrix method described in Chapter 6 and its attendant references, and practical application, e.g. to explain various kinds of defects.

The authors, as research engineers, have for several years worked in this area, and as university teachers have been preoccupied with the understanding of the mechanics of industrial metal-forming operations and related design situations, with the aim of imparting an appreciation of the principles involved to their students. The number of papers in this area is now very large, and as many teachers of the mechanics of deformable solids are now lecturing this particular topic at advanced first degree and post-graduate-degree level it seemed very worthwhile to update the catalogue of contributions to the field which we first made eleven years ago. The present monograph comprises our previous one,† describes most of the advances in the field developed during the last decade and includes references to many new papers which give results for specific problems. A co-author in the previous monograph was Professor J. B. Haddow of the Mechanical Engineering Department at the University of Edmonton, Canada. On this occasion he felt unable to be associated with the book but he has, none-the-less, kindly raised no objection to the incorporation of any work used in the earlier publication. As before, our prime objective has been to provide teachers and researchers with basic material and a bibliography of papers on the theory and application of plane-strain slip fields to metal-working problems.

It remains, again, to repeat an apology and make an explanation. The references are predominantly to work in the English language. There is little reference to work in Russian, Polish, Japanese and Chinese, and for this we apologise. We are certainly conscious of the great amount of work now appearing in these languages, but as before it has proved to be beyond the resources of the authors to explore in depth what has been written in foreign-language journals on Plasticity. We can but hope that this survey of the work published in the English language will provoke similar summaries in the languages referred to.

In conclusion, we have endeavoured to be as comprehensive as possible in compiling English-language references, but it is too much to hope that we have found a very great fraction of all those which are in print. Where we have omitted references this is indeed due to over-sight, and if readers will therefore bring notice of oversights (or of their own published work) to the authors' attention we shall be very grateful.

ACKNOWLEDGMENT

We would like to thank Mrs S. Purlan for typing this text for press and Mr R. Purlan for attending to the setting of the figures.

---

† *Plane Strain Slip Line Fields: Theory and Bibliography*, published by Edward Arnold, 1970.

Contents

CONTENTS

CONTENTS

CHAPTER 1

Introduction

THE METAL-FORMING PROCESS IN HISTORY

The working of metals is at least as old as recorded history, although some of the processes for doing it are not. Coining, forging and hammering, drifting or making holes, cutting or parting or indenting are clearly among the oldest processes. In the Bible, Exodus xxxix, 3, we read: ". . . and they did beat the gold into thin plates and cut it into wires . . .". Rolling, swaging and drawing were known and well developed by A.D. 1500. Extrusion, metal machining, drawing sheet and tube, and section rolling depend predominantly on applying more energy than can be supplied by one person, and these processes were the results of nineteenth-century innovation. The twentieth century has seen the working of large or strong parts and the consequent need for large sources of energy. Machines have been built which simultaneously employ a variety of the more primitive processes, e.g. planetary and pendulum mills and the use of explosive energy. References 1 to 10 are useful sources of information on technology and machine and press innovations in mechanical engineering.

PLANE-STRAIN SLIP-LINE FIELDS: HISTORICAL NOTE

Slip lines appear to have first been studied when they became obvious in catastrophies associated with soil and the foundations of structures. The history of the subject need not be developed here but the earliest original theory in this field appears to have stemmed from work by Coulomb (1773),[11] followed by Rankine (1857)[12] and later Levy (1873).[13] Mohr,[14] especially, gave a slip theory of strength and pointed to the importance of slip surfaces in about 1914. Tresca[15] also had studied slip directions in his work on extrusion, reported about 1864.

Lüders lines in strained sheets and curved spiral lines emanating from the bore of an internally pressurized cylinder or shot lines from plate penetrated by shells have been noted for more than a century.

Descriptions of the historical development of some of this work will

be found by referring to an article by Sobotka[16] and to the article
in the *Encyclopaedic Dictionary of Physics*[17] by Freudenthal and
Geiringer, both of which recount the development in detail. We refer
below only to contributions which seem to have been the most influen-
tial for contemporary work.

Prandtl's[18] consideration of the indentation of a semi-infinite block
using a slip-line field was perhaps the first practical solution to
be given in 1921. Nadai[19] adapted this to considering the crushing
of blunt wedges in 1921 and Hencky[20] in 1923 stated the well-known
equations which now carry his name, though Kotter[21] in 1903 had given
them in a more general form. Geiringer[22] in 1930 seems to have first
clearly formulated the velocity equations. Many of the early attempts
at solutions to metal-forming problems considered only the stress
boundary conditions and failed to establish a kinematically acceptable velocity field. The book by van Iterson (1946),[23] which carries
many potential but incorrect solutions, has been a successful starting
point for many, while Sokolovskii's[24] Russian monograph of 1946
marked a great advancement in the whole subject, despite some few
errors which it carried. Books by Tomlenov,[25] Gubkin[26] and Unksov[27]
greatly contributed to the work, and Hill, Lee and Tupper and others
appear to have brought the subject very prominently to the fore,
especially when they succeeded in solving a number of very practical
problems and thereby showing the power of the technique. The book
by Hill,[28] and that by Prager and Hodge,[29] first presented systematic
accounts of slip-line theory and showed the engineering worth of the
approach. Prager's introduction of the hodograph - discernible in
Hill's unit diagram - or velocity-plane diagram in 1953 introduced
a vast and welcome simplification into the handling of slip-line
field solutions and removed, what were to many, conceptual difficulties.
(The use of the cycloid in the stress plane was a further but later
innovation of Prager.[30]) Many solutions and much useful discussion
of the subject was given by Lee, and a series of solutions presented
by A. P. Green in the early 1950s were notable achievements. In the
same period certain aspects of the theory which were imperfectly
understood, or where theoretical weaknesses were known to exist -
for example, that materials might be undergoing a negative rate of
working, or concerning questions of overloading - were removed.

Since the first printing of this monograph the principal advance in
s.l.f.t. has been the development of the matrix method especially
in respect of the solution of statically indeterminate problems.
This has been achieved mainly by methods devised by I. F. Collins;
the method rests on work by Hill and Ewing with some notable contributions by Dewhurst. The matrix method is now so important that we
considered it warranted a separate chapter in this monograph, see pp.
160-265. It would be invidious to select further the names of men
who have made distinctive contributions in the last fifteen years
but these will be clear from references scattered through the text.

The collection of slip-line solutions now available is large and they
have been steadily extended since the first edition of this book.
Fields analysed and problems understood have become more complex
especially because of the availability of the matrix method and
modern computers. The latter has raised the level of problem solving
by the use of slip-line fields to a new level of sophistication.
The formulation of a matrix solution itself for a given specific
circumstance followed by programming for the computer have tended to

make this theatre of research now more the province of the applied mathematician than the engineer.

PHYSICAL OBSERVATIONS

The primary objective in working metal is to secure a specific shape, and secondarily and occasionally it is to secure certain properties in the worked metal. How the sought shape is arrived at is often of subsidiary importance. However, a desire to know - curiosity - a search for the origin of certain product failures and defects as a result of certain forming processes, the wish to improve product quality and eventually the need to be able to predict the load on machines in order to assess probable design performances, are all stimuli for studying the details of metal flow. It thus transpires that at a low level of sophistication there are several categories of physical observation which have contributed substantially to the progress of research into metal deformation, and these deserve to be listed. They are:

(i)   Surface Coatings

When working hot steel, as say in hammering, the black oxide coating falls away in a manner which depends on the geometry of the tools and workpiece, and to some extent the flaking reflects the surface plastic deformation undergone by the workpiece.

Painting a part which is to be stressed with some material which is brittle when it is dry, such as whitewash or a varnish or Stress Coat, can be used to reveal critically stressed regions. Cracking of the whitewash is characteristic, and distinctive patterns will indicate regions of severe deformation. The use of coatings is of limited value because only (literally) superficial information is forthcoming and even this is crude.

(ii)   Surface Markings on the Metal

Of particular and outstanding value for work on slip-line fields is the use of Lüders bands (or stretcher-strain markings). The network of lines which appear on the surface of certain steels when the material undergoes yielding were first publicized by Lüders[31] in 1860. They were also studied in detail by Hartmann[32] and independently again by Chernov.[33] The lines on the surface of the material can also be made clear by etching with a weak solution of nitric acid.

Fry[34] perfected an etching technique (see also Chapter 5) for revealing what he termed strain markings on the surface of some steels. The technique, however, is not limited to surface markings; a deformed component can be cut along any appropriate section and the yielded zones revealed by the etching reagent. The etch patterns, which usually appear black against a grey background, are often similar in shape and size to slip-line field patterns proposed for accounting for the deformation mode, see Plates 1, 2 and 3. Certainly the characteristic Lüders bands and the etching technique of Fry were known long before slip-line-field theory as such was invented. However, these methods are now of great importance, both for suggesting the

form of theoretical slip-line-field patterns and for corroborating
those which have been proposed. Specific etching and ageing techniques are:

(a)   <u>Mild steel</u>

(i)   Annealed mild steel with a high nitrogen content, e.g.
0.021%, responds well to etching. After unloading, specimens
are "aged" for about 30 minutes at 250°C in an electric furnace and then air cooled. After sectioning, the new surface
is highly polished by grinding-down with emery papers to 00
or 000 grade. Etching is performed by immersing the specimen
in Fry's reagent, a mixture of 45 g of cupric chloride crystals,
180 ml hydrochloric acid and 100 ml of water for a few (say 3
or 4) minutes. After etching, a specimen is swilled with
concentrated hydrochloric acid or methyl alcohol to prevent
staining and then washed thoroughly with water, swilled in
alcohol and dried.

In practice, due to the expansion of plastically deformed zones
with increases in load, it is difficult to choose the appropriate point at which to cease increasing it in order to secure
the best result. Experience and practice are unavoidable.

(ii)   A highly polished, mirror-like surface when viewed optically at glancing incidence after being subjected to deformation will also reveal a deformation zone in form and size.

(b)   <u>Aluminium</u>

To reveal macroscopically the plastic regions in an aluminium
specimen, before loading, one procedure is to anneal it for
4 hours at 450°C in a muffle-type electric furnace and then
furnace cool. The specimen is then loaded and if, say, this
was already in two parts, it is separated and mechanically
polished by grinding-down with emery paper to 000 grade and
polishing on rotating pads impregnated with diamond; a final
polish uses 0.5 μm diamond powder. The newly polished surface
is macro-etched by immersing the specimen in a solution of
approximately HNO_3 : 30%; HC : 20%; H_2O : 50% and HF (hydro-
fluoric acid) : 5%. The resultant plastically deformed and
etched surface is usually quite distinct. (Note that HF is
extremely dangerous and great care must be taken in handling
it. Masks should be worn.)

(iii)   <u>Grids or Nets of Lines</u>

Grids of rectangular lines (and circles) may be scribed or printed[3,5,51]on
to   various surfaces and examined before and after deformation to
reveal strain distribution patterns (see Plates 4-6).   More directly,
the pattern of deformation of a rectangular grid may be compared with
that which would be predicted by a particular pattern of slip lines.
The use of grids on the outside stress-free surface of metal being
processed should,however,be viewed with caution because the condition
there may not be precisely that which is being assessed theoretically.

Blocks of metal about to be processed may be divided usually on a

d = 1/4" dia.

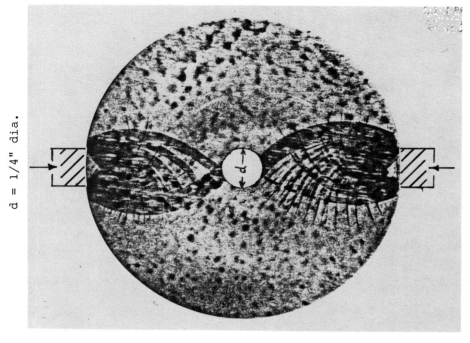

d = 1/16" dia.

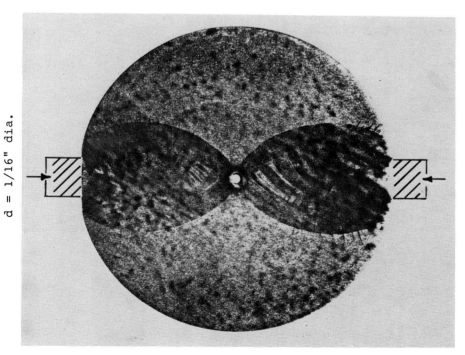

PLATE 1(c). DEFORMATION PATTERNS IN RINGS COMPRESSED BETWEEN DIES OF ¼ in. WIDTH.

LINE OF APPLICATION
OF LOAD

ENLARGED DETAIL
OF SIDE HINGE

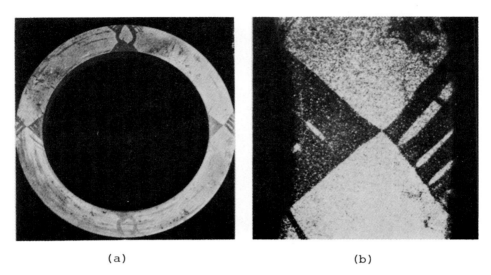

(a)

(b)

PLATE 1. Diametral compression of a ring by a point load.

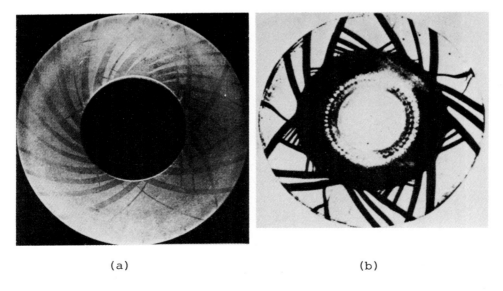

(a)

(b)

PLATE 2. (a) Thick-walled cylinder under internal pressure, showing
slip lines in the wall of the cylinder. (b) Slip-line field
in flange of a drawn cup.

PLATE 3

(a) Bending of a cantilever - initial stages of the
deformation process.

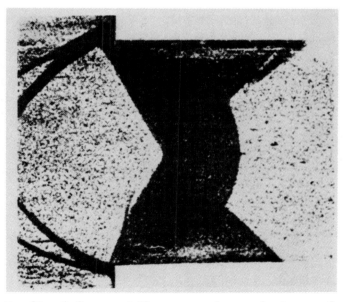

(b) Bending of a cantilever - advanced stage of
deformation process.

PLATE 4

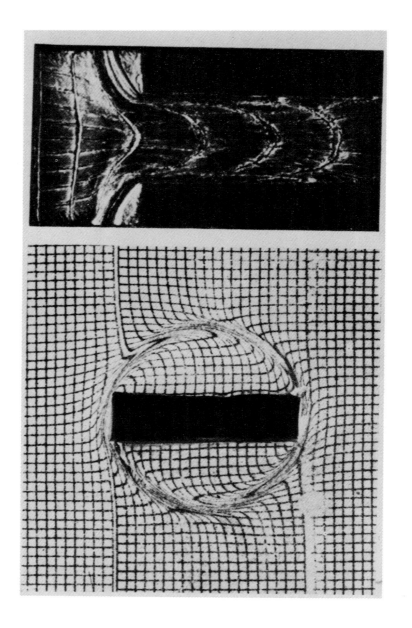

(a)

(b)

(a) Rotation of an imbedded rectangular punch in a block of Plasticine.
(b) Symmetrical end extrusion of lead from a smooth container.

PLATE 4

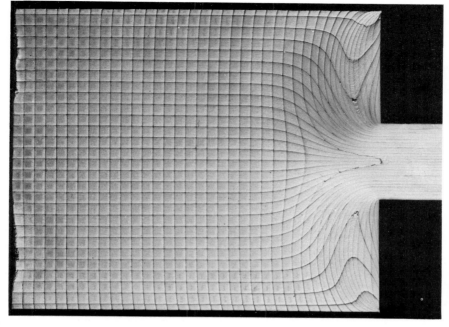

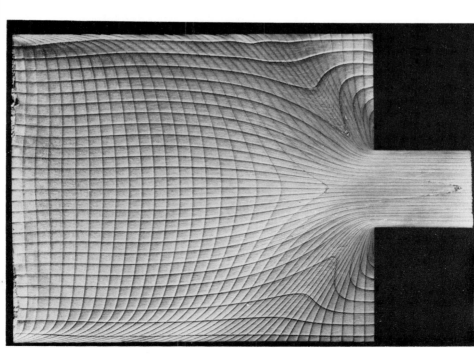

(c) Direct extrusion of aluminium.
(Courtesy of Dr. F. Gatto)

(d) Reverse extrusion of aluminium.
(Courtesy of Dr. F. Gatto)

PLATE 4

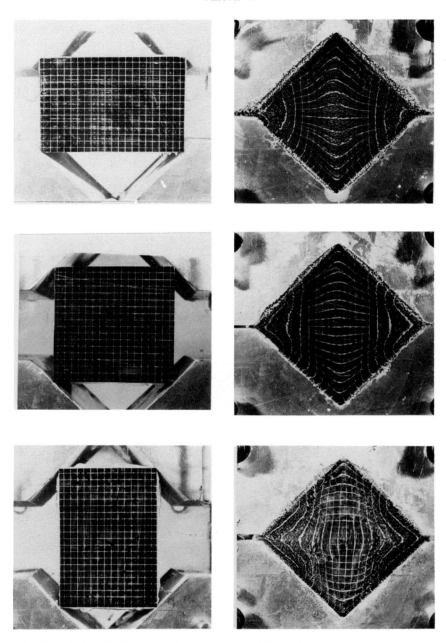

Initial billet geometry   Die closure complete

(e) Grid deformation for various initial workpiece geometries:
forging between wedge-shaped dies.

(Courtesy of K. Isobe)

PLATE 5

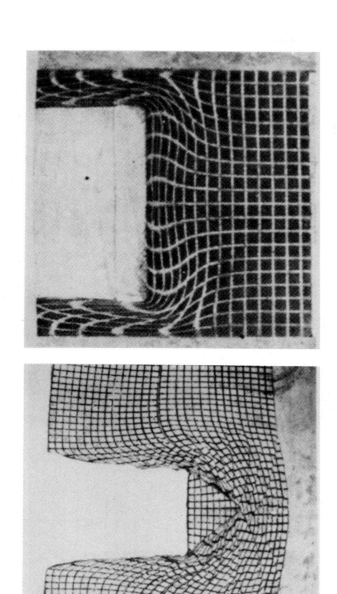

(a)

(b)

(a) Piercing of a block of Plasticine with $r < \frac{1}{2}$.
(b) Axisymmetric piercing of a block of lead $r > \frac{1}{2}$.

PLATE 6

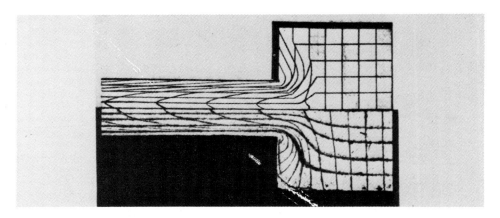

(a) Comparison of the theoretically predicted and experimentally determined grid pattern when extruding through a frictionless square die of fractional reduction $\frac{2}{3}$. Model material is Plasticine.

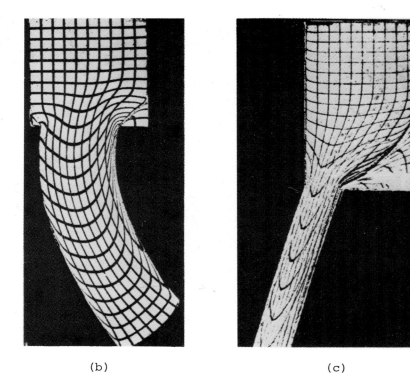

(b)   (c)

(b) Unsymmetrical end extrusion of Plasticine with smooth container walls.
(c) Unsymmetrical end extrusion of Plasticine with rough container walls.

PLATE 6

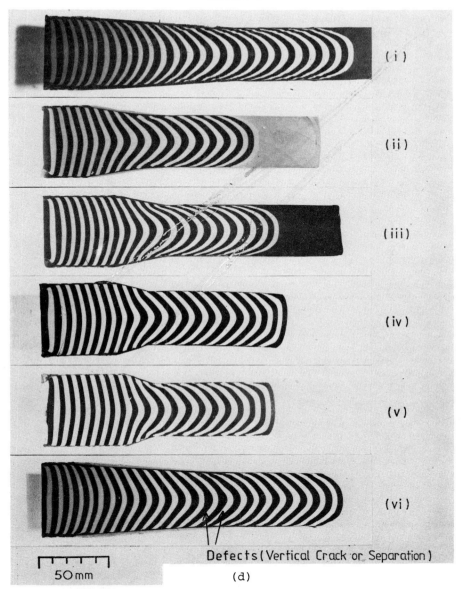

Defects (Vertical Crack or Separation)

50mm

(d)

Cross-sectional view when extruding layered Plasticine.
(Initial cross-section circular, final cross-section square.)
Various die semi-angles α,

(i) 5°; (ii) 7.5°; (iii) 10°; (iv) 15°; (v) 20°;

(vi) Showing defects on the axis when α = 5°.
Fractional reduction in area, 0.363.

(Courtesy of K. Isobe)

central plane (out of which no material is known to flow) and the grid placed on one of two such interfaces may, after working, be viewed to reveal the deformation undergone. This arrangement is often very successful and useful. It has been called visio-plasticity; it has been used to deduce, experimentally, slip-line-field directions and to determine strain distribution generally.[36]

(iv) Heat Lines and Zones

The plastic work done in a metal-forming operation largely reappears as heat; where deformation is enforced will often be apparent from a temperature rise, and therefore in hot working a zone which is brighter in colour than surrounding unworked zones can be observed. In a hot rolling operation the sudden brightening of the hot steel as it passes through the gap is unmistakable. More remarkably, "heat" lines have been seen to appear between generally worked regions and identified with lines of tangential velocity discontinuity; this was first recorded by Massey,[37] although only given currency a few years ago.[38,39]

(v) The Use of Plasticine and Wax

The use of a single mass of clay or Plasticine, or of layers of different colours, to study the plastic flow of metals was perhaps the first method of doing so. The first published reference to the use of clay seems to be that of Tresca in 1868.[15] Early notable instances of its use were by Massey,[37] Bower[40] and van Iterson.[23] Plasticine was used particularly effectively by A. P. Green.[41] Square grids are frequently printed in ink on to Plasticine to show deformation, see Plates 4(a,e), 5(a) and 6. Strain gauges may be implanted into Plasticine blocks so that the pressure distribution can be determined.[†] (It is to be noted that Plasticine is strain-rate sensitive.) Wax rather than clay has been employed by some research workers.[42,43]

(vi) Measurement of Friction Coefficient (see the bibliography of Ref. 44)

(a) Two strain-gauged probes or pins may be inserted in a large tool surface, one normally and the other obliquely. Normal pressure is measured by aid of the former and frictionless stress with the latter.

(b) An average friction coefficient may be deduced from die load and tension measurements after drawing wide strip through wedge-shaped dies.

(c) In the Cigar test, a flat rectangular block of length greater than about ten times its width is compressed between flat overhanging dies. The friction influences the spread and a simple expression between shape change and friction coefficient can be used.

---

†See Ref. 49.

(d) In the ring test, introduced by Male and Cockcroft[4][5] axial compression of a short ring or hollow cylinder between flat parallel dies causes the internal and external diameter ratio to alter according to the friction present.

(e) A steadily increasing back tension may be applied to strip passing through a roll gap until the neutral point coincides with the exit from the roll throat. The friction force then acts in the same direction over the whole surface and the friction coefficient can be found from the ratio of torque to roll load.

(vii)   PVC : Chromoplasticity

Polyvinylchloride may be effectively used as in tubes undergoing axial plastic collapse (buckling) to show up plastic hinge lines; the latter appear as dark lines.[46a] This material allows very large ("ductile") strain without fracture and thus permits complete folding patterns to be obtained.

The change in colour (mainly darkening) due to stress which occurs in some polymers has been used for plastic stress analysis; it is referred to as chromoplasticity.[46b]

(viii)   Defects: Voids or Cavities, Cracks, De-densification, Piping

Worked ductile products may be carefully examined visually to search out defects which are a result of the mode of plastic deformation enforced and invariably of the metallurgical structure of the material used. The defects, typically, may be small voids or cavities and cracks, see the discussion in Ref. 47.

(ix)   Anisotropy

A detailed discussion of the causes of anisotropy, and its influence on metal forming processes, is to be found in Chapter 7 of this monograph. A well-known manifestation is the appearance of "ears" when deep-drawing cylindrical cups from circular blanks, which is a consequence of the material being *planar anisotropic*. A practice which has developed from observations made when deep-drawing sheet steel, is the use of empirical expressions which purport to characterize the degree of both *planar* and *normal* anisotropy, see Chapter 7. These expressions involve the plastic strain ratio, the so called r-value, determined from tensile specimens cut at different orientations in the plane of the sheet. The r-value is defined as the ratio of natural width strain to natural thickness strain, and is determined at a particular level of axial strain in the tensile test. Significant changes in r-value with orientation implies *planar* anisotropy and the probability of earing. At the same time as the r-value increases the *normal* anisotropy increases, and deeper cups can be drawn, i.e. larger blank diameters can be drawn. Moiré techniques† have been used to help determine r-values.

---

†See also Moiré and grid methods of plastic strain analysis and their application to extrusion, in Ref. 48, p. 323.

(x)   Thermography[48]

Instruments for identifying surface temperature differences over a whole surface as cinematographic pictures are available, but seem not yet to have found application in metal processing.

Recently, infra-red photography has been used to obtain the temperature distribution in deformed bodies during hot forging.

(xi)   Load-punch Travel Diagrams[48]

Rapid changes in the slope of load-travel diagrams are frequently indications of a change in deformation mode, e.g. as in extrusion when there is a cessation of steady-state extrusion and the onset of an unsteady-state followed by the development of piping.

(xii)   Hardness Traverses[48]

By making a plot of hardness variation on a cold worked part, the degree of plastic working or strain it has received may be assessed; the higher the hardness number, the more intense the working.

A part long worked at a high temperature when hardness tested may show a variation which is indicative of the total temperature of the part; it may have been the more softened the higher the temperature.

(xiii)   Photoplasticity

Many efforts have been made to develop a material whose birefringence would facilitate stress distribution determination in plastically strained regions. The book by Javornicky (Ref. 48, p. 322) is perhaps the best starting point for this topic.

Unksov and Safarov (Ref. 48, p. 322) have experimentally determined contact stresses in extrusion processes by using optically insensitive material ONS (organic glass with 11% dibutyl-phthalate) glued to both sides of an optically active plate.

(xiv)   Photostress

A thin plate (about 1 mm thick) of photoelastic material may be cemented to the surface of an object to be examined and by using a reflexion polariscope, the surface strain of the object is revealed as a fringe pattern in the cemented resin plate. Direct measurement of the stresses in the actual element renders the method superior to the usual photoelastic method; see also Ref. 23 cited in Ref. 48.

Recently, it has been claimed that this technique may be applicable to plasticity investigations with the help of large strain elasticity.†

───────────────────────────

†Private communication from Professor Bayoumi of Cairo University to the authors.

(xv)   Residual Stresses[50]

These may be found by either (i) etching away layers from a deformed
specimen and following the elastic changes in strain, (ii) by machining
away specific layers and (iii) by x-ray analysis.

(xvi)   Photoelasticity[48]

The birefringence of certain polymeric materials may be used to determine plastic stress distribution along tool-workpiece interfaces in
model tests. This has been used with special care for accuracy and
interpretation and relevance to forming processes by Unksov and his
colleagues. He has frequently used photoelastic tests on workpieces
or tools to give indications of stress distributions in a plastically
deforming body and on its boundary for determining frictional behaviour.

(xvii)   Temperature-sensitive Paints

These have long been available but have found limited application in
the metal-processing field.

(xviii)   Thermocouples[48]

These may be inserted to determine temperature changes due to working.
If, however, they are set in a region of the workpiece which will be
plastically strained, they are likely to be rendered useless because
they will be plastically deformed.

(xix)   Inserts[48]

Blocks of like metal and wires have frequently been inserted into
deforming plastic masses to show up gross deformation, e.g. as in ring
rolling, see ref. 33 of Ref. 48.

INTRODUCTION

REFERENCES

1. Burstall, A. F., *History of Mechanical Engineering*. Faber, London (1963).
2. Usher, A. P., *Mechanical Engineering Invention*. Harvard University Press (1962).
3. Keller, A. B., *A Theatre of Machines*. Chapman & Hall, London (1964).
4. Chaloner, W. H. and Musson, A. E., *Industry and Technology*. Vista Books, London (1963).
5. Bertrand, G., *The Renaissance Engineers*. Lund Humphries, London (1966).
6. Crombie, A. C., *Augustine to Galileo*. Falcon Educational Books, London (1952).
7. Tatton, R. (editor), *A General History of the Sciences*. (Four volumes.) Thames & Hudson, London (1963).
8. Swainger, K., *Analysis of Deformation*. (Four volumes.) Chapman & Hall,London (1954-59).
9. Singer, C., (editor), *History of Technology*. (Five volumes.) Oxford University Press (1956-65).
10. Hodges, H., *Technology of the Ancient World*. Penguin Books (1971).
11. Coulomb, C. A., "Test on the application of the rules of maxima and minima to some problems of the statics relating to architecture." *Mem. Acad. Sci. Savants Estrangers*, 7, 343 (1773). Published Paris 1776.
12. Rankine, W. J. M., "On the stability of loose earth". *Phil. Trans. Roy. Soc. London*, 147, 9 (1857).
13. Levy, M., "Test on a rational theory of recently turned earth, and its application to the calculation of the stability of retaining walls". *Journal de Liouville*, 18, 241 (1873).
14. Mohr, O., *Papers from the Field of Applied Mechanics*, (2nd edn.) Ernst, Berlin (1914).
15. Tresca, H., "On the flow of solid bodies subjected to high pressures". *C. r. Acad. Sci., Paris*, 59, 754 (1864). Other closely connected work by Tresca is reported in *C. r. Acad. Sci.*,64, 809 (1867); *Mem. Sav. Acad. Sci., Paris*, 18, 733 (1868) and 20, 75 (1872).
16. Sobotka, Z., "The slip lines and slip surfaces in the theory of plasticity and soil mechanics". *Appl. Mech. Rev.* 14, 753 (1961).
17. Thewlis, J. *et al* (editors), *Encyclopaedic Dictionary of Physics*. Nine volumes with five supplementary volumes up to 1975. Pergamon Press, Oxford and New York (1961-1975).
18. Prandtl, L., "On the penetration hardness of plastic materials and the hardness of indentors". *Z. angew. Math. Mech.* 1, 15 (1921).
19. Nadai, A., "Experiments on the plastic deformation of wedge-shaped mild steel bodies". *Z. angew. Math. Mech.* 1, 20 (1921).
20. Hencky, H., "Concerning a few statically determinant cases in plastic bodies". *Z. angew. Math. Mech.* 3, 241 (1923).
21. Kotter, F., "The determination of the stresses on fragmented slip planes, from the theory of earth pressures". *Berl. akad. Berichte*, 229 (1903).
22. Geiringer, H., "Complete solutions to the plane plasticity problem". *Proc. 3rd Int. Congr. Appl. Mech.* 2, 185, Stockholm (1930).
23. van Iterson, F. K. J., *Plasticity in Engineering*. Blackie, Glasgow (1947).
24. Sokolovskii, V. V., *Theory of Plasticity* (in Russian), (2nd edn.)

Gostechteorizdat, Moscow (1950).

25. Tomlenov, A.D., *Theory of Plastic Deformations in Metals* (in Russian). Mashgiz, Moscow (1951).

26. Gubkin, S. I., *Plastic Deformation of Metals* (in Russian), Vols. 1-3. Metallurgizdat, Moscow (1961).

27. Unksov, E.P., *An Engineering Theory of Plasticity*. Butterworths, London (1961).

28. Hill, R., *The Mathematical Theory of Plasticity*. Oxford University Press (1950).

29. Prager, W. and Hodge, P. G. Jr., *Theory of Perfectly Plastic Solids*. Wiley, New York (1951).

30. Prager, W., "A geometrical discussion on the slip line field in plane plastic flow". *Trans. R. Inst. Tech., Stockholm*, No. 65 (1953).

31. Lüders, W., "Demonstrating the elasticity of iron and steel bars and observing the molecular slip when bending these bars". *Dinglers Journal*, 155, 18 (1860).

32. Hartmann, L., *Distribution of Strain in Metals Under Stress*. Bergen-Levrault, Paris (1896).

33. Chernov, D. K., *The Science of Metals* (in Russian). Metallurgizdat, Moscow (1950).

34. Fry, A., "Strain figures in ingot iron and steel brought out by a new etching process". *Stahl und Eisen*, 41, 1093 (1921).

35. Baraya, G. L., Parker, J. and Flowett J., "Mechanical and photographic processe for producing a grid of lines". *Int. J. Mech. Sci.* 5, 365 (1963).

36. Thompsen, E. G., Yang, C. T. and Kobayashi, S., *Mechanics of Plastic Deformation in Metal Processing*. MacMillan, N.Y. (1965).

37. Massey, H. F., "The flow of metal during forging". *Proc. Manchester Ass. Engrs.*, November 1921.

38. Johnson, W., Baraya, G. L. and Slater, R. A. C., "On heat lines or lines of thermal discontinuity". *Int. J. Mech. Sci.* 6, 409 (1964).

39. Slater, R. A. C., "Velocity and thermal discontinuities encountered during the forging of steels". *Proc. Manchester Ass. Engrs.*, No. 5 (1965-66).

40. Bower, C. O., *Practical Shell Forging*. The Library Press Limited London (1919).

41. Green, A. P., "The use of Plasticine models to simulate the plastic flow of metals". *Phil. Mag.* 42, 365 (1951).

42. Bodsworth, C., Halling, J. and Barton, J. W., "The use of paraffin wax as a model to simulate the plastic deformation of metals: Part 1". *J.Iron Steel Inst.* 185, 375 (1957).

43. Dankert, T. and Wanheim, T., "Slip line wax". *Expt. Mechs.* 16, 318 (1976).

44. Johnson, W. and Mellor, P. B., *Engineering Plasticity*, van Nostrand-Reinhold (1973).

45. Male, A. T. and Cockcroft, M. G., "A method for the determination of the friction of metals under conditions of bulk plastic deformation". *J. Inst. Metals*, 91, 38 (1964-65).

46(a) Soden, P. D., and Al-Hassani S. T. S., and Johnson, W., "The crumpling of polyvinyl-chloride tubes". *Proc. Mech. Prop. of Materials, Inst. P.A.Y.S. Conf.* 21, 327 (1974).

46(b) Rautu, S., "Chromorheology: a new experimental method". *Mechs. Res. Communications*, 6, 353 (1979).

47. Johnson, W. and Mamalis, A. G., "A survey of some physical defects arising in metal working processes". *Proc. 17th M.T.D.R. Conf.*, 113. Manchester, 1976, MacMillan Press (1977).

48. Johnson, W. and Mamalis, A. G., in *Engineering Plasticity: Theory of Metal Forming Processes*, Vol.2 (edited by H. Lippmann), 1. CISM Courses and Lectures No. 139. Springer-Verlag, (1977).

49. Mihara, Y. and Johnson, W., "Crop loss: front and back end deformation during slab and bloom rolling". *Metall. Metal Forming*, 44, 332 (1977).

50. Denton, A. A., "Determination of residual stresses". *Met. Revs.* 11, 1 (1966).

51. Farmer, L. E. and Conning, S. W., "Numerical smoothing of flow patterns". *I.J.M.S.*, 21, 577-596, 1979.

CHAPTER 2

General Plasticity Theory

INTRODUCTION

Although this monograph is mainly concerned with the two-dimensional flow of a rigid, perfectly plastic solid, some general theory is given in this chapter. It is not intended to provide a complete introduction to the basic theory of classical plasticity since this can be obtained from the references given. However, certain basic aspects are presented because they are necessary for the development of the methods of solution of the two-dimensional problems discussed in later chapters.

The theorems presented in this chapter are for a rate-independent, rigid-plastic, incompressible solid with a yield criterion that is not influenced by the hydrostatic part of the stress tensor. It is usually assumed that metals do not undergo plastic volume changes when subjected to hydrostatic pressure of the order of the uniaxial yield stress. Also, Bridgman,[1] Pugh, Crossland and others[2] have shown that a superimposed hydrostatic pressure of this order does not influence the yield stress although it results in an increase in ductility. Consequently, the theory of plasticity applied to metals is based on the assumption that the yield criterion, which is a relationship of the form $f(\sigma_{ij}) = 0$† satisfied at the onset of yielding, is independent of the hydrostatic part of the stress tensor, i.e. one-third the sum of the three direct stresses or $\sigma_{kk}/3$. Thus, it is assumed that for a metal the yield criterion is a function of the components of the deviatoric stress, σ'_{ij} (or s_{ij}) $= \sigma_{ij} - \delta_{ij}\sigma_{kk}/3$, where $\sigma'_{ii} = 0$. It becomes a matter of choice whether the yield criterion is expressed in terms of deviatoric stresses or the components of σ_{ij}.

---

†The suffix notation, as used in this chapter, is described in Appendix 1. The Appendix also provides a brief account of second-order Cartesian tensors including a discussion about the hydrostatic and deviatoric parts of the stress tensor.

A rigid plastic solid is a hypothetical solid which, under any stress system, would be rigid when stressed below the yield point, that is, the elastic moduli are infinitely large. For problems involving the unconstrained plastic flow of an elastic-plastic solid, the elastic parts of the strains are small compared with the plastic parts and may be neglected when considering the stress and velocity distributions. Consequently, the use of the rigid plastic model is justified for these problems. For other problems, such as the indentation of a surface by a flat punch, where the elastic and plastic strains are of the same order, plasticity theory based on the rigid plastic model can give useful results. The yield point of a rigid plastic body is that load in the loading sequence for which deformation or plastic flow first becomes possible. If an elastic-plastic body is subjected to a certain loading sequence, the point in the loading sequence at which the strains in the plastic region are no longer constrained to be of an elastic order of magnitude by the adjacent elastic material is usually indicated by a sharp bend in the load-displacement curve, provided the rate of work-hardening† is low.[3] This point in the loading sequence is usually very nearly equal to the yield-point load calculated by assuming the body to be rigid plastic. Also, at the instant unconstrained plastic flow of an elastic-plastic body becomes possible, the changes in the geometry of the surface of the body are usually negligible and, consequently, the boundary conditions can be referred to the original configuration.

STRAIN RATE

There is a unique state of strain corresponding to every state of stress in the isothermal (or adiabatic) deformation of an elastic solid. This is not so for plastic deformation; the strain increment or strain rate (not the strain) is related to the current state of stress.

Referring to a rectangular Cartesian coordinate system Ox_i, if du_i is the infinitesimal displacement in time dt of a particle, with current position vector x_i, in a deforming medium the infinitesimal strain increment tensor for time dt is

$$d\varepsilon_{ij} = \frac{1}{2}\left\{\frac{\partial\ (du_i)}{\partial x_j} + \frac{\partial\ (du_j)}{\partial x_i}\right\}.$$

It is often more convenient to refer to velocities rather than displacement increments, and strain rates instead of strain increments. Many plasticity problems are quasi-static, that is, the inertia forces due to plastic flow may be neglected. If the dimensionless parameter $\rho v^2/Y \ll 1$, where ρ is the density, v is a characteristic velocity and

---

†For an isotropic material the current rate of work-hardening can be obtained from the slope (tangent) of the uniaxial true stress-plastic strain curve, at any given stress (strain) state. In general, the slope decreases with increasing plastic strain.

Y the uniaxial yield stress, then the problem may be considered quasi-static. An ideal plastic solid exhibits no viscous effects and, consequently, the velocities and strain rates for quasi-static flow may be referred to some suitable monotonically varying parameter of the problem considered. For example, during a direct extrusion the ram position is a suitable time-like parameter.

The rate of deformation tensor (or strain-rate tensor) $e_{ij} = d\varepsilon_{ij}/dt$, where the differentiation follows the particle, is given by[†]

$$e_{ij} = \frac{1}{2}\left\{ \frac{\partial}{\partial x_j}\left(\frac{du_i}{dt}\right) + \frac{\partial}{\partial x_i}\left(\frac{du_j}{dt}\right) \right\}$$

$$= \frac{1}{2}\left\{ \frac{\partial v_i}{\partial x_j} + \frac{\partial v_j}{\partial x_i} \right\}, \tag{2.1}$$

where t is time or a time-like parameter and velocity $v_i = du_i/dt$ is the velocity of the particle with current position vector x_i.

The velocity gradient tensor $\partial v_i/\partial x_j$ may be written as the sum of symmetric and anti-symmetric parts, thus

$$\frac{\partial v_i}{\partial x_j} = \frac{1}{2}\left\{ \left(\frac{\partial v_i}{\partial x_j} + \frac{\partial v_j}{\partial x_i}\right) + \left(\frac{\partial v_i}{\partial x_j} - \frac{\partial v_j}{\partial x_i}\right) \right\}$$

$$= e_{ij} + \omega_{ij},$$

the strain rate tensor being the symmetric part. The anti-symmetric part corresponds to a rigid body rotation of the element of material considered and a necessary and sufficient condition for rigid body motion of this element is $e_{ij} = 0$. If $\omega_{ij} = 0$ the flow is said to be irrotational.

Later in this chapter the components of the rate of deformation tensor are related to the current state of stress, the simple relationships so derived being sufficient for the purposes of the present text. A more general treatment would consider the elastic-plastic continuum, as well as give more detailed considerations to finite deformation. Such an approach leads to several proposals for finite strain tensors (and their rates), depending upon the choice of the coordinate system and whether reference is made to the deformed or undeformed configuration. In turn, several corresponding definitions

---

[†]In Newton's fluxion notation a dot above a symbol is used to denote differentiation with respect to time. This is not done in this monograph for strain rate and rate of rotation, but no confusion should arise since different symbols, ε_{ij} and e_{ij}, are used for strain and strain rate respectively and the symbol ω_{ij} is reserved for the rate of rotation or vorticity tensor.

of stress and stress rate arise. For a more detailed discussion see Refs. 4-12.

EQUILIBRIUM AND THE VIRTUAL WORK EQUATIONS

The equations of equilibrium are

$$\frac{\partial \sigma_{ij}}{\partial x_j} + X_i = 0, \tag{2.2}$$

where σ_{ij} is the stress tensor and X_i the body force per unit volume. The condition for equilibrium on a surface element either in the interior or on the boundary of the body is

$$T_i = \sigma_{ij} n_j, \tag{2.3}$$

where T_i is the stress vector acting on the element and n_j is the outward unit normal.

If σ_{ij} is any stress field in equilibrium with both the tractions T_i on the surface of a body and the body forces X_i, and if v_i is any continuous velocity field, it follows from equations (2.2) and (2.3) and the symmetry of the stress tensor that

$$\int_V X_i v_i dV + \int_S T_i v_i dS = \int_V \sigma_{ij} e_{ij} dV, \tag{2.4}$$

where e_{ij} is given by equation (2.1), V is the volume of the body and S the surface. Equation (2.4) is known as the virtual work equation. The proof is as follows:

$$\int_S X_i v_i dV + \int_S T_i v_i dS = \int_V X_i v_i dV + \int_S \sigma_{ij} n_j v_i dS$$

$$= \int_V X_i v_i dV + \int_V \frac{\partial(\sigma_{ij} v_i)}{\partial x_j} dV$$

$$= \int_V \left(X_i v_i + \frac{\partial \sigma_{ij}}{\partial x_j} v_i + \sigma_{ij} \frac{\partial v_i}{\partial x_j} \right) dV$$

$$= \int_V \left(X_i + \frac{\partial \sigma_{ij}}{\partial x_j} \right) v_i dV + \int_V \sigma_{ij} e_{ij} dV$$

$$= \int_V \sigma_{ij} e_{ij} dV.$$

Equation (2.4) is valid regardless of the connection between σ_{ij} and e_{ij}.

SURFACES OF STRESS DISCONTINUITY

Surfaces of stress discontinuity are sometimes encountered in problems of the quasi-static flow of a rigid plastic solid. Such a surface may be considered as the limit of a thin elastic region which contains a large stress gradient and which separates two plastic regions. The equilibrium requirement for a surface of stress discontinuity is that at all points on the surface the stress vector acting on one side must be equal in magnitude and opposite in direction to the stress vector acting on the other side. This means that $\sigma_{ij}n_j$ must be continuous across the surface. It is easy to show that equation (2.4) is valid when the equilibrium stress field σ_{ij} contains surfaces of stress discontinuity.

SURFACES OF VELOCITY DISCONTINUITY

Surfaces of velocity discontinuity are permissible in the quasi-static flow of a rigid plastic solid since there are no viscosity effects. Equation (2.4) must be modified if the velocity field contains such surfaces.

Let the body under consideration be divided into two parts, 1 and 2, by a surface of velocity discontinuity S_D in an otherwise continuous velocity field v_i and let v_i^1 and v_i^2 be the velocity vectors as S_D is approached from parts 1 and 2 respectively. By applying equation (2.4) to parts 1 and 2 separately and adding, the following equation is obtained

$$\int_S T_i v_i \, dS + \int_V X_i v_i \, dV = \int_V \sigma_{ij} e_{ij} \, dV + \int_{S_D} \sigma_{ij} n_j (v_i^2 - v_i^1) \, dS, \quad (2.5)$$

where n_j is the unit vector normal to S_D and pointing into part 2.

For metals incompressibility is assumed and the velocity fields used in equations (2.4) and (2.5) must satisfy the conditions

$$v_{i,i} = 0 \qquad (2.6)$$

and

$$v_i^1 n_i = v_i^2 n_i. \qquad (2.7)$$

Equation (2.7) states that when the solid is incompressible the component of velocity normal to a surface of discontinuity S_D is continuous across S_D, that is, only the component of velocity tangential to S_D can be discontinuous. The last term in equation (2.5) can be

16

re-written as

$$\int_{S_D} \tau[v]\, dS,$$

where τ is the shear stress component of σ_{ij} along S_D in the direction of $v_i{}^2 - v_i{}^1$ and $[v] = v_i{}^2 - v_i{}^1$. Also for the particular case where σ_{ij} is an equilibrium plastic stress field and v_i is a velocity field associated with it,

$$\int_{S_D} \tau[v]\, dS = \int_{S_D} k[v]\, dS,$$

where k is the yield stress in pure shear.

MAXIMUM WORK PRINCIPLE

A yield criterion is assumed to exist for a solid in the form

$$f(\sigma_{ij}) = 0,$$

and plastic flow to occur when,

(i) $f=0$ and $\dfrac{\partial f}{\partial \sigma_{ij}} d\sigma_{ij} \left(\text{or } \dfrac{\partial f}{\partial \sigma_{ij}} \dot{\sigma}_{ij} \right) > 0$

for a work hardening solid or

(ii) $f=0$ and $\dfrac{\partial f}{\partial \sigma_{ij}} d\sigma_{ij} = 0$

for a non-hardening or perfectly plastic solid. f is a function of the nine components of σ_{ij}, whose symmetry demands that $\sigma_{ij}=\sigma_{ji}$. In a stress space of nine dimensions $f(\sigma_{ij}) = 0$ is a closed surface, known as the yield surface which is either plane or convex, that is, concave to some origin. The function should describe the initial yield behaviour of the solid and is therefore subject to certain con-straints, such as whether the material is initially isotropic or anisotropic. For complete generality it should also encompass the subsequent work-hardening behaviour of the material and thus charact-erize how the initial yield surface changes in form as a consequence of plastic deformation. For example, if the yield surface merely increases in size about the origin then the material is said to harden isotropically, regardless of whether the material is initially isotro-pic or anisotropic. More general hardening behaviour is accounted for by allowing the yield surface to shift relative to the origin, as well as to change in shape. A more detailed discussion on anisotropy is to be found in Chapter 7.

Note that if the solid is isotropic then $f(\sigma_{ij})=0$ is a function of the second (J_2) and third (J_3) invariants of the deviatoric stress tensor.[13] With the additional assumption of isotropic hardening the yield criterion is often given in the following form:

$$f = f^*(J_2, J_3) - c = 0 \tag{2.8}$$

or

$$f^*(J_2, J_3) = c, \tag{2.9}$$

where c is a parameter which depends on the plastic strain history.

It is often convenient to have a geometrical representation of any yield surface plotted in three-dimensional principal stress space, rather than the mathematical representation in a general nine-dimensional space. Thus, any yield stress state can be represented by a vector reaching from the origin to the yield surface, where the principal stresses are taken as Cartesian coordinates.

According to the concept of plastic potential, the tensor components of the plastic-strain rate during plastic flow are given by

$$e_{ij} = \lambda \frac{\partial f}{\partial \sigma_{ij}}, \tag{2.10}$$

where λ is positive . When the yield surface has edges or corners at which $\partial f/\partial \sigma_{ij}$ is not uniquely defined, e_{ij} is given at these points (which are known as singular points) by the generalization of equation (2.10) due to Koiter.[14] If it is assumed that in the neighbourhood of a singular point the yield surface is the join of a number[‡] of surfaces given by $f_r(\sigma_{ij})=0$, then at the singular point the generalization of equation (2.10) is

$$e_{ij} = \sum_r \lambda_r \frac{\partial f_r}{\partial \sigma_{ij}} . \tag{2.11}$$

---

†This relationship implies that solids which have a yield criterion that is not influenced by hydrostatic stress are incompressible and vice versa.

‡If the solid is incompressible, two surfaces meet at a singular point.

The sum is taken over all the surfaces that meet at the singular point. Equations (2.10) and (2.11) indicate that the vector representation of e_{ij} corresponding to a plastic state of stress σ_{ij} is normal to the yield locus at the point σ_{ij} when this normal is defined, or is within the fan of normals to the surfaces meeting at a singular point.

The Maximum Work Principle follows from equations (2.10) and (2.11) and the convexity of the yield surface, and is

$$(\sigma_{ij} - \sigma_{ij}*)e_{ij} \geqslant 0, \tag{2.12}$$

where σ_{ij} is a yield state of stress, e_{ij} is the associated strain rate and $\sigma_{ij}*$ is any other state of stress represented by a point either on or inside the yield surface. The equality sign holds when $\sigma_{ij} = \sigma_{ij}*$ or when $\sigma_{ij}*$ and σ_{ij} lie on the same flat of a yield surface or if σ_{ij} and $\sigma_{ij}*$ differ only by a hydrostatic stress for an incompressible solid. Drucker[15] arrived at (2.12) from a definition of a stable plastic material. Convexity of the yield surface and the normality of e_{ij} are natural consequences of assuming material stability.

UNIQUENESS

The uniqueness theorem presented in this section is concerned with a rigid plastic isotropic incompressible body that yields under the action of prescribed surface tractions T_i over area S_T of the boundary surface S, and prescribed velocities v_i over area S_v†.

The stress field for the body which is yielding must satisfy the equilibrium conditions (2.2) and (2.3) at every point in the body, the yield criterion where plastic deformation is occurring, and must not violate it elsewhere. The associated velocity field must satisfy the incompressibility requirements, the velocity boundary conditions, and must be related to the stress field where deformation is occurring according to equation (2.10). Let σ_{ij}^1, v_i^1 and σ_{ij}^2, v_i^2, be two

---

†The theorem is valid if body forces, except inertia forces due to the plastic flow, are included and also if certain components of the surface tractions T_i and the complementary components of the displacements are prescribed on part of S.

possible stress and associated velocity fields for the body at the yield point under the specified tractions and velocities on the surface. It follows from the virtual work equation (2.5) that

$$\int_S (T_i^1 - T_i^2)(v_i^1 - v_i^2)dS = \int_V (\sigma_{ij}^1 - \sigma_{ij}^2)(e_{ij}^1 - e_{ij}^2)dV$$

$$+ \int_{S_D^1} (k - \tau^2)[v^1]dS_D$$

$$+ \int_{S_D^2} (k - \tau^1)[v^2]dS_D, \qquad (2.13)$$

where S_D^1 and S_D^2 are surfaces of velocity discontinuity in the velocity fields v_i^1 and v_i^2 respectively. (v^1) and (v^2) are the magnitudes of the corresponding tangential velocity discontinuities and τ^1 and τ^2 are the shear stress components of the stress fields σ_{ij}^1 and σ_{ij}^2 on S_D^2 and S_D^1 respectively. The left-hand side of equation (2.13) is identically zero since,

$$T_i^1 = T_i^2 = T_i \text{ on } S_T$$

and

$$v_i^1 = v_i^2 = v_i \text{ on } S_v.$$

The Maximum Work Principle and the inequality $k \geqslant \tau$ indicate that each term on the right-hand side of equation (2.13) is non-negative and, consequently, each term is identically equal to zero. This implies that $\sigma_{ij}^1 = \sigma_{ij}^2$ except† possibly in the common rigid region of the velocity fields v_i^1 and v_i^2 and possibly where both stress states lie on the same flat of a yield surface.

The uniqueness theorem for a rigid plastic solid may be stated as follows:

If two or more complete solutions to a problem can be obtained the stress fields of the solutions are the same, except possibly in the common non-deforming regions of the solutions and possibly

---

†If the velocity is prescribed on the whole surface the stress fields σ_{ij}^1 and σ_{ij}^2 can differ by a constant hydrostatic stress. The velocity cannot be prescribed arbitrarily over the whole surface since the assumption of plastic incompressibility requires that $\int_S v_i n_i dS = 0$.

when the stresses lie on the same flat of a yield surface.

A complete solution consists of an equilibrium stress field and an associated velocity field satisfying the boundary conditions and the stress field satisfies the yield criterion where deformation occurs in the associated velocity field and does not violate the yield criterion in the rigid regions.

To sum up, the specification of the surface tractions and velocities on the surface of a rigid plastic body that is at the yield point uniquely defines the stress field in the deformable region; where the deformation mode is not uniquely defined it must, however, be compatible with the stress field.

Bishop *et al*[16] have shown that if one complete solution is known for plane strain, plane stress or axial symmetry the deformable zone can be uniquely determined. Hill[17] has shown that if the traction rate T_i is specified on S_T the deformation mode in then unique.

EXTREMUM PRINCIPLES

Two extremum principles due to Hill[3] can be used to obtain lower and upper bounds for the loads required to produce plastic flow. The practical application of these principles to bounding loads for problems of steady motion is limited to a non-hardening solid. However, despite their specific application for load bounding, the extremum principles are of fundamental theoretical importance.

Let σ_{ij}, v_i denote a complete solution to the problem of a rigid plastic body yielding under prescribed surface tractions T_i over part surface S_T with prescibed velocities v_i on the part surface S_v of the surface S. Also, let $\sigma_{ij}{}^0$ be an equilibrium stress field, satisfying the boundary conditions on S_T and nowhere violating the yield criterion†. The principle of virtual work gives

$$\int_S (T_i - T_i{}^0) v_i dS = \int_V (\sigma_{ij} - \sigma_{ij}{}^0) e_{ij} dV + \int_{S_D} (k - \tau^0)[v] dS$$

where τ^0 is the shear stress component of $\sigma_{ij}{}^0$ which acts along the discontinuity $[v]$ on S_D. Then,

$$\int_{S_v} (T_i - T_i{}^0) v_i dS \geqslant 0 \qquad (2.14)$$

since
$$k \geqslant \tau^0,$$

$$(\sigma_{ij} - \sigma_{ij}{}^0) e_{ij} \geqslant 0$$

and
$$T_i{}^0 = \sigma_{ij}{}^0 n_j = \sigma_{ij} n_j = T_i \text{ on } S_T.$$

---

†Such a stress field is said to be statically admissible.

Equation (2.14) is the first extremum principle and it shows that a lower bound for $\int_{S_v} T_i v_i \, dS$ - the rate of work of the unknown surface tractions on S_v - can be obtained from a statically admissible stress field.

Now let v_i^* be a velocity field that satisfies the incompressibility requirements and the velocity boundary conditions on S_v; such a velocity field is said to be kinematically admissible. The principle of virtual work now gives

$$\int_S T_i v_i^* \, dS = \int_V \sigma_{ij} e_i^*{}_j \, dV + \int_{S^*_D} \tau [v^*] \, dS,$$

where τ is the shear-stress component of the stress σ_{ij} along the discontinuity $[v^*]$ on S^*_D. If σ_{ij}^* is the stress field, not necessarily statically admissible, which is required to produce the strain-rate field

$$e_{ij}^* = \frac{1}{2} \left(\frac{\partial v_i^*}{\partial x_j} + \frac{\partial v_j^*}{\partial x_i} \right),$$

then,

$$\int_S T_i v_i^* \, dS = \int_V \sigma_{ij} e_{ij}^* \, dV + \int_{S_D^*} \tau [v^*] \, dS,$$

$$\leqslant \int_V \sigma_{ij}^* e_{ij}^* \, dV + \int_{S_D^*} k [v^*] \, dS,$$

since

$$k \geqslant \tau$$

and

$$(\sigma_{ij}^* - \sigma_{ij}) e_{ij}^* \geqslant 0.$$

On S_v, $v_i = v_i^*$, consequently

$$\int_{S_v} T_i v_i \, dS \leqslant \int_V \sigma_{ij}^* e_{ij}^* \, dV + \int_{S_D} k [v^*] \, dS - \int_{S_T} T_i v_i^* \, dS. \qquad (2.15)$$

Equation (2.15) is the second extremum principle and it shows that an upper bound to the rate of work of the unknown surface tractions on S_v can be obtained from a kinematically admissible velocity field.

The two extremum principles are also valid when certain components of the surface tractions T_i and the complementary components of velocity are prescribed on part of the surface.

Often the velocity of S_v is uniform or is equivalent to a rigid-body rotation. The extremum principles can then be used to obtain lower and upper bounds for the yield-point load or moment.

It may be deduced from the extremum principles that if a complete solution is found, the yield point load of the complete solution is both a lower and an upper bound and is thus exact.

The two extremum principles are closely related to two limit theorems which may be deduced from them. The first limit theorem states that a rigid plastic body will be capable of supporting, without plastic flow, a given system of external loads if a statically admissible stress field that is in equilibrium with the external loads exists. The second limit theorem states that a rigid plastic body cannot support, without plastic flow, a given system of external loads if a kinematically admissible velocity field v_i* exists for which the rate of working of the external loads exceeds the rate of plastic energy dissipation, i.e. for the field

$$W_D = \int_V \sigma_{ij}* e_{ij}* dV + \sum \int_{S_D*} k[\, v \,] dS.$$

A different approach to the limit theorems is given in refs. 18 and 19.

SUMMARY

This chapter provides some of the basic aspects of the mathematical theory of plasticity which are necessary for the theoretical development of the subject. However, for those readers who have difficulty in understanding the mathematics the following summary is provided to give a physical interpretation of some of the concepts covered.

Tensor Calculus and Suffix Notation

The suffix notation, as applied to tensor calculus, is a convenient and shorthand way of writing down certain mathematical expressions or equations. Because of the adherence of many textbooks to this type of notation, an appendix to this one covers the principles of suffix notation. The appendix does not develop the theory of tensor calculus but it is hoped provides sufficient information to enable the reader ultimately to interpret this type of notation readily.

Surfaces of Stress and Velocity Discontinuities

The concept of discontinuities in stress and velocity should not present too many difficulties. Possible discontinuities are discussed in the following chapters and numerous examples are given of their occurence. The assumption of a rigid-perfectly plastic material implies that the discontinuity occurs across an infinitely thin line within the material, whilst in a real elastic-plastic material the discontinuity would be replaced by a narrow transition region through which the stress or velocity varies rapidly.

Plastic Potential and Flow Rule

Plastic potential is the name given to a function $g(\sigma_{ij})$ of the stresses σ_{ij}, such that the components of the plastic rate of deformation tensor are proportional to the components of $grad\ g$,

$$e_{ij} = \lambda\ \frac{\partial g}{\partial \sigma_{ij}}\ . \tag{2.16}$$

In assuming the existence of a plastic potential the simplest hypothesis is to take g equal to the yield function f, which is of course equation (2.10). This is particularly valuable since the principle of maximum work, the uniqueness proof and extremum principles all follow, as derived earlier.

The use of (2.10) permits a convenient and general relationship between stress and plastic strain rate, i.e. the flow rule. The flow rule is developed below (without recourse to indicial notation) for the von Mises yield criterion[20], which is the most widely applied criterion for an isotropic metal. With this criterion yielding is deemed to occur when the second invariant of the deviatoric stress tensor (J_2) reaches a critical value, in particular

$$6J_2 = 6[\ \sigma_{xy}^2 + \sigma_{yz}^2 + \sigma_{zx}^2 - \sigma_{xx}'\sigma_{yy}' - \sigma_{yy}'\sigma_{zz}' - \sigma_{zz}'\sigma_{xx}'\ ] = 2\bar{\sigma}^2 = 6k^2, \tag{2.17}$$

where the components of stress are referred to a Cartesian x, y, z coordinate system. The quantity $\bar{\sigma}$ is the uniaxial yield strength and k is the yield shear strength. The above expression can be recast in the more familiar form,

$$6J_2 = (\sigma_{xx} - \sigma_{yy})^2 + (\sigma_{yy} - \sigma_{zz})^2 + (\sigma_{zz} - \sigma_{xx})^2 + 6(\sigma_{xy}^2 + \sigma_{yz}^2 + \sigma_{zx}^2) = 2\bar{\sigma}^2 = 6k^2. \tag{2.18}$$

In keeping with the definition of the yield function it follows that

$$f = 6J_2 - 2\bar{\sigma}^2 = 0. \tag{2.19}$$

From (2.10), (2.18) and (2.19)

$$e_{xx} = \lambda\ \frac{\partial f}{\partial \sigma_{xx}} = \lambda\ (4\sigma_{xx} - 2\sigma_{yy} - 2\sigma_{zz}) = 6\lambda\sigma_{xx}'\ ,$$

and similarly for the other components. Written out in full this is[†]

[†]Note that from the symmetry of the stress tensor the shear stress terms in $6J_2$ can be expressed as $3(\sigma_{xy}^2 + \sigma_{yx}^2 + \sigma_{yz}^2 + \sigma_{zy}^2 + \sigma_{xz}^2 + \sigma_{zx}^2)$.

When this is differentiated, the e_{xy} ratios, etc., in (2.20) are obtained.

$$\frac{e_{xx}}{\sigma'_{xx}} = \frac{e_{yy}}{\sigma'_{yy}} = \frac{e_{zz}}{\sigma'_{zz}} = \frac{e_{xy}}{\sigma_{xy}} = \frac{e_{yx}}{\sigma_{yx}} = \frac{e_{yz}}{\sigma_{yz}} = \frac{e_{zy}}{\sigma_{zy}} = \frac{e_{xz}}{\sigma_{xz}} = \frac{e_{zx}}{\sigma_{zx}} = 6\lambda. \qquad (2.20)$$

The above equation expresses the Levy-Mises flow rule; it states that the ratio of the components of the plastic rate of deformation tensor is determined from current deviatoric and shear stresses.

If (2.19) is expressed in terms of principal stresses only, the geometric representation of the yield surface is a right circular cylinder of radius $\sqrt{2/3}\bar{\sigma}$ (or $\sqrt{2}k$), whose axis is equally inclined to each of the coordinate axes.

Consider any point on this yield surface and permit a small change in the principal stresses, i.e. $d\sigma_{11}$, $d\sigma_{22}$, $d\sigma_{33}$ along or tangential to the yield surface. Since the surface has not changed in size (no change in $\bar{\sigma}$), and since $df = 0$ it follows that

$$\frac{\partial f}{\partial \sigma_{11}} d\sigma_{11} + \frac{\partial f}{\partial \sigma_{22}} d\sigma_{22} + \frac{\partial f}{\partial \sigma_{33}} d\sigma_{33} = 0. \qquad (2.21)$$

The above equation expresses the condition that the direction $d\sigma_{11}$: $d\sigma_{22}$: $d\sigma_{33}$ be perpendicular to the direction

$$\left(\frac{\partial f}{\partial \sigma_{11}}\right) : \left(\frac{\partial f}{\partial \sigma_{22}}\right) : \left(\frac{\partial f}{\partial \sigma_{33}}\right),$$

which is therefore the direction of the normal to the surface at that point. From (2.10) the principal components of the strain rate vector are in the ratio

$$e_{11} : e_{22} : e_{33} = \left(\frac{\partial f}{\partial \sigma_{11}}\right) : \left(\frac{\partial f}{\partial \sigma_{22}}\right) : \left(\frac{\partial f}{\partial \sigma_{33}}\right),$$

and therefore the strain rate vector is normal to the yield surface.

Representative Stress and Representative Plastic Strain Increment

The quantity $\bar{\sigma}$ in (2.21) has been used to define the current uniaxial yield strength of a material. It has also been termed, variously, the representative or equivalent stress. The reader will encounter such expressions in many texts on plasticity. As stated previously the assumption of isotropic hardening permits one hypothesis that σ is a function of the plastic strain history. This leads to the definition of an equivalent or representative plastic strain increment, $d\bar{\varepsilon}$, such that

$$\bar{\sigma} = H(\int d\bar{\varepsilon}), \qquad (2.22)$$

where the form of the function H could be determined from a single tensile test. Implicit in (2.22) is the notion that there exists a universal stress-strain curve for the material, since it covers all possible combined stress loadings through $\bar{\sigma}$. The quantity $d\bar{\epsilon}$ is taken as a multiple of the second invariant of the plastic strain increment tensor, analogous to $\bar{\sigma}$ as a function of the second invariant of the deviatoric stress tensor. Due to plastic incompressibility the components of the plastic-strain-increment tensor are deviatoric. The representative plastic strain increment is written,

$$d\bar{\epsilon} = [\frac{2}{9}\{(d\epsilon_{xx} - d\epsilon_{yy})^2 + (d\epsilon_{yy} - d\epsilon_{zz})^2 + (d\epsilon_{zz} - d\epsilon_{xx})^2$$

$$+ 6 (d\epsilon_{xy}^2 + d\epsilon_{yz}^2 + d\epsilon_{zx}^2)\}]^{\frac{1}{2}}. \tag{2.23}$$

The numerical factor $\frac{2}{9}$ ensures that $d\bar{\epsilon}$ is equal to the longitudinal strain increment in a tensile test. By using suffix notation,

$$d\bar{\epsilon} = [\frac{2}{3}d\epsilon_{ij}d\epsilon_{ij}]^{\frac{1}{2}}. \tag{2.24}$$

With the aid of (2.10) (expressed in terms of plastic strain-increment components) it is easy to show the following equivalence for an increment of plastic work per unit volume of material

$$\bar{\sigma} \; d\bar{\epsilon} = \sigma_{ij}d\epsilon_{ij}.$$

Under the special case of proportional or radial loading (implying proportional straining), the representative strain increment can be integrated to provide a representative total strain,

$$\bar{\epsilon} = \int d\bar{\epsilon}.$$

The principal components of the total strain can be identified with logarithmic or natural strains.

The Extremum Principles

The extremum principles establish that an underestimate or an overestimate can be obtained for the loads required to cause plastic flow in certain plastic boundary-value problems.

The lower-bound approach is not dealt with in this monograph. A lower-bound requires a statically admissible stress field to be found throughout the entire material (stress discontinuities being permitted). If equilibrium of the stress field, which nowhere exceeds the yield criterion, can be established, then the resulting working loads are always underestimates of the actual or true plastic collapse loads; no attempt is made to ensure that the velocity conditions are satisfied at any point in the material.

The alternative approach, as used throughout this monograph, is to establish a kinematically admissible velocity field (discontinuities in the tangentail component of velocity being permitted) and to leave the stress-equilibrium conditions unsatisfied in certain regions of the material. As shown by the second extremum principle, this method

26

will result in an overestimate of the load required to cause plastic flow.

If the upper and lower bounds give the same values of load to cause plastic flow, the load is exact.

The extremum principles do not indicate how to formulate a solution to a problem and this is left to the skill and experience of the investigator. However, if the load to cause plastic flow is bounded by means of an upper- and lower-bound approach, it will enable the investigator to assess the accuracy of any other proposed solution. If upper-and lower-bounds coincide then we can assert that the load is exact and from the uniqueness theorem it follows that a complete solution has been obtained if the statically admissible stress field and the kinematically admissible velocity field are related according to the plastic potential flow rule. From a practical point of view the upper-bound technique is usually the best one to employ in metal processing, since calculations based on this method will always result in an overestimate of the load that a press or machine will be called upon to deliver or sustain.

REFERENCES

1. Bridgman, P. W., *Studies in Large Plastic Flow and Fracture with Special Emphasis on the Effects of Hydrostatic Pressure*. McGraw-Hill, New York (1952).
2. Pugh, H. Ll. D. (Ed.), *Mechanical Behaviour of Materials under Pressure*. Elsevier Publ., Amsterdam, New York (1970).
3. Hill, R., "On the state of stress in a rigid-plastic body at the yield point". *Phil. Mag.*, **42**, 868 (1951).
4. Prager, W., "An elementary discussion of definitions of stress rate". *Q. Appl. Math.* **18**, 403 (1961).
5. Masur, E. F., "On tensor rates in continuum mechanics". *Zeit. ang. Math, Phys. (ZAMP)*, **16**, 191 (1965).
6. Green, A. E. and Naghdi, P. M., "A general theory of an elastic-plastic continuum". *Arch. Rational Mech. Anal.* **18**, 251 (1965).
7. Hill, R., "Some basic principles in the mechanics of solids without a natural time". *J. Mechs. Phys. Solids*, 7, 209 (1959).
8. Hill, R., "On constitutive inequalities for simple materials - I". *J. Mechs. Phys. Solids*, **16**, 229 (1968).
9. Malvern, L. E., *Introduction to the Mechanics of a Continuous Medium*. Prentice-Hall, Englewood-Cliffs, N. J. (1969).
10. Hutchinson, J. W., in *Numerical Solution of Nonlinear Structural Problems* (edited by R. F. Hartung), 17. A.S.M.E., New York (1973).
11. Bathe, K. J. and Ozdemir, H., "Elastic-plastic large deformation static and dynamic analysis". *Computers and Structures*, 6, 81 (1976).
12. Lee, E. H., in *Engineering Plasticity: Theory of Metal Forming Process*. Vol. I (edited by H. Lippmann), 81. C.I.S.M. Courses and Lectures No. 139. Springer Verlag, (1977).
13. Hill, R., *The Mathematical Theory of Plasticity*. Oxford University Press, London (1950).
14. Koiter, W. T., "Stress-strain relations, uniqueness and variational theorems for elastic-plastic materials with a singular yield surface". *Q. Appl. Math.* **11**, 350 (1953).
15. Drucker, D. C., "A more fundamental approach to plastic stress-strain relations". *Proc. 1st U. S. Natl. Congress Appl. Mechs.* 487. A.S.M.E., New York (1951).
16. Bishop, J. F. W., Green, A. P. and Hill, R., "A note on the deformable region in a rigid plastic body". *J. Mech. Phys. Solids*, **4**, 256 (1956).
17. Hill, R., "On the problem of uniqueness in a rigid plastic solid - I". *J. Mech. Phys. Solids*, **4**, 247 (1956).
18. Drucker, D. C., Greenburg, H. J. and Prager, W., "The safety factor of an elastic-plastic body in plane stress". *Trans. A.S.M.E., J. Appl. Mech.* **18**, 371 (1951).
19. Drucker, D. C., Prager, W. and Greenburg, H. J., "Extended limit design theorems for continuous media". *Q. Appl. Math.* **9**, 381 (1952).
20. von Mises, R., "Mechanik der festern Korper in plastisch deformablen Zustand". *Gottinger Nachricten, math.-phys. Klasse*, **562** (1913).

CHAPTER 3

Basic Theory of Plane Plastic Flow

INTRODUCTION

This chapter is concerned with the governing equations of the plane plastic flow of a rigid-perfectly plastic solid. In the plane of flow the velocity vector is everywhere parallel to a certain plane, say the (x,y)† plane, and is independent of the distance from the plane. The velocity components v_x and v_y are functions of x and y, but not z, and v_z is zero; consequently the non-zero components of the strain rate tensor are e_x, e_y and e_{xy} and $e_x = -e_y$.

STRESS EQUATIONS

In principal stress space, with the principal stresses σ_1, σ_2, σ_3 taken as rectangular Cartesian coordinates, the Mises yield criterion is represented by the surface of a circular cylinder with its axis passing through the origin and having direction cosines $(1/\sqrt{3}, 1/\sqrt{3}, 1/\sqrt{3})$. The Tresca yield criterion is represented by the surface of a regular prism which is inscribed in the Mises cylinder if the uniaxial yield stress Y is the same for both criteria.

The intersections of the yield surfaces and a plane σ_3 = constant are shown in Fig. 3.1. In Fig. 3.1 the position of the point $(\sigma_3, \sigma_3,)$ depends on the hydrostatic part of the stress tensor. If σ_1 is the algebraically greater principal stress and σ_2 the algebraically smaller principal stress in the (x,y) plane, that is if

---

†In this chapter the summation convention is not used and the subscripts x, y and z are used to denote Cartesian components.

29

$$\sigma_{1,2} = \frac{\sigma_x + \sigma_y}{2} \pm \left\{ \left(\frac{\sigma_x - \sigma_y}{2} \right)^2 + \tau_{xy}^{\;2} \right\}^{\frac{1}{2}},$$

it may be deduced from the flow rule that the stress point $(\sigma_1, \sigma_2,)$ is at point G of the ellipse for the Mises criterion and lies on the flat AF of the hexagon for the Tresca criterion.

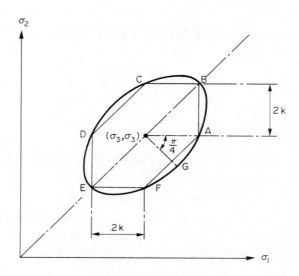

Fig. 3.1.   Intersection of the Tresca and von Mises
yield surfaces by a plane σ_3 = constant.

The flow rule for the Mises yield criterion gives the following results for plane flow:

$$\tau_{xz} = \tau_{yz} = 0$$

and

$$e_z = \lambda \{ \sigma_z - \tfrac{1}{3}(\sigma_x + \sigma_y + \sigma_z) \} = 0,$$

where λ is a non-negative parameter; consequently,

$$\sigma_z = \tfrac{1}{2}(\sigma_x + \sigma_y) = \sigma_3.$$

Substitution of these results into the Mises yield criterion gives

$$\left(\frac{\sigma_x - \sigma_y}{2} \right)^2 + \tau_{xy}^{\;2} = k^2,$$

where $k = Y/\sqrt{3}$ is the yield stress in pure shear.

For the Tresca yield criterion the principal stress σ_3, corresponding to the zero component of strain rate $e_z = e_3$, is the intermediate principal stress. Consequently for plane plastic flow parallel to the (x,y) plane the Tresca yield criterion may be written as

$$\tfrac{1}{2}(\sigma_1 - \sigma_2) = \left\{ \left(\frac{\sigma_x - \sigma_y}{2} \right)^2 + \tau_{xy}^2 \right\}^{\frac{1}{2}} = k,$$

where $k = Y/2$ is the yield stress in pure shear. This is the same as the expression for the Mises criterion but the appropriate value of k must be used.

The three stress equations for the plane plastic flow are the equilibrium equations,

$$\left. \begin{aligned} \frac{\partial \sigma_x}{\partial x} + \frac{\partial \tau_{yx}}{\partial y} &= 0 \\[2mm] \frac{\partial \tau_{yx}}{\partial x} + \frac{\partial \sigma_y}{\partial y} &= 0 \end{aligned} \right\} \tag{3.1}$$

and the yield criterion

$$(\sigma_x - \sigma_y)^2 + 4\tau_{xy}^2 = 4k^2 . \tag{3.2}$$

These three equations contain three unknowns, σ_x, σ_y and τ_{xy}, but in general the three equations and the stress boundary conditions are not sufficient to obtain a solution for the stresses. A problem is said to be statically determined if equations (3.1) and (3.2) and the stress boundary conditions are sufficient to provide a solution for the stresses, but in general this is not true.

The yield criterion is satisfied by,

$$\left. \begin{aligned} \sigma_x &= -p - k \sin 2\phi, \\[2mm] \sigma_y &= -p + k \sin 2\phi, \\[2mm] \tau_{xy} &= k \cos 2\phi, \end{aligned} \right\} \tag{3.3}$$

and

where $-p = \tfrac{1}{2}(\sigma_x + \sigma_y)$ is the hydrostatic part† of the stress tensor and $(\phi + \pi/4)$ is the anti-clockwise rotation of the direction of the

---

†Strictly $-p$ is the hydrostatic part of the stress tensor only when $\sigma_z = \tfrac{1}{2}(\sigma_z + \sigma_y)$, which is always true for the Mises yield criterion but is not necessarily true for the Tresca criterion. For the Tresca criterion the only restriction on σ_z is that it must be the intermediate principal stress.

algebraically greatest principal stress σ_1 measured form the positive
direction of the x-axis as shown in Fig. 3.2. Substitution of equations (3.3) in equations (3.1) gives,

$$-\frac{\partial p}{\partial x} - 2k \cos 2\phi \frac{\partial \phi}{\partial x} - 2k \sin 2\phi \frac{\partial \phi}{\partial y} = 0$$

and

$$-\frac{\partial p}{\partial y} - 2k \sin 2\phi \frac{\partial \phi}{\partial x} + 2k \cos 2\phi \frac{\partial \phi}{\partial y} = 0.$$

(3.4)

Equations (3.4) are hyperbolic[1] and can be solved by the method of
characteristics, see Appendix 6. The characteristic directions of
equations (3.4) are found from,

$$\begin{vmatrix} dx & dy & 0 & 0 \\ 0 & 0 & dx & dy \\ 1 & 0 & 2k\cos 2\phi & 2k\sin 2\phi \\ 0 & 1 & 2k\sin 2\phi & -2k\cos 2\phi \end{vmatrix} = 0,$$

which is a quadratic equation in dy/dx with roots

$$\frac{dy}{dx} = \tan \phi$$

and

$$\frac{dy}{dx} = \tan (\phi + \pi/2),$$

which show that the two families of characteristics form an orthogonal
network. The members of the family given by the parameter ϕ will
henceforth be called α- lines and those given by the parameter $(\phi + \pi/2)$,
β-lines. Clearly the α- and β-lines coincide with the trajectories
of maximum shearing stress. At any point in the (x,y) plane the direction of the algebraically greatest principal stress bisects the right
angle between the α and β directions as shown in Fig. 3.2. Referring

32

to Fig. 3.2, the α and β directions at any point are parallel to PI and PII respectively where P is the pole of the Mohr circle and I is the point $(-p, k)$ and II the point $(-p, -k)$ in the Mohr circle diagram

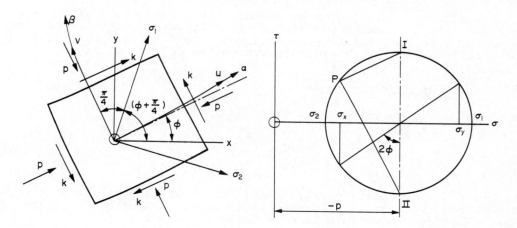

Fig. 3.2. Stress system in plane plastic flow showing the physical plane and Mohr's circle.

For a stress solution to be possible it is necessary that,

$$\begin{vmatrix} dx & dy & 0 & dp \\ 0 & 0 & dx & d\phi \\ 1 & 0 & 2k \cos 2\phi & 0 \\ 0 & 1 & 2k \sin 2\phi & 0 \end{vmatrix} = 0,$$

i.e.

$$-dp/dx - 2k \cos 2\phi \, dx/d\phi - 2k \sin 2\phi \, dy/d\phi = 0,$$

or

$$dp + 2k \, d\phi = 0 \text{ on } dy/dx = \tan \phi$$

and

$$dp - 2k \, d\phi = 0 \text{ on } dy/dx = \tan (\phi + \pi/2).$$

Integration gives,

$$\left. \begin{array}{l} p + 2k\phi = \text{constant on an } \alpha\text{-line} \\[8pt] p - 2k\phi = \text{constant on a } \beta\text{-line.} \end{array} \right\} \tag{3.5}$$

and

Equations (3.5) are known as the Hencky equations and are a form of the plane-strain equilibrium equations for material which has yielded plastically.

The form of the Hencky equations as given in (3.5) is standard in most

txt books. However, by altering the sign convention, the signs in
3.5) can be reversed, as illustrated in reference 2. In this monograph p is defined as $-(\sigma_x + \sigma_y)/2$ and hence tensile hydrostatic
stresses carry a minus sign and compressive hydrostatic stresses a
plus sign in the Hencky equations. The direction of the algebraically
greatest principal stress passes through the first and third quadrant
of a right-handed α-β coordinate system, as defined in Fig. 3.2.

VELOCITY EQUATIONS

The continuity equation

$$\frac{\partial v_x}{\partial x} + \frac{\partial v_y}{\partial y} = 0, \tag{3.6}$$

is one of the velocity equations and the other is obtained on the
assumption that for an isotropic rigid-plastic material the principal
axes of stress and strain rate coincide ; consequently,

$$\frac{2\tau_{xy}}{\sigma_x - \sigma_y} = \frac{\partial v_x/\partial y + \partial v_y/\partial x}{\partial v_x/\partial x - \partial v_y/\partial y}, \tag{3.7}$$

which yields the isotropy equation,

$$\frac{\partial v_x}{\partial y} + \frac{\partial v_y}{\partial x} = -\left(\frac{\partial v_x}{\partial x} - \frac{\partial v_y}{\partial y}\right)\cot 2\phi. \tag{3.8}$$

Equation (3.7) may be written in the form[†]

$$\frac{e_{xy}}{\tau_{xy}} = \frac{e_x - e_y}{\sigma_x - \sigma_y} = \frac{e_x - e_y}{\sigma_x' - \sigma_y'} = \frac{e_x}{\sigma_x'} = \frac{e_y}{\sigma_y'},$$

and this shows that the Levy-Mises equations are valid for the plane
flow of an isotropic rigid-plastic material regardless of the yield
criterion.

Equations (3.6) and (3.8) are hyperbolic and the characteristic directions are found from

---

[†]This is not necessarily true for the flow of an isotropic elastic-
plastic solid.
[‡]This set of equations has been given in Chapter 2, see equation (2.20).
Note that the prime represents a deviatoric stress, e.g. $\sigma_x' = \sigma_x + p$,
where $p = -\frac{1}{2}(\sigma_x + \sigma_y)$.

$$\begin{vmatrix} 1 & 0 & 0 & 1 \\ \cot 2\phi & 1 & 1 & -\cot 2\phi \\ dx & dy & 0 & 0 \\ 0 & 0 & dx & dy \end{vmatrix} = 0,$$

which is a quadratic equation in dy/dx with roots

$$\frac{dy}{dx} = \tan \phi$$

and

$$\frac{dy}{dx} = \tan \left(\phi + \frac{\pi}{2} \right).$$

This shows that the characteristics of the stress and velocity equations coincide.

For a velocity solution to be possible it is necessary that,

$$\begin{vmatrix} 1 & 0 & 0 & 0 \\ \cot 2\phi & 1 & 1 & 0 \\ dx & dy & 0 & dv_x \\ 0 & 0 & dx & dv_y \end{vmatrix} = 0,$$

i.e.
$$dv_x dx + dv_y dy = 0.$$

Consequently,

$$dv_x + \tan\phi \, dv_y = 0 \quad \text{on an } \alpha\text{-line}$$

and
$$dv_x - \cot\phi \, dv_y = 0 \quad \text{on a } \beta\text{-line.} \qquad (3.9)$$

If u and v are the velocity components in the α and β directions respectively

$$v_x = u \cos\phi - v \sin \phi,$$
$$v_y = u \sin\phi + v \cos \phi, \qquad (3.9a)$$

and substituting in equations (3.9) gives

$$du - v \, d\phi = 0 \quad \text{on an } \alpha\text{-line}$$

and
$$dv + u \, d\phi = 0 \quad \text{on a } \beta\text{-line.} \qquad (3.10)$$

Equations (3.10) are known as the Geiringer equations. The rate of extension along a slip line is zero since $e_x = -e_y$ and equations (3.10) may be derived from this (see Ref. 3, p. 107). A similar analysis leading to equations (3.5) and (3.10) has been given by Halling[4].

Note that if v acted in the opposite direction to that shown in Fig. 3.2, then it would have a negative value. This point is illustrated in Chapter 5 in the section dealing with Pressure Vessels.

The field of characteristics of stress and velocity is known as a slip-line field and the characteristics as slip lines. In general, both the stress and velocity boundary conditions must be used to obtain a slip-line field which then constitute a solution to a given problem.

Referring to Fig. 3.3, a velocity field in the curvilinear quadrilateral $ABCD$, bounded by the α-line AB, the β-line AD, and the slip lines through B and D, can be found by applying equations (3.10) in finite difference form if arbitrary distributions of v along AB and u along AD are prescribed. If there is a discontinuity at point E of the pre-scribed distribution of v on AB, the discontinuity is propagated along the β-line through E. Also, since u must be continuous across the β-line[†] it may be deduced from the second of equations (3.10) that the discontinuity in v is constant along the β-line. It is also evident that in plane plastic flow velocity discontinuities can occur only across slip lines.

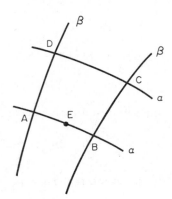

Fig. 3.3.   Element of a slip-line field net.

HENCKY'S FIRST THEOREM

In Fig. 3.3 the region $ABCD$ is bounded by two α-lines AB and DC and two β-lines AD and BC. The difference in p between A and C can be found from equations (3.5) and is

---

†It has already been noted in Chapter 2 that only the tangential component of velocity can be discontinuous.

$$p_C - p_A = (p_C - p_D) + (p_D - p_A) = 2k(2\phi_D - \phi_C - \phi_A);$$

also, $\quad p_C - p_A = (p_C - p_B) + (p_B - p_A) = 2k(\phi_C + \phi_A - 2\phi_B).$

Consequently,
$$\left. \begin{aligned} \phi_D - \phi_A &= \phi_C - \phi_B \\ \phi_C - \phi_D &= \phi_B - \phi_A. \end{aligned} \right\} \qquad (3.11)$$

and

Equations (3.11) show that there is a constant angle between the tangents to two slip lines of one family at their intersection with a slip line of the other family. This is Hencky's First Theorem, which is of considerable importance in the numerical and graphical construction of slip-line fields. A useful deduction from Hencky's First Theorem is that if a segment of a slip line, cut off by two slip lines of the other family, is a straight line then all the other segments cut off by the same two slip lines of the other family are straight. The straight segments are the common normals of the intersecting slip lines of the other family, and so these slip lines have a common evolute and the straight segments are all of the same length.

HENCKY'S SECOND THEOREM

Let the radii of curvature of the α- and β-lines be R and S respectively, the positive sense being as shown in Fig. 3.4 Then,

$$\frac{1}{R} = \frac{\partial \phi}{\partial S_\alpha}$$

and

$$\frac{1}{S} = -\frac{\partial \phi}{\partial S_\beta},$$

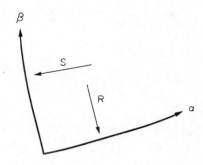

Fig. 3.4. Showing the convention for positive
radius of curvature of slip lines.

where S_α and S_β are the distances along the α- and β- lines respectively. In Fig. 3.5, $ABCD$ is an infinitesimal curvilinear quadrilateral and ΔS_β is the length of the element of a β-line cut off by α-lines AB and DC. Since

$$-S.\,\Delta\phi = \Delta S_\beta$$

where

$$\Delta\phi = \phi_D - \phi_A = \phi_C - \phi_B$$

is a constant, and from Fig. 3.5

$$\frac{\partial(\Delta S_\beta)}{\partial S_\alpha} = \Delta\phi,$$

it follows that

$$\frac{\partial S}{\partial S_\alpha} = -1. \tag{3.12}$$

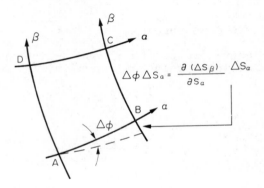

Fig. 3.5. Concerning the proof of Hencky's Second Theorem.

Similarly it may be shown that

$$\frac{\partial R}{\partial S_\beta} = -1. \tag{3.13}$$

Equations (3.12) and (3.13) are known as Hencky's Second Theorem and may also be expressed as

$$dS + R\,d\phi = 0 \quad \text{on an } \alpha\text{-line}$$

and

$$dR - S\,d\phi = 0 \quad \text{on a } \beta\text{-line}.$$

Hencky's Second Theorem shows that in moving along one set of slip lines, the radius of curvature of the intersecting slip lines of the other family changes by an amount equal to the distance travelled; if the travel is far enough in the appropriate direction and the plastic region

extends sufficiently far, the radius of curvature of the intersecting
slip line becomes zero. Also, in moving along one slip line, the
centres of curvature of the intersecting slip lines form an involute
of the given slip line.

A field that occurs frequently in problems, consists of radii and
concentric arcs, the centre being a singularity of stress. This
field clearly satisfies equations (3.12) and (3.13) and is a degenerate
case of the slip lines of a family meeting an envelope tangentially.

HODOGRAPHS

The velocity field corresponding to a slip-line-field can be represented
by a hodograph. The use of the hodograph was apparently first used (p. 6)
by Green[5] who showed that a velocity field for plane plastic flow can
be transformed into a slip-line field.

Referring to Fig. 3.6, consider two points P and Q an infinitesimal
distance apart on a slip-line. The rate of extension in the direction
tangential to the slip line is zero and consequently the velocity of
Q relative to P is normal to QP. In the velocity plane a fixed origin
representing zero velocity is chosen and from this bound vectors that
represent the velocity at points in the slip line field can be drawn.
A point in the slip-line-field maps in the velocity plane as the term-
inus of the corresponding bound vector. For example, the points P
and Q map as the points P' and Q' in the velocity plane, as shown in
Fig. 3.6, where $\overline{OP'} = \bar{v}_p$ and $\overline{OQ'} = \bar{v}_Q$ are the velocities of P and Q
respectively. The vector $\overline{P'Q'} = \bar{v}_{Q/P}$, which is the velocity of Q
relative to P, is normal to PQ, and the element PQ of the slip-line
maps as the element $P'Q'$ in the velocity plane. It may be deduced that
if an α-line maps as, say, an α'-line in the velocity plane and a β-
line as a β'-line, the α'- and β'-lines form an orthogonal network
with the same geometrical properties as the slip-line field.

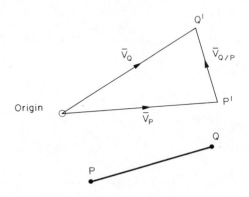

Fig. 3.6. A line element of the slip-line field
PQ and corresponding hodograph mapping
$P'Q'$.

A non-deforming region that is moving in translation maps as a point
in the velocity plane. An α-line across which there is a velocity

discontinuity maps as two parallel α'-lines connected by straight β'-lines of length equal to the magnitude of the velocity discontinuity. This is exemplified in Fig. 3.7, where the curve AB represents a slip line across which there is a velocity discontinuity. In the hodograph, with 0 as the origin, the lines ab and $a'b'$ are two parallel curves orthogonal to the slip line AB, separated by a velocity discontinuity of magnitude V^*, say. The lines aa' and bb' have the same direction as the tangent to the slip line at points A and B respectively and represent the magnitude of the velocity discontinuity.

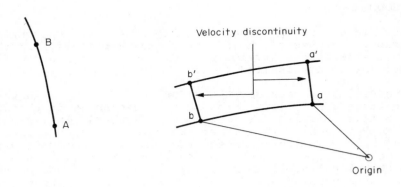

Fig. 3.7.   The representation of a velocity
            discontinuity in the hodograph.

STRESS PLANE

The normal stress-shearing stress plane containing the Mohr circle that represents the state of stress (σ_x, σ_y, τ_{xy}) at any point in plane plastic flow is known as the stress plane. For a rigid-perfectly plastic material the radius of this Mohr circle cannot exceed the yield shear stress k, and if the radius is less than k the material is not deforming.

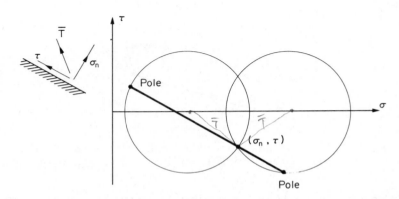

Fig. 3.8.   Strong and weak solutions in the stress
            plane.

Suppose that for the plane flow of a rigid plastic material the stress vector $\bar{T}$ at a point P on an elemental plane normal to the plane of flow is known. Referring to Fig. 3.8, σ_n and τ are the normal and shear stress components respectively of T. If $\tau < k$ two Mohr circles of radius k can be drawn through the point (σ_n, τ) in the stress plane†.

The state of stress corresponding to the right-hand circle is known as the strong solution and that corresponding to the left-hand circle as the weak solution. In most applications it is physically evident which solution should be chosen. The point (σ_n, τ) and the poles of the Mohr circles for the strong and weak solutions are collinear.

The existence of strong and weak solutions suggests that surfaces of stress discontinuity are possible in a rigid plastic solid. A surface of stress discontinuity in a rigid plastic solid may be considered as the limit of a layer in an elastic-plastic solid across which there is a very large stress gradient. An example occurs in the pure bending of an elastic-plastic prismatic bar. The outer fibres become plastic, as shown in Fig. 3.9(a), when the elastic limit is exceeded. If the bending moment is increased eventually there is only a very thin layer

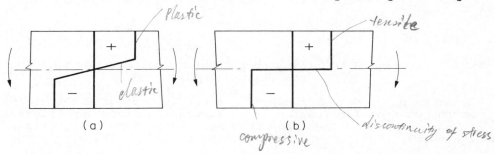

(a)   (b)

Fig. 3.9. Pure bending of an elastic, perfectly plastic, strip.

about the neutral surface which is elastic and the axial stress changes rapidly from compressive to tensile across this layer. In the limit, for a rigid plastic beam, this layer can be considered to be a surface of stress discontinuity as shown in Fig. 3.9(b). A fundamentally different situation is that of the bending of a semi-circular beam under the action of compressive (or tensile) point loads, as shown in Fig. 3.10. The maximum bending moment obviously occurs across section XX and if the deformation takes place under conditions of plane strain the theoretical slip line field in this region is a network of logarithmic spirals, as shown in Fig. 3.10. Point 0 is a singular point and there is no neutral axis through this point, the material on each side being rigid. Both the horizontal component of stress, σ_x, and the vertical component of σ_y, can be discontinuous at a singular point.

This is not so for a surface of stress discontinuity, as is explained below. Experimental verification of the physical existence of a singular point such as is referred to in Fig. 3.10 is shown in Plate 1. The photograph is reproduced from reference 6, which is concerned with the diametral compression of mild steel rings by point loads.

---

†The usual Mohr circle convention for shearing stress is used.

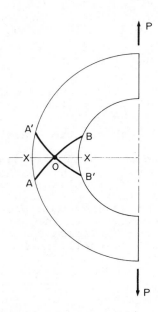

Fig. 3.10. Bending of a semi-circular bar under
the action of diametral point loads.

At every point on a surface of stress discontinuity the stress vector
acting on one side must be equal in magnitude and opposite in direction
to that acting on the opposite side. This means that for plane flow
the normal stress σ_n and the shearing stress τ are continuous across
the discontinuity, but the tangential stress σ_t may be discontinuous,
as shown in Fig. 3.11. It follows from the yield criterion that if
the material on each side of the stress discontinuity is plastic,

$$\sigma_t = \sigma_n \pm 2\sqrt{(k^2 - \tau^2)}$$

or

$$\sigma_t^{(1)} = \sigma_n + 2\sqrt{(k^2 - \tau^2)},$$

corresponding to the weak solution, and

$$\sigma_t^{(2)} = \sigma_n - 2\sqrt{(k^2 - \tau^2)}$$

corresponding to the strong solution. The Mohr circles for the states
of stress on the two sides of the discontinuity are shown in Fig. 3.11.
In Fig. 3.11, OA represents the magnitude of the stress vector on each
side of the discontinuity and

P^1 is the pole for side 1,
P^2 is the pole for side 2,
$P^1 I^1$ is the α-direction for side 1,
$P^2 I^2$ is the β-direction for side 2,
$p_1 = -\frac{1}{2}(\sigma_n + \sigma^{(1)}_t)$ for side 1,

and

$p_2 = -\frac{1}{2}(\sigma_n + \sigma^{(2)}_t)$ for side 2.

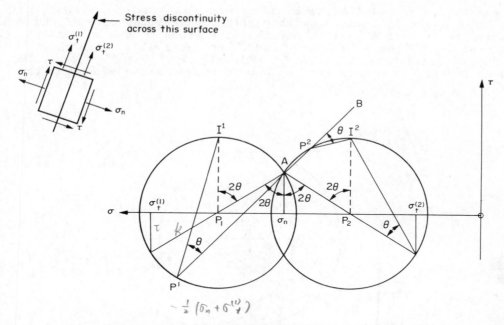

Fig. 3.11.   A stress discontinuity represented on
Mohr's circle.

It follows from elementary geometry that,

$$\angle I^1 P^1 A = \angle I^2 P^2 B = \theta,$$

and consequently the α-lines on each side of the discontinuity make
an angle θ with $P^1 A P^2$, which is parallel to the tangent to the discontinuity. Also, the relationship

$$2\sqrt{(k^2 - \tau^2)} = p_1 - p_2 = 2k \sin 2\theta, \qquad (3.14)$$

which gives the jump in p across the discontinuity, may be obtained
from the Mohr circle diagrams. Equation (3.14) shows that there can
be no stress discontinuity across an α-line. Similarly, it may be shown
that there can be no stress discontinuity across a β-line.

A stress discontinuity in the plane plastic flow of a rigid-perfectly
plastic solid can undergo a rigid body motion but no deformation since
it is the limit of a narrow band across which the stress changes
rapidly from a strong solution to a weak solution and the stress state
in this narrow band is not a plastic state.

The yield state of stress at a point in plane plastic flow is completely determined by the centre $(-p, 0)$ of the Mohr circle of radius k
and the pole of the Mohr's circle. The Hencky equations show that as
the point considered moves along an α-line the rate of change of p is
$-2k\phi$ and as it moves along a β-line the rate of change is $2k\phi$.   Now,
consider two points Q' and Q'' a small distance apart on an α-line and
let $\phi_{Q''} - \phi_{Q'} = \Delta\phi$.   In Fig. 3.12, $\Delta\phi$ is positive and the circles, centre

O' and O'', represent the states of stress at Q' and Q'' respectively. The pole of the Mohr circle with centre O' is P', the pole of the Mohr circle centre with O'' is P'' and the directions of the tangents to the α-lines are $P'I'$ and $P''I''$ at Q' and Q'' respectively. Through I'', $I''P'''$ is drawn parallel to $I'P'$. Clearly, $\angle P''O''P''' = 2\Delta\phi$, and it may be deduced from this that as a point moves along an α-line the

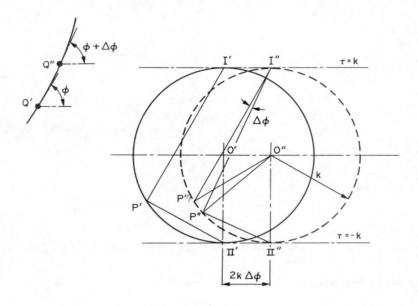

Fig. 3.12. Development of the stress plane by
            rolling Mohr's stress circles along
            the axis $\tau = +k$.

Mohr circle corresponding to the state of stress rolls along the line $\tau = k$ with the pole describing a cycloid. If ϕ increases, the circle rolls so that the radius turns anticlockwise and if ϕ decreases the radius turns clockwise. Similarly, as a point moves along a β-line the Mohr circle rolls along the line $\tau = -k$ and the pole describes a cycloid. A point in the slip line field is mapped in the stress plane by the pole of the corresponding Mohr circle. The rules for mapping the slip line field in the stress plane may be stated as follows:

(a) To map an α-line, roll the Mohr circle along $\tau = k$.
(b) To map a β-line, roll the Mohr circle along $\tau = -k$.
(c) When ϕ increases the circle rolls so that a radius turns anti-
     clockwise at a rate 2ϕ and when ϕ decreases the circle rolls
     so that a radius turns clockwise at a rate 2ϕ.

The concept of the stress plane was introduced by Prager[7] and is used in Prager's well-known geometrical method for constructing slip-line fields. Prager[3] also uses the stress plane to derive the Hencky equations. In this monograph an alternative geometrical procedure for the construction of slip lines is presented.

BASIC THEORY OF PLANE PLASTIC FLOW

REQUIREMENTS FOR A COMPLETE SOLUTION

A complete solution to a problem of the deformation of a rigid plastic solid consists of:

(a) a statically admissible stress field, that is, a stress field that satisfies the equilibrium equations and stress boundary conditions and nowhere violates the yield criterion, and

(b) a kinematically admissible velocity field that is compatible with the stress field according to the appropriate stress-strain rate relations and such that the rate of plastic energy dissipation is positive wherever deformation occurs.

Many slip-line-field solutions that have been proposed for problems of plane flow do not include a statically admissible extension of the stress field into all the non-deforming zones of the solution. If such a solution, which can be described as an incomplete solution is kinematically admissible then it gives an upper bound for the rate of working of the unknown surface tractions. For example, an incomplete slip-line-field solution for an extrusion problem gives an upper bound for the ram force. A slip-line-field solution that is kinematically admissible, that includes a statically admissible extension of the stress field into the non-deforming regions and has positive plastic energy dissipation everywhere that deformation occurs, is a complete solution. The rate of working of the unknown surface tractions given by a complete solution is exact. If two or more complete slip-line-field solutions to a problem can be found, the stress fields are unique except possibly in the common non-deforming regions, and Bishop *et al*[8] have shown that the possible deformable zone can be uniquely determined from one complete solution.

It is not always necessary to be able to extend the stress solution throughout the assumed rigid region in order to ascertain whether the yield criterion has been violated at a certain point. Use can be made of equations obtained by Hill[9] for checking the stress conditions inside wedge-shaped zones†, where the tip of the wedge is invariably a point of stress singularity.

The mathematical analysis developed by Hill is not reproduced here. However, some of the results, i.e. those which are most commonly met with in slip-line field analysis, are presented and it is left to the interested reader to consult the original work of Hill or the book by Ford[2] (p. 525) for a comprehensive treatment of the analysis.

It may be shown from Hill's criterion that, for the existence of a stress system which satisfies the conditions of equilibrium and does not violate the yield condition, a wedge

(i) bounded by a pair of slip lines must have an included angle, ψ, equal to or larger than $\pi/2$,

(ii) bounded by one slip line, on which the hydrostatic pressure‡ is p, and one stress-free surface (or one frictionless tool surface) should include an angle equal to or larger than $\pi/4$.

---

†Note that the stress conditions are only checked at the wedge tip and not elsewhere in the rigid region.

‡Obviously, limits must be imposed upon p in order that the yield and equilibrium conditions are satisfied.

These two conditions cover a surprisingly large number of cases in metal-forming problems and are well worth committing to memory. It is to be reiterated that statement (ii) is only true for frictionless tool faces; the included angle of the wedge is not limited to being more than $\pi/4$ when the tool face is rough (see p. 31 of ref. 10).

A further consequence of Hill's analysis concerns the limits imposed on the magnitude of the permissible discontinuity in stress arising at a stress singularity. It has already been mentioned that the included angle, ψ, of a wedge bounded by a pair of slip lines cannot be less than $\pi/2$. It follows from the work of Hill that the jump (or discontinuity) in hydrostatic pressure in rotating through the wedge angle ψ must not exceed that prescribed by the Hencky equations along a slip line that turns through the same angle, i.e. $\Delta p \leqslant 2k\psi$. An example of the application of this theorem is to the bending of the curved beam of Fig. 3.10. The two slip lines AO and $B'O$ bound the wedge whose included angle here is $\pi/2$, with O the point of stress singularity, Hence, the difference in hydrostatic pressure on the slip lines AO and BO at point O cannot exceed $2k(\pi/2)$. Further illustrations of the technique are to be found in Chapter 5, in the section dealing with the bending of notched bars.

The possibility of discontinuities in stress and velocity in a complete solution has already been mentioned. Such discontinuities can exist but it is reiterated that a discontinuity in stress cannot occur across a slip line. Furthermore, as illustrated by Green[11], no velocity discontinuities can pass through a singular point such as in Fig. 3.10, i.e. a discontinuity in the tangential component of velocity cannot be permitted across the slip lines passing through point O. Note that this statement is only true when applied to a singular point, i.e. where discontinuities are permitted in the σ_x and σ_y component of stress.

Many examples are to be found where four slip lines meet at a point and a tangential velocity discontinuity exists across them, e.g. point F of Fig. 5.21, Chapter 5. However, there is no discontinuity in stress at point F. A discontinuity in stress, either across a surface or at a point, is easily revealed if the slip lines can be identified. Note, that in Fig. 3.10 the slip line $B'OA$ is not a continous slip line, i.e. BO is a β-line and OA an α-line.

A necessary condition for a complete solution is that the velocity boundary conditions must always be satisfied and, amongst other things, this imposes a limitation on the permissible velocity discontinuities that can occur in a slip-line field. In the solution of many metal-forming problems it is common for certain zones of the worked metal to have a rigid-body movement†; an obvious example would be the metal entering and leaving an extrusion or drawing die. This point is exemplified in Fig. 3.13 which represents drawing or extrusion through a wedge-shaped die; only the upper half of the die is shown. Lines ABC and XYZ are a schematic representation of the entry and exit slip lines. The network of slip lines in between the bounding slip lines, which would normally represent the deforming zone, have not been shown for reasons of clarity. Depending on the precise nature of the problem, ABC and XYZ may or may not be slip lines across which there is a

---

†The translational movement of a rigid zone is represented by a single point in the hodograph.

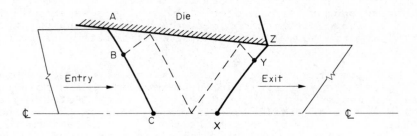

Fig. 3.13. The schematic representation of a slip-
line field in a drawing or extrusion
process.

discontinuity in the tangential component of velocity. However, because
the metal to the left of *ABC* and to the right of *XYZ* moves as a rigid
body, no slip line can either commence at a point such as *B* or terminate
at a point such as *Y* and have a discontinuity in the tangential component
of velocity across it. This statement is easily verified by considering
the velocities at points *B* or *Y*. If the slip line meeting these points
is a line of velocity discontinuity then this would be incompatible
with the rigid body movement of the entry and exit material.

In general, once a velocity discontinuity is established across a slip
line there always exists a velocity discontinuity across any extension
to the slip line. The exception to the rule is the case where the slip
line meets a perfectly rough die or tool face tangentially; the slip
line normal to the face at that point need not be a line of velocity
discontinuity; see the problem on compression with rough flat platens
in Chapter 5. Another general rule concerning slip lines across which
there is a discontinuity in the tangential component of velocity, is

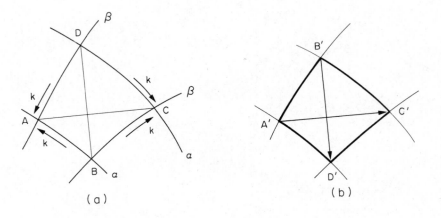

Fig. 3.14.(a) A curvilinear quadrilateral in the
slip-line-field.
(b) Hodograph to (a).

47

that these slip lines either form the boundary of a deforming region or originate and/or terminate at a point of stress singularity within the field. These restrictions are generally necessary, otherwise compatibility of the velocity solution is violated, as described earlier.

Green[5] has given the condition that must be satisfied in order that the rate of plastic energy dissipation be positive. A simple test for this has been suggested by Ford[2], and is as follows. Referring to Fig. 3.14(a), $ABCD$ is a curvilinear element bounded by two α-lines and two β-lines. Figure 3.14(b) represents the hodograph and there is positive dissipation of plastic energy in the element provided the component in the direction $\overline{AC}$ of $\bar{v}_{C/A}$, i.e., of velocity of C relative to A, is positive or if the component in the direction $\overline{DB}$ of $\bar{v}_{D/B}$ is positive in keeping with the sign of the shear stress in Fig. 3.14(a). A mathematical method for determining the sign of the energy dissipation has been given by Rychlewski[12].

REFERENCES

1. Smith, G. D., *Numerical Solutions of Partial Differential Equations*. Oxford University Press (1965).
2. Ford, H., *Advanced Mechanics of Materials*. Longmans Green, London (1960).
3. Prager, W., *An Introduction to Plasticity*. Addison-Wesley, Massachusetts (1959).
4. Halling, J., "The characteristic method of solution for the problem of plane plastic strain". *Engineer*, 207, 250 (1959).
5. Green, A. P., "On the use of hodographs in problems of plane plastic strain". *J. Mech. Phys. Solids*, 2, 73 (1954).
6. Sowerby, R., Johnson, W. and Samanta, S. K., "The diamentral compression of circular rings by 'point' loads". *Int. J. Mech. Sci.* 10, 369 (1968).
7. Prager, W., "A geometrical discussion of the slip line field in plane plastic flow". *Trans. R. Inst. Tech., Stockholm*, No. 65 (1953).
8. Bishop, J. F. W., Green, A. P. and Hill, R., "A note on the deformable region in a rigid-plastic body". *J. Mech. Phys. Solids*, 4, 256 (1956).
9. Hill, R., "On the limits set by plastic yielding to the intensity of singularities of stress". *J. Mech. Phys. Solids*, 2, 278 (1954).
10. Johnson, W. and Kudo H., *The Mechanics of Metal Extrusion*. Manchester University Press (1962).
11. Green, A. P., "Plastic yielding of notched bars due to bending". *Q. Mech. Appl. Math.* 6, 223 (1953).
12. Rychlewski, J., Comment on "Plane-flow extrusion or drawing", by Kronsjo, L. J. and Mellor, P.B. Letter to the editor, *Int. J. Mech. Sci.* 10, 669 (1968).

CHAPTER 4

Application to Specific Problems

INTRODUCTION

In this chapter methods for the solution of problems of plane plastic flow of a rigid-perfectly plastic solid are considered. A solution consists of a statically admissible stress field† and a kinematically admissible velocity field that is related to the stress field according to the flow rule, there being positive plastic energy dissipation where deformation occurs. If it is shown that the stress field can be extended in a statically admissible manner into the non-defroming regions, then a complete solution has been found and the stress field of this complete solution is unique in the deforming regions. It is possible that more than one kinematically admissible velocity field associated with the stress field of a complete solution can be found, for example, in the plane strain indentation of a semi-infinite mass by a frictionless flat rigid punch; however, the stress fields for the various velocity solutions must be identical except perhaps in the common non-deforming regions. Bishop[1] *et al* have given a theorem that determines the maximum extent of the deformable regions and it follows from the uniqueness theorems that the stress field in then unique in these regions.

A solution that does not include an extension of the stress field into all the non-deforming regions of the velocity field but is otherwise complete yields an upper bound for the surface tractions on the part of the surface S_v of the boundary-value problem†.

In the section immediately following a number of boundary-value problems are examined with the aim of showing how solutions may be developed

---

†A statically admissible stress field is taken here to mean a stress field that satisfies the equilibrium equations and the stress boundary conditions and does not violate the yield criterion.
†Such a solution may reasonably be described as an upper-bound solution. Unfortunately, this term is often used imprecisely in the literature to describe arbitrary, kinematically admissible velocity fields which are used correctly in certain boundary-value problems for a rigid-perfectly plastic solid , and incorrectly for problems with work-hardening and rate rate-sensitive materials, to obtain upper bounds for loads from the second extremum principle.

(through the construction of a slip-line-field) by a straightforward step-by-step procedure. The technique is utilized in Chapter 5, where a number of forming processes are considered with the boundary conditions sufficient to allow the complete determination of an appropriate slip-line field and from which the associated hodograph can be derived. The slip-line fields so constructed are usually geometrically simple, being comprised of regions of constant state (both families of slip-lines straight), centred fan zones and nets of logarithmic spirals, etc. Solutions of this kind are said to be of the 'direct type', and a problem is statically determined when the slip-line field is defined uniquely by the stress boundary conditions. In certain cases it is possible to start the solution by first constructing the hodograph particularly when this is made up to zones of simple geometry and then to deduce the appropriate or accompanying slip-line field. This provides a variation on the 'direct type' of solution[2], see also reference 3.

There are many problems where there are insufficient known starting conditions for the determination of the slip-line field (or hodograph) by the intuitive procedures of Chapter 5. Solutions to these type of problems are said to be of the 'indirect type', and until relatively recently have been proceeded with in a rather laborious trial and error approach, witness the computational effort involved in the solution by Green[4] for frictionless compression and that for hot-rolling due to Alexander[5].

In Chapter 6 of this monograph a systematic computational procedure is described which greatly facilitates the solution to problems of the *indirect* type. As discussed in Chapter 6, and the references therein, the method is not suited to *all* problems in this class. Nevertheless, the technique (like many other numerical procedures) has found favour because of the growing size and availability of computers; it has provided solutions to a number of problems that until fairly recently were regarded as being too complex to treat by trial and error procedures either graphically or numerically.

CONSTRUCTION OF SLIP-LINE FIELDS

Analytical integration of the plane-flow equations is possible for certain problems with very simple boundary conditions, but it is usually necessary to obtain the slip-line field by numerical or graphical methods. Hill[6] has given in detail procedures for the numerical determination of the nodal points of a slip-line field for three boundary-value problems. One of the numerical procedures which may easily be performed graphically is outlined here. Essentially, it consists of replacing an element of slip line by a straight line or chord that makes an angle ϕ for an α-line and $(\phi + \pi/2)$ for a β-line with a positive x direction, where ϕ is the mean of the values of ϕ at the ends of the element.

The *first boundary-value problem* is the determination of the slip-line field defined by two intersecting slip lines which are given. Referring to Fig. 4.1, if the α-line AB and the β-line AC are given, then the field in the region bounded by AB, AC, the β-line through B and the α-line through C is defined and can be obtained numerically or graphically. Consider the point E on AB and F on AC; the mesh point D which is the intersection of the β-line through E and the α-line through F

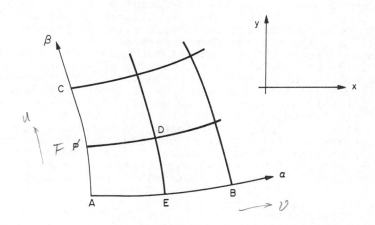

Fig. 4.1. First boundary-value problem: two
intersecting slip lines given.

can be obtained as follows: from Hencky's First Theorem,

$$\phi_D = \phi_E - \phi_A + \phi_F,$$

and the coordinates of D are given approximately by,

$$y_D - y_F = (x_D - x_F) \tan \tfrac{1}{2}(\phi_D + \phi_F),$$

and

$$y_D - y_E = (x_D - x_E) \tan \left\{ \tfrac{1}{2}(\phi_D + \phi_E) + \frac{\pi}{2} \right\}$$

$$= -(x_D - x_E) \cot \tfrac{1}{2}(\phi_D + \phi_E).$$

Since ϕ_A, ϕ_E, ϕ_F and the coordinates of E and F are known these equat-
ions can be solved for (x_D, y_D); the smaller are $|\phi_E - \phi_A|$ and $|\phi_F - \phi_A|$
the greater is the accuracy.

The procedure can be repeated in an obvious manner to obtain other
nodal points in the region. It is often convenient to make $\phi_E - \phi_A$
$= \phi_F - \phi_A = \Delta\phi$ and to use this value throughout the construction.
This results in an equiangular mesh and, as Hill has observed, "one
family of diagonal curves passing through opposite nodal points are
contours of constant p, the other family being contours of constant ϕ".
The values of p at the nodal points can be obtained by a simple application of the Hencky equations.

For an equiangular mesh the point D can be obtained as follows. A
straight line through E is drawn at an angle $\Delta\phi$ to the straight line

joining A to F and in the same sense as the angle between the normals to the slip line AB at A and E. Similarly a straight line through F is drawn that makes an angle $\Delta\phi$ with the straight line joining A to E. These two straight lines intersect at D.

Prager[7] suggested a graphical method for the construction of slip lines. His method involves the stress plane and is more complicated than the method just described but of course gives the same nodal points.

Often the normal components of velocity are known along the given intersecting slip lines AB and AC, that is v is known along AB and u along AC. The components u along AB and v along AC can be found very simply by applying the Geiringer equations. The velocity components at the previously calculated mesh point D can be obtained from a finite difference representation of the Geiringer equations by solving the simultaneous equations for u_D and v_D,

$$u_D - u_F = \tfrac{1}{2}(v_D + v_F)(\phi_D - \phi_F)$$

and

$$v_D - v_E = -\tfrac{1}{2}(u_D + u_E)(\phi_D - \phi_E).$$

The component of normal velocity along a slip line may have discontinuities at certain points on the slip line, that is the tangential component of velocity across an intersecting slip line of the other family may be discontinuous. In the above numerical procedure the finite difference intervals should be chosen so that discontinuities of tangential velocity across a slip line lie at the ends of intervals.

A special case of the first boundary-value problem occurs when one of the slip lines, say AC, degenerates to a point. It follows from Hencky's Second Theorem that by moving in the appropriate direction along slip line AB the radius of curvature of an intersecting slip line eventually becomes zero. If the β-line AC degenerates to a singular point A at which the range of ϕ is known to be from ϕ_A, corresponding to AB to ϕ_A', the field given by AB, the α-line through A corresponding to ϕ_A' at A and the β-line through B, is defined as shown in Fig. 4.2. The procedure for obtaining the nodal points is the same as already described except that all the points on the β-line, AC, coincide.

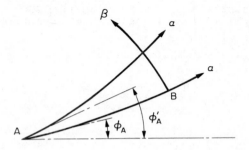

Fig. 4.2. First boundary-value problem: one slip line and a singularity in the slip-line field given.

The second boundary-value problem concerns the determination of the slip-line field defined by a curve along which the stresses are known and which satisfies the yield criterion. It is assumed the curve does not cut any slip line more than once and consequently lies either entirely in the first and third quadrants or the second and fourth

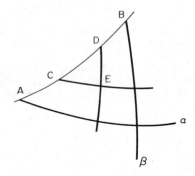

Fig. 4.3. Second boundary-value problem: extension
of a slip-line field from a boundary on
which p and ϕ are known.

quadrants formed by the α and β lines, taken as a right-handed pair, that pass through any point on it. In Fig. 4.3 the curve AB is shown in the first quadrant and, provided the whole region is plastic, the curve determines the slip-line field in the curvilinear quadrilateral bounded by the α and β lines through A and B. Since the stress components σ_x, σ_y, τ_{xy} are known along the curve, p and ϕ are known. If C and D are two adjacent points on the curve, as shown in Fig. 4.3, the nodal point E, which is the intersection of the α-line through C and the β-line through D, can be obtained approximately as follows. From the Hencky equations, the value of ϕ at E is,

$$\phi_E = \frac{1}{4k} (p_C - p_D) + \tfrac{1}{2}(\phi_C + \phi_D).$$

The coordinates of E can be found by replacing the segments of slip lines CE and ED by straight lines passing through C and D that make angles ϕ and $(\phi' + \pi/2)$ with the positive x-direction where

$$\phi = \frac{\phi_E + \phi_C}{2}$$

and

$$\phi' = \frac{\phi_D + \phi_E}{2}.$$

Often AB is a straight line (or surface) and is stress free, and then $p = k$, if the weak solution is chosen, so that ϕ is constant. Consequently, the slip-line field consists of straight lines that intersect AB at $\pi/4$.

The third boundary-value problem arises when a slip line *OA*, see Fig. 4.4, and a curve *OB*, along which ϕ but not p is known, are given. First assume that the value of ϕ at *O* given on *OB* is the same as that on *OA* at *O* and that the angle between the tangent to *OA* and *OB* is acute.

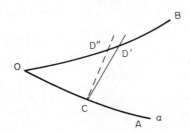

Fig. 4.4. Third boundary-value problem: one slip
line and a curve along which ϕ is known
is given.

At a mesh point *C* on *OA* adjacent to *O* construct a straight line in the β-direction (if *OA* is an α-line) to intersect *OB* at *D'*. A further straight line through *C* to meet *OB* in *D''* is drawn so that it makes an angle ($\phi + \pi/2$) with the positive x-direction where $\phi = \frac{1}{2}(\phi_C + \phi_{D'})$.

This procedure is repeated until the desired accuracy is obtained. In many problems the value of ϕ on *OB* is constant and the iterative procedure is not required. If the value of ϕ at *O* is different on *OA* and *OB*, but the α-direction corresponding to ϕ at *O* on *OB* lies in *OAB*, a slip-line field in *BOA* can be obtained. There is then a singularity at *O* and the field in *BOA* can be obtained by first determining the field *AOA'*, as shown in Fig. 4.5. The field *AOA'* is defined by the α-line, *OA*, and the singularity at *O*; *OA'* is the α-line whose direction at *O* corresponds with the given α-direction on *OB*. The construction

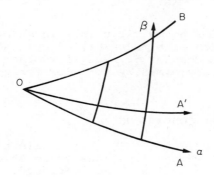

Fig. 4.5. A singularity in the third boundary-value
problem.

of this type of field has already been described as for the special case of the first boundary-value problem. It then remains for the field *OA'B* to be constructed and the method has been described in the first part of this section, see Fig. 4.4.

KINDS OF SLIP-LINE FIELDS

Slip-line fields can be broadly classified into four categories which account for the form of the field during the deformation process. These are,
- (a) incipient fields,
- (b) steady-state fields,
- (c) unsteady-state fields, and
- (d) geometrically similar fields.

The term incipient is applied to certain slip-line fields that account for the *beginning* of a plastic deformation process; it follows that they prevail only at a particular moment in time. The shape of this slip-line field changes as the deformation continues, and an example is that of the classical indentation of a half-space by a flat-ended punch, see Chapter 5. Group (b), as the name implies, refers to fields that do not change with time. The stress and velocity vector at some fixed point, referred to a particular coordinate system, remain invariant. Typical examples of this are to be found in steady-state drawing and extrusion processes.

Very few solutions have been given to metal-forming problems which adequately account for the change in geometry of the boundary, i.e. (c) or post-(b) cases. These types of problems are invariably complex and usually recourse is made to a step-by-step procedure to effect a solution, i.e. the stress and velocity conditions have to be solved simultaneously at a particular instant of time; a small change is then made in the shape of the boundary with the stress and velocity equations then being redetermined.

Geometrically similar fields are those which merely change in size as the deformation proceeds. A classical example of this type of field is that of indenting a semi-infinite mass by a frictionless wedge-shaped indenter. A detailed description of this particular process is given in Chapter 5.

A *simple* illustration of a geometric change in shape of boundary is the plane-strain expansion of a thick-walled cylinder under internal pressure as described in Chapter 5. Very few other problems exist which possess the necessary symmetry to allow for geometry changes in this manner.

STRESS BOUNDARY CONDITIONS

As mentioned at the end of Chapter 3, certain limitations have to be imposed on the angles at which slip lines can meet certain boundaries in order that the yield criterion is not violated. A few examples of the various boundaries, which are most frequently encountered in slip-line-field theory, are given below.

(i) Stress-Free Surface

A plastic zone sometimes extends to the free surface of a metal beyond the confines of a tool. This is illustrated by the solution to the problem of the indenting of a semi-infinite mass with a flat-bottomed punch, witness Fig. 5.12 of Chapter 5.

At the free surface there is no normal and no shear component of stress, so that the normal and tangential directions at the free surface are directions of principal stress. Hence, since the slip lines, by definition, are directions of the maximum shear stress at any point in the material, they intersect the free surface at $\pm\pi/4$. If the surface yields under the action of a compressive force then, as shown in Fig. 4.6, the normal stress $\sigma_2 = 0$.

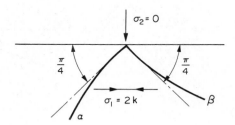

Fig. 4.6. Intersection of the slip lines with a free surface.

Thus, from the yield criterion, $\sigma_1 = 2k$ (compressive) and the hydrostatic component of stress at the point in question is k (compressive). It was pointed out in Chapter 3 that the sign convention adopted in this monograph assumes the maximum algebraic principal stress to fall in the first and third quadrant of the $\alpha - \beta$ coordinate system, see Fig. 3.2. Hence the α- and β- slip lines are as shown in Fig. 4.6, since $\sigma_2 = 0$ is the maximum algebraic principal stress. If the surface had yielded in tension then the α- and β-slip lines would have been interchanged.

(ii)   Frictionless Interface

A smooth die or tool face constitutes a frictionless interface. By definition there can be no resultant shear force parallel to the interface and hence the slip lines meet the interface at $\pm\pi/4$. However, unlike the free surface, the normal stress on a tool is seldom zero. The normal and tangential stresses at a point on the interface have to satisfy the yield criterion and hence a knowledge of the magnitude of these stresses will allow the slip lines to be identified.

(iii)   Interface with Coulomb Friction

Coulomb friction implies that the coefficient of friction, μ, is a constant at every point on the interface, i.e. the ratio (shear stress) /(normal stress) is a constant. The resultant shear force over any element of the interface is balanced by the resolved components of the forces along the slip lines, which meet the interface at some angle

$\phi < \pi/4$, as shown in Fig. 4.7. From the equilibrium of forces acting on the element shown in Fig. 4.7,

$$\cos 2\phi = \frac{\mu q}{k}, \qquad (4.1)$$

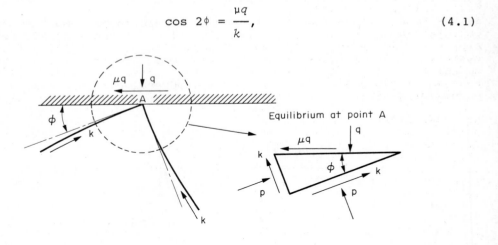

Fig. 4.7. Intersection of the slip lines with a partially rough boundary.

where q is the normal pressure. In general q will vary from point to point along the interface and hence the slip lines will meet the interface at continuously changing angles. Alexander[8] has given a solution to the problem of compression between partially rough platens assuming Coulomb friction to act over the metal-platen interface.

(iv) Full Shearing along an Interface

The maximum possible value of the frictional stress at any interface is k, i.e. the yield shear stress of the material. When the frictional stress reaches the value k the metal will shear at the interface and so, in this case, the coefficient of friction is arrived at in a different way from that associated with Coulomb friction. The slip lines meet the interface normally and tangentially, as seen from equation (4.1), when $\mu q = k$ and then,

$$\cos 2\phi = 1 \quad \text{or} \quad \phi = 0. \qquad (4.2)$$

Under these conditions the surface is often referred to as being "perfectly rough".

The two extreme interface conditions, i.e. the frictionless and the "perfectly rough", are the ones most often encountered in slip-line-field analysis primarily because they constitute the simplest and widest apart stress boundary conditions.

CONSTRUCTING THE HODOGRAPH

The word hodograph was the name given by Prager to the graphical representation of the kinematically admissible velocity field associated with the slip-line field. The use of the hodograph was first suggested by Green[9] who showed that the velocity field can be transposed into a slip-line field and vice-versa. Prior to the introduction of the hodograph, velocity boundary conditions were always shown to be satisfied by using the Geiringer equations, as described in the book by Hill[6] and wherein numerous metal-forming problems are solved correctly without actually constructing a hodograph. Hill, however, did introduce the "unit diagram" method, for analysing the deformation mode in problems where the configuration remains geometrically similar at all stages, and thus making implicit use of a kind of hodograph.

As shown by the simple geometric construction in Chapter 3, corresponding elements of the slip-line field and hodograph are orthogonal. It is usual to build up slip line fields using equi-angular networks, say, of 15, 9, 5, 4½ or 2½ degree intervals, depending upon the required accuracy. The associated hodograph will consequently have the same equi-angular mesh. The treatment or inclusion of tangential velocity discontinuities in the velocity solution can often give rise to confusion. However, as the name tangential implies, the velocity vector representing the tangential velocity discontinuity is drawn tangential to the element of the slip line in question. This point is well illustrated in Fig. 3.7 of the preceding chapter.

When the boundary conditions are particularly simple (most often where tool surfaces are frictionless) the slip-line field and hodograph have *identical* geometric configurations (with certain boundaries interchanged); see, for example, Figs. 5.7 and 5.8 in Chapter 5. This observation was first made by Green[9]; however, it must be emphasized that in general such an identity does not occur.

A number of processes involve rotating elements, and an example of a direct solution for indentation with a rotating tool is given in Chapter 5. Another obvious example is met with in rolling where the rotation of the roll has to be accounted for in the hodograph. Quite often rotating tools, etc., give rise to problems which are of the indirect type, and in such cases the computational procedures of Chapter 6 are likely to have advantage over alternative trial-and-error methods. As already mentioned, the technique of Chapter 6 is not suited to all problems of the indirect type and a case in point is the solution for the hot rolling of plate given by Alexander[5] where the curved boundary of the roll gives rise to non-linear conditions. If a dead metal zone is assumed to embrace the whole roll contact surface the solution is greatly simplified; it is, however, still of the indirect type. Chitkara and Johnson[10] originally proposed a solution based on a trial-and-error graphical procedure, which is illustrated in Chapter 5, Fig. 5.51 of this book. However, a solution is effected much more rapidly by the procedures of Chapter 6, as first demonstrated by Dewhurst, Collins and Johnson[11].

SOLUTIONS TO PROBLEMS USING THE UPPER-BOUND METHOD

This monograph is intended to illustrate the solution of problems using slip-line-field analysis as opposed to applying the "upper-bound"† method. However, for the sake of completeness a brief discussion of the upper-bound approach will be given here.

As with slip-line field (s.l.f.) solutions the upper-bound method, described herein, subdivides the deforming zone into a number of finite regions. In nearly all cases straight lines are considered to separate the various regions which are each assumed to be rigid. The intersecting lines in the physical plane need not be orthogonal, as required by a s.l.f. solution, and furthermore a discontinuity in the tangential component of velocity exists across every line. Although a discontinuity in the tangential component of velocity can exist across a slip line, as discussed in Chapter 3 yet in a s.l.f. solution as such, each slip line does not, in general, have a finite velocity discontinuity across it. Both the s.l.f. solution and upper-bound method provide kinematically admissible velocity fields, but only the former is called upon also to satisfy the stress boundary conditions and the yield criterion. In this book the term "slip-line field" has been given to solutions which are not necessarily complete as defined at the end of Chapter 3, i.e. that a check that a positive rate of working exists throughout the deformation zone and that a statically admissible extension of the stress field into all the non-deforming zones of the solution is taken not to be mandatory. In addition to the references quoted in Chapter 3, the reader is also referred to the work of Refs. 12 and 13 for examples of certain checks on complete solutions.

Slip-line-field solutions which are incomplete in the above sense are strictly upper bounds. Nevertheless, they are to be preferred to upper-bound solutions which make no attempt to satisfy either the equilibrium equations or the yield criterion. There is no systematic manner in which a s.l.f. solution (complete or otherwise) can be established from an arbitrary pattern of lines in the physical plane which provide an upper-bound solution. However, it is always possible to start with a s.l.f. solution and generate an upper-bound solution. As mentioned earlier (see also the discussion at the beginning of Chapter 5) a slip-line field can be constructed graphically by replacing elements of curved slip lines by straight lines or chords. If a discontinuity in the tangential component of velocity is now permitted across each of these lines an upper-bound solution is revealed; the technique is illustrated later in this chapter. Such upper-bound solutions might be regarded as "near" s.l.f. solutions. Indeed, if the subdivision (or s.l.f. mesh) of the deformation zone is made fine enough, the discontinuity in the tangential component of velocity across many lines in the zone becomes vanishingly small. In the limit the upper-bound solution quite naturally recovers the s.l.f. solution. Examples are to be found in the work by Johnson and Sowerby.[14,15]

The upper-bound method, as the name implies, always gives an over-estimate to the unknown surface tractions acting over part of the boundary. Thus equation (2.13) of Chapter 2 can be written as,

$$\int_{S_v} T_i v_i \, dS \leqslant \int_{S_D} k \, [v*] \, dS - \int_{S_T} T_i v_i * \, dS, \qquad (4.3)$$

---

†The term "upperbound" is used here to describe any arbitrary kinematically admissible velocity field applied to a deforming rigid-perfectly plastic solid; no attempt is made to satisfy the yield condition and equilibrium equations at any point in the field of deformation.

since the term $\int_V \sigma_{ij}^* e_{ij}^* dV$ is zero for the method described here, i.e. modes of deformation comprised of rigid blocks separated by lines of velocity discontinuity. Furthermore, the term $\int_{S_T} T_i v_i^* dS$ can generally be equated to zero, both for the slip-line-field solution and the upper-bound method, since often the part S_T of the boundary remains stationary. Consequently, for the upper-bound method, equation (4.3) can often be written as

$$\int_{S_v} T_i v_i dS \leq \int_{S_D} k \, [v*] \, dS, \tag{4.4}$$

where the right-hand side of (4.4) is the energy dissipated at the velocity discontinuities.

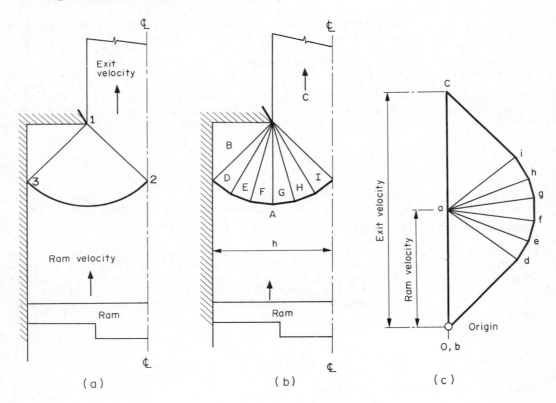

Fig. 4.8. (a) Slip-line field for extrusion through a square die of 50% reduction.

(b) Upper-bound solution for the die shown in (a).

(c) Hodograph to (b).

61

The distinction between the slip-line-field and the upper-bound approach can be further illustrated by a simple example. Figure 4.8(a)
shows the slip-line field and hodograph for extrusion through a frictionless square die of 50 per cent reduction. If the α-line 23 is
replaced by straight lines obtained from a 15° mesh the result is as
shown in Fig. 4.8(b). The regions designated by capital letters in
Fig. 4.8(b) can be regarded as rigid regions bounded by velocity discontinuities. A hodograph can now be constructed, Fig. 4.8(c), in a
way exactly analogous to the construction of the force diagram for a
plane, statically determinate, pin-jointed structure. Bow's notation
is used, and a line in the hodograph, designated for example by ad,
represents the velocity discontinuity between regions A and D in the
physical plane.

The semi-height, h, of the extrusion chamber can be selected as unity,
and all the lines separating the rigid zones in the physical plane of
Fig. 4.8(b) can be measured directly. The velocity of the extrusion
ram can also be chosen arbitrarily (say unity), and the hodograph of
Fig. 4.8(c) is constructed by drawing lines parallel to the corresponding lines in the physical plane. Most of the lines in the hodograph
represent the velocity discontinuity between adjacent rigid regions
in the physical plane, and these can be measured directly from the
diagram. The rate of external working at the ram is then equated to
the rate of internal energy dissipated by shearing across each of the
lines in the physical plane. Thus, for line AD in the physical plane
the energy dissipated is the product of, the line length AD, the velocity discontinuity across it, $\vec{ad}$, and the yield shear stress of the
material, k. If the mean ram pressure is denoted by p, this can be
evaluated from,

$$p.h.\ \vec{oa} = k \sum_{i=1}^{n} L_i . V_i^{*}. \tag{4.5}$$

In the above expression n is the total number of lines in the physical
plane, L_i the length of the i th line and V_i^{*} the corresponding tangential velocity discontinuity (t.v.d.) across it.

Whilst an upper-bound solution is generally easily obtainable, it must
be pointed out that to arrive at an optimal solution (the lowest upper
bound) is less rapid. When the starting point is a valid, but arbitrarily chosen, kinematically admissible velocity field, there can
result a considerable amount of computation in order to minimize the
energy dissipated, i.e.

$$\sum_{i=1}^{n} L_i . V_i^{*},$$

particularly where n is large.

The book by Johnson and Mellor[16] provides several examples of solutions
obtained using the upper-bound method.

APPLICATION TO SPECIFIC PROBLEMS

REFERENCES

1. Bishop, J. F. W., Green, A. P. and Hill, R., "A note on the deformable region in a rigid-plastic body". *J. Mechs. Phys. Solids*, **4**, 256 (1956).
2. Collins, I.F., in *Applications of Numerical Methods to Forming Processes* (edited by H. Armen and R. F. Jones), p. 129. Winter Ann. Meeting A.S.M.E., Dec. 1978, California. A.S.M.E. (1978).
3. Johnson, W., "Some slip-line fields for swaging or expanding indenting, extruding and machining for tools with curved dies". *Int. J. Mech. Sci.* **4**, 323 (1962).
4. Green, A. P., "A theoretical investigation of the compression of a ductile material between smooth flat dies". *Phil. Mag.*, **42**, 900 (1951).
5. Alexander, J. M., "A slip-line field for the hot rolling process". *Proc. Inst. Mech. Engrs.*, **169**, 1021 (1955).
6. Hill, R., *The Mathematical Theory of Plasticity*. Oxford University Press (1950).
7. Prager, W., "A geometrical discussion of the slip-line field in plane plastic flow". *Trans. R. Inst. Tech. Stockholm*, No. 65, (1953).
8. Alexander, J. M., "The effect of Coulomb friction in the plane strain compression of a plastic-rigid material". *J. Mechs. Phys. Solids*, **3**, 233 (1955).
9. Green, A. P., "On the use of hodographs in problems of plane plastic strain". *J. Mech. Phys. Solids*, **2**, 73 (1954).
10. Chitkara, N. R. and Johnson, W., "Some results for rolling with circular and polygonal rolls". *Proc. 5th M.T.D.R. Conf.*, 391 (1964).
11. Dewhurst, P., Collins, I. F. and Johnson, W., "A class of slip-line field solutions for the hot rolling of strip". *J. Mech. Engng. Sci.* **15**, 439 (1973).
12. Dodd, B. and Scivier, D. A., "On the static inadmissibility of some slip line fields for sheet drawing". *Int. J. Mech. Sci.* **17**, 663 (1975).
13. Dodd, B. and Shiratori, M., "The plane strain general yielding of notched members due to combined axial force and bending - I and II". *J. Mech. Sci.* **20**, 451 and 465 (1978).
14. Johnson, W. and Sowerby, R., "An analysis of a rigid-plastic thick walled cylinder using slip line field theory". *Bull. Mech. Engng. Education*, **6**, 201 (1967).
15. Johnson, W. and Sowerby, R., "Upper bound techniques applied to plane strain extrusion, minimum weight two dimensional frames and rotationaly symmetric flat plates". *Bull. Mech. Engng. Education*, **8**, 269 (1969).
16. Johnson, W. and Mellor, P. B., *Engineering Plasticity*. Van Nostrand-Reinhold (1973).

CHAPTER 5

Applications to Specific Processes: Bibliography

1.   CENTRED-FAN FIELDS

Chapters 2, 3 and 4 have dealt with basic plasticity theory and this chapter is devoted to the application of the theory to specific problems of plane plastic flow. In this section we consider a type of slip line field which, because of its frequent use, is well worth studying in detail.

If the radius of curvature of one of a family of slip lines becomes zero then there arises a singularity at some point in the field through which all the slip lines of the other family pass. In particular, if the family of, say, α-slip lines passing through the singularity are straight, then the β-slip lines are circular arcs. This type of field is known as a centred-fan and is often encountered in solutions to plane-strain problems. Singular points usually occur at die corners or at sudden changes in cross-section and physically they represent relatively small zones at which there is a rapid change in stress, velocity and strain-rate.

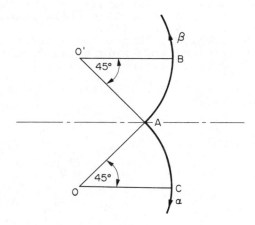

Fig. 5.1.   Two centred-fans of equal radius.

64

Figure 5.1 shows two centred-fan fields each of equal radius and angular span 45° and where O and O' are singular points. To effect a solution to many plane-strain-forming problems, as shown below, it is essential to know how the above field can be extended. In the authors' opinion the simplest method is to use a small-arc approximation, i.e. to approximate the curved element of a slip line by a chord that makes an angle ϕ for an α-line, or $(\phi + \pi/2)$ for a β-line, with the positive x direction; ϕ is the mean of the values of ϕ at the nodal points.

To illustrate the extension of the field using the small-arc approximation choose, arbitrarily, OAB to be a β-line line and $O'AC$ to be an α-slip line. The centred-fan fields are subdivided into 15° arcs, as shown in Fig. 5.2(a), and the resulting field will now be an equiangular mesh of 15° intervals. The chain-dotted line passing through point A in Fig. 5.2(a) represents a line of symmetry and therefore all

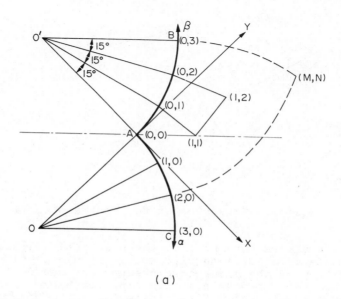

(a)

Fig. 5.2(a).   Extension of the centred-fan field.
Method I.

slip lines will intersect this line at ±45°. In what follows, angles measured anticlockwise from the axis of symmetry are considered positive and those measured clockwise as negative. To locate the nodal point $(1,1)$ draw from point $(0,1)$ a chord with a mean slope of $-37\frac{1}{2}°$ i.e. $(45° + 30°)/2$, to meet the axis of symmetry in $(1,1)$. For point $(1,2)$ draw from $(0,2)$ a chord with a mean slope of $-22\frac{1}{2}°$, i.e. $(30° + 15°)/2$, and from $(1,1)$ a chord with a mean slope of $52\frac{1}{2}°$, i.e. $(60° + 45°)/2$, to meet in $(1,2)$. The remainder of the field can be built-up in a similar manner. Because mean values of ϕ are used, the slip lines will not meet orthogonally and the position of the nodal points will not be exact. However, the slip line field can be drawn to increasing degrees of accuracy by using, say, 15°, 9°, 5° and $2\frac{1}{2}°$, etc., equiangular nets†. Obviously the smaller the angle the more accurate the

---

†These numbers are so chosen because they are aliquot parts of 45°.

solution, although the labour involved is considerably increased.

An alternative construction is illustrated in Fig. 5.2(b) where the slip lines are made to meet orthogonally at each of the nodal points†. To locate the nodal point (1,1) the line through point (0,1) is extended, at a slope of -30⁰, to an *estimated* position mid-way between (0,1) and the point of intersection on the axis of symmetry. This line is then broken at the mid-way point and continued with a slope of -45⁰ to meet the axis of symmetry at (1,1). It requires very little practice to estimate a mid-way position (between the anticipated nodes) at which to change the slope of the slip lines. This method tends to be more accurate than the former, particularly when coarse equi-angular nets are employed.

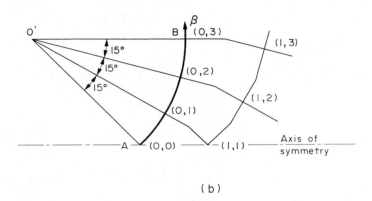

(b)

Fig. 5.2(b). Extension of the centred-fan field.
Method II.

Hill[7] has given several examples of the numerical calculation of slip-line fields made up of equi-angular nets. He has also attempted analytical integration of the plane-strain equations and derived exact expressions for the coordinates, slip-line curvatures and velocity components at any point of a field in terms of the boundary values. The expressions, however, contain integrals which can only be evaluated in finite form if the boundary conditions are especially simple. When the slip-line field is defined by two circular arcs, as in Fig. 5.2(a), the analytical expressions can be solved to yield the values of the coordinates at a general point in the field. Hill has compared the exact solution with the numerical solution based on an equi-angular 5⁰ net, and concludes that the error is less than 1% over the field defined by two circular arcs of 45⁰ span‡.

---

†Slip line fields can be constructed using Ringleb's theorem which states: "If four circles be constructed such that each pair of adjacent circles intersect orthogonally, then the four intersection points must lie on another circle". In Ref. 176 it is demonstrated how this property can be utilized to construct an orthogonal network which also satisfies Hencky's Second Theorem.
‡In the authors' experience an equi-angular net of 9⁰ (or even 15⁰) provides results which are correct to 2½% and thus perfectly satisfactory for engineering purposes.

We give in Appendix 3 the values of the nodal points defined in terms of the coordinate system (x,y), see Fig. 5.2(a). The nodal points are given for an equi-angular net of 15° over a field defined by 90° circular arcs, each of unit radius. The figures quoted have been taken from reference 158, which gives the results of numerical calculations based on a 5° equi-angular net. Ewing[170] also gives the coordinates of the nodal points for a 10° mesh. Ewing's calculations are based on a power series method developed for the numerical computer construction of slip-line-field networks.

It will be seen in the following examples that centred-fan fields not of equal radius, are often required, see Fig. 5.3; this usually arises when problems involving constant friction at a flat surface are encountered. The results of the calculations for the nodal points, when the radius ρ is held constant at unity and the radius r, varied between 0 and 1.0 in steps of 0.1, are also given in Appendix 7 along with the corresponding boundary values, i.e. the coordinates of points on the circular arcs.

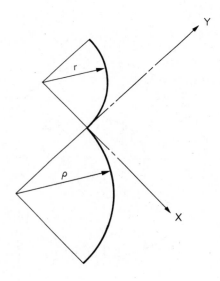

Fig. 5.3. Two centred-fans of unequal radius.

2. PRESSURE VESSELS

Consider a thick walled cylinder made from a rigid-perfectly plastic material subjected to internal and external normal pressures of P and zero respectively. No deformation of the cylinder will occur until it has everywhere just become plastic. We restrict our attention to the determination of the yield-point pressure P and the deformation mode at at the onset of yield or collapse.

The problem is statically determinate and the yield-point pressure can be obtained without recourse to slip-line-field theory. However, because the problem and its solution are well known to students of elementary Strength of Materials, the techniques of slip-line-field theory may therefore be better exemplified by applying them to a case with which they are very familiar.

Symmetry requires that the hoop and radial directions are directions of principal stress and thus that the slip lines make an angle of $\pm 45^\circ$ with these directions. Consequently, it is easily verified that the slip lines are logarithmic spirals.[167] Figure 5.4 shows an orthogonal net of slip lines covering part of the cylinder wall, though the whole cylinder wall will be covered by such a net. At point C on the external surface of the cylinder the radial stress is zero and hence from the yield criterion the hoop stress is $2k$ and obviously tensile, so that ABC is an α-slip line† and AB_1C_1 a β-slip line.

Taking OD, Fig. 5.4, as the positive x-direction and ϕ as the angle between the x-direction and the α direction, then the change in the angle $\Delta\phi$ between two adjacent points when moving along the α-slip line AC has the same numerical value and is in the same sense as the change in angle $\Delta\theta$ between the radius vectors to the points from origin, O.

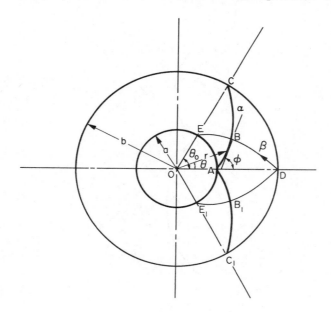

Fig. 5.4. Slip-line field for a thick-walled
cylinder under internal normal pressure
only.

Experimental evidence of the validity of the theoretical slip-line field pattern is given in Plate 2(a). The experimental result was obtained by pressurizing a long, mild steel, thick-walled tube until yielding occured. The cylinder was then sectioned mid-way along its

---

†Note the sign convention for the determination of the α- and β-slip lines. The direction of the maximum algebraic principal stress lies in the first and third quadrants - adopting the usual mathematical convention - of the α, β coordinate system.

axial length, and the newly formed surface first machined, then polished and finally etched in Fry's reagent to reveal the slip-line-field pattern. The experimental details are described in the article by Johnson and Sowerby.[212]

The polar equations of the slip lines are

$$\theta \pm \ln \frac{r}{a} = \text{constant.} \tag{5.1}$$

The constant is zero if θ is prescribed as zero when $r = a$. The relationship between a and b, the internal and external radii of the cylinder respectively, is

$$b = a \exp \theta_0 \quad \text{or} \quad \theta_0 = \ln \frac{b}{a}, \tag{5.2}$$

where θ_0 is the angular span of the slip line, as shown in Fig. 5.4.

It follows from the *Hencky equations* that the hydrostatic pressure at A is given by

$$p_A = -k + 2k\theta_0.$$

The internal pressure, which is the compressive normal stress acting on the bore, is from (5.2)

$$p = (-\sigma_r)_{r=a} = k + p_A = 2k \ln \frac{b}{a}.$$

Similarly it follows that the stress distribution throughout is

$$\left. \begin{array}{l} \sigma_\theta = -2k\left(\ln \frac{b}{r} - 1\right) \\[2ex] \sigma_r = -2k\ln \frac{b}{r} \, . \end{array} \right\} \tag{5.3}$$

and

From symmetry it follows that the velocity of a particle is radially outwards, and consequently if the positive α and β directions are as shown in Fig. 5.4,

$$u = -v = \frac{V}{\sqrt{2}}, \tag{5.4}$$

where V is the magnitude of the velocity vector in the radial direction. Applying the *Geiringer equations* - see (3.10), Chapter 3 - to the α-line ABC,

$$du - v \, d\phi = 0.$$

Consequently, from (5.4) the above equation can be written as

$$du + u \, d\phi = 0. \tag{5.5}$$

The integral of (5.5) is

$$u = c \exp (-\phi), \tag{5.6}$$

where c is a constant which can be determined if V is known at $r = a$

or $r = b$. The value of ϕ can be taken as zero at the bore, the starting point of the slip line ABC. Similarly, starting with a β-slip line it follows that

$$v = c \exp(-\phi).\tag{5.7}$$

Clearly the hodograph is formally the slip-line field of Fig. 5.4 redrawn to some appropriate scale but with the internal and external boundaries reversed, as in Fig. 5.5.

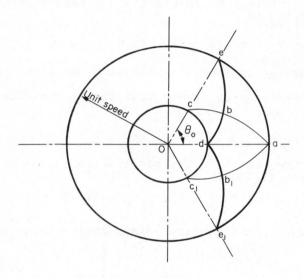

Fig. 5.5. Hodograph to Fig. 5.4.

Note that once deformation starts, the ratio of the current outer to inner radius of the tube decreases and the process becomes unstable. In the absence of work-hardening the internal pressure would have to be gradually reduced as the tube continued to expand. However, the theoretical slip-line field remains a network of logarithmic spirals in the cylinder wall regardless of the extent of the expansion.

The preceding analysis holds equally well, but with a reversal in sign, for inward radial flow. The adaptation of this type of flow to sheet drawing is discussed on page 89.

A similar analysis can be applied for calculating the stresses in the flange of a circular disc when deep-drawing a cylindrical cup. The net of spiral slip lines that exist in the flange are shown in Plate 2(b) at an early stage in the drawing process. The condition of plane strain can only be maintained in the flange of the blank if the stress exerted by the blank holder is compressive, and this requires that ln $(b/a) \leqslant \frac{1}{2}$ or $b \leqslant 1.65a$ where b is the initial radius of the blank and a the radius of the cylindrical cup.

Slip line field patterns in the flange of variously shaped blanks, when drawing circular and non-circular cups, are to be found in Refs.

211 and 213. The latter reference employs slip-line-field analysis as an aid to blank development for industrial pressings. Instantaneous deformation modes and incipient slip-line fields only apply and these will, in general, change as the material boundary changes so that they are not totally representative of the entire deformation history.

Johnson and Sowerby, *op cit.*, have given slip-line-field solutions for multi-hole pressure vessels, i.e. vessels of either square or circular cross-section containing either a number of circular holes variously located within the section or one centrally located non-circular hole, all internally loaded by hydrostatic pressure. Experimental verification of the proposed solutions was obtained using the etching techniques referred to earlier.

A slip-line field has been given[210] for the circumstance in which, as well as uniform internal normal pressure, uniform but unequal internal and external shear stresses are applied.

Attention is drawn to the interesting force plane representation of those problems, see Refs. 188 and 214.

COMPRESSION

(i) *Perfectly Rough Parallel Dies*

The compression of a rectangular block of metal between rough, rigid, parallel dies was first investigated by Prandtl[216] who deduced that the slip lines were cycloids, and later Prager[151] showed that this type of field can be obtained as a simple geometric property of Mohr's circle. As shown by Hill, Lee and Tupper,[221] Prandtl's solution is only valid when the material and the die are of infinite width. However, as might be expected, the wider the block of material compared with its thickness the more uniform does slip-line field become with increasing distance from either edge and the closer is Prandtl's original solution approached.

The problem considered by Hill *et al*[221] is that of the compression of a rectangular block of material between perfectly rough (that is, the slip lines meet the dies normally and tangentially)† parallel dies

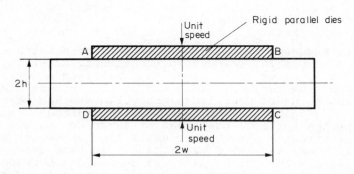

Fig. 5.6. Compression of a block between rough, rigid, parallel platens.

†There may be relative movement between the die and the material.

which approach each other with a relative speed of two units, as in Fig. 5.6. The material overhangs the dies and the die width exceeds the material thickness. The corners of each die, A, B, C and D, constitute singularities in the stress distribution and are therefore the most likely starting points in the construction of the slip line field. It is important to recognize the constraining role played by the rigid end blocks. Because of symmetry we can confine our remarks to one half of Fig. 5.6, and this has been redrawn to a larger scale in Fig. 5.7. A suitable trial hypothesis would be to draw straight lines from A and D to meet the centre line in G at $\pm 45°$. The overhanging material moves outwards as a rigid body against zero horizontal force and hence the hydrostatic pressure on the exit slip lines is k.

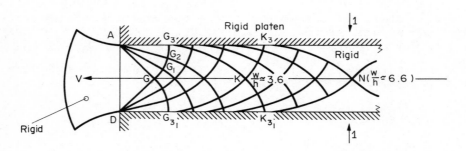

Fig. 5.7. Slip-line field for compression between rough, parallel platens.

All slip lines meet the dies normally or tangentially, and hence the field can be extended around A and D as circular arcs, (centred-fan fields) meeting the dies in G_3 and G_{3_1}. The centred-fan field can then be extended in the manner described in Section 1 as far as point K. From the *Hencky equations*, and because the slip-line net is equiangular, both ϕ and the pressure distribution are known along $AG_3 K_3$ and $DG_{3_1} K_{3_1}$. We then have a boundary-value problem in which ϕ and p are known along a slip line and ϕ along the rigid platen (third boundary-value problem, see Chapter 4). Hence the field can be extended by the small-arc approximation as indicated earlier, see also Refs. 7 and 89. The slip-line field shown in Fig. 5.7 is a $15°$ equi-angular net. However, smaller intervals could be selected to increase accuracy if required. The slip-line field has been extended as far as point N where $w/h \doteq 6.6$. Material above and below NK_3 and NK_3 respectively are rigid zones assumed fixed to the dies and moving with the same speed. Hence a tangential velocity discontinuity occurs across the aforementioned slip lines which separate the rigid material from the plastically deforming region. Since the precise stress distribution in the rigid zones is not calculable, only the average stress applied over the surface of contact with the dies is obtained. This is obtained after resolving the vertical component of force due to the pressure p and the shear stress k acting over small line elements in the slip line NK_3; this is exactly the same situation as that described in the Section on *Cutting*. The normal pressure on the die between points K_3 and A is found quite simply from the *Hencky equations*. The variation of the normal die pressure with w/h is derived in detail in Ref. 89.

Note that when w/h is less than about 3.6 but greater than unity a rigid zone extends over the entire platen.

The hodograph corresponding to the slip-line field of Fig. 5.7 is given in Fig. 5.8.

When the dies are of unequal width the slip-line field is no longer symmetrical about an axis midway between the upper and lower platens. The problem has been discussed by Johnson and Kudo,[231] who show that at large values of w/h the slip-line field becomes increasingly symmetrical.

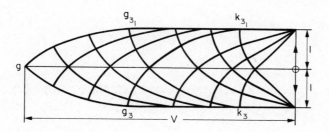

Fig. 5.8.   Hodograph to Fig. 5.7.

(ii) *Perfectly Rough Inclined Dies*

This problem has been examined in Ref. 230, the solution being a simple adaptation of the solution to the problem of compression between rough parallel dies.

Figure 5.9 shows one-quarter of the slip-line field, when the upper die is inclined at 9° to the horizontal. The slip-line field has been constructed using a 9° equi-angular net. The similarity to the preceding solution to that obtained with parallel dies is obvious.

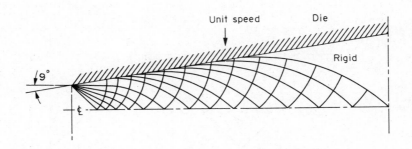

Fig. 5.9.   Slip-line field for compression between perfectly rough inclined platens.

(iii) *Frictionless Parallel Dies*

When the dies are frictionless the slip lines meet them at ±45°. For integral values of w/h the slip-line field solution consists of straight lines, as shown in Fig. 5.10. The physical solution is simply that of the material deforming as a succession of rigid triangular blocks each separated by a velocity discontinuity. If the dies move with unit speed the discontinuity is of amount $\sqrt{2}$, initiated at the centre of the block and propagated by successive reflection from the dies along their whole length. The hodograph is shown in Fig. 5.11. The normal pressure on the dies is uniformly distributed and is $2k$.

The latter solution is only valid for integer values of w/h because for all other dimensions the discontinuity terminates on the exit slip lines, which is of course incompatible with the rigid-body motion of the overhanging ends.

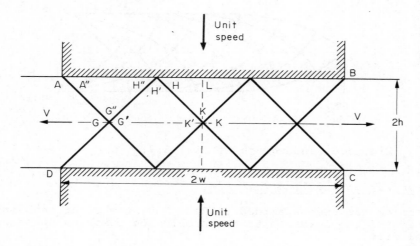

Fig. 5.10. Slip-line field for compression between frictionless parallel platens for integral values of w/h.

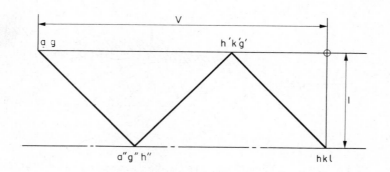

Fig. 5.11. Hodograph to Fig. 5.10.

74

For non-integer values of w/h neither the slip lines nor their traces
in the hodograph are known in shape at the outset. This problem is
then one of *indirect* type and requires or lends itself to the computational scheme described in Chapter 6, in which a solution to this
particular problem is given. Collins[237] first investigated the properties of the slip-line field for frictionless compression, using the
matrix operational method. Without recourse to the matrix method it
has been customary to seek a solution by trial-and-error procedures,
as first demonstrated by Green[222] for non-integer values of w/h between
1 and 2. However, the computational effort involved is considerable.
The work of Green, *op cit.*, clearly illustrates the transformation of
the velocity field (or hodograph) into the slip-line field and vice-versa
- which observation has served to facilitate the solution to many
plasticity problems.

The work of Ref. 232 is of interest since a simplified approach is
used to arrive at an approximate value for the mean die pressure and
is satisfactory for revealing the interesting manner in which the
latter varies with geometrical ratio, w/h.

Alexander[224] has used slip-line-field theory to study the effect of
Coulomb friction at the faces of parallel rigid dies, on the compression
load. This provides an "intermediate" solution between frictionless
and perfectly rough dies. Thomason[244] has considered a similar situation but permitted the coefficient of friction to vary over the compression platens; it is claimed that this provides a more realistic
approximation to the frictional conditions which prevail in the presence
of a viscous lubricant.

Shabaik[243] has predicted the geometry changes of the free surface during
the plane-strain compression of a strip between parallel, overhanging,
platens. The shear stress at the material-platen interface was deduced
with the aid of the visio-plasticity technique (see Chapter 1). More
recently Das *et al*[246] have analysed the compression of a strip between
parallel platens with Coulomb friction, using the matrix technique;
see also Chapter 6.

Collins[240] has provided solutions for the compression of strip between
parallel, rotating, frictionless platens. The deformation field is
found to consist of alternate rigid and deforming zones.

(iv) Compression of Other Than Slabs

The compression of slabs has constituted a very widely investigated
class of s.l.f. problems but industrially there are many other interesting shapes which are subjected to compressive action during forging,
hammering and similar kinds of action. References 197, 219, 227, 233,
238, 239 and 241 provide slip-line field solutions for the compression
of wedges; different interfacial frictional conditions are assumed
and a number of possible deformation modes are presented.

The compression of a circular cylinder between rigid parallel platens
is less rigorously amenable to analysis than the wedge. Although
qualitative deformation modes can be found in the literature very few
quantitative solutions exist. Jain and Kobayashi[242] have proposed
three basic slip-line fields (or deformation modes) depending upon
the ratio of the width to the amount of separation of the compression
platens. Similar fields have been given by Aksenov *et al*[245] for

compressing a circular section bar to form turbine blades; in this latter case the compression platens were curved.

Harvey and Palmer[278] have provided a novel solution for the compression of a tube, seated on a curved mandrel, between parallel platens; it applies to the tube-relieving process, i.e. the process of facilitating the removal of a thick tube from a circular mandrel.

The compression of a circular ring (and a shackle) is treated by Sowerby *et al.*[236a], the plastic deformation being confined to four plastic hinges which form at the quarter-points of the ring as shown in Plate 1. When the ring is sufficiently thick, the two side hinges do not form; and two zones under the loading areas enforce a forging kind of deformation, see Plate 1(c) and Refs. 236b.

INDENTATION OF A SEMI-INFINITE MEDIUM

The indentation of a rigid-plastic semi-infinite medium was first investigated by Prandtl,[247] who suggested the stress field defined by the slip lines in the region *AFEGD* of Fig. 5.12. This indentation problem is statically determined in the sense that a unique stress field in *AFEGDA* can be obtained from the stress boundary conditions,

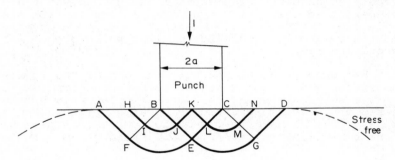

Fig. 5.12. Slip-line field for the indentation
of a semi-infinite mass.

namely the stress-free surfaces *BA* and *CD*. Bishop[148] has obtained a statically admissible extension of this stress field into the region below *AFEGD*.

The extension of the stress field below *AFEGD* indicates that a block of finite depth on a frictionless plane foundation may be considered semi-infinite if the depth is at least 8.75a.[294]

The yield point load, *P*, obtained from an application of the *Hencky equations*, is given by

$$\frac{P}{4ka} = 1 + \frac{\pi}{2}.$$ (5.8)

There is an infinity of admissible velocity fields that satisfy the boundary condition of an uniform normal velocity component on *BC*.

76

It may be deduced from a theorem due to Bishop[148] that the plastically deforming region of any admissible velocity field cannot extend beyond the region *AFEGDA*. The velocity field implied by Prandtl's solution

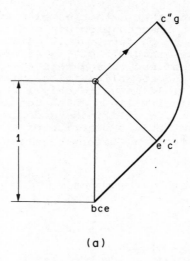

(a)

Fig. 5.13(a). Hodograph to Fig. 5.12 assuming a dead-metal cap to cover the punch face.

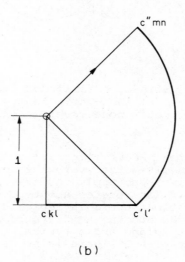

(b)

Fig. 5.13(b). Alternative hodograph to Fig. 5.12 for a frictionless punch.

involves a dead-metal wedge *BEC*;[†] the hodograph for the solution is shown in Fig. 5.13(a). This velocity field is strictly valid for *any* punch roughness since there is no relative movement between the punch and the metal and no shearing traction is required to maintain the equilibrium of wedge *BEC*.

It has been pointed out[7] that with the velocity field of Fig. 5.13(a) considerable plastic deformation probably occurs before the plastic region covers the whole punch face. Hill[7] suggested the velocity field represented by the hodograph of Fig. 5.13(b). With this velocity field, deformation is confined to the region *HIJKLMN* of Fig. 5.12 and the rigid elements *BJK* and *KLC* slide frictionlessly over the punch surface; this velocity field is valid only if the punch is frictionless. An admissible velocity field which combines both the latter solutions is shown in Fig. 5.14(b); the hodograph is drawn for a dead-metal zone extending over only a fraction of the punch face whilst over the remainder the material slides frictionlessly, see Fig. 5.14(a)

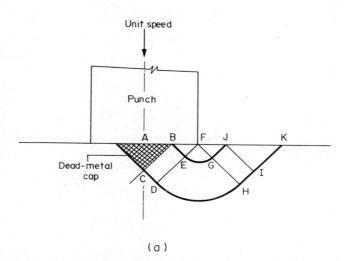

(a)

Fig. 5.14(a). Slip-line field for the indentation of a semi-infinite mass, when a dead-metal zone covers a part of the punch face.

The stress field in region *AFEGDA*, Fig. 5.12, is also compatible with velocity fields which involve other velocity-boundary conditions on *BC*, and it has been shown[2 6 9] to apply for example, see Fig. 5.15, to the case in which a rigid die rotates about point *B* with an angular velocity ω. The deformation occurs in region *BEGDB* and the hodograph is shown in Fig. 5.16. Points on the die surface *BHC* are mapped along *ohc* in the velocity plane and a typical α-line *HIJK* is mapped by *hh'ijk* in the velocity plane. There is no velocity discontinuity

---

[†]Note the similarity in the slip-line field of Fig. 5.12 to that of Fig. 5.35 (see the section on *Piercing*). Both solutions involve the existence of a dead-metal wedge under the punch.

along α-line *BEGD* which maps as the origin in the velocity plane.

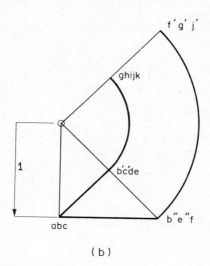

(b)

Fig. 5.14(b). Hodograph to Fig. 5.14(a).

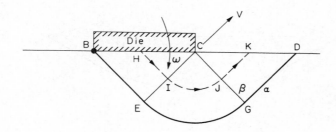

Fig. 5.15. Slip-line field for a die rotating
about an edge.

The preceding slip-line fields are all incipient solutions since the
process is non-steady; the slip-line fields no longer apply when the
original stress-free surface, adjacent to the punch, is deformed -
as it must be immediately penetration starts.

Hill, Lee and Tupper[250] have proposed a slip-line field solution for
the indentation of a semi-infinite block of rigid-plastic material
with a wedge-shaped indenter. Here, a frictionless symmetrical wedge
of semi-angle θ is pushed normally into the plane surface of the
material. The solution allows for the "piling-up" of material on
either side of the indenter but in such a way that geometric similarity
is preserved, i.e. the slip-line field does not change in shape but
merely in size as the penetration increases. The slip-line field is
shown in Fig. 5.17 and the hodograph in Fig. 5.18.

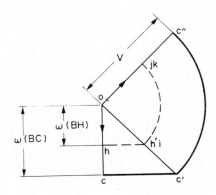

Fig. 5.16. Hodograph to Fig. 5.15.

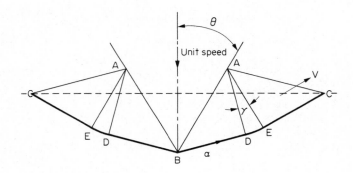

Fig. 5.17. Slip-line field for indenting a semi-
            infinite mass for a frictionless,
            acute-angled, wedge-shaped punch.

For a pair of rigid straight dies BA, pivoted at B and rotating outwards with angular speed ω, Fig. 5.17, the hodograph is given by
$Oqa'a''$ in Fig. 5.18, where $Oq = BA.\omega$.

The process represented by Fig. 5.17 is the two-dimensional analogue
of the Vickers pyramid hardness test. The preservation of geometric
similarity, using the theoretical slip-line field, results in a constant
punch pressure and can be interpreted as a measure of constant hardness
(pressure) with penetration of the wedge. This is typical, in general,
of the results from a Vickers hardness test in that the indentation
load can be varied over a wide range and yet the same hardness number
is computed. This is not true of the Brinell hardness test where a
spherical indenter is employed with the consequence that geometric
similarity of the plastically deformed zone is not preserved during
the indentation process. Readers familiar with the test will recognize

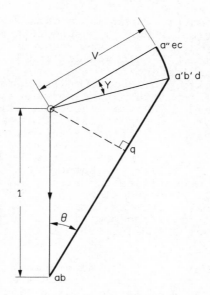

Fig. 5.18. Hodograph to Fig. 5.17.

that it is on the basis of experimental evidence only that a standard
has evolved which specifies the ball sizes and indentation loads to
be used for specific materials in order to obtain repeatable hardness
numbers. Its success depends on the ball mainly functioning as a
flat-headed punch, without the penetration to width of contact becom-
ing large. It will also be appreciated that to obtain a reliable
measure of hardness,irrespective of the type of indenter used, the
plastic zone must be confined to the vicinity of the indenter and
must not spread either through the thickness of the material or to
the sides but only up to the surface. Some theoretical limits to
the specimen size for reliable hardness measures have been given by
Hill.[251]

The stress field inside region $ABDECA$ of Fig. 5.17 can be obtained
from the knowledge that the surface AC is stress free. The pressure,
q, on the wedge face, AB, is uniformly distributed and can be obtained
by applying the *Hencky equations*.

The magnitude is given by

$$q = 2k(1 + \gamma).\qquad(5.9)$$

The load per unit width to cause penetration is

$$P = 2qAB. \sin\theta.\qquad(5.10)$$

As θ approaches 90° so too does the angle γ and the slip-line-field
approaches that for indenting with a frictionless flat punch as shown

81

in Fig. 5.12. Similarly, equation (5.10) reduces to (5.8).†

Hill and Lee[249] have extended the above analysis to the case where a frictionless, symmetrical wedge is pushed into material obliquely, i.e. with the axis of symmetry of the wedge no longer perpendicular to the material surface. Meguid and Collins[289] have also given results for different wedge angles and different angles of obliquity. The latter authors have also provided calculations for the critical depth of the material, at which deformation spreads through the thickness of the material so that a *cutting* action commences; see the next section in this monograph. Experimental fields were obtained by the etching technique and these vindicated the proposed fields.

When the wedge face is rough the slip lines no longer intersect it at ± 45 degrees. A field similar to that of Fig. 5.17 would continue to be valid even though the α-lines intersect BA at more than 45^0, i.e. $45^0 \leqslant LABD \leqslant 90^0$. If the condition $LDBD < 90^0$ prevails the material at point B is *overstressed*. This leads to the requirement, for certain combinations of wedge angle and coefficient of friction, of a dead cap of metal extending over the wedge tip; as an example see reference 277.

Dodd and Osakada[288] have recalculated a number of statically admissible slip-line fields for rough wedges. Fields are established for the *indentation* process, as well as the *indentation - cutting* transition, for different wedge angles and coefficients of friction. The work verifies some of the results of earlier investigations, and these are cited in the article.

CUTTING

The slip-line-field solution for indenting with a frictionless wedge-shaped tool can be extended to explain the mechanics of the cutting process.[294]

Consider the indented block to be of finite thickness and to rest on a frictionless foundation. When the wedge indenter first enters the block the mode of deformation is identical with that given for *indentation*, i.e. material piles up at the side of the wedge, geometric similarity is preserved, and the slip-line field merely grows in size as the penetration increases. However, at some stage of the indentation process, because the block is of finite thickness, the plastic region will extend through the whole thickness of the block. Consequently, a new deformation mode can be envisaged particularly as no increase in load is required to maintain it. Experimental evidence verifies that a new deformation mode comes into being. The material no longer piles up at the sides of the wedge and the indentation causes each half of the block to move oppositely outwards, sliding horizontally over the frictionless foundation. The applicable slip-line field

---

†For a blunt indenter (approximated by a wedge with a flat tip) the indentation pressure at the start will be given by (5.8), and will approach that given by (5.10) when the penetration becomes large in relation to the flat tip, see Ref. 94, Vol. 2, p. 195 where fields are also provided for the simple circumstance in which a rough flat-bottomed wedge is inserted into a prepared cavity.

and hodograph are given in Figs. 5.19 and 5.20 respectively. The
critical thickness of the block, i.e. the change-over point between

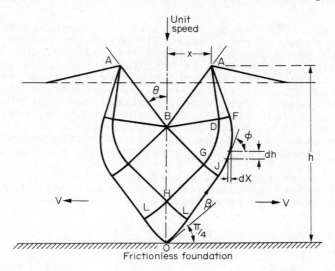

Fig. 5.19. Indentation of a block of finite depth
resting on a frictionless foundation.

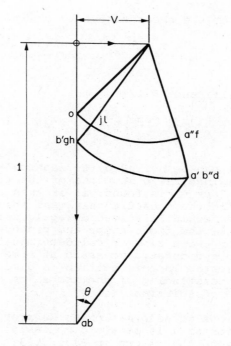

Fig. 5.20. Hodograph to Fig. 5.19.

the deformation mode, which allows piling-up of the material, and that
shown in Fig. 5.19, is given in Ref. 251 for punches with various
wedge angles.

To calculate the indenting force it is first necessary to find the
stress as some point in the plastically deforming region. The most
convenient starting point is to obtain the value of the hydrostatic
pressure at point O, p_0. This is obtained after observing that the
total horizontal force on the portion of the block to the right of
the bounding slip line $OLJFA$ is zero. By considering the equilibrium
of forces on the wedge face AB it is established that $ADGH$ and hence
$AFJLO$ are β-slip lines. The direction of the shear stress is as yet
undetermined, but if we consider the region $HLOL$, the shear-stress
directions (in keeping with the positive work requirement) must be
such as to allow the points L to separate and H to approach point O.

At a line element on the slip line $AFJLO$, inclined at an angle ϕ to
the chosen reference direction, the hydrostatic stress is given by
the *Hencky equations* and is of amount

$$p_0 - 2k \frac{\pi}{4} + 2k\phi.$$

The horizontal component of force due to the normal stresses is therefore,

$$\int_0^h \left[p_0 - 2k \frac{\pi}{4} + 2k\phi \right] dh; \tag{5.11}$$

Additionally from the shear stress k acting over the line element,
we have

$$\int_0^x k \, dx. \tag{5.12}$$

Hence, from (5.11) and (5.12)

$$\left(\frac{p_0}{2k} - \frac{\pi}{4} \right) h + \int_0^h \phi \, dh = \frac{x}{2}. \tag{5.13}$$

Equation (5.13) can be solved by a graphical-numerical procedure,[89]
having once obtained the dimensions of the field from a graphical
construction. Once p_0 is found, it is then easy to use the Hencky
equations to find the pressure on AD and thence the indenting loads.
The same problem could be solved directly using the procedures described in Chapter 6; the field shape and proportions can be determined
numerically along with a numerical determination - which could employ
(5.13) - of the hydrostatic pressure at some point in the field.
The method presented in this section is aimed at providing the reader
with a clear understanding of the mechanics of the problem along with
a viable method of solution.

The preceding mode of deformation holds providing the stress normal
to the foundation at O is always compressive. The slip-line field may
be extended beyond that shown in Fig. 5.19, by continuing the slip-
line field at O to form a right isosceles triangle meeting the

foundation at ± 45°. The stress normal to the foundation is then zero and that parallel to it just the tensile yield stress $2k$. The hodograph for this instance shows that the material in the right of the isosceles triangle rises vertically, causing contact with the foundation to cease.

Fields not dissimilar to that of Fig. 5.19 exist when using a cutting tool with a flat bottom. The fields can be obtained by extending the solution for indenting given in Fig. 5.12, through the thickness of the material; piling-up of the material is ignored.[89] In particular, the field surrounding the dead-metal zone (*BEC* of Fig. 5.12) is extended, using any range of the arcs *FE* and *EG* up to the limiting slip lines *BF* and *CG*. At a certain ratio of material thickness to semi-width of punch (actually 4.86) lift-off from the base will occur, and the slip-line field can be extended in the manner discussed for the wedge indenter in order to model the separation. In the light of this discussion on the flat-bottomed tool and lift-off, it will be the easier to appreciate the kinematics of the tube-relieving process.[278]

For certain ratios of material thickness to punch width, it has been demonstrated experimentally that the two sides of the material rotate towards the indenter. There is no obvious way of modifying the known fields for indenting or cutting with a flat-bottomed tool in order to model the bending-up phenomenon. As demonstrated by Dewhurst,[287] the problem is of the *indirect* type and can be solved using the computational procedures described in Chapter 6. Dewhurst, *op cit.*, using a criterion of reduced indentation pressure for a given ratio of material thickness to semi-width of punch, showed that rotation can occur if this ratio lies between 1 and 4.07. As mentioned earlier, lift-off from the base commences when this ratio reaches 4.86.

SHEET DRAWING

Hill and Tupper[300] constructed the first slip-line field for the sheet-drawing process which satisfied both stress and velocity requirements and adequately accounted for inhomogeneous deformation. Inhomogeneous deformation is an undesirable feature because non-useful or redundant work is expended, in achieving the overall desired change of shape. (The same desired overall change in shape could be achieved more efficiently in work terms though not so in terms of production.) However, by specially shaping the drawing die profile non-useful work can be minimized, to lead to homogeneous deformation and a minimum drawing stress.

The slip-line field proposed by Hill and Tupper is shown in Fig. 5.21 and is the two-dimensional analogue of a round-wire drawing process. The die has frictionless wedge-shaped walls of included angle 2α. The slip lines therefore meet the wall at ±45° and the points A and B are singularities for the stress distribution. The whole slip-line field comprises the extension of the centred-fan fields as illustrated in Section 1. Symmetry requires that at point F the slip lines be inclined at 45° to the axis. The corresponding hodograph is shown in Fig. 5.22, for an assumed drawing speed of unity. There is a tangential velocity discontinuity (t.v.d.) across the slip lines *ADF* and *BEF*, and from the hodograph this is seen to be of magnitude $r/\sqrt{2}$, where r is the fractional reduction.

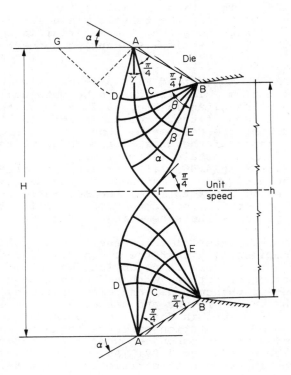

Fig. 5.21.   Slip-line field for drawing (or
             extrusion) through a frictionless
             wedge-shaped die of small reduction.

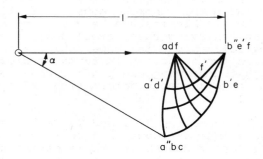

Fig. 5.22.   Hodograph to Fig. 5.21.

In order to satisfy the equilibrium requirements on the undrawn part
of the material we have to equate to zero the longitudinal component
of the total force over ADF; this is done by integrating, along ADF,
the resolved horizontal components of the hydrostatic pressure p and
the shear stress k.   The pressure p at a general point on ADF can be
found in terms of p_F, the pressure at point F, from the *Hencky equations*. p_F is obtained by satisfying the equilibrium requirements along

ADF, in the same manner as described in Section 5; thence the stress can be determined at any point in the field. The force needed to draw the sheet is then simply the horizontal component of the force acting on the die face, and if this does not exceed $2kh$ the solution is valid, i.e. the tensile stress in the drawn sheet cannot exceed the yield stress. Note, that since the slip lines in ABC are straight, the pressure on the die face is uniform.

The maximum fractional reduction, r, for which the field of Fig. 5.21 is valid, for geometrical reasons alone, is

$$r = 1 - \frac{h}{H} = \frac{2 \sin \alpha}{1 + 2 \sin \alpha} ; \qquad (5.14)$$

this corresponds to $\gamma = 0$ and $\theta = \alpha$ so that points E and F coincide, see, for example, Fig. 5.34(a).

It is easily verified that the mean tensile stress, t, in the drawn sheet is given by

$$\frac{t}{2k} = \frac{2(1 + \alpha) \sin \alpha}{1 + 2 \sin \alpha} \qquad (5.15)$$

for the reduction given by (5.14).

Larger reductions can be realized and possible slip-line fields are obtained by extending the field of Fig. 5.34(a) as in Figs. 6.28 (b) and (c). To continue to extend the field in the same manner beyond that shown in Fig. 6.28(c) provides admissible fields for certain reductions only, i.e. when using straight starting slip lines no solutions of this type exist for certain ranges of reduction and this thus leads on to problems of the *indirect* type; these are discussed in Chapter 6 with Figs. 6.28 (e) to (h) illustrating some of the admissible fields. Note that for the strip-drawing problem, $t/2k < 1$, so that if the reduction was given by (5.14), i.e. for the triangle and sector s.l.f., the limiting angle of α would be 42^0 $45'$ and the reduction 0.57. This may be contrasted with $r = 0.638$, regardless of die angle, by assuming the deformation to be attained entirely homogeneously.†

A limit is also imposed on the minimum reduction that can be achieved with the slip-line field of Fig. 5.21. At small reductions it can be conceived that the slip-line field could extend, as shown chain-dotted in Fig. 5.21, to meet the surface of the undrawn material. This imposes a limit on the maximum normal stress, q_{max}, on the die face. It is easily verified from the Hencky equations that

$$q_{max} = 2k\left(1 + \frac{\pi}{2} - \alpha\right). \qquad (5.16)$$

As α approaches zero, q_{max} approaches the flat-bottomed punch pressure for indenting a semi-infinite medium.

---

†Some possible limiting reductions for a work-hardening material are calculated in Ref. 89, where the stress-strain curve is assumed to be of the form $\sigma = A\varepsilon^n$.

At very small reductions there is a tendency for a bulge to form on the surface of the metal immediately at entry to the die. Consequently, the surface of the sheet entering the die does not remain flat, as implied by the surface GA of Fig. 5.21, but piles-up rather like the material adjacent to the flank of a wedge-shaped indenter. The formation of the bulge in strip drawing has, most recently, been discussed in detail by Rowe and Johnson.[321] Further, at these small reductions the hydrostatic stress at point F in Fig. 5.21 can become tensile, and this can result in voids opening up along the centre-line of the drawn stock.

Dodd and Kudo[328] have recently proposed a possible slip-line field which accounts for the splitting or voiding phenomenon. The field is shown in Fig. 6.27(a) and since the problem is of the *direct* type it can be constructed graphically. However, as discussed in Chapter 6, possible extensions of the field are expedited by using the matrix method.

In principle, it is not difficult to assess the influence of friction in drawing through wedge-shaped dies. The slip lines no longer meet the die face at ±45° and the angle CBA, see Fig. 5.21, becomes less than 45°. From the equilibrium requirements of region ABC, if μ is the coefficient of friction, q the normal pressure on the die face and $\angle ABC = \gamma$ then

$$q = \frac{k \cos 2\gamma}{\mu} .$$ (5.17)

The die pressure can be determined in the manner already described above, by requiring that the equilibrium requirements on the drawn and undrawn material are satisfied. The computation involved is not inconsiderable since the field, corresponding to DCEF in Fig. 5.21, has to be continually recalculated for a given angle of γ until (5.17) is satisfied. A range of solutions is likely to be reached more readily if the fields are constructed numerically, as opposed to being constructed graphically. This statement holds equally for many of the *direct* problems presented in this Chapter, when a range of tool geometries has to be inspected; see the discussion in Chapter 6 of the numerical determination of slip-line fields.

Rogers and Coffin[323] have investigated the influence of die friction on the stress distribution during strip drawing, based on the type of field shown in Fig. 5.21. Among other things, they found that for a given die angle and reduction increasing the coefficient of friction reduced the hydrostatic pressure at the centre line of the drawn strip, i.e. the tensile hydrostatic stress is increased when other things remain the same. It follows that the probability of internal structural damage is increased by die friction.

Kudo *et al.*[324] pointed out that not all the fields proposed in Ref. 323 were statically admissible. The material to the right of the slip line BE, see Fig. 5.21, should not be *overstressed*, and this condition must be met whether drawing with or without friction.

Kudo *et al.*[324] determined the overstressing limits by the method of Hill,[152] and showed graphically the domain of admissible fields as a function of reduction and die angle for frictionless drawing. These calculations have been repeated by Dodd and Scivier;[325] they also plotted regions of statically admissible fields as a function of reduction and coefficient of friction for a selected number of die angles.

Richmond and Devenpeck[313] constructed an *ideal* frictionless die profile, which required no expenditure of redundant work on material as it is drawn through the die. The drawing stress, t, when the height of the strip is reduced from H to h, is given by

$$\frac{t}{2k} = \ell n \left(\frac{H}{h} \right).$$

The above expression is the same as that for the work done in plane strain uniaxial tension for the same reduction. Since no redundant work is involved it is the most efficient way of reducing the dimensions of the strip. Note that $\ell n(H/h) \leqslant 1$, otherwise the mean drawing stress will exceed the yield stress of the material.† In Ref. 313 the profile was constructed analytically, based on the assumption that at every point in the zone of deformation the velocity vector coincides with the greatest principal stress direction. The same profile is developed below using a graphical construction, based on the slip-line-field solution for the radially inward flow of a thick-walled cylinder under plane-strain conditions; see Section 2 of this Chapter.

Select the slip-line region $ABDB_1$, of Fig. 5.4, Section 2, and build-on to it a bell-mouthed die, as shown in Fig. 5.23(a). The shape of

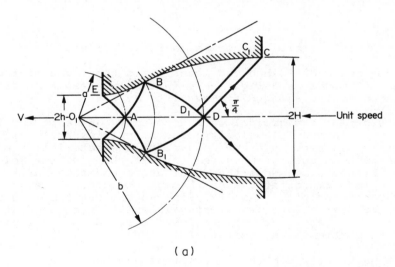

(a)

Fig. 5.23(a). Ideal die for plane strain drawing
or extrusion.

---

†As pointed out earlier the limiting reduction for homogeneous *drawing* is 0.638. When this kind of die is used for *extrusion*, the maximum reduction is limited to 0.865 with this type of field for geometrical reasons.[89]

the die is as yet unspecified; however, because the flow is assumed frictionless all slip lines meet the wall at ±45°. The volume of the material is assumed constant, and hence for a given speed of entry into the die its width at entry and exit is determined in terms of a and b, the dimensions of the slip-line net $ABDB_1$. It is easily shown that the reduction H/h is equal to b/a.[†] If a straight slip line is drawn from point D at 45° to the axis, to meet the die wall at C, all other slip lines drawn normally to the logarithmic spiral slip line DB will also be straight. The flow of material in the region $ABDB_1$ is radial and directed towards point O_1, and hence the direction of the flow along all the straight slip lines such as $D_1 C_1$ is known. Thus, with the aid of the hodograph given in Fig. 5.23(b), the profile BC could be determined graphically[167] and similarly on the exit side

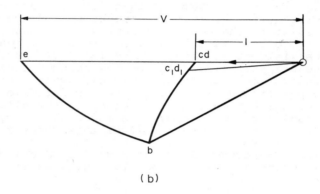

(b)

Fig. 5.23(b). Hodograph to Fig. 5.23(a).

of the die below B. Since the material to the right of the entry slip line DC moves as a rigid body (with zero resultant force) the hydrostatic stress along DC is equal to k.

The die profile is sigmoidal with zero entry and exit angles and therefore no tangential velocity discontinuities are introduced. The profile constitutes a *streamline* for the material, i.e. a line whose tangent at each point gives the direction of the velocity vector. Figure 5.24 shows the deformation undergone by an initially vertical line, xy, as it passes through the die. Lines $x' y'$, $x'' y''$, etc., show the original vertical line at various times in its passage through the die; note that a vertical line is recovered at exit. The lines $11'$, $22'$, etc., are streamlines, i.e. the path travelled by individual particles in their passage through the die.

For this particular die the streamlines and the lines $x' y'$, $x'' y''$ etc., are always orthogonal. At any point they bisect the slip line directions and thus the tangents to these curves are coincident with the direction of the principal stresses.

[†]In Ref. 167 it is shown that $2H = b \; ln \; (b/a)$ and
$2h = a \; ln \; (b/a)$.

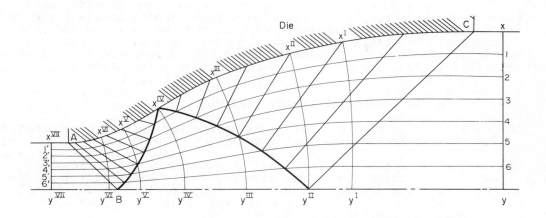

Fig. 5.24. Deformed grid pattern when drawing
through an ideal die.

Since the deformation process involves no redundant work the structural
damage incurred by the material would therefore be expected to be
minimal. An improvement in certain mechanical properties, particularly
fatigue life, might be anticipated with material drawn (or extruded)
through the *ideal* die *vis-à-vis* other die profiles; experimental evidence to this effect may be found in reference 316 and 390. As pointed
out by Hill,[374] a variety of ideal profiles are possible for a given
reduction. From a practical point of view the shortest axial length
of die should be the most desirable since this would generally assist
in minimizing any frictional work generated at the die-workpiece interface, which will always be present in fact. Sowerby *et al.*[390] have
proposed an *ideal* die shorter in length than the sigmoidal profile,
but the hodograph retains the form of Fig. 5.23(b). The die has a
finite exit angle and zero entrance angle; a centred fan field radiates
from the exit point of the die. See the discussion in Chapter 7 which
treats of *ideal* dies for axi-symmetric drawing and extrusion.

The construction of slip-line fields for drawing or extrusion through
convex- or concave-shaped dies is generally difficult because of the
need to satisfy a complete set of boundary conditions, particularly
those which exist along the curved profile. Solutions which are based
on trial-and-error graphical procedures have generally not specified
the die shape *a priori*, but rather constructed a profile as part of
the problem-solving process.[187] Note that this was the procedure
adopted earlier in this section when constructing the sigmoidal die
profile, and likewise in the analytical determination of the same
profile.[313]

Solutions to certain problems can be facilitated by first specifying
a simple field of characteristics in the hodograph plane, as was done
by Sokolovskii[365] and Johnson,[427] and working backwards to construct
the physical plane. These methods were not followed by Samanta,[381]
Samanta and Bachrach[187,389] and Fenton and his co-workers,[185,385] who
specified the curved die profile and the friction conditions at the
outset. These workers used the finite difference form of the equations

due to Hencky and Geiringer, along with expressions for the nodal
points. Their solution proceeded on a trial-and-error basis and by
continuously adjusting the shape of some guessed starting slip line
in the field until all the boundary conditions were met. In references 187 and 389 the solution of the finite difference form of the
equations is facilitated by the use of optimization techniques.

EXTRUSION AND EXTRUSION FORGING

The literature on this process is extensive and up to 1960 the mechanics of it is summarized in the monograph by Johnson and Kudo.[62]

The mechanics of the extrusion and the drawing process (Section 6) are
in many ways interrelated. For example, the proposed slip-line field
of Fig. 5.21, for drawing through wedge-shaped dies, could be equally
well applied to the extrusion process with only the stress conditions
on the bounding slip lines being modified.†

We give, however, another example of the extrusion process, i.e. that
of extrusion through a frictionless square die, from a frictionless
container when the fractional reduction is 2/3; this is originally
due to Lee.[1] The slip-line field is shown in Fig. 5.25, with A a
point of singularity for the stress distribution. The region ABC is
a centred-fan field consisting of straight and circular slip lines.
The slip lines are extended to form the region ACD which is a right
isosceles triangle made up of straight slip lines meeting the die
face at ±45°. The region ACD is therefore a region of constant hydrostatic pressure. Slip lines AB and BCD are lines of tangential velocity discontinuity. Material crossing the slip-line boundary CD is
constrained to move parallel to the die face; it is then turned as
it passes through the region ABC and on crossing the exit slip line
AB experiences a velocity jump in its tangential component of velocity
and emerges parallel to the centre line. The hodograph is shown in
Fig. 5.26.

---

†In the nomenclature of the "upper-bound" approach, see Chapter 4, p.
62 for frictionless drawing and extrusion with identical slip-line
fields, where u and v denote entry to and exit speed from the die,
with t the tensile drawing stress and p the compressive extrusion
pressure,

$$t.h.v = k \ \Sigma \ L_i V_i = p.H.u.$$

Since
$$hv = Hu,$$

then
$$t = p.$$

Simple adaptations of this approach allow of calculations made for
one process, with or without friction, easily being transformed to
apply for those of another.

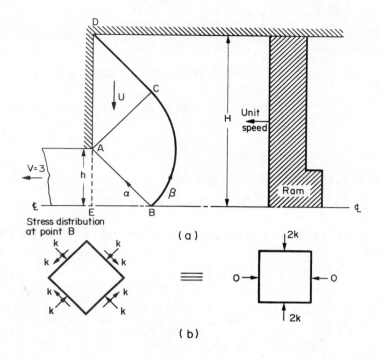

Fig. 5.25. Extrusion through a frictionless square
die when $r = 2/3$.

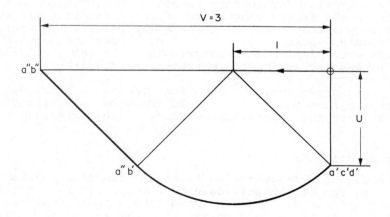

Fig. 5.26. Hodograph to Fig. 5.25.

The exit slip line AB is straight, and symmetry demands that it intersects the centre line at 45°. Since there is no horizontal force on
the material to the left of AB, the hydrostatic pressure on the slip
line AB is equal to k. Figure 5.25 shows the stress system at the

the point B, and establishes the fact that AB is an α-slip line and BCD a β-slip line. A discontinuity in stress occurs across the chain-dotted line AE, see Fig. 5.25; this is valid providing equilibrium is maintained and the yield criterion not violated.

From the *Hencky equations* the hydrostatic pressure at point C is given by

$$p_C - 2k \, \frac{\pi}{2} = p_B.$$

Hence,
$$p_C = k(1 + \pi) \qquad\qquad (5.18)$$

and thus the normal stress on the die face, q, is

$$q = k(2 + \pi). \qquad\qquad (5.19)$$

Thus the mean extrusion pressure or the normal stress on the ram, P, is given by

$$P = \frac{2}{3}k(2 + \pi). \qquad\qquad (5.20)$$

In Ref. 344 slip-line fields for reductions $\geq$ 2/3 are given and the extrusion pressures calculated. The slip-line fields are logical extensions of Fig. 5.25, i.e. the extension of the centred-fan field as discussed in Section 1 of this Chapter. For a fractional reduction of 1/2, point C terminates on the container wall and a dead-metal zone covers the die face with shearing occurring along the slip line AC. The reader's attention is drawn to these two apparently completely different modes of deformation at 1/2 and 2/3 reduction. As mentioned in the preceding section, when straight starting slip lines are employed no solutions exist for certain ranges of reduction. Solutions for problems in the latter ranges are of the *indirect* type, and W. A. Green[366] first provided them using the numerical trial-and-error procedures introduced earlier by A. P. Green;[222] see the section dealing with frictionless, plane-strain compression. Latterly Collins[237] has analysed the same problem by the matrix-operator method.

Alexander[360] has shown that the solutions for the 1/2 and 2/3 reduction are complete, in that the fields can be extended in a statically admissible manner into the non-deforming zones of the material.

(i)   Inverted Extrusion

A simple example of this extrusion technique can be obtained from Fig. 5.25. The ram (or in this case the bottom of the container) is stationary and the die faces AD move down into the material. The slip-line field and the hodograph are the same except for a reversal in sign of the unit speed. The pressure on the die face remains the same as that given by (5.19) and this is the extrusion pressure.

(ii) Extrusion Forging

The preceeding slip-line field solutions can be extended to allow simultaneous forward and backward extrusion. Figure 5.27 shows a

94

simple slip-line-field solution for this particular process, assuming the walls of the container to be frictionless. The plastically deforming region is encompassed by two centred-fan fields ABC and CDE. Since the thickness X is continuously changing, so must the shape of the slip-line field; the state is an unsteady one. The slip-line field has been constructed for the instance in which $X/D = 3$ and with $h_1 = h/2 = H/8$. Because rigid zones of metal cover the face of both the ram and the container, the precise pressure distribution over these faces is not calculable. The hydrostatic pressure normal to the straight slip lines AB and DE is equal to k and this is compatible with the assumed rigid body motion of the extruded material and zero resultant force; the pressure distribution throughout the deforming region can easily be determined using the *Hencky equations*.

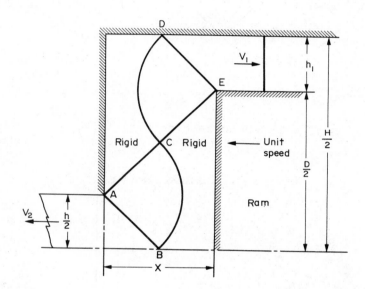

Fig. 5.27. Slip-line field for the simultaneous backward and forward extrusion under frictionless conditions.

A discontinuity in the tangential component of velocity occurs across all the bounding slip lines; the corresponding hodograph is given in Fig. 5.28.

(iii) <u>Grid Distortion</u>

For the simple type of slip-line field shown in Fig. 5.25 it is possible to calculate analytically the form that an initially square grid will take on passing through the die.[11,396] Consider a partially rough wedge-shaped die of semi-angle α; see Fig. 5.29. The square die of Fig. 5.25 is then a special instance of this case with $\alpha = 90°$ and no friction on the die face. The slip line AC no longer meets the die face at $45°$ but at some angle η where $\eta < 45°$. The coefficient of friction, μ, between the metal and the die is given by

$$\mu = \frac{\cos 2\eta}{1 + 2(\alpha - \eta) + \frac{\pi}{2} + \sin 2\eta}. \qquad (5.21)$$

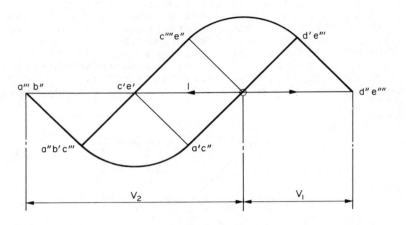

Fig. 5.28. Hodograph to Fig. 5.27.

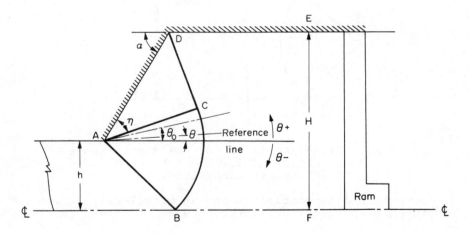

Fig. 5.29. Slip-line field for extrusion through a partially rough wedge-shaped die of moderate reduction.

The fractional reduction, $r = (1 - h/H)$, is of amount

$$\frac{1}{1 + \dfrac{\cos \eta}{\sqrt{2} \sin \alpha}}. \qquad (5.22)$$

In order to calculate the path of a particle as it travels through the deforming region, the easiest approach is to consider simultaneously both the slip-line field and the hodograph which are shown in Figs. 5.29 and 5.30 respectively.

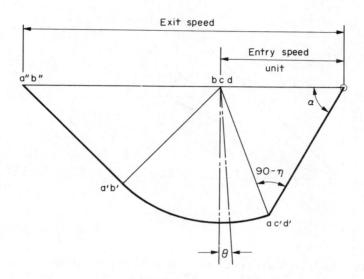

Fig. 5.30. Hodograph to Fig. 5.29.

A particle after entering the plastic region across DC proceeds parallel to the die face, AD, until it enters the plastic sector across AC. If the ram speed is unity, the speed of a particle within the triangle ADC, as obtained from the hodograph, is $\cos(\eta - \alpha).\sec\eta$.

Figure 5.31 shows an enlarged region of the sector ABC of Fig. 5.29 and the chain-dotted line represents the path of a particle as it passes through part of the sector. By considering the small element $JKLM$ as shown in Fig. 5.31,

$$\frac{JM}{JK} = \frac{dr}{r\,d\theta} = \tan\xi; \tag{5.23}$$

from the corresponding part of the hodograph it can be deduced that

$$\tan\xi = \frac{\cos\theta}{c - \sin\theta}, \tag{5.24}$$

where $c = \sin\alpha\,\sec\eta$.

From (5.23) and (5.24) it follows that the path described by a particle which enters the plastic sector across arc CB is given by

$$\int_{a}^{r}\frac{dr}{r} = \int_{\theta_0}^{\theta}\frac{\cos\theta}{(c - \sin\theta)}\,d\theta, \tag{5.25}$$

97

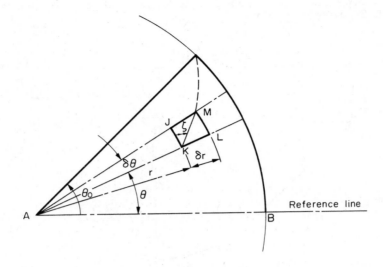

Fig. 5.31. Enlarged detail of part of the circular
sector of Fig. 5.29.

where (r,θ) are the polar coordinates of a point in the sector, a the
radius AB of the sector and θ_0 defines the point where the arc CB is
crossed by the particle, as shown in Figs. 5.29 and 5.31. Integration
of (5.25) gives

$$r = \frac{a(c - \sin\theta_0)}{(c - \sin\theta)} . \qquad (5.26)$$

Note that particles entering the plastic sector across AC pursue curves similar to that travelled by a particle entering at point C. The
time, t, taken to move over a given arc from θ_0 to θ in the plastic
sector is given by

$$\int_0^t dt = a(c - \sin\theta_0) \int_{\theta_0}^\theta \frac{d\theta}{(c - \sin\theta)^2} . \qquad (5.27)$$

The solution of (5.27) is[†]:

$$t = \frac{a(c - \sin\theta_0)}{(1 - c^2)} \left[\frac{\cos\theta}{(c - \sin\theta)} + \frac{2c}{\sqrt{c^2 - 1}} \tan^{-1} \sqrt{\frac{c + 1}{c - 1}} \tan\left(\frac{\pi}{4} - \frac{\theta}{2}\right) \right]_{\theta_0}^\theta ,$$

$$(5.28)$$

[†]Equations (5.28) and (5.29) have been given in a British Iron and
Steel Research Association report, number MW/E/54/54, W. Johnson.

when $c > 1$;

$$t = \frac{a(c - \sin \theta_0)}{(1 - c^2)}\left[\frac{\cos \theta}{(c - \sin \theta)} - \frac{2c}{\sqrt{1 - c^2}} \coth^{-1}\sqrt{\frac{1 + c}{1 - c}} \tan\left(\frac{\pi}{4} - \frac{\theta}{2}\right)\right]_\theta^{\theta_0},$$

(5.29)

when $c < 1$; and

$$t = 2a(1 - \sin \theta_0)\left[\frac{1}{(\tan[\theta/2] - 1)} + \frac{1}{(\tan[\theta/2] - 1)^2} + \frac{2}{3(\tan[\theta/2] - 1)^3}\right]_\theta^{\theta_0},$$

(5.30)

when $c = 1$.

By starting from an initial vertical line such as EF, Fig. 5.29, the position of selected points on EF can be determined after given times using the above expressions, and used so as to construct the form that a square grid takes.

Figure 5.32 shows the grid distortion for the slip-line field of Fig. 5.25. Here $\alpha = 90^0$ and $\eta = 45^0$ and hence the value of c is $\sqrt{2}$ and equation (5.28) is employed. Apart from the cusp on the axis of symmetry there is a close resemblance to most experimentally determined deformations - see Plates 3(a) and 4(b).

The cusp is less pronounced when the reduction is small and better and better agreement is thus obtained between theoretical and experimental results. The angle of the cusp can be determined as follows.

Figure 5.33(a) shows an enlarged view of a very small region around point B on the centre line of Fig. 5.29, and Fig. 5.33(b) shows the corresponding hodograph.

It is assumed that a particle on crossing the entry slip line at C proceeds in a straight line to emerge parallel to the axis at A after encountering the exit slip, BA. From the geometry of Fig. 5.33(a),

$$AC^2 = (2H^2 + 2h^2),$$

(5.31)

where H and h are related through the die reduction, r, by

$$h = (1 - r)H.$$

(5.32)

From the hodograph of Fig. 5.33(b) the velocity of the particle along the path CA is

$$\left(\frac{v^2 + u^2}{2}\right)^{\frac{1}{2}},$$

(5.33)

where

$$u = (1 - r)v.$$

(5.34)

The time, T, for the particle to travel from C to A is therefore the length from (5.31) divided by the time from (5.33). Using (5.32) and

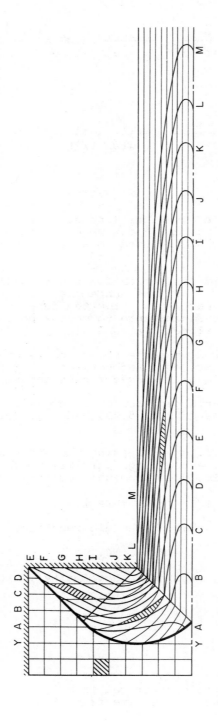

Fig. 5.32. Deformed grid pattern for extrusion through a frictionless square die of fractional reduction 2/3.

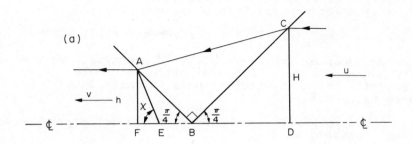

(a)

Fig. 5.33(a). Enlarged detail of region about
point B in Fig. 5.29.

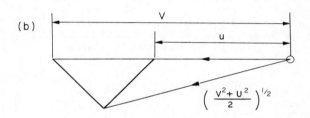

(b)

Fig. 5.33(b). Hodograph to Fig. 5.33(a).

(5.34) and simplifying gives

$$T = \frac{2H}{v}. \tag{5.35}$$

If T_1 is the time taken for a particle on the axis to travel from D
to B, then the distance EB can be expressed as

$$(T - T_1)v \tag{5.36}$$

where $T_1 = H/u$. Substituting for T and T_1 in (5.36) and using (5.34)
shows

$$EB = H\frac{(1 - 2r)}{(1 - r)}. \tag{5.37}$$

From Fig. 5.33(a),

$$\tan \chi = \frac{AF}{FE} = \frac{h}{h - EB}, \tag{5.38}$$

where χ is taken to be the angle of the cusp. Substituting for EB in
(5.38) gives

$$\cot \chi = \left(\frac{H}{h} - 1\right)^2 = \left(\frac{r}{1 - r}\right)^2. \tag{5.39a}$$

In Fig. 5.32, the cusp angle at the axis is $\cot^{-1} 4 \approx 14°$. If in Fig. 5.33(a), $\angle ABE = \theta$ and $\angle CBD = \phi$, then

$$\cot \chi = r[(1 - r) \cot \theta - \cot \phi]/(1 - r)^2. \qquad (5.39b)$$

Cusps occur whenever two lines of t.v.d. intersect whether or not they are bounding lines. Cusps at different angles in the same workpiece may also arise in circumstances in which these lines cross the axis more than once.

Conspicuous cusps have been observed in the hot extrusion of aluminium;[†] see also Ref. 383.

(iv) Energy-Dissipation Rate

When the slip-line field for frictionless extrusion consists only of circular arcs and triangles, the time rate of energy dissipation is easily calculated.[380] We consider a wedge-shaped die of semi-angle α, Fig. 5.34(a), and show that the rate of working at the ram equals the rate at which work is done on the material in the deforming region. Figure 5.25 is a special case of extrusion where $\alpha = 90°$. The die

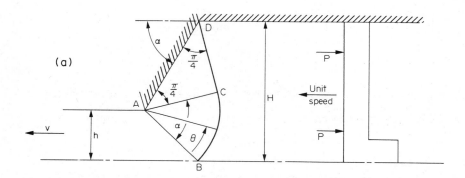

Fig. 5.34(a). Slip-line field for extrusion through a frictionless wedge-shaped die.

reduction defined in (5.14) is given by

$$\frac{2 \sin \alpha}{1 + 2 \sin \alpha}; \qquad (5.40)$$

after using the *Hencky equations* the mean pressure on the ram is

$$P = 4k\frac{(1 + \alpha) \sin \alpha}{(1 + 2 \sin \alpha)}. \qquad (5.41)$$

[†]See the article by R. E. Medrano *et al.*, *Int. J. Mech. Sci.*, **15**, 955 (1973).

If both the ram speed and the half-width at entry to the die are taken as unity, then the rate of working by the ram is

$$\frac{(1 + \alpha)\ \sin \alpha}{(1 + 2\ \sin\ \alpha)}\ ,$$ (5.42)

for just one-half of the die.

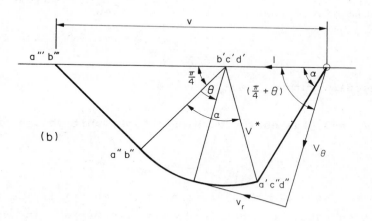

Fig. 5.34(b).   Hodograph to Fig. 5.34(a).

With a ram speed of unity the hodograph corresponding to the slip-line field of Fig. 5.34(a) is shown in Fig. 5.34(b). As determined from the hodograph the magnitude of the tangential velocity discontinuity, V^*, across the slip lines AB and DCB is $\sqrt{2}\ \sin\ \alpha$. Hence the energy-dissipation rate per unit thickness of material at the discontinuities is

$*V. \quad k$. length of slip lines AB and DCB,

which leads to

$$\frac{2k(2 + \alpha)\ \sin\ \alpha}{(1 + 2\ \sin\ \alpha)}.$$ (5.43)

There is no energy dissipated in the triangular region ADC because the material moves as a rigid mass parallel to the die face.

For the sector ACB let r and θ be plane polar coordinates with origin A, with θ measured positive, counter-clockwise from AB. The shear strain rate is given by†

$$e_{r\theta} = \frac{1}{2}\left\{\frac{\partial V_\theta}{\partial r} - \frac{V_\theta}{r} + \frac{1}{r}\frac{\partial V_r}{\partial \theta}\right\}.$$ (5.44)

V_r and V_θ represent the r and θ components of velocity respectively.

---

†This is the tensor definition, see Chapter 2.

It is easily verified from the hodograph of Fig. 5.34(b) that

$$V_\theta = -\left\{V^* + \cos\left(\frac{\pi}{4} + \theta\right)\right\}$$

and

$$V_r = -\sin\left(\frac{\pi}{4} + \theta\right).$$

By substituting for V_r and V_θ into (5.44) gives

$$e_{r\theta} = \frac{1}{2}\frac{V^*}{r} . \tag{5.45}$$

(Note that strain rate $e_{r\theta} \to \infty$ as $r \to 0$.)

Since $e_r = e_\theta = 0$, the energy dissipation per unit volume of material in ABC is

$$2\tau_{r\theta}e_{r\theta} = 2ke_{r\theta} , \tag{5.46}$$

where $\tau_{r\theta} = k$, the yield shear stress of the material. The total ene-rgy-dissipation rate, per unit thickness of material, in ABC is

$$2k\int_0^a\int_0^a e_{r\theta}r \ d\theta \ dr , \tag{5.47}$$

where a is the radius of the sector equal to $\sqrt{2}/(1 + 2\sin\alpha)$. Substituting for $e_{r\theta}$ in (5.47) and integrating gives

$$kV^*a\alpha. \tag{5.48}$$

Substituting for V^* and a into (5.48) gives

$$\frac{2k\alpha \sin \alpha}{(1 + 2 \sin \alpha)}. \tag{5.49}$$

Adding (5.43) and (5.49) yields

$$\frac{4k(1 + \alpha) \sin \alpha}{(1 + 2 \sin \alpha)}. \tag{5.50}$$

(5.50) is the same quantity as given in (5.42) for the rate at which energy is being supplied by the punch or ram.

PIERCING

The mechanics of *Indenting*, *Extrusion* and *Piercing* are very similar and are all inter-related. Specific points of similarity are raised later in this section.

The simplest form of the piercing process is one where the billet is

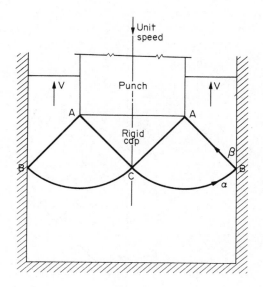

Fig. 5.35. Slip-line field for piercing when the
container wall is frictionless.

held in a container and penetrated by a punch. Sometime after the
punch has penetrated the mass, the process can be regarded as a steady-
state one since the material flows upwards past the punch and the zone
of deformation does not change in form or extent with time. A slip-
line field solution is given in Fig. 5.35 for a fractional reduction,
i.e. (punch width)/(width of container) of ½, assuming frictionless
conditions at the container walls. The slip lines meet the container
walls at ±45° and points A are singularities of stress. A 90° wedge
of dead metal, ACA, becomes attached to the face of the punch and moves
downwards with the same speed. Shearing of the material occurs along
the faces AC and a discontinuity in the tangential component of velocity occurs across the slip lines AB and CB. The hodograph is shown
in Fig. 5.36.

Because the material crossing the exit slip lines AB moves as a rigid
body, the resultant vertical force on it is taken as zero. The hydrostatic pressure on AB is thus equal to k. By examining the state of
stress at point B it is easily verified that AB is a β-slip line and
CB an α-slip line. Using the *Hencky equations* the pressure at point
C (and hence along the face CA) is

$$p_C = k(1 + \pi).$$ (5.51)

The mean punch pressure, P, is thus

$$P = 2k\left(1 + \frac{\pi}{2}\right).$$ (5.52)

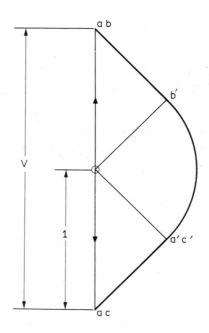

Fig. 5.36.   Hodograph to Fig. 5.35.

In Figs. 6.25 (a) and (b) fields are presented for fractional reductions greater and less than 50% respectively. These fields were first
proposed by Hill[7,396] for rough punches; note that a dead-metal zone
exists under the punch face. The punch pressure has a minimum value
of $2k(1 + \pi/2)$ corresponding to a fractional reduction of $\frac{1}{2}$. The
curve of punch pressure versus fractional reduction as derived from
the fields shown in Figs. 6.25 (a) and (b) is symmetrical about this
latter point.

The slip-line fields presented for the *Piercing* operation are formally
identical to those which could occur for *Inverted Extrusion* from a
frictionless container if the die faces in this latter process were
supporting dead-metal zones. All that has to be appreciated is the
interchange as between the axis of symmetry and the wall of the container in each process. Thus, the mean punch pressure and the extrusion
die pressure are the same for identical fields.

It also follows that the slip lines proposed for extrusion through a
frictionless square die, for reductions greater than $\frac{1}{2}$, should be kinematically acceptable for *Piercing* with a frictionless punch. In this
case no dead-metal cap would appear on the punch face. This latter
statement is partly, but interestingly, verified by Plate 5(b), which
shows the distortion undergone by an initially square grid of lines
scribed on the meridian section of a lead billet in lubricated, axisymmetric, piercing.[62]

In Ref. 398 the matrix method has been employed to develop slip-line-
field solutions for a range of reductions in the piercing operation.

FORGING

Forging is the process by which metal is altered in shape or form as
a result of being struck by a hammer or squeezed in a press. The
reader could therefore consider the examples given for *Compression*,
and, to a lesser extent, the examples of *Indenting* and *Cutting* to be
forging operations. We give here as an example, the solution to the
problem of forging using parallel unequal rigid dies.

Figure 5.37(a) shows metal of thickness H indented by unequal dies of
width $2a_1$ and $2a_2$. If H is somewhat larger than $(a_1 + a_2)$ the slip-
line field for forging a rigid, perfectly plastic material is as given.
The field is a more general form of one proposed originally for forging
with equal width parallel rigid dies. The mode of deformation assumed
is one where the two blocks of material to the right of *BOD* and to the
left of *AOC* move as rigid bodies outwards and downwards under the influence of the wedge action of the rigid zones of dead metal which are
assumed to be attached to the face of the indenters. The reader
should have no difficulty in recognizing the shape of the field. It
consists of four centred-fan fields extended to meet in *O*; the concept
of a $90°$ wedge of rigid material adhering to the face of the punch
has been previously used in connection with *Piercing*. The identification of the slip lines, apart from determining the stress magnitude

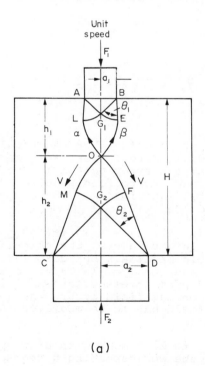

(a)

Fig. 5.37(a). Slip-line field for the forging of
strip between opposed parallel tools
of unequal width.

107

at a point, can be obtained intuitively. This can be done by reasoning that the pressure at E is certainly greater than that at point O and hence by a trial use of the *Hencky equations BEO* is established as a β-slip line.

The pressure on the dies can be calculated in the following manner. (We neglect considerations of moment equilibrium.) If p_0 denotes the pressure at point O, then by traversing a β-line from O to E and from E to G_1 along an α-line, the pressure at G_1 from the *Hencky equations* is

$$p_{G_1} = p_0 + 4k\theta_1 . \tag{5.53}$$

Hence the pressure on the upper die is

$$P_1 = p_0 + k(1 + 4\theta_1) . \tag{5.54}$$

Similarly the pressure on the lower die, P_2, is

$$P_2 = p_0 + k(1 + 4\theta_2) . \tag{5.55}$$

Vertical force equilibrium demands that

$$a_1 P_1 = a_2 P_2 \tag{5.56}$$

Thus,

$$p_0 = \frac{4k(n\theta_1 - \theta_2)}{(1 - n)} - k , \tag{5.57}$$

where $n = a_1/a_2$.

p_0 is also determined by assuming that the total horizontal force on the boundary BOD or AOC is zero. (See, for example, the section on *Cutting*.) Thus a trial-and-error method is necessary which involves varying the angles θ_1 and θ_2, to find a value of p_0 satisfying (5.57) and requiring horizontal equilibrium. The computation is considerable, as will be evident from Ref. 401.

Providing $P_1/2k$ is less than $(1 + \pi/2)$ the slip-line field of Fig. 5.37(a) is valid. At larger values, the slip-line field no longer passes through the whole material, but deformation occurs locally around the upper die, and $P_1/2k = (1 + \pi/2)$ is the yield-point pressure for a flat-faced rigid punch pressed into a rigid- plastic material. A further restriction on the field occurs when points O and G_1 coincide. In this instance the field has to be modified in the manner suggested in Ref. 401.

Assuming the upper die to move down with unit speed and the lower die to remain stationary, the corresponding hodograph is as in Fig. 5.37(b). The hodograph provides a kinematically admissible velocity field, but displays a rather interesting feature. The vector V indicates the velocity of the right-hand half of the displaced material; it can be seen that it is possible for a small amount of material to be expelled across the upper slip lines at O into the rigid region and subsequently back into the lower slip-line field region. Similar situations for

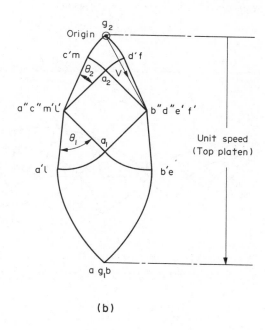

(b)

Fig. 5.37(b). Hodograph to Fig. 5.37(a).

possible geometries in sideways extrusion have been noted.[350]

In Fig. 5.38(a) the slip-line field for a closed die forging is shown
(neglecting die lands). For free, sideways expulsion of metal through
each orifice, the two fields must be of the same *shape*. The hodograph
is shown in Fig. 5.38(b).

It is interesting to compare the normal pressure which exists at the
tool-workpiece interface when *indenting*, *compressing* and *forging* with
flat-face tools, as a function of the tool-workpiece geometry.[7,87]
As will be gathered from the preceding examples, the tool pressure is
high in the case of the *indentation* process but the ratio of the punch
width to the material height (or depth) is then small. In general it
follows that in processes which can be regarded as ones of indentation
only, e.g. hardness testing, that the forming loads are relatively
small and the deformation is a local event with material merely being
displaced around the indenter. This type of deformation can be related
to the thread-rolling process,[292] where only the surface layers are
deformed to become the thread profile, without changing the mean diameter of the bar stock. Another example is that of embossing.

When the requirement is a change in the overall dimensions of the
workpiece, e.g. reducing the height of material stock with an attendant increase in the lateral dimensions, the plastic zone has to spread
completely through the thickness of the material. In such cases the
ratio of tool width to material thickness is usually much greater
than that encountered in the indentation process. As seen in the
section on *Compression*, under frictionless conditions the normal
platen pressure is $2k$ for integer values of w/h, and this does not

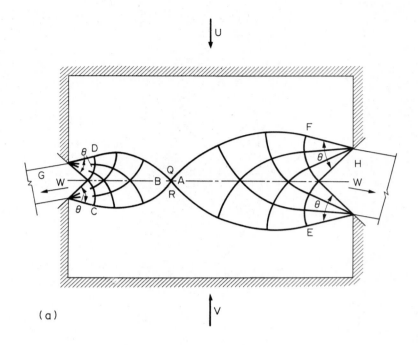

(a)

Fig. 5.38(a).   A possible slip-line field for a
closed die forging operation.

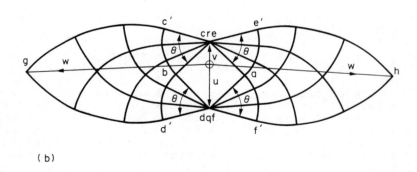

(b)

Fig. 5.38(b).   Hodograph to Fig. 5.38(a).

change much for non-integer values larger than unity. Although the
tool pressure is much less than that arising when *Indenting*, nearly
all practical situations would demand a much larger press capacity
for the compression operation due to an order of magnitude difference
in the size of the tools. Furthermore, in an actual process friction
cannot be avoided, and its presence usually results in a build-up of
the normal pressure from an edge to the centre of the tool - the
"friction-hill" effect - thus adding to the press requirements.

Consequently, high forming loads cannot be avoided in open and closed die-forging operations when wide tools (or dies) are employed.

The forging operation illustrated by Fig. 5.37(a) could represent one stage in a cogging process, i.e. where material is fed under tools (or a hammer) to reduce the stock height. In effect this is an incremental forging operation since selected zones of the workpiece are deformed in sequence to achieve the overall dimensional changes. It will be appreciated that there will be a trade-off between the amount of material deformed in a single stroke and the associated forming load, since both are a function of the tool width.

Incremental forging machines have been developed suitable for the manufacture of symmetric and unsymmetric components, whose lateral dimensions are large compared with the thickness. In these machines the tool sweeps over the surface of the workpiece in a regular and repeated fashion. The pressure is intensified in the zone of contact between the tool and the workpiece but excessive overall loads are avoided. The process has also been referred to as "rocking-die" or "orbital" forging.[407,408]

ORTHOGONAL MACHINING

In orthogonal machining the cutting edge of the tool is perpendicular to the direction of feed, see Fig. 5.39.

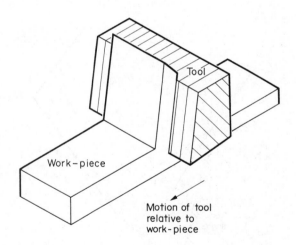

Fig. 5.39. Orthogonal machining.

As early as 1870 experimenters suggested deformation modes for machining based on the existence of a single shear plane.† Ernst and Merchant[409] attempted to determine the cutting forces on the tool using the single shear-plane hypothesis and more recently several investigators have proposed slip-line-field solutions. A completely satisfactory

---

†This is the simplest hypothesis.

solution has yet to be found which explains in full the mechanics of
machining. The main criticism levelled against slip-line-field models
among other things (see below) is that they are too idealized and do
not take account of the complicated interplay of friction, temperature
at the tool-material interface, strain hardening and strain rate
during the process. However, as in many other problems, slip-line-
field solutions may be used as a first approximation with which to
predict loads and deformation modes.

We give as an example the slip-line field proposed by Johnson[427] and
Usui and Kikuchi[429] for machining with a restricted-edge cutting tool
(a Klopstock tool), as shown in Fig. 5.40. Note the similarity, in
part, to the slip-line-field solution for indenting with rough wedge-
shaped dies. Assuming some degree of friction between the tool and
the workpiece, the slip lines in the region ABC do not meet the tool
face at $\pm 45^{\circ}$. The closer ψ approaches zero the more nearly does the
shear stress on the material along the die face approach the limiting
value, k. A is a point of stress singularity and hence region ABC
can be extended around A to form the sector ACD. The point E is then
located with AD equal to DE. The position of point E is not as critical as in the problem of wedge indentation because

    (i)   point A need not lie on the original surface EF produced,
           and
    (ii)   surface EF may or may not be parallel to the direction
           of travel, but if it is, point A may be above or below it.

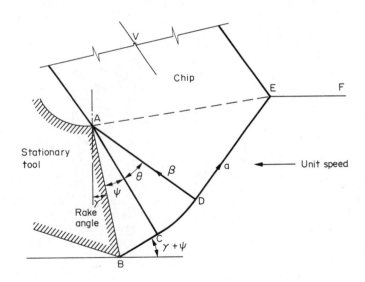

Fig. 5.40. Slip-line field for cutting with a
            Klopstock tool.

Evidently a discontinuity in the tangential component of velocity
occurs across the slip line $BDCE$, which separates the rigid region
from the plastically deforming one. Assuming the tool to remain
stationary and the workpiece to approach it with unit speed, the
corresponding hodograph is shown in Fig. 5.41.

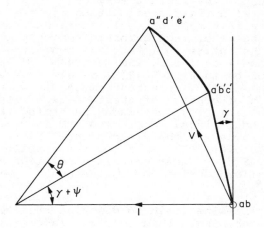

Fig. 5.41.   Hodograph to Fig. 5.40.

Beyond the slip lines AD and DE the chip moves as a rigid body. The only manner in which the chip can be in equilibrium and still satisfy the condition that there is zero resultant force on it, is for the hydrostatic pressure to be k along AD and DE. $EDCB$ is therefore identified as an α-slip line and, using the Hencky equations, the pressure at point B, p_B, is given by

$$p_B = p_D + 2k\theta = k(1 + 2\theta).\qquad(5.58)$$

The normal pressure on the tool face, q, is then of amount

$$\frac{q}{2k} = \frac{\sin 2\psi}{2} + \frac{1}{2} + \theta.\qquad(5.59)$$

The horizontal cutting force, F_H, is found to be

$$\frac{F_H}{kt} = 1 + 2\theta + \sin 2\psi + \tan \gamma \cos 2\psi,\qquad(5.60)$$

where from Fig. 5.40, $t = AB \cos \gamma$. The coefficient of friction is then given by

$$\mu = \frac{k \cos 2\psi}{q}.\qquad(5.61)$$

Kudo[432] has found more elaborate slip-line-field solutions for ortho-gonal machining with restricted-edge cutting tools which, in some cases, yield lower cutting forces than are obtained by using the present fields. More recently, some slip-line-field solutions for turning, milling and boring operations involving rotation of either or both the workpiece and the tool have been proposed.[438,439]

113

The application of slip-line-field theory to machining problems is
not limited to tools with restricted cutting edges but one of the
values of considering this type of tool, at least from a theoretical
viewpoint, is that the deforming region in the chip can be assumed
to take place over the entire tool face and hence the extent of the
deforming region is well defined. The length of the contact zone
between chip and tool as in Fig. 5.42(a) is always even experimentally
obscure. Most of the earlier solutions given did not impose any restriction on the length of contact of the tool face. Lee and Shaffer[411]
proposed a slip-line field for continuous machining which consists of
a triangle of orthogonal lines, see region ABC in Fig. 5.42(a), wherein
all the material is raised to the yield point. The field can also be
readily extended around point A, to allow for a built-up nose on the
tool tip see Fig. 5.42(b). Under certain conditions this latter solution can provide smaller cutting forces and hence a more likely deformation mode.

Lee[412] has given a slip-line field to describe the formation of a discontinuous chip in machining. This solution is clearly a modification
of a slip-line field given in a paper by Hill, Lee and Tupper[250] concerning the wedge indentation of ductile materials. Rowe and Wetton[317]
have also given similar fields for the drawing of brittle materials
through wedge-shaped dies - a process which could be regarded as akin
to cutting with a negative-rake tool.

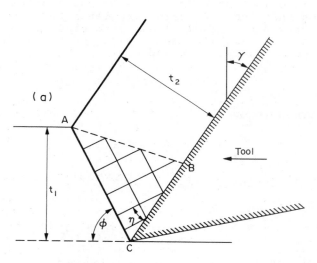

Fig. 5.42(a). Slip-line field proposed by Lee and
Shaffer for continuous machining.

In general there exists a large disparity between experimental measurements of cutting force and theoretical predictions based on the rigid-
plastic, non-hardening solid. This is commonly attributed to the
exclusion of the effects of temperature, strain-rate and strain-hardening from the analysis, and an inadequate representation of the true
frictional conditions at the tool-material interface, Many investi-

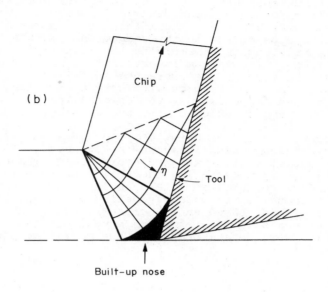

Fig. 5.42(b). Possible slip-line field for machining
with a built-up nose.

gators, notably Oxley and his co-workers,† have attempted to account
for some of these factors in order to resolve some of the disparities
between theory and experiment. By so doing the problem becomes analytically difficult, and recourse is made to the experimental determination of the details of the mode of plastic deformation in the vicinity
of the chip-tool interface. This is achieved by first photographically
printing or electrochemically etching a grid pattern on the surface
of the workpiece,[186,446] and then filming the ensuing distortion or
"freezing" the distorted net by rapidly removing the cutting tool -
the so-called "quick-stop" method.[443,447] It is to be noted that such
tests are, however, often run at industrially unrealistic slow cutting
speeds. Nonetheless the visual observations permit the construction
of a possible slip-line field and corresponding hodograph. The first
attempts to incorporate strain-hardening into the *Hencky equations*
are to be found in Refs. 417 and 419. The modified Hencky equations
are then applied (usually in their finite difference form) to the
constructed slip-line field, and thus it is possible to obtain estimates of cutting forces. As would be anticipated the experimental observations reveal a deformation zone which is finite in extent and this
therefore places in question single shear-plane hypotheses. A finite
zone is also required in theoretical modelling in order to allow for
the effects of strain-hardening and the like. Nevertheless, how well
the constitutive equation(s) used in these models reflect the actual
material characteristics in the deformation zone is a moot point.

The reader is referred to a paper by Roth and Oxley[446] wherein a
slip-line field for orthogonal machining is determined by the above-

---

†Some of this work is summarized in Ref. 448.

mentioned procedures. Very slow cutting speeds were employed (12.7 mm/min), but very good agreement between theoretical and measured cutting forces was obtained. The method is rather tedious and this may prove to be a deterrent to investigations of this nature. In addition, inconsistencies remain with the latter proposed solution, in that the rigid chip was not in equilibrium and certain boundary conditions at the free surface were not satisfied. However, it could be argued that the results vindicate the method, and that only through a detailed inspection of the deformation zone will a better understanding of the kinetics of the process be realized.

In a very recent article Dewhurst[450] proposed a slip-line field for orthogonal machining, which is shown in Fig. 5.43. The field varia-bles are the angles θ, ψ, η and the hydrostatic pressure at point A, with the cutting parameter being the tool rake face friction τ, where $0 \leqslant \tau \leqslant k$, associated with some rake angle.[†] With this type of field the cutting process is not uniquely defined. Ranges of permissible solutions were found, based on the criterion that the vertices at either side of the slip line at point A were not overstressed. The field variables were determined using the matrix method.

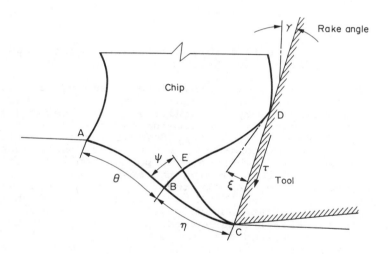

Fig. 5.43. Possible slip-line field for curly chip formation.

Dewhurst, *op cit.*, proposed that the steady-state machining mode is dependent upon the manner in which the region of plastic deformation develops from the time the tool contacts the workpiece. Since the developing zone is largely unconstrained, and since it will also be influenced by random disturbances, the steady-state mode is not likely

---

[†]The reader interested in the physical realities of machining should refer to the book by Trent,[449] for photographs and discussions of the complex interaction which may take place on the tool face, due to a constant scouring of the tool face by the chip and involving pressure, temperature and possible metallurgical phase changes along the inter-face.

to be unique. Dependent upon the rake angle and angle of friction, two distinct machining conditions were identified in the paper. One, in which the chip will always curl and a second, which is bounded at the lower end by the Lee and Shaffer[411] slip-line field, which corresponds to straight chip formation.

SWAGING†

In most practical cases the expansion or swaging operation is a non-steady process, which may or may not preserve the geometric similarity of any slip-line-field solution which is used. Following Hill[7,219] we can study one situation by considering the expansion of a semi-cylindrical cavity in the surface of an infinite block of material. The cavity is assumed to be preformed and with a coronet of piled-up material against it. In Fig. 5.44 *ABC* is the coronet and *BEB* the frictionless cylindrical surface.

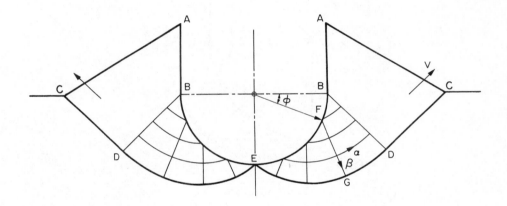

Fig. 5.44. Slip-line field for the swaging or
expansion of a cylindrical cavity.

A suitably distributed normal pressure is now applied over the surface *BEB* (and *not* over *AB*), and a search is made for a possible deformation mode. All slip lines meet the cylindrical surface at ±45° and a start is made by assuming that the plastic-rigid boundary joins up through points *E* and *C*. A natural trial hypothesis is to have two straight slip lines through *B* and *C* meet in *D*. Since *BD* is a straight slip line all other β-lines in the region *BDE* are straight. This assumption provides a simple geometric form for the α-slip lines which are then involutes of a circle, centre *O* and radius $1/\sqrt{2}$, if the radius of the cavity is taken as unity. The coronet *ABC*, by hypothesis, has stress-free surfaces, so that part of it at least must move out as a rigid body separated from the plastically deforming material by a slip line. If this slip line is taken to be *CD* then region *ABDC* moves out as a rigid body. The only way in which this region can now be in

---

†As with many processes examined in this chapter, descriptions and diagrams of types of machines for performing them are to be found in the *ASM Handbook*, Vol. 4 - *Forming*, ASM (1976).

equilibrium is by having a normal pressure equal to k along the surfaces BD and DC. A discontinuity in the tangential component of velocity occurs across the slip line EDC and hence the velocity component v on each of the straight β-lines in the region EBD is zero. Thus if the cavity expands radially with unit speed the component of velocity u along the α-lines is equal to $\sqrt{2}$ on BE. Because v is zero on all the β-lines, then from the *Geiringer equations* u is a constant along all the α-lines. The hodograph is shown in Fig. 5.45 and can only be satisfied by taking the height BA of the coronet equal to the radius of the cavity.

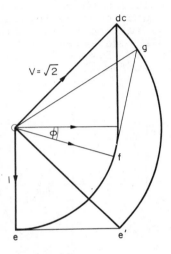

Fig. 5.45. Hodograph to Fig. 5.44.

Define ϕ as the angular coordinate of a point on the surface of the cavity measured around O from the horizontal, as shown in Fig. 5.44. Then noting that $p = k$ on the slip lines BD and DC, by the *Hencky equations* the hydrostatic pressure on the surface of the cavity is distributed according to

$$p = k \ (1 + 2\phi),\qquad (5.62)$$

and the normal pressure by

$$P = 2k \ (1 + \phi).\qquad (5.63)$$

In Ref. 427 a connection between this swaging situation and the squashing of a wedge by a flat rigid die is found.

YIELDING OF NOTCHED BARS IN TENSION

The tensile specimen shown in Fig. 5.46 is symmetrical about YY and XX and the notch is sufficiently deep for the plastic region to be localised around the core. The specimen is of sufficient length for the state of stress in the neighbourhood of the notch to be independent of the precise distribution of the end load, which is equipollent to an axial pull parallel to XX.

As the load on the specimen is increased the plastic region spreads across the notch, so that when the neck is fully plastic the ends of the specimen can move apart. The slip-line field consists of a family of logarithmic spirals,[453] as in Fig. 5.46. There is a discontinuity

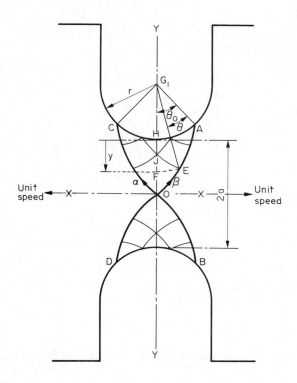

Fig. 5.46. Slip-line field for a symmetrically deep-notched specimen under uniaxial tension.

in the tangential component of velocity across the bounding slip lines AOB and COD; if the ends of the bar move away from YY with unit speed the discontinuity is of amount $\sqrt{2}$. The corresponding hodograph is given in Fig. 5.47.

At point A the boundary is stress-free, the stress is tangential to the boundary and tensile and consequently AO is a β-line and BO an α-line. The angular span of these slip lines is taken to be θ_0 and hence in the same manner as that described in the section on *Pressure Vessels*, the change in angle ϕ between two points along the β-slip line AO is numerically the same as the change in angle θ of the radius vector of the slip line, with G_1 as the origin.

From the *Hencky equations* the hydrostatic pressure at 0 is

$$o = p_A - 2k\theta_0$$

$$= -k(1 + 2\theta_0).$$

119

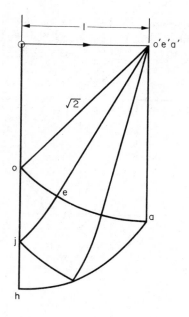

Fig. 5.47.   Hodograph to Fig. 5.46.

The hydrostatic stress at point E on the slip line AO and at any point on the circular arc EF with centre G_1 is

$$p_E = -k(1 + 2\theta).$$

It follows from the polar equation of the slip line OA that

$$\frac{a}{r} = \exp \theta_0 - 1,$$

and therefore,

$$\theta_0 = \ln \left(\frac{a}{r} + 1 \right).$$

If the radius of $G_1 E$ is $(r + y)$ then

$$\theta = \ln \left(\frac{y}{r} + 1 \right).$$

The longitudinal stress is thus distributed across the neck according to

$$\sigma = 2k \left[1 + \ln \left(\frac{y}{r} + 1 \right) \right].$$

By integration, the tensile yield point load is

$$P = 4ka \left(1 + \frac{r}{a} \right) \ln \left(1 + \frac{a}{r} \right),$$

or
$$P = 4k\theta_0 r \exp \theta_0 .$$

The number $P/4ka$ is termed the constraint factor; it is the factor by which the mean stress in the neck exceeds the yield stress $2k$.

The above slip-line field and analysis was first given by Hill[453] who also found the plastic collapse load for a specimen containing a deep wedge-shaped notch with a circular root. An interesting feature of this latter analysis is that when the ratio r/a approaches zero, i.e. for a vanishingly small root radius and parallel notch sides, the constraint factor has a maximum value of $(1 + \pi/2)$. This is the same value as would be obtained by indenting a semi-infinite medium with a frictionless punch of width $2a$. The distribution of stress and strain in the notched bar in this limiting case is then identical with that for a frictionless punch, apart from a change in the sign of the load.

Solutions for some sharp wedge-shaped notches have been given by Lee;[458] also Lee et al.[459,460] have extended the problem discussed above to account for the changes in geometry of the free surface of the notch under continued deformation. It will be appreciated that because the mode of deformation is non-steady the geometrical changes of boundaries, etc., have to be considered before the problem can be continued.

In all the above-mentioned solutions, the specimen is assumed so wide that the plastic zone at the onset of yielding is confined to the ligament between the notches, as shown in Fig. 5.46. As the width of the specimen considered is gradually decreased a stage is reached when this type of solution becomes inadmissible. The deformation spreads to the sides of the test piece and rigid zones of material adjacent to the notch become isolated, as shown schematically in Fig. 5.48. These rigid zones are rotated during deformation; constraint factors for these deformation modes are less than those mentioned earlier. Ewing and Hill[463] and Ewing[464] have determined the critical width of the test piece containing sharp V-notches and V-notches with a circular root, respectively.

CRACK INITIATION AND FRACTURE

In the field of Fracture Mechanics one of the prime objectives is the determination of an appropriate design criterion for predicting the stress which gives rise to rapidly propagating cracks. Experimental investigations have mainly been confined to the study of crack initiation and propagation in notched test pieces (or propagation in test pieces containing purposely pre-formed cracks), under some combination of axial load and bending. Complementary theoretical treatment has been devoted to the determination of the stress and strain fields in the vicinity of the stress raiser in terms of the applied stress system.

Much of the research has concentrated on the problem of brittle fracture treating the material as a linear elastic solid, following the early work of Griffith.[465] There also exists in the literature a number of elegant analytical solutions for the stress distribution around regularly shaped holes, slits (cracks) and the like (see, for example, the book by Savin[466]), and the application of some of these

results to the linear elastic theory of fracture mechanics is discussed
in Refs. 471 and 483.

It is generally accepted that with most metals brittle fracture is
usually preceded by a small amount of plastic deformation, at least
on a microscopic scale. Thus the fracture theory due to Griffith,
op cit., which treats of perfectly brittle materials, must be modified
mutatis mutandis when dealing with metals.[471,483] The assumption of
an elastic/plastic material model greatly increases the complexity
of ascertaining the stress distribution in cracked or notched test
pieces. Invariably, mumerical procedures are required and more rigorous solutions often employ finite difference or finite element methods,
the latter approach having been the most favoured in recent years.[487,
489] With either of these methods the formulation should be flexible
enough to deal not only with small strain problems, but also with
large displacements and/or large strains.[487,488] Knott[483] has provided
a brief survey of certain solution procedures (not only finite element
methods) for the determination of the stress determination around
cracks in elastic/plastic solids; see also the discussion in Ref. 482.

More relevant to the subject matter of this monograph is the application of slip-line-field theory (based on a rigid, perfectly-plastic,
solid) to the determination of the stress and velocity fields around
slits and notches, assuming either a plane-strain or plane-stress
condition. This model material is obviously more appropriate to
studies of ductile fracture, where general yielding has usually occurred, rather than brittle fracture. In Sections 12 and 14 of this
Chapter some simple plane-strain slip-line fields are shown for notched
members deformed in a uniaxial and a bending mode respectively. The
bibliography of these sections provides a comprehensive coverage of
the work performed in this area. In Chapter 7 further references are
provided for the plane-stress case. Knott, *op cit.*, has shown some
further slip-line fields which are to be found in the references
quoted herein, and he deals specifically with the determination of
constraint factors, i.e. a measure of the stress intensification,
for various notch geometries. A number of experimentally determined
fields, revealed by etching the specimens in Fry's reagent, are also
provided. It is to be noted that the problems are non-steady state
ones and therefore the slip-line-field method provides information
about the stress and velocity distribution at the onset of general
yielding only. The technique does not lend itself to problems where
the boundary conditions are continuously changing.

The discussion above has centred on experimental and theoretical
studies pertaining to the fracture of notched members. No regard
has been paid to the structure of the material or to the study of the
micro-mechanisms which initiate fracture though they are now heavily
researched areas. In simple terms this involves the study of the
conditions which give rise to void formation (usually around inclusions
and second-phase particles), and the growth and coalescence of the
voids which result in fracture. These investigations are less amenable
to analysis primarily because of the imprecise knowledge of the influence of the morphology and spacing of the particles, and the bond strength between particle and matrix. A number of hole-growth models,
i.e. models of the growth of existing holes, have been proposed, and
the ones due to McClintock and his co-workers (Refs. 469, 470, 472,
473) and Rice and Tracey[481] have formed the basis for many subsequent
investigations in this area.

The extent of the formation of voids, microcracks and the like is often referred to as the *damage* incurred by the material. A commonly held view is that the growth of the *damage* is strongly dependent upon the hydrostatic component of stress, and that ductile fracture will occur at a certain level of damage. This has a direct bearing on all sheet and bulk metal-forming operations, but to date no single *damage function* has been proposed which satisfies experimental observations for a range of metals, even under the most carefully controlled laboratory conditions.

The literature dealing with fracture is extensive and the number of symposia and conferences, e.g. The International Conference on Fracture (held every four years), devoted to the topic continues to increase. A limited bibliography only is supplied here but it should lead the reader to more detailed information on the various aspects discussed above.

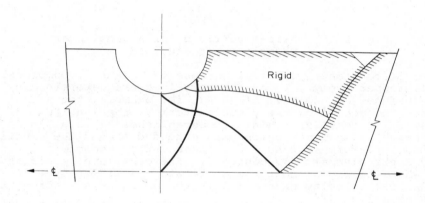

Fig. 5.48.   A schematic representation of a slip-line field for a symmetrically notched tensile bar of subcritical width.

14. BENDING

(i) Cantilevers Under Concentrated Loading

The first attempt to assess theoretically the effect of shearing loads in the theory of plastic bending in terms of slip-line-fields is reported in the papers by A. P. Green[492,493]   Following Green, we suppose that a cantilever is fixed at AB and yields under a vertical load St, applied at the other end, as in Fig. 5.49. The beam is of rectangular cross-section and of sufficient width for the assumption of plane-strain to be applicable.

If the ratio l/t is sufficiently large the beam may be expected to yield by the formation of a plastic hinge at the fixed end, where the bending moment is greatest and the remainder of the beam remains rigid. This mode of deformation suggests a slip-line field of the type shown in Fig. 5.49, where A and B are points of stress singularity. The regions BCD and AGH are right isosceles triangles, and hence are

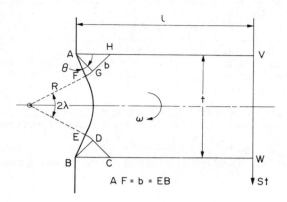

Fig. 5.49.   Slip-line field for a cantilever
under a shear end load.

regions of constant hydrostatic stress of amount k, compressive and
tensile respectively. These stress values are determined by the stress
-free surfaces AH and BC. Along AH, for example, the normal stress
is zero and hence from the yield criterion, the longitudinal yield
stress is $2k$ (tensile); this also establishes HG as a β-slip line.
The straight slip line regions are extended around the singularities
at A and B to form AFG and BDE. These latter regions are then connected by a circular arc FE, centre O. The cantilever would start to
yield when its rigid end tends to rotate by sliding over the arc FE;
a tangential velocity discontinuity therefore exists across the continuous slip line $AFEB$.

The slip-line field is symmetrical about the centre line of the beam
and hence the condition of zero horizontal force is seen to be satisfied. The dimensions of the field are obtained in terms of the thickness of the beam, t. There are two equilibrium equations and one geometrical condition for obtaining the three unknowns, viz. b/t, R/t and
S, see Fig. 5.49, in terms of l/t.

Since the hydrostatic pressure varies from k (tensile) to k (compressive) along line $GFED$, then expressions

$$\left.\begin{aligned} \theta &= \frac{\pi}{8} - \frac{1}{4} \\[2mm] 2\lambda &= \frac{\pi}{4} + \frac{1}{2}, \end{aligned}\right\} \qquad (5.64)$$

and

may be obtained by using the *Hencky equations*.

The expression

$$St = kt - 2k(1 + 2\theta)b \, \cos\left(\frac{\pi}{4} + \theta\right) + 2Rk(2\lambda \cos \lambda - 2 \sin \lambda), \qquad (5.65)$$

is obtained by equating the resolved vertical components of the

124

hydrostatic pressure p and the shear stress k on $AFEB$ to St, and the expression

$$St\left[l - b \cos\left(\frac{\pi}{4} + \theta\right) + R \cos\lambda\right] = kR^2\,2\lambda + k(1 + 2\theta)b^2 + 2kbR \quad (5.66)$$

is obtained by taking moments about O.

From the geometry of the field it follows that

$$b \sin\left(\frac{\pi}{4} + \theta\right) + R \sin\lambda = \frac{t}{2}. \quad (5.67)$$

Equations (5.63) to (5.67) are sufficient to provide a solution to the problem. The hodograph for the slip-line field of Fig. 5.49 is shown in Fig. 5.50. With increasing l/t, R/t approaches zero, and the

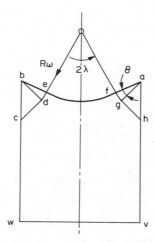

Fig. 5.50. Hodograph to Fig. 5.49.

points F and E then meet on the centre line of the beam. At still larger values of l/t the angle θ decreases until the limiting case is reached when points G and D meet on the centre line. The problem is then reduced to that of the simple theory of plastic bending when the yield moment becomes $\frac{1}{4}kt^2$, corresponding to S/k equal to zero and l/t approaching infinity.

The solution of Fig. 5.49 is incomplete since it has not been shown that the stress can be extended into the rigid zones, and consequently the calculated yield-point loads are upper bounds which may or may not be also lower bounds and hence exact. However, Plate 6(a) shows excellent experimental corroboration of the proposed deformation mode. With a real material a small degree of deformation in the deforming regions will cause it to harden, and if the applied loads have to be increased in order to maintain plastic flow, a new mode of deformation may occur in regions that were previously assumed rigid. Green[493] suggested a solution of the type shown in Fig. 5.51 involving deformation of the support material. The rigid material then rotates over

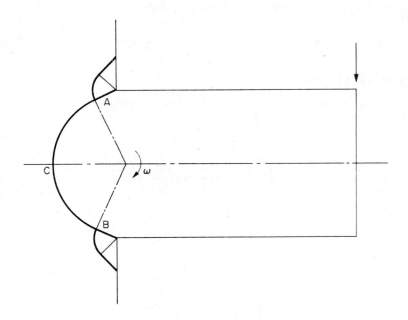

Fig. 5.51.   Slip-line field for a cantilever under
a shear end load with yielding of the
support material.

the circular arc ACB. A paper by Hundy[494] which presents experimental
confirmation of Green's slip-line field is shown in Plate 6(b). Detailed calculations for this type of field have also been given by Johnson
and Sowerby.[508]

It is common structural steel construction practice to cut openings into
the webs of beams to facilitate the passage of utility components,
e.g. pipes, electrical conduits, ventilation ducts and the like. Similarly, perforated structures are made up as castellated beams for
purposes of economy. Ranshi, Chitkara and Johnson[513,514] have studied
the plastic collapse-load consequences of providing these perforated
beams. They have calculated the collapse load for end-loaded cantilever beams containing variously shaped holes, circles and rectangles,
located along the beam centre-line. The proposed solutions were compared with experimentally determined fields using the etching technique.
The latter authors have also extended many of the solutions given
earlier by Green[492,493] for the bending of beams under *plane-stress*
conditions. The reader is referred to Chapter 7 of this monograph for
further discussion.

(ii) Pure Bending of Notched Bars

Consider the pure bending of a bar, with a semicircular root notch,[491]
as shown in Fig. 5.52. For particular values of r/a the slip-line
field is as given in Fig. 5.52. The slip-line region DOA under the
notch is made up of logarithmic spirals, as for the notched specimen.

pulled in tension.

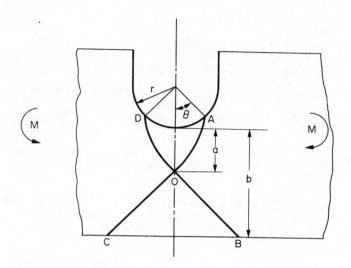

Fig. 5.52.   Pure bending of a single notched specimen.

The resultant vertical and horizontal forces along the axis of symmetry are zero.   If the bending moment is applied as shown in the diagram, $p = k$ (compressive) in OCB and k (tensile) at A. OA is a β-line and OC an α-line.   Hence point O is a singularity in the stress distribution.   Consequently, in order that the rate of plastic work be everywhere positive, there is no discontinuity in the tangential component of velocity when crossing the bounding slip lines.   In addition, the solution is only valid if the rigid material at the corner O bounded by slip lines OA and OB is not overstressed.   As given by Hill[152] the discontinuity in the hydrostatic component of stress across O cannot exceed that given by the Hencky equations in turning through an angle equivalent to that subtended by the slip lines AO and OB - in this instance 90°.   Hence the jump in hydrostatic pressure, Δp, across O is limited to

$$\Delta p = \pi k.\tag{5.68}$$

Hence,
$$\theta \leqslant \left(\frac{\pi}{2} - 1\right).\tag{5.69}$$

The vertical equilibrium equation is seen to be satisfied.   Also, satisfying the horizontal equilibrium equation, provides the dimensions of the field.   For the field DOA the horizontal force is given by

$$2k\theta r.\exp \theta.\tag{5.70}$$

The reader is referred to Section 12 of this Chapter, for verification of (5.70).   Similarly, for the compression region, COB, the horizontal force is

$$2k(b - a).\tag{5.71}$$

Equating (5.70) and (5.71) we have

$$(1 + \theta). \exp \theta = \frac{b + r}{r} . \qquad (5.72)$$

Substituting for θ from (5.69) shows that for values of $[b/(r + b)] > 0.64$ the field of Fig. 5.50 is no longer valid.

Taking moments about point O provides the following expression for M:

$$M = k\theta r^2. \exp 2\theta + \frac{kr^2}{2} - \frac{kr^2 \exp 2\theta}{2} + k(b - a)^2 . \qquad (5.73)$$

The only compatible velocity field for the slip-line field of Fig. 5.50 is that which requires rotation of the rigid regions of the bar about O.

The reader is referred to the paper by Green[491] for possible deformation modes when $[b/(b + r)]$ exceeds 0.64, and to Refs. 496, 497 and 500 for possible slip-line-field solutions to a variety of notch geometries.

Analyses of the bending of Izod and Charpy specimens will be found in Refs. 497, 500, 505 and 508. In Refs. 496 and 497 it was first pointed out that when the notch is sufficiently shallow the plastic zone can extend to the free surface of the specimen above the notch, so that an alternative deformation mode arises with specimens of critical or subcritical depth.

Ewing[510] has determined the critical depth of specimens containing a single V-notch with a circular root under four-point bending. Detailed calculations are also provided in his article for the three-point bending of a single-notched member, corresponding to the standard Charpy test. The slip-line fields were constructed numerically and the method improves upon the accuracy of graphical procedures. As a consequence, the dimensions of certain fields proposed by earlier investigators are refined.

More recently Shiratori and Dodd[515-518] have analysed the yield behaviour of symmetrical notched and single-notched members, under combined axial force and bending. The results are presented in the form of a yield locus which relates the constraint factor due to axial force with that due to bending. In all cases the notches were considered to be sufficiently deep for the plastic zone to be confined to the ligament between the notches (double-notched specimens) or the notch and opposing face (single-notched specimens).

15. ROLLING

Slip-line-field solutions for plate rolling are generally very complicated. The problems posed are of the *indirect* type, i.e. no slip line or its trace in the velocity plane are known in shape at the outset. As remarked previously, the matrix method of Chapter 6 requires the matrix operators to be linear, and problems involving curved boundaries or boundaries with Coulomb friction violate this condition. An exception occurs when a dead-metal zone embraces the entire curved boundary and this is significant in establishing solutions for certain circumstances of hot rolling. Some admissible fields for hot rolling cases are presented in Chapter 6 and consequently no details about the method of their construction will be given at this point. Instead, we give later in this section one particular field from a class presented in Chapter 6, which was first solved by a trial-and-error graphical procedure. More recent references to the solution of certain rolling problems which involve the matrix method are also deferred until Chapter 6.

The first slip-line field for the hot rolling of plate was given by Alexander.[519] A trial-and-error graphical procedure was used to arrive at a solution and the resulting slip-line field involved a dead-metal zone which covered only part of the roll contact surface. The labour involved was considerable since, in keeping with the preceding remarks on the matrix method, the problem was of the *non-linear, indirect* type. The numerical techniques employed for investigating extrusion through curved dies[123] may facilitate the resolution of this type of rolling problem. The authors are not aware, however, of any solution to the rolling of plate which does not involve a dead-metal zone over some part of the roll contact surface.†

As implied earlier, when a dead-metal zone covers the entire roll-plate contact surface the problem is greatly simplified; the matrix method of Chapter 6 then leads on to a relatively straightforward solution.[535] This is not the case with trial-and-error graphical procedures, since continual readjustment of the field is a time-consuming and tedious task. Chitkara and Johnson[527] used the graphical technique to arrive at the slip-line field and hodograph shown in Figs. 5.53 and 5.54 respectively. The roll radius is 2, the entry thickness 0.195, exit thickness 0.126 and the angle of contact 10.75 degrees. Particular features of their solution are

(a) dead metal covering the whole of the roll contact surface (compare the section on Compression when $1 < w/h < 3.6$);
(b) the existence of curved slip lines at entry and exit – though this is a feature of all slip-line-field solutions to the hot-rolling problem;
(c) at entry to the plastically deforming zone a region of continuous plastic deformation, but at exit plastic deformation occuring at a velocity discontinuity across the exit slip line;
(d) The influence of rotation on the shape of the hodograph; the effect of rotation increases the difficulty of transforming the slip-line field to the hodograph;
(e) equilibrium demands that there is zero resultant horizontal force on the material to the left of the entry slip line and to the right of the exit slip line.

The stress distribution throughout the whole field can be found from the *Hencky equations* in terms of p_6, the hydrostatic pressure at point 6. As described in Section 5, p_6 is obtained by satisfying the equilibrium requirements along the entry and exit slip lines.

---

†A solution proposed by Firbank and Lancaster,[528-530] based on a trial-and-error graphical procedure, comes close to achieving this. The proposed slip-line field does not involve dead-metal zones or velocity discontinuities. However, slight errors exist in their solution and a fully compatible hodograph was not obtained.

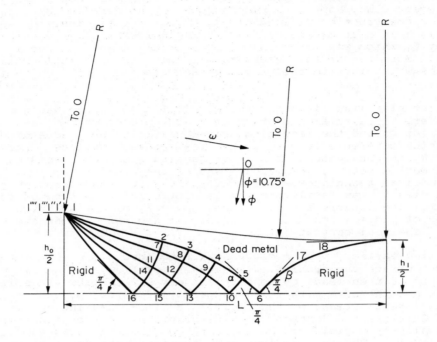

Fig. 5.53. A slip-line field for hot rolling.

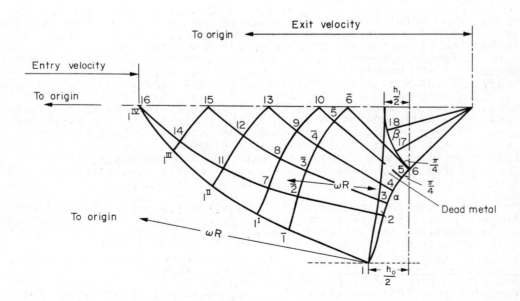

Fig. 5.54. Hodograph to Fig. 5.53.

In the present problem it is not possible to ascertain the precise distribution of pressure over the roll surface because it is covered by a dead-metal zone. Only the total vertical force on the roll, per unit width, is calculable.† The torque is obtained by taking moments about the centre of the roll, of the forces acting over the entry and exit slip lines.

Alexander and Ford[525] have attempted to reduce the amount of work involved in the computation of the roll force and roll torque by constructing a slip-line field with a straight entry slip line (the curvature of entry slip lines is frequently very small) and an exit slip line which is a curcular arc. They employ the term "slip line" loosely and use it in effect to obtain a kind of lower bound, i.e. only the equilibrium conditions are satisfied. These authors assert that very little difference was found between their calculations of roll force and roll torque and those determined from slip-line-field solutions. The computational time required is also considerably less.

16. BLANKING AND SHEARING

A. P. Green[536,537] first applied slip-line-field theory to the shearing of metal junctions. He was concerned with friction and wear studies and proposed various "junction models" to explain interfacial friction between two sliding bodies.

Jimma,[539] following Maeda,[538] proposed similar fields to explain the mechanics of the blanking process. It is not possible here to describe the full analysis of Jimma; however, we give one of his solutions and the original paper should be consulted for further details.

The ratio of the tool or punch width (or diameter) to thickness is considered large enough to enable one to assume that the material near to the tool edges is approximately in a state of plane strain. Jimma proposed that during the first stage of the blanking process there was simple shear of the metal, as shown in Fig. 5.55. Simple shearing occurs in the plastic region II, the rigid region I is stationary and III moves down at the speed of the punch.

In the second stage of the process the punch is assumed to have penetrated the material and the deformed surface arising from the first stage of the process is taken to be an oblique straight line. Figure 5.56 shows the geometry of the punch and workpiece and the proposed slip-line field for this stage of the process. Triangles *ABC* and *GEF* encompass regions of constant hydrostatic stress, and if friction is assumed the slip lines in these regions will not meet the die and punch face at ±45⁰. The recess in the punch and die, as shown in Fig. 5.56, is only essential in order to specifically localize the deformation zone and to clearly define the slip-line field; in practice such recesses are not generally used.

The plastic regions in contact with the punch and the die have a downward speed on unity and zero respectively. However, because penetration

---

†It is possible to determine a realistic pressure distribution over the roll surface if it can be established that the whole of the material within the dead-metal zone is on the point of yielding.

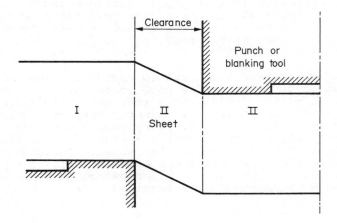

Fig. 5.55. Onset of the blanking process.

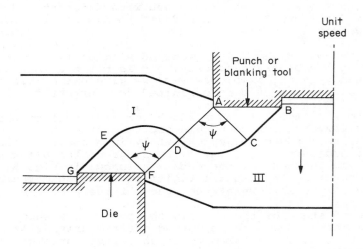

Fig. 5.56. A later stage in the blanking process.

of the material occurs, the rigid region I will have a downward velocity; similarly, the rigid region III will move downwards but at a
speed less than the punch speed. The corresponding hodograph is
drawn in Fig. 5.57.

At first sight Jimma's proposed solution appears perfectly acceptable
since the punch load is obtained by equating the rates of energy
dissipation, i.e. equating the rate of energy supplied to the punch
to the rate of energy dissipated in the slip-line field. However,
Jimma does mot mention the existence of a clamping pressure without
which a resultant couple would exist on the material to the left of
AF and this is not compatible with the downwards motion. Intuitively,
the hydrostatic stress at point D is tensile or, more certainly, one

132

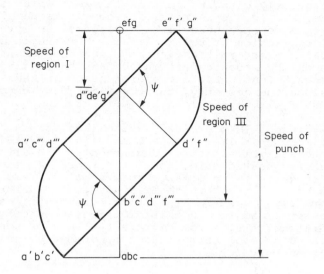

Fig. 5.57.   Hodograph to Fig. 5.56.

of the principal stresses at this point is tensile.† This establishes
GEDCB as a β-line and that the resultant couple on the material to the
left of *AF* is in a clockwise direction.

Jimma's solution would be acceptable if Fig. 5.56 represented one of
a row of punches and dies. By ignoring the configuration at each end
of the row there would then be no out-of-balance couple on the material
between the punches and hence it could be assumed that there was zero
resultant force on the material to the left of *AF*. By adjusting the
geometry, i.e. clearance, penetration, length of *AB*, etc., and allowing
(if necessary) for friction over the punch and die face, the hydrostatic
pressure at point *D*, p_D, could be determined to satisfy the above equilibrium requirement. The punch pressure could then be obtained via
the Hencky equations.

Alternatively, a clamping pressure could be imposed on the material
to the left of *AF*. This would result in the slip-line field being
unsymmetrical, i.e. *GF* > *AB*. Again an assumption could be made that
there is zero horizontal force on the material to the left of *AF*.
Similarly, by suitable adjustment of the geometry and of the position
and magnitude of the clamping pressure, the pressure on the punch face
could be obtained by the method previously outlined.

Blanking and shearing are well-developed industrial processes and it
is certain that their success has relied more on technical expertise
than detailed analysis. The process is, however, exceedingly complex
and invariably involves initial indentation by the tools, followed

---

†In many practical applications cracks occur in the material, approximately in the direction *AF*, emanating either from the sharp corner
of the die or punch.

by a continuously changing deformation zone which decreases in area as the punch (blade) penetrates. Microcracks develop within the deformation zone and these finally coalesce and propagate leading to the final separation of the material. Notwithstanding the importance of material characteristics, the tooling does exert a very strong influence on the mode of deformation and the appearance of the final sheared edge. Considerable research has been made into the design of tooling since the geometry, the clearance between punch and die and the method of clamping, are all crucial to the success of the operation.

Since the process is non-steady state (and strain hardening plays an important role), it is arguable that slip-line-field theory is an appropriate analytical tool. Undoubtedly, the slip-line field presented here is questionable, and furthermore it deals only with one specific stage in the process. More complex fields have been proposed by Kasuga *et al.*[543,544] in their study of the deformation arising in a "scissors-type" shear. Kinematically and statically admissible fields are provided for an initial indentation stage, followed by three additional fields for different stages of penetration by the blade. The degree of correspondence between experiment[543] and theory[544] is said to be very good.

BIBLIOGRAPHY

The authors have attempted to compile a reasonably comprehensive bibliography of slip-line-field theory as applied to various metal deformation processes, and in general they have grouped the references according to the individual process, e.g. *Indenting, Drawing, Extrusion* and the like. However, they acknowledge that their search has not been exhaustive. Much of the work published in foreign languages has not been investigated and reports of various research organizations, e.g. BSC (formerly BISRA), PERA,[†] NEL,[††]etc., have in general been omitted. All of the references given below have not been referred to in the text but many of these are works which provide some background to the subject matter and are listed under *Books, Reviews, Theory,* etc. Not all of these references are necessarily devoted to slip-line-field analysis *per se*, but they do deal either with the foundations of plasticity theory, observations of material flow or associated forming processes. Finally, since Chapter 6 of this monograph deals with the development and application of slip-line-field theory based on matrix operator methods, the majority of the references in that area are presented in the following Chapter.

Books

1. Pearson, C. E., *The Extrusion of Metals*. Chapman and Hall, London (1944).
2. van Iterson, F. K. J., *Plasticity in Engineering*. Blackie, Glasgow (1947).
3. Ilyushin, A. A., *Plasticity Part I - Elastic-Plastic Deformations*. OGIZ, Moscow and Leningrad (1948).
4. *Courant Anniversary Volume: Studies and Essays Presented to R. Courant on his Sixtieth Birthday*. Interscience, New York (1948).

---

†Production Engineering Research Organization.
††National Engineering Laboratory.

5. van der Brock, John A., *Theory of Limit Design*. Wiley, New York (1948).

6. Freudenthal, A. M., *Inelastic Behaviour of Engineering Materials and Structures*. Wiley, New York; Chapman & Hall, London (1950).

7. Hill, R., *The Mathematical Theory of Plasticity*. Oxford University Press (1950).

8. Nadai, A., *Theory of Flow and Fracture of Solids*, Vol. I. McGraw-Hill, New York (1950).

9. Sokolovskii, V. V., *The Theory of Plasticity* (in Russian), 2nd edn. Gostechteorizdat, Moscow (1950).

10. *Proceedings of the First U.S. National Congress of Applied Mechanics*. Held at Illinois Institute of Technology, Chicago, Illinois, June 11-16, 1951. Published by A.S.M.E.

11. Prager, W. and Hodge, P. G., Jr., *Theory of Perfectly Plastic Solids*. Chapman & Hall, London (1951).

12. Tabor, D., *Hardness of Metals*. Oxford University Press (1951).

13. Andrade, E. N. Da C., *Viscosity and Plasticity*. Chemical Publishing, New York (1951).

14. Heyman, J., *Plastic Design of Portal Frames*. Cambridge University Press (1951).

15. Tomlenov, A. D., *Theory of Plastic Deformation in Metals* (in Russian). Mashgiz, Moscow (1951).

16. Westergaard, H. M., *Theory of Elasticity and Plasticity*. Harvard University Press (1952).

17. Delpech, S. A., *Structural Properties and Deformation of Metals*. Alsina, Buenos Aires (1952).

18. Hoffman, O. and Sachs, G., *Introduction to the Theory of Plasticity for Mechanical Engineers*. McGraw-Hill, New York (1953).

19. Keldysch, W. M., (Ed.), *Limit Design of Structures*. V.E.B. Verlag Technik, Berlin (1953).

20. *Proceedings of the Second U.S. National Congress of Applied Mechanics*. Held at Univ. of Michigan, Ann Arbor, Michigan, June 14-18, 1954. Published by A.S.M.E.

21. Siebel, E. and Beisswangen, H. (Eds.), *Deep Drawing: Research papers in the field of deep drawing*. Sponsored by the Research Society on Sheet Metals. Carl Hensen, Munich (1955).

22. *Proceedings Eighth International Congress on Theoretical and Applied Mechanics*. Istanbul, Turkey, August 20-28, 1952. Vol. I. Faculty of Science, University of Istanbul (1956).

23. Phillips, A., *Introduction to Plasticity*. Ronald Press, New York (1956).

24. Baker, J. Horne, M. R. and Heyman, J., *The Steel Skeleton*, Vols. I and II. Cambridge University Press (1956).

25. Jaeger, J. C., *Elasticity, Fracture and Flow*. Methuen, London (1956).

26. Batchelor, G. K. and Davies, R. M. (Eds.), *Surveys in Mechanics: G. I. Taylor Anniversary Volume*. Cambridge University Press (1956).

27. Neal, B. G., *The Plastic Methods of Structural Analysis*. Wiley, New York (1957).

28. Belyayev, N. M., *Papers on the Theory of Elasticity and Plasticity*. (in Russian). Gostechteorizdat, Moscow (1957).

29. Uzhik, G. V., *Strength and Plasticity of Metals and Low Temperatures*. (in Russian). Izdatel'stvo Akademii Nauk S.S.S.R., Moscow (1957).

30. Goodier, J. N. and Hodge, P. G. Jr., *Elasticity and Plasticity*. Wiley, New York (1958).

31. *Proceedings of the Third U.S. National Congress of Applied Mechanics*. Held at Brown University, Providence, Rhode Island,

June 11-14, 1958. Published by A.S.M.E.

32. Strel'bitskaya, I. A., *Investigation of the Strength of Thin-walled Beams Beyond the Limit of Elasticity*. Kiev Akad Nauk, S.S.S.R. (1958).

33. Prager, W., *Problems of Theoretical Plasticity*. Dunod, Paris (1958).

34. Batchelor, G. K. (Ed.), *The Scientific Papers of G. I. Taylor: Vol. I - Mechanics of Solids*. Cambridge University Press (1958).

35. Olszak, W. (Ed.), *Non-homogeneity in Elasticity and Plasticity*. Proceedings of I.U.T.A.M. Symposium, Warsaw, 1958. Pergamon Press, Oxford and New York (1959).

36. Averbach, B. L., Felbeck, D. K., Hahn, G. T. and Thomas, D. A. (Eds.), *Fracture*. Technology Press, M.I.T. and Wiley, New York; Chapman & Hall, London (1959).

37. Prager, W., *Probleme der Plastizitatstheorie* (with summary in English). Birkhauser, Basle (1959).

38. Godfrey, D. E., *Theoretical Elasticity and Plasticity for Engineers*. Thames & Hudson, London (1959).

39. Prager, W., *An Introduction to Plasticity*. Addison-Wesley, Massachusetts (1959).

40. Feldmann, D.H., *Extrusion of Steel*. Springer, Berlin (1959).

41. Crandell, S. H. and Dahl, N. C., *Introduction to the Mechanics of Solids*. McGraw-Hill, New York (1959).

42. Szabo, I., *Advanced Engineering Mechanics*, 3rd edn. Springer-Verlag, Berlin (1960).

43. Yamada, Y. and Nakahara, M., *Soseigaku* (Mathematical Theory of Plasticity). Japan Society Mechanical Engineers (1960).

44. Pearson, C. E. and Parkins, R. N., *The Extrusion of Metals*. Chapman & Hall, London (1960).

45. Sneddon, I. N. and Hill, R. (Eds.), *Progress in Solid Mechanics* Vol. 1. Interscience, New York (1960).

46. Goodier, J. N. and Hoff, N. J. (Eds.), *Structural Mechanics*. Proceedings of First Symposium on Naval Structural Mechanics, Stanford University, August 11-14, 1958. Pergamon Press, New York and Oxford (1960).

47. Dieter, G. E., *Mechanical Metallurgy*. McGraw-Hill, New York (1961).

48. *Volume dedicated to N. I. Muskheilishvili on his Seventieth Birthday*. Philadelphia Society Industrial and Applied Mathematics (1961).

49. *Collected Works - Problems in the Theory of Plasticity*. Izdatel'-stvo Akademii Nauk S.S.S.R., Moscow (1961).

50. Thomas, T. Y., *Plastic Flow and Fracture of Solids*. Academic Press, New York (1961).

51. Lee, E. H. and Symonds, P. S. (Eds.), *Plasticity*. Proceedings of the Second Symposium on Naval Structural Mechanics, Brown University. Pergamon Press, Oxford and New York (1961).

52. Unskov, E. P., *An Engineering Theory of Plasticity*. Butterworths, London (1961).

53. Gubkin, S. I., *Plastic Deformation of Metals* (in Russian), Vols. 1-3. Metallurgizdat, Moscow (1961).

54. Hill, R. and Sneddon I. N. (Eds.), *Progress in Solid Mechanics*, Vol. II. Interscience, New York (1961).

55. Prager, W., *Introduction to the Mechanics of Continua*. Birkhauser, Basle (1961).

56. Massonnet, C. E. and Save, M., *Plastic Design of Construction: Vol. I: Two-dimensional Frames*. Bruxelles Centre-Belgo, Luxembourgeons d'Information de l'Acier (1961).

APPLICATIONS TO SPECIFIC PROCESSES: BIBLIOGRAPHY

57. Stippes, M. *et al.*, *An Introduction to the Mechanics of Deformable Bodies*. Merril Books, Columbus, Ohio (1961).
58. *Proceedings of Fourth U.S. National Congress of Applied Mechanics.* Held at the University of California, Berkeley, California, June 18-21, 1962. Published by A.S.M.E.
59. Mandel, J., Epain, R., Lubliner, J., Parsy, F. and Radonkovic, D., *Seminar in Plasticity* (in French). Publ. Sci. Tech. Min. Air, France, N.T. 116 (1962).
60. Krzya, W. and Zyczkowski, M., *Elasticity and Plasticity: Problems and Examples*. Panstwowe Wydawnictwo Naukowe, Warsaw (1962).
61. Johnson, W. and Mellor, P. B., *Plasticity for Mechanical Engineers*. Van Nostrand, London (1962).
62. Johnson, W. and Kudo, H., *The Mechanics of Metal Extrusion*. Manchester University Press (1962).
63. *Proceedings of the International Production Engineering Research Conference.* Held at the Carnegie Institute of Technology, Pittsburgh, September 1963.
64. Nadai, A., *Theory of Flow and Fracture of Solids*, Vol. II. McGraw-Hill, New York (1963).
65. Ford, H. and Alexander, J.M., *Advanced Mechanics of Materials*. Longmans Green, London (1963) and reprinted by Ellis Horwood, Chichester, 1978.
66. Alexander, J. M. and Brewer, R. C., *Manufacturing Properties of Materials*. Van Nostrand, London (1963).
67. Olszak, W., Mroz, Z. and Parzyna, P., *Recent Trends in the Development of the Theory of Plasticity*. Polish Academy of Sciences. Pergamon Press, Oxford and New York (1963).
68. Parkes, E. W., *Braced Frameworks: An Introduction to the Theory of Structures*. Pergamon Press, Oxford and New York (1965).
69. Thomsen, E. G., Yang, C. T. and Kobayashi, S., *Mechanics of Plastic Deformation in Metal Processing*. Macmillan Co., New York; Macmillan-Collier, London (1965).
70. Vinokurov, L. P., *Theory of Elasticity and Plasticity* (in Russian). Khar'hov Izdatel'stvo Khar'kovskogo Ordena Trudovogo Krasnogo Znameni Gosudarstvennogo Universiteta im. A.M. Gor'kogo (1965).
71. Massonnet, C. E. and Save, M. A., *Plastic Analysis and Design* Vol. I: *Beams and Frames*. Blaisdell, New York (1965).
72. Rowe, G. W., *An Introduction to the Theory of Metalworking*. Edward Arnold, London (1965).
73. *Proceedings of Fifth U.S. National Congress of Applied Mechanics.* Held at the University of Minnesota, Minneapolis, Minnesota, June14-17, 1966. Published by A.S.M.E.
74. *Applied Mechanics Survey 1966*. Published by A.S.M.E.
75. Zorev, N. N., *Metal Cutting Mechanics*. Pergamon Press, Oxford and New York (1966).
76. McClintock, F.A. and Argon, A.S., *Mechanical Behaviour of Materials*. Addison-Wesley, Massachusetts (1966).
77. Drucker, D. C., *Introduction to the Mechanics of Deformable Bodies*. McGraw-Hill, New York and London (1967).
78. Lippmann, H. and Mahrenholtz, O., *The Mechanics of the Plastic Forming of Metals* (in German). Springer, Berlin (1967).
79. Mendelson, A., *Plasticity: Theory and Application*. Collier-Macmillan, London (1968).
80. Washizu, K., *Variational Methods in Elasticity and Plasticity*. Pergamon Press, Oxford and New York (1968).
81. Parkins, R. N., *Mechanical Treatment of Metals*. Allen & Unwin, London (1968).
82. Avitzur, B., *Metal Forming Processes and Analysis*. McGraw-Hill

(1968).

83. Spencer, G. C., *An Introduction to Plasticity*. Chapman & Hall Ltd., London (1968).

84. Calladine, C. R., *Engineering Plasticity*. Pergamon Press (1969).

85. Johnson, W., Sowerby, R. and Haddow, J. B., *Plane Strain Slip Lines Fields: Theory and Bibliography*. Edward Arnold (1970).

86. Kachanov, L. M., *Foundations of the Theory of Plasticity*. North-Holland (1971).

87. Backofen, W. A., *Deformation Processing*. Addison-Wesley (1972).

88. Sawczuk, A. (Ed.), *Foundations of Plasticity*. Symposium in Warsaw (1972). Noordhoff Int. Pub. (1973).

89. Johnson, W. and Mellor, P. B., *Engineering Plasticity*. Van Nostrand-Reinhold (1973).

90. Martin, J. B., *Plasticity: Fundamentals and General Results*. M.I.T. Press (1975).

91. Blazynski, T. Z., *Metal Forming: Tool Profiles and Flow*. The Macmillan Press, London (1976).

92. Rowe, G. W., *Principles of Industrial Metalworking*. Edward Arnold (1977).

93. Slater, R. A. C., *Engineering Plasticity: Theory and Application to Metal Forming Processes*. The Macmillan Press, London (1977).

94. Lippmann, H. (Ed.), *Engineering Plasticity: Theory of Metal Forming Processes*, Vols. 1 and 2. C.I.S.M. Courses and Lectures No. 139. Springer-Verlag (1977).

95. Armen, H. and Jones, R. F. (Eds.), *Application of Numerical Methods to Forming Processes*. Winter Annual Meeting A.S.M.E., San Francisco, 1978. A.S.M.E. (1978).

96. Szczepinski, W., *Introduction to the Mechanics of Plastic Forming of Metals*. Sijthoff & Noordhoff, Netherlands (1979).

97. Avitzur, B., *Metal Forming. The Application of Limit Analysis*. Marcel Dekker (1980).

98. Avitzur, B., *Metal-forming Processes*. Wiley-Interscience, New York (1981).

Bibliographies and Reviews

99. Nakahara, M., *The Theory of Plasticity: Bibliography of Scientific and Industrial Reports*. U.S. Office of Technical Services, No. 52364, 875 (Sept. 1946).

100. Kececioglu, Dimitri, *Bibliography on Plasticity-Theory and Application*. A.S.M.E. (1950).

101. Prager, W., "Recent contributions to the theory of plasticity". *Appl. Mech. Rev.* 4, 11 (1951).

102. Prager, W., "The theory of plasticity: a survey of recent achievements". *Proc. Inst. Mech. Engrs.* 169, 41 (1955).

103. Keldi, Arpad, "Soil mechanics". *Appl. Mech. Rev.* 8, 357 (1955).

104. Hill, R., "The mechanics of quasi-static plastic deformation in metals", in *Surveys in Mechanics: G. I. Taylor Seventieth Anniversary*, Vol. 7 (edited by G. K. Batchelor and R. M. Davies). Cambridge University Press (1956).

105. Finnie, I., "Review of the metal cutting analysis of the past hundred years". *Mech. Engng.* 78, 715 (1956).

106. Bishop, J. W. F., "The theory of extrusion". *Metall. Rev., Inst. Metals,* 2, 361 (1957).

107. Ford, H., "The theory of rolling". *Metall. Rev., Inst. Metals,* 2, 1 (1957).

108. Lindstrand, E., "Wire drawing - a literature survey" (in Swedish). *Jernkontorets Ann.* 142, 105 (1958).

109. Boulger, F. W., "1958 Review of Metal Processing Literature (Plastic Working). A.S.M.E. Production Engineering Conference, Detroit, Michigan, May 1959. Paper 59-PROD-5.
110. Slibar, A. and Steck, E., "Theory of plasticity - a survey". *ZVDI*, 103, 31 (1961).
111. Sobotka, Z., "slip lines and slip surfaces in theory of plasticity and soil mechanics". *Appl. Mech. Rev.* 14, 753 (1961).
112. Szcepinski, W., "Recent advances in the drawing of thin shells". *Appl. Mech. Rev.* 14, 173 (1961).
113. Hockett, John E., "Recent research in metal forming". *Appl. Mech. Rev.* 15, 157 (1962).
114. Wennberg, J. L., "1964 Review of materials processing literature". *Trans. ASME, J. Engng. Ind.* 87B, 511 (1965).
115. Johnson, W. and Sowerby, R., "The mechanics of wire drawing. Recent contribution made by plasticity theory". *Wire Ind.* 36, 137 and 249 (1969).
116. Johnson, W., "The mechanics of metalworking plasticity". *Appl. Mech. Revs.* 24, 977 (1971).
117. Sowerby, R. and Johnson, W., "A review of texture and anisotropy in relation to metal forming". *Mats. Sci. Engng.* 20, 101 (1975).
118. Alexander, J. M., "New techniques in metalworking". *Metals Technology*, 3, 393 (1976).
119. Sowerby, R., "New techniques of metalforming". *Science Progress*, 64, 117 (1977).
120. Schey, J. A.,(Coordinating Ed.), "Progress report on recent advances in bulk metal deformation processes" (Four reviews presented). *Int. Metals Revs.* 22, 302 (1977).
121. Johnson, W., *Advances in Deformation Processing* (edited by J. J. Burke and V. Weiss,), 1. 21st Sagamore Conf., Racquette Lake, N. Y., 1974. Plenum Press (1978).

Theory

122. Hencky, H., "Concerning a few statically determinant cases in plastic bodies". *Z. angew. Math. Mech.* 3, 241 (1923).
123. Geiringer, H., "Complete solutions to the plane plasticity problem". *Proc. 3rd Int. Cong. Appl. Mech.* 2, 185. Stockholm (1930).
124. Geiringer, H., "Foundation of the mathematical theory of isotropic plastic bodies". *Memorial des Sciences Mathematiques*, Fascicule 86 (1937).
125. Sadowsky, M. A., "Equiareal pattern of stress trajectories in plane plastic flow". *Trans. ASME, J. Appl. Mech.* 8, 74 (1941).
126. Prager, W., "Streamlines and lines of principal stress". *Rev. math. Un. interbalk.* 3, 63 (1941).
127. Ament, W. S., "The lines of principal stress in the plane problem of Plasticity". *Q. J. Appl. Math.* 1, 278 (1943).
128. Sokolovskii, V. V., "The theory of plasticity - outline of work done in Russia". *Trans. ASME, J. Appl. Mech.* 13, 1 (1946).
129. Hill, R. and Lee, E. H., Discussion of E. Siebel's paper: "The application to shaping processes of Hencky's laws of equilibrium". *J. Iron Steel Inst.* 156, 511 (1947).
130. Prager, W., "Discontinuous solutions in the theory of plasticity", in *Courant Anniversary Volume: Studies and Essays Presented to R. Courant on his Sixtieth Birthday*, p. 289. Interscience, New York (1948).
131. Prager, W., "Problem types in the theory of perfectly plastic solids". *J. Aeronaut. Sci.* 15, 337 (1948).

132. Hill, R., "A variational principle of maximum plastic work in classical plasticity". *Q.J. Mech. Appl. Math.* **1**, 18 (1948).

133. Winzer, A. and Carrier, G. F., "Discontinuities of stress in plane plastic flow". *Trans. ASME, J. Appl. Mech.* **16**, 346 (1949).

134. Prager, W., "Recent developments in the mathematical theory of plasticity". *J. Appl. Phys.* **20**, 235 (1949).

135. Drucker, D. C., "Relation of experiments to the mathematical theories of plasticity". *Trans. ASME, J. Appl. Mech.* **16**, 349 (1949).

136. Drucker, D. C., "Discussion of the theories of plasticity". *J. Aeronaut. Sci.* **16**, 547 (1949).

137. Prager, W., "Discontinuities solutions in the theory of plasticity". *Proc. Symp. Appl. Math.* **1**, 211 (1949).

138. Coburn, N., "A graphical method for solving problems in plane plasticity". *Proc. Symp. Appl. Math.* **3**, 201 (1950).

139. Hodge, P. G., Jr., "Approximate solutions of problems of plane plastic flow". *Trans. ASME, J. Appl. Mech.* **17**, 257 (1950).

140. Geiringer, H., "On the Plane Problems of a Perfect Plastic Body". *Grad. Div. Appl. Math.*, Brown Univ., Tech. Rep. A11-55 (1950).

141. Lee, E. H., "On stress discontinuities in plane plastic flow". *Proc. Symp. Appl. Math.* **3**, 213 (1950).

142. Drucker, D. C., Greenberg, H. J. and Prager, W., "The safety factor of an elastic-plastic body in plane strain". *Trans. ASME, J. Appl. Mech.* **18**, 371 (1951).

143. Hill, R., "On the state of stress in a plastic-rigid body at the yield point". *Phil. Mag.* **42**, 868 (1951).

144. Lee, E. H., "The theoretical analysis of metal forming problems in plane strain". *Trans. ASME, J. Appl. Mech.* **19**, 97 (1952).

145, Swift, H. W., "On the foothills of the plastic range". *J. Inst. Metals*, **81**, 109 (1952).

146. Geiringer, H., "On the characteristics of the complete plasticity problem". *Z. angew Math. Mech.* **32**, 379 (1952).

147. Hill, R., "On Inoue's hydrodynamic analogy for the state of stress in a plastic solid". *J. Mech. Phys. Solids*, **2**, 110 (1954).

148. Bishop, J. F. W., "On the complete solution to problems of deformation of a rigid-plastic material". *J. Mech. Phys. Solids*, **2**, 43 (1953).

149. Green, A. P., "On the use of the hodograph in plane plastic strain". *J. Mech. Phys. Solids*, **2**, 73 (1954).

150. Geiringer, H., "Some recent results in the theory of an ideal plastic body". *Adv. Appl. Mech.* **III**, 197 (1953).

151. Prager, W., "A geometrical discussion of the slip line field in plane plastic flow". *Trans. R. Inst. Technol.*, Stockholm, No. 65 (1953).

152. Hill, R., "On the limits set by plastic yielding to the intensity of singularities of stress". *J. Mech. Phys. Solids*, **2**, 278 (1954).

153. Drucker, D. C., "On obtaining plane strain or plane stress conditions in plasticity". *Proc. 2nd U.S. Nat. Cong. Appl. Mech.*, June 1954, 485. A.S.M.E. (1955).

154. Hill, R., "On the problem of uniqueness in the theory of a rigid-plastic solid - I". *J. Mech. Phys. Solids*, **4**, 247 (1956).

155. Bishop, J. F. W., Green, A. P. and Hill, R., "A note on the deformable region in a rigid-plastic body". *J. Mech. Phys. Solids*, **4**, 256 (1956).

156. Hill, R., "On the problem of uniqueness in the theory of a

rigid-perfectly plastic solid - II, III, IV". *J. Mech. Phys. Solids*, 5, 1 (1956); 5, 153 (1957); 5, 312 (1957).

157. Thomsen, E. G., "A new method for the construction of Hencky - Prandtl nets". *Trans. ASME, J. Appl. Mech.* 24, 81 (1957).

158. Downie, T. M., "Numerical Calculation of Slip Line Fields". Tech. Rep. No. 45, NR-064-406, Div. Appl. Maths., Brown Univ. (November 1958).

159. Halling, J., "The characteristic method of solution for the problem of plane plastic strain". *Engineer*, 207, 250 (1959).

160. Spencer, A. J. M., "Perturbation methods in plasticity - I". *J. Mech. Phys. Solids*, 9, 279 (1961).

161. Spencer, A. J. M., "Perturbation methods in plasticity - II". *J. Mech. Phys. Solids*, 10, 17 (1962).

162. Spencer, A. J. M., "Perturbation methods in plasticity - III". *J. Mech. Phys. Solids*, 10, 165 (1962).

163. Rychlewski, J., "The plane plastic strain problem of a wedge with jump non-homogeneity". *J. Mecan.* 3, 461 (1964).

164. Nepershin, R. I., "Application of the method of R. Sauer to calculations of static processes in plane plastic strain". *Mashinovedenie*, No. 6, 79 (1965).

165. Severenko, V. P., Makushom, E. M. and Segal, V. M., "Integration of the equations of a field of slip lines". *Dokl. Akad. Nauk. SSSR*, 9, 454 (1965).

166. Rychlewski, J., "Plane plastic strain for jump-homogeneity". *Int. J. Non-linear Mechanics*, 1, 57 (1966).

167. Johnson, W. and Sowerby, R., "The yielding of a rigid-plastic thick-walled cylinder analysed using slip line theory". *Bull. Mech. Engng. Educ.* 6, 201 (1967).

168. Johnson, W. and Sowerby, R., "On the yielding of a wide plate having an initial curvature subjected to pure bending". *Bull. Mech. Engng. Educ.* 6, 307 (1967).

169. Halling, J. and Mitchell, L. A., "The effect of variation in yield stress on slip line field solutions". *Int. J. Prod. Res.* 5, 249 (1967).

170. Ewing, D. J. F., "A series method for contstructing slip line fields". *J. Mech. Phys. Solids*, 15, 105 (1967).

171. Hill, R., "On the vectorial superposition of Hencky - Prandtl nets". *J. Mech. Phys. Solids*, 15, 255 (1967).

172. Lippmann, H., "On the compression of a plastic layer". *Int. J. Mech. Sci.* 9, 223 (1967).

173. Collins, I. F., "An optimum loading criterion for rigid-plastic materials". *J. Mech Phys. Solids*, 16, 456 (1968).

174. Collins, I. F., "The algebraic-geometry of slip line fields with applications to boundary value problems". *Proc. R. Soc.* A, 303, 317 (1968).

175. Ewing D. J. F., "A mass flux method for deducing dimensions of plastic slip line fields". *J. Mech. Phys. Solids*, 16, 267 (1968).

176. Llorens, R. E. and Koenig, H. A., "The application of an orthogonal net of circles to the problem of plane strain in plasticity". *Trans. ASME, J. Appl. Mech.* 36, 736 (1969).

177. Johnson, W., "Upper bounds to the load for the transverse bending of flat rigid-perfectly plastic plates - I and II". *Int. J. Mech. Sci.* 11, 913 (1969).

178. Bedso, D., "Principal and slip line methods of numerical analysis in plane and axial-symmetric deformations of rigid/plastic media". *J. Mech Phys. Solids*, 19, 313 (1971).

179. Collins, I. F., "On an analogy between plane strain and plane bending solutions in rigid/perfect plasticity theory". *Int. J.*

Solids Structs. 7, 1057 (1971).

180. Johnson, W., Chitkara, N. R., Reid, S. R. and Collins, I. F., "The displacement field and it significance for certain minimum weight two-dimensional frames using the analogy with perfectly plastic flow in metalworking". *Int. J. Mech. Sci.* 13, 547 (1971).

181. Burnat, M., "The method of Riemann invariants and its applications to the theory of plasticity". *Arch. Mech. Stos.* 24, 1 (1972).

182. Dewhurst, P. and Collins, I. F., "A matrix technique for constructing slip line field solutions to a class of plane strain plasticity problems". *Int. J. Num. Meth. Engng.* 7, 357 (1973).

183. Romiti, A., "A graphical analysis of plastic plane stress fields". *Annals CIRP.*, 23, 49 (1974).

184. Czyz, J., "Construction of a flow of an ideal plastic material in a die, on the method of Riemann invariants". *Arch. Mech. Stos.* 26, 589 (1974).

185. Fenton, R. G. and Durai Swamy, B., "Slip line field solution of strain rate sensitive materials". *Int. J. Mach. Tool Des. Res.* 15, 105 (1975).

186. Farmer, L. E. and Oxley, P. L. B., "A computer-aided method for calculating the distributions of strain-rate and strain from an experimental flow field". *J. Strain Analysis,* 11, 26 (1976).

187. Bachrach, B. I. and Samanta, S. K., "A numerical method for computing plane plastic slip line fields". *Trans. ASME, J. Appl. Mech.* 43, 97 (1976).

188. Johnson, W. and Mamalis, A. G., "Some force plane diagrams for plane strain slip line fields". *Int. J. Mech. Sci.* 20, 47 (1978).

189. Thomason, P. F., "Riemann-integral solutions for the plastic slip line fields around elliptical holes". *Trans. ASME, J. Appl. Mech.* 45, 678 (1978).

190. Johnson, W. and Mamalis, A. G., "Force polygons to determine upper-bounds and force distribution in plane strain metal forming processes". *Proc. 18th MTDR Conf.* 456. London 1977. Macmillan Press (1978).

191. Chakrabarty, J., "Exact solutions for certain slip line fields". *Int. J. Mech. Sci.* 21, 477 (1979).

192. Petryk, H., "On slip line field solutions for steady state and self similar problems with stress free boundaries". *Arch. Mech. Stos.,* 31, 861 (1979).

General

193. Turner, T. H. and Jevons, J. D., "The detection of strain in mild steels". *J. Iron Steel Inst.* 111, 169 (1925).

194. Jevons, J. D., "Strain detection in mild steel by special etching". *J. Iron Steel Inst.* 111, 191 (1925).

195. Prager, W., "What does the theory of plasticity offer the designer?" *Trend Engng. Univ. Wash.* 3, 8 (1951).

196. Yamada, Y., "On theory and its application of two-dimensional plasticity". *Tokyo Univ. Inst. Indust. Sci. Rep.* 1, 151 (1951).

197. Green, A.P., "The use of plasticine models to simulate the plastic flow of metals". *Phil. Mag.* 42, 365 (1951).

198. Nye, J. F., "The flow of glaciers and ice sheets as a problem in plasticity". *Proc. R. Soc.,* A, 207, 554 (1951).

199. Johnson, W., "Research into some metal forming and shaping operations". *J. Inst. Metals*, 84, 165 (1956). (Contributed to the Symposium on the final forming and shaping of wrought non-ferrous metals in April 1956).

200. Johnson, W., "Research into some metal forming and shaping operations". *Sheet Metal Industries*, 34, 41 and 121 (1957).

201. Alexander, J. M., "Deformation modes in metal forming processes". *Proceedings Conference on Technology of Engineering Manufacture, London, 25-27 March 1958*, 63. Institution Mechanical Engineers (1958).

202. Johnson, W. and Tanner, R. I., "Temperature distribution in some fast metalworking operations". *Int. J. Mech. Sci.* 1, 28 (1960).

203. Johnson, W., "Slip line field and discontinuous velocity solutions for some metal forming operations". Parts I and II, No. 3, 180; Part III, No. 4, 275. *Annals Cirp*, 10 (1963).

204. Bodsworth, C., Halling, J. and Barton, J. W., "The use of paraffin wax as a model to simulate the plastic deformation of metals: Part I". *J. Iron Steel Inst.* 185, 375 (1957).

205. Barton, J. W., Bodsworth, C. and Halling, J., "The use of paraffin wax as a model material to simulate the plastic deformation of metals: Part II". *J. Iron Steel Inst.* 188, 321 (1958).

206. Nye, J. F., "Plastic solution for a glacier snout". *J. Glaciology*, 6, 695 (1967).

207. Collins, I. F. and Swithinbank, C., "Rifts at the foot of Bear dmore Glacier, Antarctica". *Commission of Snow and Ice*, 109, Gen. Ass. Bern, Sept-Oct. (1967).

208. Thomason, P. F., "Plastic flow and fracture in fibre composites". *J. Mech. Phys. Solids*, 20, 19 (1972).

209. Danckert, J. and Wanheim, T., "Slip line wax". *Expt. Mechs.*, 16, 318 (1976).

Pressure Vessels

210. Freudenthal, A. M. and Geiringer, H., "Elasticity and Plasticity", Vol. VI, *Encyclopedia of Physics*, Ed. S. Flugge, Springer-Verlag, Berlin, 365, 1958.

211. Sowerby, R. and Johnson, W., "Analysing flange drawing in non-circular cups using slip line fields". *Annals CIRP*, 19, 491 (1970).

212. Sowerby, R. and Johnson, W., "Use of slip line field theory for the plastic design of pressure vessels". *Proc. 4th Int. Conf. on Expt. Stress Analysis*, 301. Cambridge, 1970. Pub. by I. Mech. E. (1971).

213. Hasek, V. V. and Lange, K., "Use of the slip line field method in deep drawing of large irregular shaped components". *Proc. 7th North Am. Metal-working Res. Conf.* 65. S.M.E. (1979).

214. Boer, C. and de Malherbe, M. C., "A note on force plane diagrams for elastic and elastic-plastically stressed thick walled cylinders". *Int. J. Mech. Sci.* 21, 23 (1979).

Compression

215. Nadai, A., "Experiments on the plastic deformation of wedge-shaped mild steel bodies". *Z. Angew. Math. Mech.* 1, 20 (1921).

216. Prandtl, L., "On the penetration hardness of plastic materials and the hardness of indentors". *Z. angew. Math. Mech.* 1, 15 (1921).

217. Prandtl, L., "Practical application of the Hencky equation to plastic equilibrium". *Z. angew. Math. Mech.* 3, 401 (1923).

218. Geiringer, H. and Prager, W., "Mechanics of isotropic bodies in a plastic state". *Ergebnisse der exacten Naturwissenschaften,* 13, 310 (1934).

219. Hill, R., "Some special problems of indenting and compression in plasticity". *Proc. 7th Int. Congr. Appl. Mech.* 1, 365 (1948).

220. Hill, R., "On the inhomogeneous deformation of a plastic laminar in a compression test". *Phil Mag.* 41, 733 (1950).

221. Hill, R., Lee, E. H. and Tupper, S. J., "A method of numerical analysis of plastic flow in plane strain and its application to the compression of a ductile material between rough plates". *Trans. ASME, J. Appl. Mech.* 18, 46 (1951).

222. Green, A. P., "A theoretical investigation of the compression of a ductile material between smooth flat dies". *Phil Mag.* 42, 900 (1951).

223. Nye, J. F., "Experiments on the plastic compression of a block between rough plates". *Trans. ASME, J. Appl. Mech.* 19, 337 (1952).

224. Alexander, J. M., "The effect of Coulomb friction in the plane-strain compression of a plastic-rigid material". *J. Mech. Phys. Solids,* 3, 233 (1955).

225. Murdi, B. B. and Tong, K. N., "Yielding in compression of strip between smooth dies". *J. Mech. Phys. Solids,* 4, 121 (1956).

226. Ross, E. W., "On the plane plastic flow of an inset block". *Trans. ASME, J. Appl. Mech.* 24, 457 (1957).

227. Ota, T., Shindo, A., Fukuoka, H. and Sugimoto, K., "Compression of a wedge by a flat rigid die". *Trans. Soc. Mech. Engrs. Japan,* 23 242 (1957).

228. Ivlev, D. D., "Certain particular solutions of equations for the axi-symmetrical problem in the theory of ideal plasticity and generalisation of Prandtl's solution of compression of plastic layer between rough plates". *Prikl. Mat. Mekh.* 22, 943 (1958).

229. Van Rooyan, G. T. and Backofen, W. A., "Distribution of inter-face stress in plane strain and compression". *J. Mech. Phys. Solids,* 7, 163 (1959).

230. Johnson, W. and Kudo, H., "Plane strain compression between rough inclined plates". *Appl. Scient. Res.* A9, 206 (1960).

231. Johnson, W. and Kudo, H., "The compression of rigid-perfectly plastic materials between rough parallel dies of unequal width". *Int. J. Mech. Sci.* 1, 336 (1960).

232. Johnson, W. and McShane, I. E., "A note on calculations concerning the plastic compression of thin material between smooth plates under conditions of plane strain". *Appl. Scient. Res.* A, 9, 169 (1960).

233. Shindo, A., "General considerations on the compression of a wedge by a rigid flat die". 1st and 2nd reports, *Bull. JSME,* 5, 21 and 30 (1962).

234. Takahashi, H., "The plane strain compression between V-shaped dies with Coulomb friction". *Int. J. Mech. Sci.* 5, 1 (1963).

235. Toth, L., "Calculation of the deformation resistance of prismatic bodies to compression by parallel plates". *Acta tech. Akad. Sci. Hung., Budapest,* 51, 105 (1965).

236a. Sowerby, R., Johnson, W. and Samanta, S. K., "The diametral compression of circular rings by point loads". *Int. J. Mech.*

Sci. 10, 369 (1968).

236b. Johnson, W. and Rees,P. E., "Plastic collapse of short hollow cylinders or rings under diametral load". Nat. Symposium of Large Deformations, Delhi, 1979. (In press).

237. Collins, I. F., "Geometric properties of some slip line fields for compression and extrusion". *J. Mech. Phys. Solids*, 16, 137 (1968).

238. Johnson, K. L., "Deformation of a plastic wedge by a rigid flat die under the action of a tangential force". *J. Mech. Phys. Solids*, 16, 395 (1968).

239. Suh, N. P., Lee, R. S. and Rogers, C. R., "The yielding of truncated solid cones under quasi-static and dynamic loading". *J. Mech. Phys. Solids*, 16, 357 (1968).

240. Collins, I. F., "Compression of a rigid-perfectly plastic strip between parallel rotating smooth dies". *Q. J. Mech. Appl. Math.* 23, 329 (1970).

241. Devenpeck, M. L. and Weinstein, A. S., "Experimental investigation of work hardening effects in wedge flattening with relation to non-hardening theory". *J. Mech. Phys. Solids*, 18, 213 (1970).

242. Jain, S. C. and Kobayashi, S., "Deformation and fracture of an aluminium alloy in plane strain side pressing". *Proc. 11th Int. MTDR Conf.* 1137. Univ. Birmingham, 1970. Pergamon Press (1971).

243. Shabaik, A. H., "Prediction of geometry changes of the free boundary during upsetting by slip line field theory". *Trans. ASME, J. Engng. Ind.* 93B, 568 (1971).

244. Thomason, P. F., "On the plane strain compression of a rigid-plastic material with an entrapped viscous lubricant on the platen face". *Int. J. Mech. Sci.* 14, 279 (1972).

245. Aksenov, L. B., Chitkara, N. R. and Johnson, W., "Pressure and deformation in the plane strain side pressing of circular section bar to form turbine blades". *Int. J. Mech. Sci.* 17, 681 (1975).

246. Das, N. S., Banerjee, J. and Collins, I. F., "Plane strain compression of rigid perfectly plastic strip between parallel dies with slipping friction". *Trans. ASME, J. Appl. Mech.* 46, 317 (1979).

Indenting

247. Prandtl. L., "Concerning the hardness of plastic bodies". *Nachr. Ges. Wiss. Gottingen*, 74 (1920).

248. Bishop, R. F., Hill, R. and Mott, N. F., "The theory of indentation and hardness tests". *Proc. Phys. Soc. Lond.* 57, 147 (1945).

249. Hill, R. and Lee, E. H., Ministry of Supply, A.R.D. Report 1/46 (1946).

250. Hill, R., Lee, E. H. and Tupper, S. J., "A theory of wedge indentation of ductile materials". *Proc. R. Soc.*, A, 188, 273 (1947).

251. Hill, R., "Theoretical effect of specimen size in measurement of hardness". *Phil. Mag.* 41, 319 (1950).

252. Dugdale, D. S., "Wedge indentation experiments with cold-worked metals". *J. Mech. Phys. Solids*, 2, 14 (1953).

253. Grunzweig, J., Longman, I. M. and Petch, N. J., "Calculations and measurements of wedge indentation". *J. Mech. Phys. Solids*, 2, 81 (1953).

254. Shield, R. T. and Drucker, D. C., "The application of limit analysis to punch indentation problems". Nat. Conf. Appl. Mechs. A.S.M.E. Paper No. 53-APM-21, Minneapolis (June 1953).

255. Shield, R. T., "The plastic indentation of a layer by a flat punch". *Q. J. Appl. Math.* **13**, 27 (1955).

256. Ota, T., Shindo, A., Fukuoka, H. and Sugimoto, K., "Some problems of wedge-shaped slip line fields". *Proc. 6th Jap. Nat. Congr. Appl. Mech.* 197. University Kyoto (1956).

257. Conway, H. D., "The indentation of a transversely isotropic half space by a rigid punch". *Zeit. ang. Math. Phys. (ZAMP)*, **7**, 80 (1956).

258. Tabor, D., The physical meaning of indentation and scratch hardness". *Br. J. Appl. Phys.* **7**, 159 (1956).

259. Mulhearn, T. O., "The deformation of metals by Vickers-type pyramid indentors". *J. Mech. Phys. Solids*, **7**, 85 (1958).

260. Johnson, W. and Woo, D. M., "The pressure for indenting material resting on a rough foundation". *Trans. ASME, J. Appl. Mech.* **25**, 64 (1958).

261. Johnson, W., "Indentation and forging and Nasmyth's anvil". *Engineer*, **205**, 348 (1958).

262. Ivlev, D. D., "Rigid punch indentation into a plastic half-space". *Prikl. Met. Mekh.* **23**, 394 (1959).

263. Ivlev, D. D., "Pressing a rigid stamping in a plastic half-space". *Prikl. Met. Mekh.* **23**, 274 (1959).

264. Ivlev, D. D., "Pressing of a thin body of revolution in a plastic half-space". *Zh. Prikl. Mekh. Tekh. Fiz.*, No. 4, 71 (1960).

265. Bykovstov, G. I. and Ivlev, D. D., "Determination of limiting loads on a body pressed in a plastic media". *Izv. Akad. Nauk, SSSR, Otd. Tekh. Nauk, Mekh. i Mash.* **1**, 173 (1961).

266. Hauer, P. J., "A model technique for plastic working processes: flow patterns, material constants, forming coefficients". *VDI-Forschungsheft*, **28**, 493 (1962).

267. Bocharov, Y., Kobayashi, S. and Thomsen, E. G., "The mechanics of the coining process". *Trans. ASME, J. Engng. Ind.* **84B**, 491 (1962).

268. Lockett, F. J., "Indentation of a rigid-plastic material by a conical indentor". *J. Mech. Phys. Solids*, **11**, 345 (1963).

269. Johnson, W. and Hillier, M. J., "Some slip line fields for indenting with rotating dies". *Int. J. Mech. Sci.* **2**, 191 (1963).

270. Dugdale, D. S., "Indentation of strips with flat dies on a flat anvil". *Int. J. Prod. Res.* **3**, 141 (1964).

271. Johnson, W., Mahtab, F. U. and Haddow, J. B., "The indentation of a semi-infinite block by a wedge of comparable hardness - I. Theoretical". *Int. J. Mech. Sci.* **6**, 329 (1964).

272. Hillier, M. J., "Proposed slip line fields for indenting with rough plane and curved dies". *Appl. Scient. Res.* A, **13**, 332 (1964).

273. Johnson, W. and Kudo, H., "Plane strain deep indentation". *Proc. 5th M.T.D.R. Conf.* **441**. Univ. Birmingham, 1964. Pergamon Press (1965).

274. Johnson, W., Mahtab, F. U. and Williams, A., "Experiments concerning geometric similarity in indentation". *Int. J. Mech. Sci.* **7**, 389 (1965).

275. Kolos, V. I., "On the impression of a concave stamp in a plastic medium". *Zh. prikl. Mekh. tekh. Fiz.*, No. 2, 157 (1965).

276. Johnson, W., Mahtab, F. U. and Williams, A., "Further experiments concerning geometrically similar indentations". *Int. J. Mech. Sci.* **8**, 49 (1966).

277. Haddow, J. B., "On a wedge indentation paradox". *Int. J. Mech. Sci.* **9**, 159 (1967).

278. Harvey, S. J. and Palmer, W. B., "Analysis of the tube relieving process". *Proc. 8th M.T.D.R. Conf.*, 1059. Univ. Manchester,

1967. Pergamon Press (1968).

279. Salencon, J., "Theory of limit loads: On the solution of the problem of plane strain indentation of a block by a rigid rectangular punch". *C.r. Acad. Sci., Paris*, A, 264, 613 (1967).

280. Salencon, J., "Theory of limit loads: Plane strain indentation of a block by a pair of symmetrical punches, when the thickness of the block is less than the width of the punch". *C.r. Acad. Sci., Paris*, A, 265, 869 (1967).

281. Salencon, J., "Theory of limit loads: Study of the plane strain indentation of a bi-layer". *C.r. Acad. Sci., Paris*, A, 266, 1210 (1968).

282. Salencon, J., "Theory of limit loads: Study of a class of kinematic solutions for the problems of indenting a non-homogeneous semi-infinite block". *C.r. Acad. Sci., Paris*, A, 267, 171 (1968).

283. Johnson, W. and Needham, G., "Plastic hinges in ring indentation in relation to ring rolling". *Int. J. Mech. Sci.* 10, 487 (1968).

284. Sayir, M. and Ziegler, H., "On Prandtl's punch problem". *Ingegneri Archit. Costr.* 36, 294 (1968).

285. Rowe, G. W. and Wetton, A. G., "Theoretical considerations in the grinding of metals". *J. Inst. Metals*, 97, 193 (1969).

286. Sohrabpour, S. and Kobayashi, S., "Mechanics of plane strain deep indentation with flat punches". *Proc. 13th M.T.D.R. Conf.* 491. Univ. Birmingham, 1972. The Macmillan Press (1973).

287. Dewhurst, P., "Plane-strain indentation on a smooth foundation: a range of solutions for rigid-perfectly plastic strip". *Int. J. Mech. Sci.* 16, 923 (1974).

288. Dodd, B. and Osakada, K., "A note on the types of slip line field for wedge indentation determined by computer". *Int. J. Mech. Sci.* 16, 931 (1974).

289. Meguid, S. A. and Collins, I. F., "On the mechanics of the oblique cutting of metal strips with knife edged tools". *Int. J. Mech. Sci.* 19, 361 (1977).

290. Meguid, S. A., Collins, I. F. and Johnson, W., "The co-indentation of a layer by two flat plane or spherical headed rigid punches". *Int. J. Mech. Sci.* 19, 1 (1977).

291. Tabata, T., Masaki, S. and Uozumi, Y., "An analysis of wedge indentation of a porous material". *Bull. JSME*, 20, 661 (1977).

292. Vassilaros, M., Taylor, D. W. and Kuhn, H., "Analysis of residual stresses resulting from cold rolling of threads and their effect on fatigue behaviour". *Proc. 7th North Am. Metalworking Res. Conf.* 96. S.M.E. (1979).

293. Chitkara, N. R., Johnson, W. and Saxena, S. K., "Deformation modes in the plastic yielding of deeply notched specimens when indented by flat rigid punches", *Int. J. Mech. Sci.* (To be published.)

Cutting

294. Hill, R., "On the mechanics of cutting metal with knife-edge tools". *J. Mech. Phys. Solids*, 1, 265 (1953).

295. Johnson, W., "The cutting of round wire with knife-edge and flat-edge tools". *Appl. Scient. Res.*, A, 7, 65 (1957).

296. Johnson, W. and Kudo, H., "The cutting of metal strips between partly rough knife tools". *Int. J. Mech. Sci.* 2, 224 (1961).

297. Druyanov, B. A., "Stress distribution under a punch or curvilinear profile during cutting of an ideally plastic strip". *Zh. prikl. Mekh. tekh. Fiz.*, No. 6, 155 (1961).

298. Johnson, W. and Mahtab, F. U., "The mechanics of cutting strip with knife-edge and flat-face dies". *Int. J. Mach. Tool Des. Res.* 2, 335 (1962).

299. Kudo, H. and Tamura, K., "Indentation and cutting of metal plate between knife-edged tools". *Japan Society of Mechanical Engineers Semi-international Symposium*, 139, Tokyo (1967).

Drawing

300. Hill, R. and Tupper, S. J., "A new theory of plastic deformation in wire drawing". *J. Iron Steel Inst.* 159, 353 (1948).

301. Hill, R., "The calculation of stresses in the ironing of metal cups". *J. Iron Steel Inst.* 161, 41 (1949).

302. Ansoff, H. I., "Forming of plastic sheet between fixed cylindrical dies with Coulomb friction". *Trans. Am. Soc. Mech. Engrs.* 72, 145 (1950).

303. Cook, P. M. and Wistreich, J. G., "Measurement of die pressures in wire drawing by photoelastic methods". *Br. J. Appl. Phys.* 3, 59 (1952).

304. Wistreich, J. G., "Die pressures in plane strain drawings: comparison between theory and experiment". *J. Mech. Phys. Solids*, 1, 164 (1953).

305. Hill, R., "A note on the pull back factor in strip drawing". *J. Mech. Phys. Solids*, 1, 142 (1953).

306. Green, A. P. and Hill, R., "Calculations on the influence of friction and die geometry in sheet drawing". *J. Mech. Phys. Solids*, 1, 31 (1952).

307. Bishop, J. F. W., "Calculations of sheet drawing under back tensions through a rough wedge-shaped die". *J. Mech.Phys. Solids*, 2, 39 (1953).

308. Sokolovskii, V. V., "Some remarks concerning a plane problem in the theory of plasticity". *Prikl. Mat. Mekh.* 18, 762 (1954).

309. Green, A. P., "Plane strain theories of drawing". *Proc. Inst. Mech, Engrs.* 174, 847 (1960).

310. Sokolovskii, V. V.,"A problem of plasticity theory", in *Volume Dedicated to N. I. Muskhelishvili on his Seventieth Birthday*. Philadelphia Soc. Industr. Appl. Math. (1961).

311. Sokolovskii, V. V.,"On the drawing of a plastic strip". *Prikl. Mat. Mekh.* 25, 5 (1961).

312. Druyanov, B. A., "Drawing through curvilinear die" (in Russian). *Zh. prikl. Mekh. tekh. Fiz.*, No. 1, 165 (1962).

313. Richmond, O. and Devenpeck, M. L., "A die profile for maximum efficiency in strip drawing". *Proc. 4th U.S. Congr. Appl. Mech.* 1053. Univ. California, Berkeley. A.S.M.E. (1962).

314. Firbank, T. C. and Lancaster, P. R., "Plane strain drawing between dies with a circular profile and zero exit angle". *Int. J. Mech. Sci.* 6, 415 (1964).

315. Masuda, M., Murota, T. and Jimma, T., "Sheet drawing through a wedge-shaped die". *Annals CIRP*, 13, 325 (1965).

316. Devenpeck, M. L. and Richmond, O., "Strip-drawing experiments with a sigmoidal die profile". *Trans. ASME, J. Engng. Ind.* 87B, 425 (1965).

317. Rowe, G. W. and Wetton, A. G., "A simple correlation between deformation in some sliding-wear and metal working processes". *Wear*, 8, 448 (1965).

318. Firbank, T. C., Lancaster, P. R. and McArthur, G., "An examination of the deformation during cold drawing through cylindrical dies".

Int. J. Mech. Sci. 8, 541 (1966).

319. Kovalev, V. G., "Possibility of using slip lines to determine stress fields during drawing". *Kuznechno-shtampovochnoe proizvodstvo*, 8, 17 (1966).
320. Sowerby, R., Johnson, W. and Samanta, S. K., "Plane strain drawing and extrusion of a rigid-perfectly plastic material through concave dies". *Int. J. Mech. Sci.* 10, 231 (1968).
321. Johnson, R. W. and Rowe, G. W., "Bulge formation in strip drawing with light reductions in area". *Proc. Instn. Mech. Engrs.* 182, 521 (1968).
322. Johnson, W., Sowerby, R. and Caddell, R. M., "Redundant deformation factors and maximum reduction in plane strain and axi-symmetric wire drawing. Part I". *Annals CIRP*, 19, 311 (1970).
323. Rogers, H. C. and Coffin, L. F., Jr., "An analysis of the effect of friction in sheet drawing". *Int. J. Mech. Sci.* 13, 141 (1971).
324. Kudo, H., Nagahama, T. and Yoshida, K., "Comment on a paper by H. C. Rogers and L. F. Coffin Jr.". *Int. J. Mech. Sci.* 14, 339 (1972).
325. Dodd, B. and Scivier, D. A., "On the static inadmissibility of some slip-line fields for sheet drawing". *Int. J. Mech. Sci.* 17, 663 (1975).
326. Wilson, W. R. D., "Slip line field solutions for strip drawing with arbitrary frictional conditions". *Proc. 5th North Am. Metalworking Res. Conf.* 80. S.M.E. (1977).
327. Kohser, R. A. and Chronister, D. J., "Wire and rod drawing: the process and the product". *Proc. 7th North Am. Metalworking Res. Conf.* 100. S.M.E. (1979).
328. Dodd, B. and Kudo, H., "A slip line field for mid-lane cracking or splitting in sheet drawing". *Int. J. Mech. Sci.* 22, 67 (1980).

Extrusion

329. Hill, R., "The theory of extrusion of metals". M.O.S. Armament Res. Dept., Theoretical Research Rep. No. 23/45 (1945).
330. Northcott, L., McLean, D. and Lee, O. R. J., "The effect of single and multi-hole extrusion on the properties of extruded aluminium alloy bar". *J. Inst. Metals*, 74, 81 (1947).
331. Tupper, S. J. and Purchase, N. W., "Experiments with a laboratory extrusion apparatus under conditions of plane strain". *J. Mech Phys. Solids*, 1, 277 (1953).
332. Yang, C. T. and Thomsen, E. G., "Plastic flow in lead extrusion". *Trans. Am. Soc. Mech. Engrs.* 74, 575 (1953).
333. Frisch, J. and Thomsen, E. G., "An experimental study of metal extrusions and various strain rates". Paper 53-A-154, A.S.M.E. Annual Meeting, New York, December 1953.
334. Green, A. P., "On symmetrical extrusion in plane strain". *J. Mech. Phys. Solids*, 3, 189 (1954).
335. Thomsen, E. G. and Lapsley, J. T., "Experimental stress determination within a metal during plastic flow". *Proc. Soc. Exp. Stress Analysis*, 11, 59 (1954).
336. Thomsen, E. G., Yang, C. T. and Bierbower, J. B., "An experimental investigation of the mechanics of plastic deformation". *Univ. Calif. Publs. Engng.* 5, 89 (1954).
337. Jordan, T. F. and Thomsen, E. G., "Comparison of an unsymmetrical slip line solution in extrusion with experiment". *J. Mech. Phys. Solids*, 4, 184 (1955).

338. Thomsen, E. G., "A new approach to metal forming problems". *Trans. Am. Soc. Mech. Engrs.* 77, 515 (1955).

339. Thomsen, E, G. and Frisch, J., "Stresses and strains in cold extrusion". *Trans. Am. Soc. Mech. Engrs.* 77, 1343 (1955).

340. Johnson, W., "Extrusion through wedge-shaped dies". *J. Mech. Phys. Solids,* 3, 218 (1955).

341. Johnson, W., "Extrusion through wedge-shaped dies". *J. Mech. Phys. Solids,* 3, 224 (1955).

342. Bishop, J. W. F., "An approximate method for determining the temperatures reached in steady motion problems of plane plastic strain". *Q.J. Mech. Appl. Math.* 9, 236 (1956).

343. Thomsen, E. G., "Comparison of slip line solutions with experiment". *Trans. ASME, J. Appl. Mech.* 23, 225 (1956).

344. Johnson, W., "Extrusion through square dies of larger reduction". *J. Mech. Phys. Solids,* 4, 191 (1956).

345. Johnson, W., "Experiments in plane strain extrusion". *J. Mech. Phys. Solids,* 4, 269 (1956).

346. Kudo, H., "A method for direct and continuous observation of metal flow during forming". *Rep. Inst. Sci. Technol. , Tokyo,* 11, 147 (1957).

347. Wang, J., "Plastic flow in the extrusion of ribs on flat plates" (in Chinese). *Chinese J. Mech.* 1, (1957).

348. Johnson, W., "The pressure for the cold extrusion of lubricated rod through square dies of moderate reduction at slow speeds". *J. Inst. Metals,* 85, 403 (1957).

349. Johnson, W., "The plane strain extrusion of short slugs". *J. Mech. Phys. Solids,* 5, 202 (1957).

350. Johnson, W., "Partial sideways extrusion from a smooth container". *J. Mech. Phys. Solids,* 5, 193 (1957).

351. Johnson, W. and Dodeja, L. C., "On the multiple hole extrusion of sheets of equal thickness". *J. Mech. Phys. Solids,* 5, 267 (1957).

352. Johnson, W. and Dodeja, L. C., "On the cold extrusion of circular rods through square multiple hole dies". *J. Mech. Phys. Solids,* 5, 281 (1957).

353. Johnson, W., Mellor, P. B. and Woo, D. M., "Single-hole staggered and unequal multi-hole extrusions". *J. Mech. Phys. Solids,* 203 (1958).

354. Johnson, W., "Experiments in the cold extrusion of rods of non-circular cross-section". *J. Mech. Phys. Solids,* 7, 37 (1958).

355. Johnson, W., "Estimation of upper bound loads for some extrusion and coining operations". *Proc. Instn. Mech. Engrs.* 173, 61 (1957).

356. Johnson, W., "Upper bound loads for extrusion through circular dies". *Appl. Scient. Res.* Series A, 7, 437 (1959).

357. Johnson, W., "An elementaty consideration of some extrusion defects". *Appl. Scient. Res.,* Series A, 8, 52 (1959).

358. Johnson, W., "Cavity formation and enfolding defects in plane strain extrusion using a shaped punch". *Appl. Scient. Res.,* Series A, 8, 228 (1959).

359. Backofen, W. A., "Extrusion theory and calculations". *J. Metals,* 13, 206 (1961).

360. Alexander, J. M., "On the complete solutions for frictionless extrusions in plane strain". *Q. Appl. Math.* 19, 31 (1961).

361. Treco, R. M., "Theoretical and experimental analysis of extrusion processes for metals". *Trans. Am. Soc. Metals,* 55, 697 (1962).

362. Alexander, J. M., "Application of experimental and theoretical results to practice of hot extrusion". *J. Inst. Metals,* 90, 193 (1962).

363. Alexander, J. M., "Slip line field theory of extrusion". *Metal Industry*, 100, 268 and 311 (1962).
364. Hillier, M. J., "Slip line fields for extrusion through lipped or curved dies". *Int. J. Mech. Sci.* 4, 529 (1962).
365. Sokolovskii, V. V., "Complete plane problems of plastic flow". *J. Mech. Phys. Solids*, 10, 353 (1962).
366. Green, W. A., "Extrusion through smooth square dies of medium reduction". *J. Mech. Phys. Solids*, 10, 225 (1962).
367. Kobayashi, S., "Application of theory of plasticity to extrusion problems". *Proc. Int. Prod. Eng. Res. Conf.* 356. Pittsburg, September (1963).
368. Johnson, W., and Hillier, M. J., "Plane strain extrusion through partly rough dies". *Int. J. Mech. Sci.* 5, 191 (1963).
369. Halling, J. and Mitchell, L. A., "Use of upper-bound solution for predicting the pressure for plane strain extrusion of materials". *J. Mech. Engng. Sci.* 6, 240 (1964).
370. Halling, J. and Mitchell, L. A., "An experimental study of symmetrical extrusion using paraffin wax as a model". *Proc. 5th MTDR Conf.* 353, Univ. Birmingham, 1964. Pergamon Press (1965).
371. Kudo, H. and Takahashi, H., "Effects of die or punch angle and friction in plane strain extrusion or piercing". *Annals CIRP*, 13,73 (1965).
372. Yu Alyushin, A., "Analysis of deformation processes of metals by tools with curvilinear contours" *Mashinovendenie*, No. 5, 83 (1965).
373. Johnson, W., Duncan, J. L. and Ovreset, A., "Some experiments and theory for plane strain side-extrusion". *Proc. Inst. Mech. Engrs.* 180, Part 31, 241 (1966).
374. Hill, R., "A remark on diagonal streaming in plane plastic strain". *J. Mech. Phys. Solids*, 14, 245 (1966).
375. Kronsjo, L. I. and Mellor, P. B., "Plane strain extrusion through concave dies". *Int. J. Mech. Sci.* 8, 515 (1966).
376. Johnson, W., "Plane strain extrusion of initially curved sheet". *Int. J. Mech. Sci.* 8, 163 (1966).
377. Alexander, J. M. and Whitlock, B. C., "Extrusion of a bi-metallic strip from separate containers". *Proc. Instn. Mech. Engrs.* 180, Part 31, 250 (1966).
378. Takahashi, H., "Some slip line fields for plane strain extrusion and forging". *Japan Society of Mechanical Engineers, Semi-international Symposium*, 163, Tokyo (1967).
379. Kronsjo, L. I. "Slip line field analysis of incipient plane strain extrusion through frictionless and perfectly rough wedge shaped dies". *Int. J. Mech. Sci.* 11, 281 (1969).
380. Johnson, W. and Sowerby, R., "Upper bound techniques applied to plane strain extrusion, minimum weight two-dimensional frames and rotationally symmetric flat plates". *Bull. Mech. Engng. Ed.* 8, 269 (1969).
381. Samanta, S. K., "Slip line field for extrusion through cosine dies". *J. Mech. Phys. Solids*, 18, 311 (1970).
382. Murota, T., Jimma, T. and Kato, K., "Analysis of axi-symmetric extrusion". *Bull. JSME*, 13, 1366 (1970).
383. Farmer, L. E. and Oxley, P. L. B., "A slip line field for plane strain extrusion of a strain hardening material". *J. Mech. Phys. Solids*, 19, 369 (1971).
384. Abe, T., Kubo, K. and Oyane, M., "Central cracking of extruded product of brittle metal in hydrostatic extrusion". *Bull. JSME*, 15, 1357 (1972).
385. Fenton, R. G. and Lavanchy, S. A., "Solution of plane strain extrusion problems using the method of characteristics". *Proc.*

1st Symp. Application of Solid Mech. 553. Univ. Waterloo, Canada (1972).

386. Johnson, W. and Chitkara, N. R., "Corrugated plate formed by side extrusion with two coaxial rams moving at different speeds". *Int. J. Mech. Sci.* 15, 199 (1973).

387. Newnham, J. A. and Rowe, G. W., "An analysis of compound flow of metal in a simple extrusion/forging process". *J. Inst. Metals*, 101, 1 (1973).

388. Hill, R. and Kim, D. W., "Some theoretical aspects of hydrostatic extrusion and allied processes". *J. Mech. Phys. Solids*, 22, 73 (1974).

389. Bachrach, B. I. and Samanta, S. K., "Plane strain sheet and tube extrusion through cosine dies with friction". *Proc. 2nd North Am. Metalworking Res. Conf.* 179. S.M.E. (1974).

390. Sowerby, R., Sambasivan, B. and Caddell, R. M., "The influence of the die profile on the properties of extruded aluminium". *Proc. 3rd Symp. Applications of Solid Mechs.* 27. Univ. Toronto, Canada (1976).

391. Rowe, G. W. and Hartley, P., "Computer analysis of progressive deformation in extrusion-forging". *Proc. 5th North Am. Metalworking Res. Conf.* 204. S.M.E. (1977).

392. Chenot, J. L., Felgeres, L., Lavarenne, B. and Salencon, J., "A numerical application of the slip line field method to extrusion through conical dies". *Int. J. Engng. Sci.* 16, 263 (1978).

393. Gatto, F., Barbero, A. and Murari, G., "Theoretical and experimental analysis of an extrusion process". *Proc. 7th North Am. Metalworking Res, Conf.* 72. S.M.E. (1979).

394. Farmer, L. E., "An extrusion process for uniformly working metals". *Annals CIRP*, 29 (1980).

395. Murakami, T. and Takahashi, H., "On a complete solution for frictionless non-steady state extrusion in plane strain". *Int. J. Mech. Sci.* 23, 999 (1981).

Piercing

396. Hill, R., "A theoretical analysis of the stresses and strains in extrusion piercing". *J. Iron Steel Inst.* 158, 177 (1948).

397. Johnson, W. and Haddow, J. B., "Experiments in the piercing of soft metals". *Int. J. Mach. Tool Des. and Res.* 2, 1 (1962).

398. Farahbakhsh, B., M.Sc. Thesis, Mech. Eng. Dept., U.M.I.S.T., Manchester (1979).

FORGING

399. Massey, H. F., "The flow of metal during forging". *Proc. Manchester Assoc. Engrs.* (Nov. 1962).

400. Cook, P. M., "Experiments with Plasticine models to simulate hot forging of steel". *Metal Treat. Drop Forg.* 20, 541 (1953).

401. Johnson, W., "Over-estimates of load for some two-dimensional forging operations". *Proc. 3rd U.S. Nat. Cong. Appl. Mechs.* 571. Brown University, June 1958. Published by A.S.M.E.

402. Johnson, W., "Extrusion, forging, machining and indenting minimum-weight frames and high-rate sheet metal forming". *Proc. Int. Prod. Eng. Res. Conf.* 342. Pittsburg, September 1963. Published by A.S.M.E.

403. Brovman, M. YA and Yudin, Yu S., "Certain problems of pressworking bi-metal". *Kuznechno-shtamp Proizv*, 1, 3 (1963).

404. Johnson, W., Baraya, G. L. and Slater, R. A. C., "On heat lines or lines of thermal discontinuity". *Int. J. Mech. Sci.* 6, 409 (1964).

405. Johnson, W. and Baraya, G. L., "Flat bar forging". *Proc. 5th M.T.D.R. Conf.* 449. Univ. Birmingham, 1964. Pergamon Press (1965).

406. Slater, R. A. C., "Velocity and thermal discontinuities encountered during the forging of steel". *Proc. Manchester Assoc. Engrs.*, No. 5 (1965-66).

407. Marciniak, Z., "A rocking-die technique for cold-forming operations". *Machinery and Prod. Engng.* 11, 792 (1970).

408. Appleton, E. and Slater, R. A. C., "Effects of upper platen configuration in the rotary forging process and rotary forging into a contoured lower platen". *Int. J. Mach. Tool Des. Res.* 13, 43 (1972).

Machining

409. Ernst. H. and Merchant, M. E., "Chip formation, friction and high-quality machined surfaces". *Trans. Am. Soc. Metals,* 29, 299 (1941).

410. Drucker, D. C., "An analysis of the mechanics of metal cutting". *J. Appl. Phys.* 20, 1013 (1949).

411. Lee, E. H. and Shaffer, B. W., "The theory of plasticity applied to a problem of machining". *Trans. ASME, J. Appl. Mech.* 18, 405 (1951).

412. Lee, E. H., "A plastic flow problem arising in the theory of discontinuous machining". *Trans. Am Soc. Mech. Engrs.* 76, 189 (1954).

413. Hill, R., "Mechanics of machining: a new approach". *J. Mech. Phys. Solids,* 3, 47 (1954).

414. Takeyama, H., Murai, T. and Usui, E., "Speed effect on metal machining (1)". *J. Mech. Lab., Tokyo,* 1, 59 (1955).

415. Shindo, A. *et al.*, "An investigation into the theories of orthogonal machining". *Trans. Jap. Soc. Mech. Engrs.* 24, 484 (1958).

416. Shindo, A., "Limits of validity of some solutions for orthogonal cutting 1 and 2" (in Japanese). *Kikai-no-kenkyu,* 10, 640 and 761 (1958).

417. Christopherson, D. G., Palmer, W. B. and Oxley, P. L. B., "Orthogonal cutting of work-hardening material". *Engineering,* 186, 113 (1958).

418. Zorev, N. N., "Certain results of the work in the field of mechanics of metal working processes". *Conf. on Technology of Eng. Manufacture, Inst. Mech. Engrs.* (1958).

419. Palmer, W. B. and Oxley, P. L. B., "Mechanics of orthogonal machining". *Proc. Instn. Mech. Engrs.,* 175, 623 (1959).

420. Ota, T., Shindo, A. and Fukuoka, H., "An investigation on the theories of orthogonal machining". *Bull. JSME,* 2, 115 (1959).

421. Oxley, P. L. B. and Enahoro, H. E., "An investigation of the transition from continuous to a discontinuous chip in orthogonal machining". *Int. J. Mech. Sci.* 3, 145 (1961).

422. Oxley, P. L. B., "Mechanics of metal cutting". *Int. J. Mach. Tool Des. Res.* 1, 87 (1961).

423. Okushima, K. and Hitomi, K., "Transitional phenomenon in metal cutting". *Bull. JSME,* 4, 357 (1961).

424. Oxley, P. L. B., "An analysis for orthogonal cutting with restricted tool-chip contact". *Int. J. Mech. Sci.* 4, 129 (1962).

425. Kobayashi, S. and Thomsen, E. G., "Metal cutting analysis. Part I: Re-evaluation and new method of presentation of theories. Part II: New parameters". *Trans. ASME, J. Engng. Ind.* 84B, 63 (1962).

426. Thomsen, E. G., McDonald, A. G. and Kobayashi, S., "Flank friction studies with carbide tools reveal sublayer plastic flow". *Trans. ASME, J. Engng. Ind.* 84B, 53 (1962).

427. Johnson, W., "Some slip line fields for swaging or expanding, indenting, extruding and machining, for tools with curved dies". *Int. Mech. Sci.* 4, 323 (1962).

428. Usui, E. and Hoshi, L., "Slip line fields in metal cutting involving centred fan fields". *Proc. Int. Prod. Eng. Res. Conf.* 61. Pittsburg, September 1963. Published by A.S.M.E.

429. Usui, E. and Kikuchi, K., "Theory of plasticity applied to machining mechanisms - Part I" (in Japanese). *J. Soc. Precision Mech.* 29, 26 (1963).

430. Usui, E., Kikuchi, K. and Hoshi, K., "The theory of plasticity applied to machining with cut-away tools". *Trans. ASME, J. Engng. Ind.* 86B, 95 (1964).

431. Ho, W. S. and Brewer, R. C., "A slip line field for machining with discontinuous chips". *Proc. Instn. Mech. Engrs.* 180, 791 (1965).

432. Kudo, H., "Some new slip line solutions for two-dimensional steady state machining". *Int. J. Mech. Sci.* 7, 43 (1965).

433. Shabaik, A. H. and Thomsen, E. G., "An application of potential theory to the solution of metal flow problems". *Proc. 6th M.T.D.R. Conf.* 429. Univ. Manchester, 1965. Pergamon Press (1966).

434. Bitans, K. and Brown, R. H., "An investigation of the deformation of orthogonal cutting". *Int. J. Mach. Tool Des. Res.* 5, 155 (1965).

435. Bannerjee, H. and Palmer, W. B., "Metal cutting with a discontinuous chip". *Proc. 6th M.T.D.R. Conf.* 405. Univ. Manchester, 1965. Pergamon Press (1966).

436. Bhattacharyya, A., "On the friction process in metal cutting". *Proc. 6th M.T.D.R. Conf.* 491. Univ. Manchester, 1965. Pergamon Press (1966).

437. Johnson, W. and Mahtab, F. U., "Upper bounds for restricted edge machining. Paper I". *Proc. 6th M.T.D.R. Conf.* 447. Univ. Manchester, 1965. Pergamon Press (1966).

438. Johnson, W. and Mahtab, F. U., "Some solutions using slip-line field and the method of upper bounds for milling, turning and boring". *Proc. 6th M.T.D.R. Conf.* 463. Univ. Manchester, 1965. Pergamon Press (1966).

439. Johnson, W., "Further rotational configurations: straight starting slip lines. Paper III". *Proc. 6th M.T.D.R. Conf.* 487. Univ. Manchester, 1965. Pergamon Press (1966).

440. Enahoro, H. E. and Oxley, P. L. B., "Flow along tool-chip interface in orthogonal machining". *J. Mech. Engng. Sci.* 8, 36 (1966).

441. Johnson, W., "Cutting with tools having a rounded edge: some theoretical considerations". *Annals CIRP*, 14, 315 (1966-67).

442. Palmer, W. B., "Plastic deformation when cutting into an inclined plane". *J. Mech. Engng. Sci.* 9, 1 (1967).

443. Hastings, W. F., "A new quick-stop device and grid technique for metal cutting research". *Annals CIRP*, 15, 109 (1967).

444. Fujii, Y., Kiyoshi, T., Matsuno, M. and Miura, K., "An analysis of orthogonal cutting mechanism with a Pb-Sn alloy". *Bull. JSME*, 13, 454 (1970).

445. Childs, T. H. C., "A new visio-plasticity technique and a study of curly chip formation". *Int. J. Mech. Sci.* **13**, 373 (1971).

446. Roth, R. N. and Oxley, P. L. B., "Slip line field analysis for orthogonal machining based upon experimental flow fields". *J. Mech. Engng. Sci.* **14**, 85 (1972).

447. Thomason, P. F. and Chakraborti, S. K., "A note on a strain etching method revealing the bounding slip lines to metal cutting flow zones". *Int. J. Mech. Sci.* **16**, 353 (1974).

448. Oxley, P. L. B. and Hastings, W. F., "Minimum work as a possible criterion for determining the frictional conditions at the tool/ chip interface in machining". *Phil. Trans. Roy. Soc. London*, A, **282**, 565 (1976).

449. Trent, E. M., *Metal Cutting.* Butterworths (1977).

450. Dewhurst, P., "On the non-uniqueness of the machining process". *Proc. Roy. Soc.* A, **360**, 587 (1978).

451. Dewhurst, P., "The effect of chip breaker constraints on the mechanics of the machining process". *Annals CIRP*, **28**, 1 (1979).

452. Childs, T. H. C., "Elastic effects in metal cutting chip formation". *Int. J. Mech. Sci.* **22**, 457 (1980).

Notched Bars Pulled in Tension

453. Hill, R., "The plastic yielding of notched bars under tension". *Q.J. Mech. Appl. Math.* **2**, 40 (1949).

454. Lee, E. H., "Plastic flow in V-notched bar pulled in tension". *Trans. ASME, J. Appl. Mech.* **19**, 331 (1952).

455. Drucker, D. C. and Brady, W. G., "An experimental investigation and limit analysis of net area in tension". *Proc. Am. Soc. Civ. Engrs.* **79**, Separ. No. 296 (1953).

456. Wang, A. J., "Plastic flow in deeply notched bars with semi-circular root". *Q.J. Appl. Maths.* **11**, 427 (1954).

457. Onat, E. T. and Prager, W., "The necking of a tension specimen in plane plastic flow". *J. Appl. Phys.* **25**, 491 (1954).

458. Lee, E. H., "Plastic flow in rectangularly notched bars subject to tension". *Trans. ASME, J. Appl. Mech.* **21**, 140 (1954).

459. Lee, E. H. and Wang, A. J., "Plastic flow in deeply notched bars with sharp internal angles". *Proc. 2nd U.S. Nat. Cong. Appl. Mechs.* 489. Ann Arbor, Michigan, 1954. A.S.M.E. (1955).

460. Garr, L., Lee, E. H. and Wang, A. J., "Pattern of plastic deformation in deeply notched bar with semi-circular root". *Trans. ASME, J. Appl. Mech.* **23**, 56 (1956).

461. Zhukovskii, V. S., "On the coefficient of strengthening and character of propogations of plastic zones in notched bars". *Izv. Akad. Nauk SSSR Otd. Tekh Nauk*, **5**, 116 (1958).

462. Findley, W. N. and Drucker, D. C., "An experimental study of plane plastic straining in notched bars". *Trans. ASME, J. Appl. Mech.* **32**, 493 (1965).

463. Ewing, D. J. F. and Hill, R., "The plastic constraint of V-notched tension bars". *J. Mech. Phys. Solids*, **15**, 115 (1967).

464. Ewing, D. J. F., "Plastic yielding of V-notched tension bars with circular roots". *J. Mech Phys. Solids*, **16**, 81 (1968).

Crack Initiation and Fracture

465. Griffith, A. A., "The phenomena of rupture and flow in solids". *Phil. Trans. Roy. Soc. London*, A, **221**, 163 (1920).

466. Savin, G. N., *Stress Concentration around Holes*. Pergamon Press (1961).

467. Bilby, B. A., Cottrell, A. H. and Swinden, K. H., "The spread of plastic yield from a notch". *Proc. R. Soc.* A, 272, 304 (1963).

468. McClintock, F. A. and Irwin, G. R., "Plasticity aspects of fracture mechanics". *Symposium on Fracture Toughness Testing and Applications*. ASTM-STP-381 (1965).

469. McClintock, F. A., "Effects of root radius stress, crack growth and rate of fracture instability". *Proc. R. Soc.* A, 285, 58 (1965).

470. McClintock, F. A., Kaplan, S. M. and Berg, C. A., "Ductile fracture by hole growth in shear bands". *Int. J. Fracture Mech.* 2, 614 (1966).

471. Tetelman, A. S. and McEvily, A. J., *Fracture of Structural Materials*. Wiley-Interscience (1967).

472. McClintock, F. A., "Local criteria for ductile fracture". *Int. J. Fracture Mech.* 4, 101 (1968).

473. McClintock, F. A., "A criterion for ductile fracture by the growth of holes". *Trans. ASME, J. Appl. Mechs.* 35, 363 (1968).

474. Wilshaw, T. R., Rau, C. A. and Tetelman, A. S., "A general model to predict the elastic-plastic stress distribution and fracture strength of notched bars in plane strain bending". *Engng. Fracture Mech.* 1, 191 (1968).

475. Rice, J. R. and Rosengren, G. F., "Plane strain deformation near a crack tip in a power-law hardening material". *J. Mech. Phys. Solids*, 16, 1 (1968).

476. Hutchinson, J. W., "Plastic stress and strain fields at a crack tip". *J. Mech. Phys. Solids*, 16, 337 (1968).

477. Neimark, J. E., "The fully plastic plane strain tension or a notched bar". *Trans. ASME, J. Appl. Mech.* 35, 111 (1968).

478. Rice, J. R., "The elastic-plastic mechanics of crack tension". *Int. J. Fracture Mech.* 4, 41 (1968).

479. Rice, J. R., "A path independent integral and approximate analysis on strain concentration by notches and cracks". *Trans. ASME, J. Appl. Mech.* 35, 379 (1968).

480. Liebowitz, H. (Ed.), *Fracture: An Advanced Treatise*, 7 volumes. Academic Press, N. Y. (1968-1972).

481. Rice, J. R. and Tracey, D. M., "On the ductile enlargement of voids in triaxial stress field models". *J. Mech. Phys. Solids*, 17, 201 (1959).

482. Rice, J. R. and Johnson, M. A., in *Inelastic Behaviour of Solids* (edited by M. F. Kanninen *et al.*), 641. McGraw-Hill (1970).

483. Knott, J. F., "Mechanics and mechanisms of large-scale brittle fracture in structural metals". *Mats. Sci. Engng.* 7, 1 (1971).

484. Sih, G. C. (Ed.), *Mechanics of Fracture*, Vols. 1-5. Noordhoff Int. Pub. (1973-78).

485. Knott, J. F., *Fundamentals of Fracture Mechanics*. Butterworths (1973).

486. Sih, G. C. and Chow, C. L. (Eds.), *Fracture Mechanics and Technology*, Vols. 1 and 2. Sijthoff and Noordhoff (1977).

487. McMeeking, R. M., "Finite deformation analysis of crack tip opening in elastic-plastic materials and implications for fracture". *J. Mechs. Phys. Solids*, 25, 357 (1977).

488. Norris, D. M., Reaugh, J. E., Moran, B. and Quinones, D. F., "A plastic-strain, mean stress criterion for ductile fracture". *Trans. ASME, J. Eng. Mats. Tech.* 100H, 279 (1978).

489. Rice, J. R. and Sorensen, E. P., "Continuing crack-tip deformation and fracture for plane-strain crack growth in elastic-plastic solids". *J. Mech. Phys. Solids*, 26, 163 (1978).

490. Caddell, R. M., *Deformation and Fracture of Solids*. Prentice-Hall (1980).

Bending

491. Green, A. P., "Plastic yielding of notched bars due to bending". *Q. J. Mech. Appl. Math.* 6, 223 (1953).

492. Green, A. P., "A theory of plastic yielding due to the bending of cantilever and fixed-ended beams - Part I". *J. Mech. Phys. Solids*, 3, 1 (1954).

493. Green, A. P.,"A theory of plastic yielding due to bending of cantilevers and beams - Part II". *J. Mech. Phys. Solids*, 3, 143 (1954).

494. Hundy, B. B., "Plane plasticity". *Metallurgia*, 49, 109 (1954).

495. Onat, E. T. and Shield, R. T., "The influence of shearing forces on the plastic bending of wide beams". *Proc. 2nd U.S. Nat. Cong. Appl. Mechs.* 535. Ann Arbor, Michigan, 1954. A.S.M.E. (1955).

496. Green, A. P., "The plastic yielding of shallow notched bars due to bending". *J. Mech. Phys. Solids*, 4, 259 (1956).

497. Green, A. P. and Hundy, B. B., "Initial plastic yielding in notch bend tests". *J. Mech. Phys. Solids*, 4, 128 (1956).

498. Freiberger, W., "Plastic flow in a beam compressed by three dies". Aero. Res. Labs., Melbourne, Australia, SM Rep. No. 229, 7 (July 1955).

499. Drucker, D. C., "The effect of shear on the plastic bending of beams". *Trans. ASME, J. Appl. Mech.* 23, 509 (1956).

500. Lianis, G. and Ford, H., "Plastic yielding of single notched bars due to bending". *J. Mech. Phys. Solids*, 7, 1 (1958).

501. Lianis, G., "The plastic yielding of double notched bars due to pure bending". *Ingegneri Archit. Costr.* 29, 55 (1960).

502. Neal, B. G., "The effect of shear and normal forces on the fully plastic moment of beams of rectangular cross-section". Brown Univ. Div., Appl. Maths., TR.11 (Contract N-189 (181) -49518-A(X) (1960)).

503. Johnson, W., "A note on calculating the collapse load for knee frames". *Appl. Scient. Res.*, Series A, 11, 318 (1961).

504. Ball, R. E. and Lee, S. L., "On the effect of surface load upon the plastic yielding of simply supported beams". *J. Mech. Phys. Solids*, 10, 151 (1962).

505. Alexander, J. M. and Komoly, T. J., "On the yielding of a rigid/plastic bar with an Izod notch". *J. Mech. Phys. Solids*, 10, 265 (1962).

506. Wilshaw, T. R. and Pratt, P. L., "On the plastic deformation of Charpy specimens prior to general yield". *J. Mech. Phys. Solids*, 14, 7 (1966).

507. Shindo, A. and So, T., "Initial plastic yielding of a notched bar due to bending". *Proc. 16th Japan Congr. Appl. Mech.* 194 (1966).

508. Johnson, W. and Sowerby, R., "On the collapse load of some simple structures". *Int. J. Mech. Sci.* 9, 433 (1967).

509. Anderson, C. and Shield, R. T., "A class of complete solutions for bending of perfectly plastic beams". *Int. J. Solids Structures*, 3, 935 (1967).

510. Ewing, D. J. F., "Calculations on the bending of rigid/plastic notched bars". *J. Mech. Phys. Solids*, 16, 205 (1968).

511. Ewing, D. J. F. and Griffiths, J. R., "The applicability of slip-line field theory to contained elastic-plastic flow around a notch". *J. Mech. Phys. Solids*, 19, 389 (1971).

512. Shindo, A. and Tomita, Y., "Slip-line Eifle solution of shallow notched bar due to three point loading. (The case of shallow notch depth)". *Bull. JSME*, 15, 11 (1972).

513. Ranshi, A. S., Chitkara, N. R. and Johnson, W., "Plane strain plastic yielding due to bending of end-loaded cantilevers containing circular, triangular or diamond shaped holes". *Int. J. Mech. Sci.* 15, 329 (1973).

514. Ranshi, A. S., Chitkara, N. R. and Johnson, W., "Limit loads for the plastic bending in plane strain of cantilevers containing rectangular holes under end shear". *Int. J. Mech. Sci.* 15, 15 (1973).

515. Shiratori, M. and Dodd, B., "The plane strain general yielding of notched members due to combined axial force and bending - I. Wedge shaped notches with large flank angles". *Int. J. Mech. Sci.* 20, 451 (1978).

516. Dodd, B. and Shiratori, M., "The plane strain general yielding of notched members due to combined axial force and bending - II. Deep circular notches". *Int. J. Mech. Sci.* 20, 465 (1978).

517. Shiratori, M. and Dodd, B., "Effect of deep wedge shaped notches of small flank angle on plastic failure". *Int. J. Mech. Sci.* 22, 127 (1980).

518. Shiratori, M. and Dodd, B., "The plane strain general yielding of notched members due to combined axial force and bending - III. Comparison of theory with experiment". *Int. J. Mech. Sci.* 22, 431 (1980).

Rolling

519. Alexander, J. M., "A slip line field for the hot rolling process". *Proc. Inst. Mech. Engrs.* 169, 1021 (1955).

520. Sansome, D. H. and Lloyd, H. K., "An investigation of the Pilger process by plane strain analogue". *J. Mech. Engng. Sci.* 2, 359 (1960).

521. Tselikov, A. I. *et al.*, "The theory of transverse cold rolling in three roll mills". *Russian Engng. J.* 41, 7 (1961).

522. Milson, B. E. and Alexander, J. M., "An experimental determination of detailed distortion in hot rolling". *J. Mech. Phys. Solids*, 9, 105 (1961).

523. Yajnik, K. S. and Frisch, J., "Strain rate distribution during experimental metal rolling". *Trans. ASME, J. Engng. Ind.* 84B, 81 (1962).

524. Ford, H. and Alexander, J. M., "Simplified hot rolling calculations". *J. Inst. Metals*, 92, 397 (1963-64).

525. Alexander, J. M. and Ford, H., "Limit analysis of hot rolling". *Progress in Applied Mechanics: The Prager Anniversary Volume*, 191. Collier-Macmillan, London (1963).

526. Johnson, W., "An approximate treatment of metal deformation in rolling contact and rotary forming". *Int. J. Prod. Engng. Res.* 3, 51 (1964).

527. Johnson, W. and Chitkara, N. R., "Some results for rolling with circular and polygonal rolls". *Proc. 5th M.T.D.R. Conf.* 391. Univ. Birmingham, 1964. Pergamon Press (1965).

528. Firbank, T. C. and Lancaster, P. R., "A suggested slip line field for cold rolling with slipping friction". *Int. J. Mech. Sci.* 7, 847 (1965).

529. Firbank, T. C. and Lancaster, P. R., "On some aspects of the cold rolling problem". *Int. J. Mech. Sci.* **8**, 653 (1966).

530. Firbank, T. C. and Lancaster, P. R., "A proposed slip line field for lubricated cold rolling". *Int. J. Mech. Sci.* **9**, 65 (1967).

531. Marshall, E. A., "Rolling contact with plastic deformation". *J. Mech. Phys. Solids,* **16**, 243 (1968).

532. Crane, F. A. A. and Alexander, J. M., "Slip line fields and deformation in hot rolling of strip". *J. Inst. Metals,* **96**, 289 (1968).

533. Druyanov, B. A., "Sheet rolling under maximum friction conditions", in *Plastic Flow of Metals,* Vol. 1 (edited by A. D. Tomlenov), 80. (Translated from Russian). Consultants Bureau, N. Y. (1971).

534. Collins, I. F., "A simplified analysis of the rolling of a cylinder on a rigid/perfectly plastic half-space". *Int. J. Mech. Sci.* **14**, 1 (1972).

535. Dewhurst, P., Collins, I. F. and Johnson, W., "A class of slip line field solutions for the hot rolling of strip". *J. Mech. Engng. Sci.* **15**, 439 (1973).

Blanking, Shearing and Surface Asperities

536. Green, A. P., "The plastic yielding of metal junctions due to combined shear and pressure". *J. Mech. Phys. Solids,* **2**, 197 (1954).

537. Green, A. P., "Friction between lubricated metals: a theoretical analysis of junction models". *Proc. R. Soc.,* A, **228**, 191 (1955).

538. Maeda, T., "Theory of the shearing mechanism for sheet metals with punch and die" (in Japanese). *J. Soc. Precis. Mech.* **25**, 248 (1959).

539. Jimma, T., "Theoretical research on the blanking of sheet material". *Bull. JSME,* **6**, 568 (1963).

540. Kudo, H., "A note on the role of microscopically trapped lubricant at the tool work interface". *Int. J. Mech. Sci.* **7**, 383 (1965).

541. Masuda, M., Jimma, T. and Yammauchi, S., "Research on shaving mechanisms of sheet metal with punch and die". *Bull. JSME,* **9**, 224 (1966).

542. Edwards, C. M. and Halling, J., "An analysis of the plastic interaction of surface asperities and its relevance to the value of the coefficient of friction". *J. Mech. Engng. Sci.* **10**, 101 (1968).

543. Kasuga, Y., Tsutsumi, S. and Mori, T., "On the shearing process of ductile sheet metals - I". *Bull. JSME,* **20**, 1329 (1977).

544. Kasuga, Y., Tsutsumi, S. and Mori, T., "On the shearing process of ductile sheet metals - II". *Bull. JSME,* **20**, 1336 (1977).

545. Wanheim, T. and Bay, N., "A model for friction in metal forming". *Annals CIRP,* **28**, 189 (1978).

CHAPTER 6

Matrix-operator Methods for Solving Plane-strain Slip-line Field Problems

INTRODUCTION

In Chapters 4 and 5 reference was made to slip-line-field solutions which were either of the "direct type" or the "indirect type". This categorization is not intended to be rigid, but it can be loosely interpreted as follows. In the development of a new slip-line-field solution none of the slip lines will have a pre-defined or known shape. This difficulty can be partially overcome by examining existing solutions which provide some guidance in the construction of the possible field when considered in conjunction with a suitable interpretation of the boundary conditions as they apply to the problem under investigation. In the very simplest cases it is possible that a family of slip lines can be defined which are straight and such that the remainder of the slip-line field can be constructed in a straightforward step-by-step manner by working outwards from either a known constant state (a straight line cross-patch) or from a centred fan zone. Solutions which can be constructed directly from some knowledge of a region within the slip-line field ascertained from either the physical or velocity planes are referred to as "direct type" solutions.

When sufficient details pertaining to the shape of a number of the slip lines is not available, the complete slip-line field cannot be directly constructed as described above. The solution to this "indirect" type of problem can, however, be accomplished as a result of the mathematical formulations of the problem recently developed by Collins and Dewhurst and which are referred to as the *matrix operator methods*. For further clarification of the "direct" and "indirect" type solutions see also references 1 and 2 in which some categorization of the earlier work of Hill,[3] Green,[4] Alexander[5] and others[6-10] is provided.

Until recently, slip-line fields were constructed step-by-step from some initial known slip line using the approaches described by Hill and detailed in Chapter 4. If the boundary conditions were such that the shape of an initial slip line could not be defined, a trial-and-error procedure had to be followed to determine the shape of the initial slip line from whence the complete slip-line field could be constructed. This required a substantial computational effort and tended to detract from the usefulness of the slip-line-field method. As examples the reader is referred to the hot rolling solution by Alexander[5] in which Prager's graphical technique[7] was employed and the finite difference solutions for compression and strip drawing developed by Green.[4]

In 1967 Ewing[11] proposed a series method for constructing slip-line fields. In this approach, the radius of curvature of a **slip** line is expressed as a uniformly convergent double-power series and starting from two orthogonal slip-line field segments, the remainder of the field could be determined from this series representation. With this method, the inherent errors of the finite difference approximations are reduced; the only errors are those associated with series truncation error which can be made very small indeed. While the thrust of Ewing's work was directed towards simplifying computational methods for direct-type solutions, it afforded a convenient means, as shown by Collins and Dewhurst,[12,13] by which a slip line could be represented as a column vector of the coefficients in the series expansion of its radius of curvature. Further development by Collins, [12,14,15] in which a system of matrix operators were defined, enabled the geometric formulation of the superposition principle for slip-line fields discussed by Hill[16] to be described in the context of simple linear algebraic expressions. This matrix-operator method is particularly suited to solving problems of the "indirect type" since, by using the matrix-operators, relations can be established within the field such that the problem of determining an unknown initial slip line reduces to a simple matrix inversion.

In this chapter the matrix-operator method is presented in detail. While the method is applicable to both "direct" and "indirect" type solutions, the examples presented in this chapter will initially focus on the "direct" type solutions before examining solutions of the "indirect" type. By presenting the method in this way it is anticipated that a better understanding of the method might be obtained.

GOVERNING EQUATIONS IN SLIP-LINE-FIELD THEORY

For plane-strain conditions the equations for stress and velocity fields in the deforming regions of a non-hardening rigid plastic material are hyperbolic in nature. The characteristics define the trajectories of maximum shear strain rate and hence maximum shear stress - the slip lines - and form an orthogonal Hencky-Prandtl net of α- and β-lines as shown in Fig. 6.1. Any point, P, within the net can be defined either in terms of Cartesian coordinates (x,y) or characteristic or curvilinear coordinates (α,β). With curvilinear axes OA (an α-line) and OB (a β-line), the value of ϕ at P, where $\phi = \alpha + \beta$, is defined as the angle between the α direction at O and the α direction at P, measured anticlockwise. The coordinates (α,β) at P are defined as (α_3, β_2) where α_3 is the value of ϕ at the point where the β-line through P intersects the α base line OA, and β_2 is the value of ϕ at the point where the α-line through P intersects the β base line OB. Hence α is constant along a β-line and β is constant along an α-line.

It is convenient to represent the slip lines either by their radii of curvature R, S or by "moving coordinates".

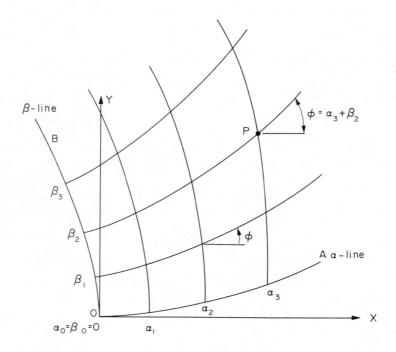

Fig. 6.1.   Hencky-Prandtl net of α- and β-lines.

(i)   Radii of Curvature

The radii of curvature for α- and β-lines represented by R and S
respectively are defined by

$$\frac{1}{R} = \frac{d\phi}{ds_\alpha} = \frac{d\alpha}{ds_\alpha} \qquad \text{along an α-line}$$

(6.1)

and

$$\frac{1}{S} = -\frac{d\phi}{ds_\beta} = -\frac{d\beta}{ds_\beta} \quad \text{along a β-line,}$$

where ds_α and ds_β are differentials of the arc lengths measured along
the α- and β-curves respectively, their sense being such that they
they define a right-handed pair of curvilinear axes as shown in Fig.
6.2.   Both S and R are positive for the curvatures shown.   This
occurs as $d\beta$ would now be negative as a result of the clockwise
rotation in moving through the arc length ds_β.

Furthermore, as has been shown previously in Chapter 3 with the proof
of Hencky's second theorem, the equations for the radius of curvature
are

$$dS + Rd\phi = 0, \quad \text{along an α-line}$$

(6.2)

and

$$dR - Sd\phi = 0, \quad \text{along a β-line.}$$

162

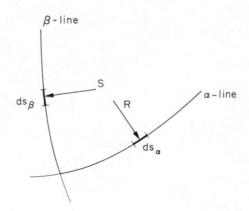

Fig. 6.2.   Definitions associated with two intersecting slip lines.

Since $d\phi = d\alpha$ along an α-line, and $d\phi = d\beta$ along a β-line, (6.2) can
be written as

$$\frac{\partial S}{\partial \alpha} + R = 0$$

$$\frac{\partial R}{\partial \beta} - S = 0.$$

and   (6.3)

Hencky's second theorem shows that in moving along a given slip line
the radius of curvature of the intersecting slip lines of the other
family change by an amount equal to the distance travelled.

(ii)   <u>Moving Coordinates</u>

The "moving coordinates" $\bar{x}$ and $\bar{y}$, often referred to as Mikhlin
coordinates, are defined by the following equations:

$$\bar{x} = x \cos \phi + y \sin \phi$$

$$\bar{y} = -x \sin \phi + y \cos \phi.$$

and   (6.4)

$\bar{x}$ and $\bar{y}$ represent the coordinates of the point P shown in Fig. 6.3
with reference to axes passing through the origin O and orientated
parallel to the slip line directions at point P.   The respective
variation of $\bar{x}$ and $\bar{y}$ along a β- and an α-line are given by

$$d\bar{x} = (\cos \phi \, dx + \sin \phi \, dy) + (-x \sin \phi + y \cos \phi)d\phi$$

$$d\bar{y} = (-\sin \phi \, dx + \cos \phi \, dy) - (x \cos \phi + y \sin \phi)d\phi.$$

and   (6.5)

However, $dy = \tan \phi \, dx$, along an α-line and $dy = -\cot \phi \, dx$ along a β-

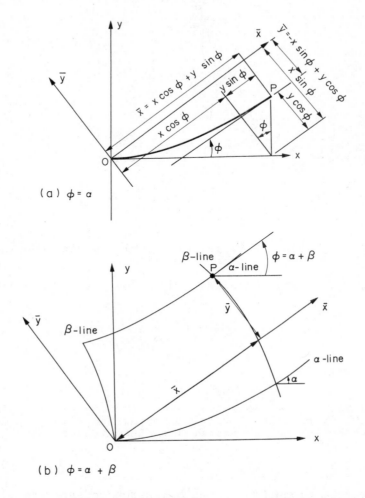

Fig. 6.3. Definition of Mikhlin or moving coordinates.

line, so that

$$d\bar{y} + \bar{x}\, d\phi = 0, \quad \text{along an } \alpha\text{-line}$$

and
$$d\bar{x} - \bar{y}\, d\phi = 0, \quad \text{along a } \beta\text{-line.} \tag{6.6}$$

Furthermore, $d\phi = d\alpha$ along an α-line and $d\phi = d\beta$ along a β-line. Hence,

$$\frac{\partial \bar{y}}{\partial \alpha} + \bar{x} = 0$$

and
$$\frac{\partial \bar{x}}{\partial \beta} - \bar{y} = 0. \tag{6.7}$$

(iii) Velocity Equations

At this point it is useful to re-introduce the velocity or Geiringer equations which are given by (3.10) as

$$du - vd\phi = 0, \quad \text{along an } \alpha\text{-line}$$

and

$$dv + ud\phi = 0, \quad \text{along a } \beta\text{-line.}$$

Since $\qquad d\phi = d\alpha$ along an α-line and $d\phi = d\beta$ along a β-line,

$$\frac{\partial u}{\partial \alpha} - v = 0, \quad \text{along an } \alpha\text{-line}$$

$$\tag{6.8}$$

and $\qquad\qquad \dfrac{\partial v}{\partial \beta} + u = 0, \quad \text{along a } \beta\text{-line.}$

Equations (6.3), (6.7) and (6.8) can be summarized as follows:

$$\frac{\partial^2 R}{\partial \alpha \partial \beta} = \frac{\partial S}{\partial \alpha} = -R \quad \text{and} \quad \frac{\partial^2 S}{\partial \alpha \partial \beta} = -\frac{\partial R}{\partial \beta} = -S, \tag{6.9a}$$

$$\frac{\partial^2 \bar{x}}{\partial \alpha \partial \beta} = \frac{\partial \bar{y}}{\partial \alpha} = -\bar{x} \quad \text{and} \quad \frac{\partial^2 \bar{y}}{\partial \alpha \partial \beta} = -\frac{\partial \bar{x}}{\partial \beta} = -\bar{y}, \tag{6.9b}$$

and

$$\frac{\partial^2 u}{\partial \alpha \partial \beta} = \frac{\partial v}{\partial \beta} = -u \quad \text{and} \quad \frac{\partial^2 v}{\partial \alpha \partial \beta} = -\frac{\partial u}{\partial \alpha} = -v. \tag{6.9c}$$

All these functional pairs (R, S), $(\bar{x}, \bar{y})$ and (u, v) satisfy the same hyperbolic system of linear partial differential equations which are of the type

$$\frac{\partial g}{\partial \alpha} = -f \quad \text{and} \quad \frac{\partial f}{\partial \beta} = g, \tag{6.10}$$

where both g and f separately satisfy the "equation of telegraphy", i.e.

$$\frac{\partial^2 f}{\partial \alpha \partial \beta} + f = 0$$

and

$$\frac{\partial^2 g}{\partial \alpha \partial \beta} + g = 0.$$

As a result of the linearity of the governing equations given by (6.10), slip-line fields are subject to the principles of superposition. A systematic investigation of the consequences of these properties was first demonstrated geometrically by Hill[16] who showed that any two Hencky-Prandtl nets can be combined to develop a third net by the addition or subtraction of position vectors to points having the same coordinate values (α, β). Collins[12] has provided an alternative algebraic formulation of this superposition principle by considering each slip line in the physical plane to be represented as an element of an infinite dimensional linear vector space. The slip lines are characterized in terms of their radii of curvature, but could equally well have been represented in terms of the "moving" coordinates as a result of the linearity of the governing equations, see (6.9a), (6.9b) and (6.10). Similarly, since the velocity components along a slip line satisfy (6.10), all properties associated with the physical plane are directly applicable to the velocity plane (hodograph) which also forms a Hencky-Prandtl net. Details of both the geometric and algebraic formulations are provided in Refs. 12 and 16.

The algebraic approach is particularly significant since it affords a means by which the construction of further slip lines can be generated from a given slip line. These constructions are represented by linear operators defined in an abstract linear vector space and consequently lead to the entirely new computational method for slip-line field construction which is referred to as the matrix-operator method. In summary, if a slip line is represented by a finite dimensional column vector, characterized by its radius of curvature, and the linear operators are characterized by square matrices, then the construction of complete slip-line fields reduces to a problem of matrix algebra.[13]

In the following sections the method of solution will be detailed. The column vector representation of the slip line will be presented and a series of matrix operators will be defined such that a working knowledge of the method can be obtained.[17] Subroutines of all matrix-operators are provided such that a convenient computational system is developed by which the slip-line fields can be generated and load requirements evaluated. Initially all examples will relate to problems of the "direct" type prior to investigating the more advantageous potential of the method for solving "indirect" problems.

SERIES EXPANSION FOR RADII OF CURVATURE

(i)   Definitions: Radius of Curvature, Base Point, Intrinsic Direction

To represent the radius of curvature of the slip lines as a series expansion it is convenient to introduce a different, and probably simpler, sign convention for both the radius of curvature and the angle through which a slip line rotates. The definition used differs from that previously given but leads directly to a numerical technique for constructing slip line fields which is independent of whether or not a slip line is an α- or a β-line.

With reference to Fig. 6.4 the following definitions, which relate to the notation to be employed in the subsequent sections, are required:

   (i)   A *base point* or starting point on the base slip line must be established. In Fig. 6.4, point 0 on the base slip line $0A$ will be defined as the base point.

   (ii)   The *intrinsic direction* is always taken as positive if motion is away from a base point. In Fig. 6.4 the intrinsic direction is therefore from 0 to A and is represented by an arrow along the slip line $0A$.

   (iii) The *inclination of a slip line* is always defined by the tangent to the slip line at its base point. The inclination will always be taken as positive and is independent

166

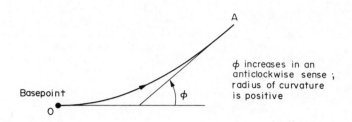

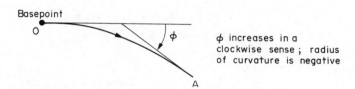

Fig. 6.4. Slip lines showing the base points,
intrinsic direction and sense of
rotation.

of the sense of rotation.

(iv)   The *radius of curvature* of a slip line is defined by

$$\frac{1}{\rho} = \pm \left| \frac{d\phi}{ds} \right| , \qquad (6.11)$$

where ϕ is the inclination of the local tangent to that
at the base point, and ds is the differential of the arc
length. The sign associated with the radius of curvature
is as follows: positive when ϕ increases in an anti-
clockwise sense along the slip line, and negative when ϕ
increases in a clockwise sense along the slip line.

(ii)   Hencky's Second Theorem

For this sign convention Hencky's second theorem, which can be described in terms of a pair of linear differential equations, can be
written as follows for the pair of base slip lines OA and OB shown in
Fig. 6.5. With reference to Fig. 6.5, $\phi = \alpha$ along the α-line OA, and
the inclination of α with respect to the base point O is clockwise
so that R is negative. Similarly along the β-line, OB, $\phi = \beta$, and
the inclination of β with respect to the base point O is anti-clockwise,
so that S is positive. Since $R(\alpha,\psi)$ and $S(\theta,\beta)$ have absolute values
which are greater than $R(\alpha)$ and $S(\beta)$ respectively, but still require
each radius of curvature to have the same sign, i.e. R negative and
S positive, the pair of linear differential equations which describe

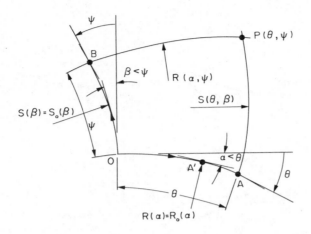

Fig. 6.5. Base slip lines *OA* and *OB* curving away from each other. The base point is *O*. The intrinsic directions are *OA* and *OB*.

Hencky's second theorem are given by

$$\frac{\partial S}{\partial \alpha} = -R \quad \text{and} \quad \frac{\partial R}{\partial \beta} = -S.$$

(6.12)

Similarly, for the pair of slip lines having the curvature shown in Fig. 6.6, R is positive and S is negative such that Hencky's second theorem is written as

$$\frac{\partial S}{\partial \alpha} = R \quad \text{and} \quad \frac{\partial R}{\partial \beta} = S.$$

(6.13)

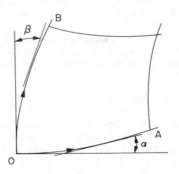

Fig. 6.6. Base slip lines *OA* and *OB* curving towards each other. The base point is *O*. The intrinsic directions are *OA* and *OB*.

A comparison of (6.3), (6.12) and (6.13) indicates that the equations are now in a form which is basically independent of whether an α- or a β-line is being considered.

(iii)   Series Representation of the Radius of Curvature

With reference to Fig. 6.5, the radii of curvature $R_0(\alpha)$ and $S_0(\beta)$ can be expanded as a power series in the angular coordinates α and β respectively as

$$R_0(\alpha) = \sum_{n=0}^{\infty} a_n \frac{\alpha^n}{n!}$$

and

$$S_0(\beta) = \sum_{n=0}^{\infty} b_n \frac{\beta^n}{n!} \ . \qquad (6.14)$$

The subscript zero refers to the base lines OA and OB.

The radius of curvature of each slip line OA and OB changes with progression from the base point O along the slip lines towards either point A or B. In moving from O to A, the value of α increases. The radius of curvature, R, at point A' is given by (6.14), where α now corresponds to the rotation of the tangent at point A' with respect to the tangent at the origin O. Hence,

$$R_0(\alpha) = R_{A'} = \sum_{n=0}^{\infty} a_n \frac{\alpha^n}{n!}$$

which in matrix notation can be written as

$$R_{A'} = \begin{bmatrix} \alpha_0 & \alpha_1 & \alpha_2 & \ldots & \alpha_n \end{bmatrix} \begin{bmatrix} a_0 \\ a_1 \\ a_2 \\ \cdot \\ \cdot \\ \cdot \\ a_n \end{bmatrix} \qquad (6.15)$$

where $\alpha_n = \alpha^n/n!$.

A slip line can therefore be considered to be represented by the column vector of coefficients in its series expansion. This can be written as

$$\chi_{OA} = \begin{bmatrix} a_0 \\ a_1 \\ a_2 \\ \cdot \\ \cdot \\ \cdot \\ a_n \end{bmatrix} \qquad (6.16)$$

where χ_{OA} now describes the particular slip line OA and the ordering

169

of the subscripts *OA* denotes the intrinsic direction, i.e. from base
point *O* to *A*. The column vector of the coefficients of the series
expansion is represented by the symbol χ rather than the symbol σ
which has been used in the literature. (This has been done to avoid
any association with stress which is usually designated by the symbol
σ.) Once the slip line is represented by this format, the radius of
curvature at any point, i.e. *A'* or *A* which is defined in terms of the
angular rotation from the base point to that point, can be obtained
directly.

(iv)   Series Representation of a Circular Arc

As a simple illustration of the column vector representation, consider
the slip line which coincides with the circumference of a circular arc
of unit radius as shown in Fig. 6.7(a).

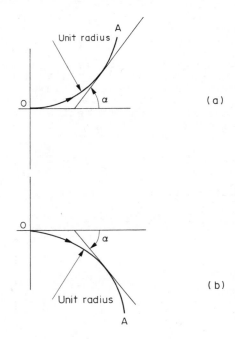

Fig. 6.7.   Positive and negative curvature for a
circular arc of unit radius.

Since the radius of curvature is constant for any value of α, the
column vector is directly given by

$$\chi_{OA} = \begin{bmatrix} 1 \\ 0 \\ 0 \\ 0 \\ 0 \\ 0 \end{bmatrix} = c.$$

From (6.15) the radius of curvature is equal to unity for all α, for $a_0 = 1$ and $a_{1,n} = 0$.

When the rotation of the slip line from the base point is in the opposite sense as shown in Fig. 6.7(b), the radius of the curvature is defined as negative, and the column vector can now accommodate this change as

$$\chi_{OA} = \begin{bmatrix} -1 \\ 0 \\ 0 \\ 0 \\ 0 \\ 0 \end{bmatrix} = -c.$$

For practical purposes, as will be shown later, the number of elements, $(n+1)$, in a column vector is usually restricted to six. However, in certain problems where the range of the slip line is large it might be necessary to increase this value to obtain an improved accuracy.[18]

(v)   Generalized radius of Curvature at a Point

It can be shown[11],[13] that the radii of curvature for the α- and β-lines through point P as shown in Fig. 6.5 are given by

$$\left. \begin{aligned} R(\alpha,\psi) &= \sum_{n=0}^{\infty} r_n(\psi) \frac{\alpha^n}{n!} \\[2em] S(\theta,\beta) &= \sum_{n=0}^{\infty} s_n(\theta) \frac{\beta^n}{n!} \end{aligned} \right\} \tag{6.17}$$

and

Note that the form of these equations is identical to that given by (6.14), where $r_n(\psi)$ and $s_n(\theta)$ are defined by

$$\left. \begin{aligned} r_n(\psi) &= \sum_{m=0}^{n} a_{n-m} \frac{\psi^m}{m!} - \sum_{m=n+1}^{\infty} b_{m-n-1} \frac{\psi^m}{m!} \\[2em] s_n(\theta) &= \sum_{m=0}^{n} b_{n-m} \frac{\theta^m}{m!} - \sum_{m=n+1}^{\infty} a_{m-n-1} \frac{\theta^m}{m!} \end{aligned} \right\} \tag{6.18}$$

and

These expressions for r_n and s_n were derived by Ewing[11] and Dewhurst and Collins.[13]

Since the radii of curvature of the base lines OA and OB, shown in Fig. 6.5, are given by (6.14), it is indeed possible to represent any other slip line in a similar manner - the only difference being that the coefficients of the column vector would now be changed to represent the new slip line. For the slip line BP in Fig. 6.5 one would anticipate that the coefficients of the column vector representation for this slip line would be a function of the angular coordinate, β, where $\beta = \psi$ for the slip line BP, as well as the coefficients of the base slip lines χ_{OA} and χ_{OB}. This representation is derivable from the solution to (6.12) and given by (6.17). By using the approaches outlined by Ewing,[11] the radii of curvature at the general point

171

$P(\theta,\psi)$ are given by

$$R(\theta,\psi) = \sum_{m,n=0}^{\infty} \left(a_n \frac{\theta^{m+n}}{(m+n)!} \frac{\psi^m}{m!} - b_n \frac{\theta^m}{m!} \frac{\psi^{m+n+1}}{(m+n+1)!} \right)$$

and

$$S(\theta,\psi) = \sum_{m,n=0}^{\infty} \left(-a_n \frac{\theta^{m+n+1}}{(m+n+1)!} \frac{\psi^m}{m!} + b_n \frac{\theta^m}{m!} \frac{\psi^{m+n}}{(m+n)!} \right)$$

(6.19)

Similarly, the radii of curvature of the α- and β-lines through the point $P(\theta,\psi)$ with $0 \leqslant \alpha \leqslant \theta$ and $0 \leqslant \beta \leqslant \psi$, are

$$R(\alpha,\psi) = \sum_{m,n=0}^{\infty} \left(a_n \frac{\alpha^{m+n}}{(m+n)!} \frac{\psi^m}{m!} - b_n \frac{\alpha^m}{m!} \frac{\psi^{m+n+1}}{(m+n+1)!} \right)$$

and

$$S(\theta,\beta) = \sum_{m,n=0}^{\infty} \left(-a_n \frac{\theta^{m+n+1}}{(m+n+1)!} \frac{\beta^m}{m!} + b_n \frac{\theta^m}{m!} \frac{\beta^{m+n}}{(m+n)!} \right),$$

(6.20)

which lead directly to the expressions given by (6.17).

CENTRED FANS AND REGULAR NETS

(i)   Centred Fans

The method by which the above definition of the radii of curvature can be used, is probably best illustrated by reducing the regular net shown in Fig. 6.5 to the more fundamental centred fan shown in Fig. 6.8.   In effect point B has collapsed to point O.   The base slip line is denoted as OA with base point O having an intrinsic direction (shown by the arrow) OA.   The rotation, α, of the tangent to this slip line from the base point to point A is θ, which is referred to as the range of the slip line, i.e. $0 \leqslant \alpha \leqslant \theta$.   The notation is the same as that

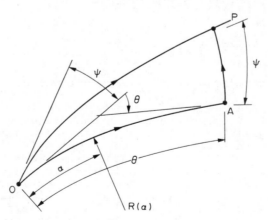

Fig. 6.8.   Centred fan.

172

previously used to describe the regular net. Again, the radius of curvature of the slip line OA is given by the series expansion

$$R(\alpha) = \sum_{n=0}^{\infty} a_n \frac{\alpha^n}{n!} , \tag{6.21}$$

which can be written as

$$R(\alpha) = \begin{matrix} \alpha_0 & \alpha_1 & . & . & . & \alpha_n \end{matrix} \begin{bmatrix} a_0 \\ a_1 \\ . \\ . \\ . \\ a_n \end{bmatrix}$$

where the coefficients of the column vector χ_{OA} are assumed to be known and $\alpha_n = \alpha^n/n!$.

The radii of curvature of the two bounding slip lines of the centred fan field based on OA are given by

$$\left. \begin{aligned} R(\alpha,\psi) &= \sum_{n=0}^{\infty} r_n(\psi) \frac{\alpha^n}{n!} \\[2mm] S(\theta,\beta) &= \sum_{n=0}^{\infty} s_n(\theta) \frac{\beta^n}{n!} , \end{aligned} \right\} \tag{6.22}$$

and

where r_n and s_n for the centred fan field are given by (6.18) as

$$\left. \begin{aligned} r_n(\psi) &= \sum_{m=0}^{\infty} a_{n-m} \frac{\psi^m}{m!} \\[2mm] s_n(\theta) &= - \sum_{m=n+1}^{\infty} a_{m-n-1} \frac{\theta^m}{m!} . \end{aligned} \right\} \tag{6.23}$$

and

Since O is the base point, the inclination increases from O to A and the intrinsic direction is OA. Similarly, since the same angular coordinates are used, the inclination increases from A to P and from O to P; the intrinsic directions are as shown in Fig. 6.8. Following the matrix representation of the slip line shown previously it follows that

$$\chi_{OA} = \begin{bmatrix} a_0 \\ a_1 \\ a_2 \\ . \\ . \\ . \\ a_n \end{bmatrix} . \text{ Also } \chi_{OP} = \begin{bmatrix} r_0 \\ r_1 \\ r_2 \\ r_3 \\ . \\ . \\ r_n \end{bmatrix} \text{ and } \chi_{AP} = \begin{bmatrix} s_0 \\ s_1 \\ . \\ . \\ . \\ s_n \end{bmatrix} . \tag{6.24}$$

173

The coefficients $r_n(\psi)$ and $s_n(\theta)$, which are required to evaluate $R(\alpha,\psi)$ and $S(\theta,\beta)$ respectively, can be expanded and given a matrix representation. This is illustrated below using (6.23) for the $r_n(\psi)$ coefficients as

$$\chi_{OP} = \begin{bmatrix} r_0 \\ r_1 \\ r_2 \\ \cdot \\ \cdot \\ r_n \end{bmatrix} = \begin{bmatrix} a_0 \psi_0 \\ a_1 \psi_0 + a_0 \psi_1 \\ a_2 \psi_0 + a_1 \psi_1 + a_0 \psi_2 \\ \\ \sum_{m=0}^{n} a_{n-m} \psi_m \end{bmatrix} , \qquad (6.25)$$

where $\psi_m = \psi^m/m!$. Equation (6.25) can now be conveniently rewritten such that the known coefficients, a_n, of the slip line OA are again represented as a column vector, and

$$\chi_{OP} = \begin{bmatrix} \psi_0 & 0 & 0 & 0 & 0 & \cdot \\ \psi_1 & \psi_0 & 0 & 0 & 0 & \cdot \\ \psi_2 & \psi_1 & \psi_0 & 0 & 0 & \cdot \\ \cdot & \cdot & & & & \\ \cdot & \cdot & & & & \\ \psi_n & & & & & \end{bmatrix} \begin{bmatrix} a_0 \\ a_1 \\ a_2 \\ \cdot \\ \cdot \\ \cdot \end{bmatrix} .$$

The slip line χ_{OP} can be expressed as a function of ψ (now formulated as a square matrix operator) and χ_{OA} (the base slip line OA).

Hence,

$$\chi_{OP} = P_{\psi}^{*} \, \chi_{OA} \qquad (6.26)$$

where

$$P_{\psi}^{*} = \begin{bmatrix} \psi_0 & 0 & 0 & 0 & 0 & \cdot \\ \psi_1 & \psi_0 & 0 & 0 & 0 & \cdot \\ \psi_2 & \psi_1 & \psi_0 & 0 & 0 & \cdot \\ \cdot & & & & & \\ \cdot & & & & & \\ \psi_n & & & & & \end{bmatrix}$$

and as before $\psi_m = \psi^m/m!$.

This is a significant result and should be clearly understood. Equation (6.26) implies that for a given slip line OA, denoted by χ_{OA},

174

it is possible to obtain directly the coefficients of the column vector x_{OP} of the slip line OP constructed on the convex side of the base line OA by simply multiplying the column vector x_{OA} by an operator P_ψ^* for a known range ψ.

When the $s_n(\theta)$ coefficients are manipulated in the same way the slip line AP can be expressed in terms of x_{OA} as

$$x_{AP} = Q_\theta^* \, x_{OA} \, , \qquad\qquad (6.27)$$

where

$$Q_\theta^* = - \begin{bmatrix} \theta_1 & \theta_2 & \theta_3 & \cdot & \cdot & \cdot \\ \theta_2 & \theta_3 & \theta_4 & \cdot & \cdot & \cdot \\ \theta_3 & \theta_4 & \theta_5 & \cdot & \cdot & \cdot \\ \cdot & \cdot & \cdot & \cdot & \cdot & \cdot \\ \cdot & \cdot & \cdot & \cdot & \cdot & \cdot \\ \theta_n & \cdot & \cdot & \cdot & \cdot & \cdot \end{bmatrix} \qquad \theta_m = \frac{\theta^m}{m!} \;\; ?$$

Once x_{AP} and x_{OP} are known the radius of curvature at any point along these lines can be evaluated.

$$\left.\begin{matrix} x_{AP} \\ x_{op} \end{matrix}\right\} \to \left.\begin{matrix} r_o \\ s_o \end{matrix}\right\} \to E(6.22) \to \begin{matrix} R(\alpha, \psi) \\ S(\theta, \beta) \end{matrix}$$

(ii)   Regular Nets

The method shown for the centred fan can be directly applied to develop a regular net once two initial base slip lines are defined. Figure 6.9 shows two base slip lines OA and OB of a regular net. x_{OA} and x_{OB}

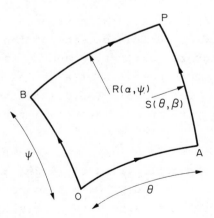

Fig. 6.9.   Regular net.

are assumed to be known. To evaluate the radii of curvature $R(\alpha,\psi)$ and $S(\theta,\beta)$ the column vectors χ_{BP} and χ_{AP} are required. From (6.18), the column vector χ_{BP} can be developed as shown below.

$$
\chi_{BP} = r_n(\psi) =
\begin{bmatrix}
r_0 \\
r_1 \\
r_2 \\
r_3 \\
r_4 \\
\cdot
\end{bmatrix}
=
\begin{bmatrix}
a_0\psi_0 \\
a_1\psi_1 + a_0\psi_1 \\
a_2\psi_0 + a_1\psi_1 + a_0\psi_2 \\
\cdot \\
\cdot \\
\cdot
\end{bmatrix}
-
\begin{bmatrix}
b_0\psi_1 + b_1\psi_2 + \\
b_0\psi_2 + b_1\psi_3 + \\
b_0\psi_3 + b_1\psi_4 + \\
\cdot \\
\cdot \\
\cdot
\end{bmatrix}
$$

$$(6.28)$$

$$
=
\begin{bmatrix}
\psi_0 & 0 & 0 & \cdot & \cdot & \cdot \\
\psi_1 & \psi_0 & 0 & \cdot & \cdot & \cdot \\
\psi_2 & \psi_1 & \psi_0 & \cdot & \cdot & \cdot \\
\cdot & \cdot & \cdot & \cdot & \cdot & \cdot \\
\cdot & \cdot & \cdot & \cdot & \cdot & \cdot
\end{bmatrix}
\begin{bmatrix}
a_0 \\
a_1 \\
a_2 \\
a_3 \\
\cdot \\
\cdot
\end{bmatrix}
-
\begin{bmatrix}
\psi_1 & \psi_2 & \psi_3 & \cdot & \cdot & \cdot \\
\psi_2 & \psi_3 & \psi_4 & \cdot & \cdot & \cdot \\
\psi_3 & \psi_4 & \psi_5 & \cdot & \cdot & \cdot \\
\cdot & \cdot & \cdot & \cdot & \cdot & \cdot \\
\cdot & \cdot & \cdot & \cdot & \cdot & \cdot
\end{bmatrix}
\begin{bmatrix}
b_0 \\
b_1 \\
b_2 \\
b_3 \\
\cdot \\
\cdot
\end{bmatrix}
$$

The square matrix operators in (6.28) have been previously defined as P^*_ψ and Q^*_ψ respectively so that

$$\chi_{BP} = P^*_\psi \chi_{OA} + Q^*_\psi \chi_{OB}. \qquad (6.29)$$

Similarly by expanding $s_n(\theta)$,

$$\chi_{AP} = P^*_\theta \chi_{OB} + Q^*_\theta \chi_{OA}. \qquad (6.30)$$

For both the centred fan and the regular nets, the column vectors for the slip lines constructed on the convex side of the base lines can be obtained directly. The square matrices P^* and Q^* are designated operators. These are but two operators of a series of such operators which subsequently will be developed. The use of these operators has become accepted as the matrix operator technique for slip-line-field construction.

A simple illustration of the application of (6.29) and (6.30) follows. Consider two base slip lines OA and OB with base point O as shown in Fig. 6.10. For the purpose of illustration, the slip lines are chosen such that their curvature coincides with the circumference of a circle of unit radius. The respective column vectors are given by

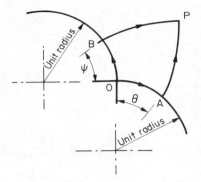

Fig. 6.10. Regular net with base lines OA and OB having unit radii.

$$\chi_{OA} = \begin{bmatrix} -1 \\ 0 \\ 0 \\ 0 \\ 0 \\ \cdot \end{bmatrix} \text{ and } \chi_{OB} = \begin{bmatrix} 1 \\ 0 \\ 0 \\ 0 \\ 0 \\ \cdot \end{bmatrix} .$$

From (6.29) and (6.30)

$$\chi_{BP} = P^*_\psi \, \chi_{OA} + Q^*_\psi \, \chi_{OB}$$

and

$$\chi_{AP} = P^*_\theta \, \chi_{OB} + Q^*_\theta \, \chi_{OA} .$$

Hence,

$$\chi_{BP} = \begin{bmatrix} \psi_0 & 0 & 0 & 0 & \cdot & \cdot \\ \psi_1 & \psi_0 & 0 & 0 & \cdot & \cdot \\ \psi_2 & \psi_1 & \psi_0 & 0 & \cdot & \cdot \\ \cdot & \cdot & \cdot & \cdot & \cdot & \cdot \\ \cdot & \cdot & \cdot & \cdot & \cdot & \cdot \\ \cdot & \cdot & \cdot & \cdot & \cdot & \cdot \end{bmatrix} \begin{bmatrix} -1 \\ 0 \\ 0 \\ 0 \\ 0 \\ \cdot \end{bmatrix} - \begin{bmatrix} \psi_1 & \psi_2 & \psi_3 & \cdot & \cdot & \cdot \\ \psi_2 & \psi_3 & \psi_4 & \cdot & \cdot & \cdot \\ \psi_3 & \psi_4 & \psi_5 & \cdot & \cdot & \cdot \\ \cdot & \cdot & \cdot & \cdot & \cdot & \cdot \\ \cdot & \cdot & \cdot & \cdot & \cdot & \cdot \\ \cdot & \cdot & \cdot & \cdot & \cdot & \cdot \end{bmatrix} \begin{bmatrix} 1 \\ 0 \\ 0 \\ 0 \\ 0 \\ \cdot \end{bmatrix}$$

$$= \begin{bmatrix} -\psi_0 \\ -\psi_1 \\ -\psi_2 \\ \cdot \\ \cdot \\ \cdot \end{bmatrix} - \begin{bmatrix} \psi_1 \\ \psi_2 \\ \psi_3 \\ \cdot \\ \cdot \\ \cdot \end{bmatrix} = - \begin{bmatrix} \psi_0 + \psi_1 \\ \psi_1 + \psi_2 \\ \psi_2 + \psi_3 \\ \cdot \\ \cdot \\ \cdot \end{bmatrix} .$$

177

Similarly,

$$\chi_{AP} = \begin{bmatrix} \theta_0 + \theta_1 \\ \theta_1 + \theta_2 \\ \theta_2 + \theta_3 \\ \cdot \\ \cdot \\ \cdot \end{bmatrix}.$$

(iii) <u>Construction on the Concave Side of the Base Line</u>

Whilst the developments given above have been applied to the construction of slip lines on the convex side of the base lines of the centred fan and the regular net, the operators can also be used to construct the slip lines on the concave side of the base lines. The centred fan shown in Fig. 6.11(a) is identical to that shown in Fig. 6.8 in which

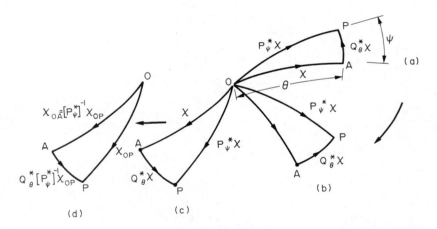

Fig. 6.11. Construction on the concave side of
the base slip line OP.

$\chi = \chi_{OA}$. If the slip line OP is now considered to be the base slip line, the rules for constructing slip lines OA and AP on the concave side of OP can be obtained simply by letting $\chi_{OP} = P_\psi^* \chi$, so that $\chi_{OA} = \chi = [P_\psi^*]^{-1} \chi_{OP}$ and $\chi_{AP} = Q_\theta^* \chi = Q_\theta^* [P_\psi^*]^{-1} \chi_{OP}$. This yields the result shown in Fig. 6.11(d) where the centred fan has simply been rotated about point O (as shown by Figs. 11 (b) and (c)) and the base slip line OP is now defined by the column vector χ_{OP}.

178

MATRIX OPERATORS

In addition to the $P*$ and $Q*$ operators, other operators will now be defined to facilitate the construction of slip-line fields. They will be of significant value in deriving solutions for both the "direct" and "indirect" type problems.

(i)   Reversion Operator, R

As will be observed later, it is often convenient to be able to reverse the intrinsic direction of a slip line. Consider a slip line OA of angular span ϕ as shown in Fig. 6.12. The radius of curvature

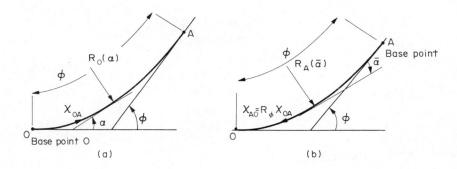

(a)   (b)

Fig. 6.12.   Definition of reversion operator.

of this slip line can be evaluated with respect to either points O or A being identified as the base points as given below. With point O as the base point, see Fig. 6.12(a), the radius of curvature R is given by

$$R_O(\alpha) = \sum_{n=0}^{\infty} a_n \frac{\alpha^n}{n!} .$$
(6.31)

With point A as the base point, see Fig. 6.12(b),

$$R_A(\bar{\alpha}) = \sum_{n=0}^{\infty} \bar{a}_n \frac{\bar{\alpha}^n}{n!} .$$
(6.32)

The angular rotation for both conditions requires that, $\alpha + \bar{\alpha} = \phi$ and $R_O = -R_A$ from the definition of the sign conventions adopted for the radii of curvature. Equation (6.31) can therefore be written as

$$R_A(\bar{\alpha}) = -\sum_{n=0}^{\infty} a_n \frac{(\phi-\bar{\alpha})^n}{n!} .$$
(6.33)

An assessment of the coefficients in (6.32) and (6.33) enables the "$\bar{a}$" coefficients to be expressed in terms of the "a" coefficients and the range ϕ, so that once the "a" coefficients are known the "$\bar{a}$" coefficients can be evaluated. They are given by

179

$$\bar{a}_n = (-1)^{n+1} \sum_{m=n}^{\infty} a_m \frac{\phi^{m-n}}{(m-n)!} \, . \tag{6.34}$$

Thus if the slip line OA is represented by the column vector χ_{OA},

$$\chi_{AO} = R_\phi \chi_{OA}, \tag{6.35}$$

where

$$R_\phi = - \begin{bmatrix} \phi_0 & \phi_1 & \phi_2 & \phi_3 & \cdot & \cdot \\ 0 & -\phi_0 & -\phi_1 & -\phi_2 & \cdot & \cdot \\ 0 & 0 & \phi_0 & \phi_1 & \cdot & \cdot \\ \cdot & \cdot & \cdot & \cdot & \cdot & \cdot \\ \cdot & \cdot & \cdot & \cdot & \cdot & \cdot \\ \cdot & \cdot & \cdot & \cdot & \cdot & \cdot \end{bmatrix} \tag{6.36}$$

and $\quad \phi_n = \phi^n / n! \, .$

(ii) Operators P and Q

The function of the reversion operator R is to reverse the intrinsic direction associated with a slip line. When used in conjunction with the $P*$ and $Q*$ operators it is convenient to define two further operators P and Q which are subscripted in accordance with the defined range of the slip line.

(a) **The centred fan.** Figure 6.13(a) illustrates the intrinsic directions and column vectors for each of the slip lines of the centred fan field. To evaluate χ_{PO} from χ_{OP} requires the use of the reversion operator. The range of the slip line is θ, so that χ_{PO}, as shown in Fig. 6.13(b), is given by

$$\chi_{PO} = R_\theta \chi_{OP} = R_\theta P^*_\psi \chi = P_{\theta\psi} \chi \, .$$

Similarly,

$$\chi_{PA} = R_\psi \chi_{AP} = R_\psi Q^*_\theta \chi = Q_{\theta\psi} \chi \, . \tag{6.37}$$

(b) **The regular net.** From (6.29) and (6.30) expressions are given for χ_{BP} and χ_{AP} as shown in Fig. 6.14(a). To reverse the intrinsic

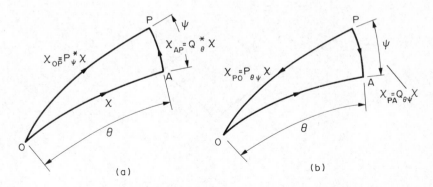

Fig. 6.13. Methods of construction of centred
fans from the base line OA.

directions of these column vectors it is necessary to operate or pre-
multiply these expressions by R_θ and R_ψ respectively, where the subscript denotes the range of the respective slip line.
Hence

$$\left. \begin{aligned} X_{PB} &= R_\theta \ X_{BP} = R_\theta \ P_\psi^* \ X_{OA} + R_\theta \ Q_\psi^* \ X_{OB} = P_{\theta\psi} \ X_{OA} + Q_{\psi\theta} \ X_{OB} \\[2mm] \text{and} \\[2mm] X_{PA} &= R_\psi \ X_{AP} = R_\psi \ P_\theta^* \ X_{OB} + R_\psi \ Q_\theta^* \ X_{OA} = P_{\psi\theta} \ X_{OB} + Q_{\theta\psi} \ X_{OA}. \end{aligned} \right\} \quad (6.38)$$

These intrinsic directions are illustrated in Fig. 6.14(b). For a
field on the concave side of a pair of base slip lines, as shown in
Fig. 6.14(c), the bounding slip lines are given by[12]

$$\left. \begin{aligned} X_{PB} &= P_{\theta\psi} \ X_{OA} - Q_{\psi\theta} \ X_{OB} \\[2mm] X_{PA} &= P_{\psi\theta} \ X_{OB} - Q_{\theta\psi} \ X_{OA}. \end{aligned} \right\} \quad (6.39)$$

and

In (6.37) and (6.38) the operators P and Q have been defined where

$$\left. \begin{aligned} P_{\theta\psi} &= R_\theta \ P_\psi^* \\[2mm] Q_{\theta\psi} &= R_\psi \ Q_\theta^*. \end{aligned} \right\} \quad (6.40)$$

and

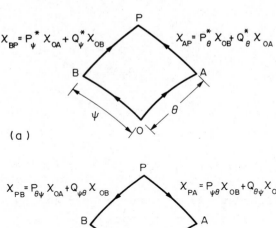

$$X_{BP} = P_\psi^* X_{OA} + Q_\psi^* X_{OB} \qquad X_{AP} = P_\theta^* X_{OB} + Q_\theta^* X_{OA}$$

(a)

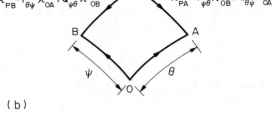

$$X_{PB} = P_{\theta\psi} X_{OA} + Q_{\psi\theta} X_{OB} \qquad X_{PA} = P_{\psi\theta} X_{OB} + Q_{\theta\psi} X_{OA}$$

(b)

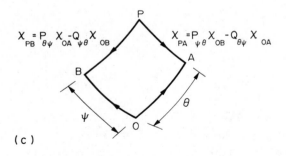

$$X_{PB} = P_{\theta\psi} X_{OA} - Q_{\psi\theta} X_{OB} \qquad X_{PA} = P_{\psi\theta} X_{OB} - Q_{\theta\psi} X_{OA}$$

(c)

Fig. 6.14. Methods of construction of a regular
net from base lines OA and OB.

If $P*$ and $Q*$ are considered as sub-operators, then these sub-operators
as shown in Figs. 6.13(a) and 6.14(a), produce intrinsic directions
away from the base slip lines, while the operators P and Q give intrinsic directions toward the base slip lines.

(iii) <u>Shift Operator, S</u>

The purpose of the shift operator, S_ϕ, is simply to provide an operator which permits the base point of the slip line to be moved through
an angle ϕ so that the column vector is now defined with respect to a

new base point. The operator can be evaluated in a manner similar to that by which R_ϕ was obtained and is given by[13]

$$
S_\phi = \begin{bmatrix}
\phi_0 & \phi_1 & \phi_2 & \phi_3 & \cdot & \cdot \\
0 & \phi_0 & \phi_1 & \phi_2 & \cdot & \cdot \\
0 & 0 & \phi_0 & \phi_1 & \cdot & \cdot & \cdot \\
0 & 0 & 0 & \phi_0 & \cdot & \cdot \\
\cdot & \cdot & \cdot & \cdot & \cdot & \cdot \\
\cdot & \cdot & \cdot & \cdot & \cdot & \cdot
\end{bmatrix}
$$

For a slip line OB as shown in Fig. 6.15 with radius vector χ_{OB}, the column vector χ_{AB} with new base point, A, is given by

$$\chi_{AB} = S_\phi \, \chi_{OB}, \tag{6.41}$$

where χ_{AB} is now defined with respect to the new base point A.

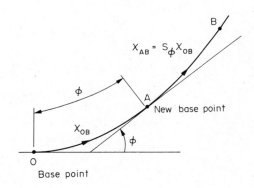

Fig. 6.15.   Definition of shift operator.

(iv)   Numerical Application of the Operators R_ϕ and S_ϕ

To consolidate the understanding of the use of the matrix operators the following elementary example can be investigated. Consider a slip line OB which exactly coincides with the circumference of a circular arc of radius a as shown in Fig. 6.16. The column vector which describes this slip line is given by

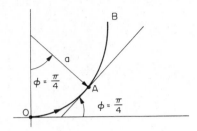

Fig. 6.16. Slip line OB of constant radius a.

$$\chi_{OA} = \chi_{OB} = \begin{bmatrix} a \\ 0 \\ 0 \\ 0 \\ 0 \\ 0 \end{bmatrix}.$$

(i)   From (6.21), the radius of curvature at point A, where $\phi = \pi/4$, is given by

$$R_A = [\, \phi_0 \quad \phi_1 \quad \phi_2 \quad \phi_3 \quad \phi_4 \quad \phi_5 \,] \begin{bmatrix} a \\ 0 \\ 0 \\ 0 \\ 0 \\ 0 \end{bmatrix}$$

where $\phi_m = \phi^m/m!$ and hence $R_A = (\pi/4)^0 a/0! = a$.

This result was previously known, but the same approach can be used when the slip line is not a circular arc, and all the coefficients of χ_{OA} are non-zero.

(ii)   Using the reversion operator R_ϕ, χ_{AO} can be found from (6.36).^{35} χ_{AO} implies that the base point is now defined as point A and hence for $\phi = \pi/4$,

$$\chi_{AO} = R_\phi \, \chi_{OA}$$

$$= - \begin{bmatrix} \phi_0 & \phi_1 & \phi_2 & \phi_3 & \cdot & \cdot \\ 0 & -\phi_0 & -\phi_1 & -\phi_2 & \cdot & \cdot \\ 0 & 0 & \phi_0 & \phi_1 & \cdot & \cdot \\ \cdot & \cdot & \cdot & \cdot & \cdot & \cdot \\ \cdot & \cdot & \cdot & \cdot & \cdot & \cdot \\ \cdot & \cdot & \cdot & \cdot & \cdot & \cdot \end{bmatrix} \begin{bmatrix} a \\ 0 \\ 0 \\ 0 \\ 0 \\ 0 \end{bmatrix} = - \begin{bmatrix} a\phi_0 \\ 0 \\ 0 \\ 0 \\ 0 \\ 0 \end{bmatrix}$$

where $\qquad \phi_m = \phi^m/m!$,

so that $\qquad\qquad\qquad \chi_{AO} = \begin{bmatrix} -a \\ 0 \\ 0 \\ 0 \\ 0 \\ 0 \end{bmatrix}$.

The radius of curvature at O can again be evaluated using χ_{AO}, with $\phi = \pi/4$ as was previously shown for finding the radius of curvature at point A from χ_{OA}. If this is carried out the radius of curvature at O is now equal to $-a$ with A as the base point.

(iii) Using the shift operator S_ϕ, χ_{OA} can be operated on to shift the base point from point O to A and hence for $\phi = \pi/4$, χ_{AB} is given by

$$\chi_{AB} = S_\phi \, \chi_{OA}$$

$$= \begin{bmatrix} \phi_0 & \phi_1 & \phi_2 & \phi_3 & \cdot & \cdot \\ 0 & \phi_0 & \phi_1 & \phi_2 & \cdot & \cdot \\ 0 & 0 & \phi_0 & \cdot & \cdot & \cdot \\ \cdot & \cdot & \cdot & \cdot & \cdot & \cdot \\ \cdot & \cdot & \cdot & \cdot & \cdot & \cdot \\ \cdot & \cdot & \cdot & \cdot & \cdot & \cdot \end{bmatrix} \begin{bmatrix} a \\ 0 \\ 0 \\ 0 \\ 0 \\ 0 \end{bmatrix} = \begin{bmatrix} a\phi_0 \\ 0 \\ 0 \\ 0 \\ 0 \\ 0 \end{bmatrix}$$

where $\qquad \phi_m = \phi^m/m!$,

185

so that,

$$\chi_{AB} = \begin{bmatrix} a \\ 0 \\ 0 \\ 0 \\ 0 \\ 0 \end{bmatrix}.$$

This result was previously known since $\chi_{OA} = \chi_{OB} = \chi_{AB}$ and the slip line OB is a circular arc.

It is believed that the above demonstration of the application of the R_ϕ and S_ϕ operators will illustrate the simplicity by which these and other operators can be employed.

(v)   Frictionless Boundary Operator, T

The frictionless boundary operator, T_ϕ, constructs the field between a slip line and a straight frictionless boundary or line of symmetry. In the field shown in Fig. 6.17(a), OB and OC are perpendicular frictionless boundaries or lines of symmetry, while OA is the base line with base point O. OA' is the reflection of OA in OB. The operator T_ϕ is defined as the operator which constructs the line BA on the concave side of the base slip line. Hence from (6.39) for the regular net $BAOA'$

$$\chi_{BA} = P_{\phi\phi} \chi_{OA'} - Q_{\phi\phi} \chi_{OA} = T_\phi \chi_{OA} \quad , \tag{6.42}$$

where $\psi = \theta = \phi$. Also $\chi_{OA'} = -\chi_{OA}$ since OA' is geometrically similar to OA but its curvature is of opposite sign.
Therefore,

$$\left. \begin{array}{c} T_\phi \chi_{OA} = -P_{\phi\phi} \chi_{OA} - Q_{\phi\phi} \chi_{OA} \\ \\ \\ T_\phi = -P_{\phi\phi} - Q_{\phi\phi}. \end{array} \right\} \tag{6.43}$$

or

Similarly χ_{CA} on the convex side of χ_{OA} can be constructed where

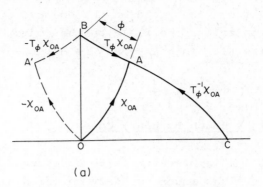

(a)

Fig. 6.17 (a). Definition of the frictionless boundary operators T_ϕ and T_ϕ^{-1}.

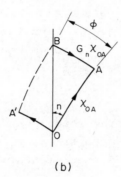

(b)

Fig. 6.17 (b). Definition of the straight rough boundary operator G.

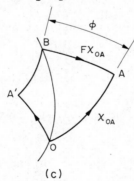

(c)

Fig. 6.17 (c). Definition of the stress free surface operator F.

$$X_{CA} = T_\phi^{-1} \, X_{OA}$$

and

$$T_\phi^{-1} = -P_{\phi\phi} + Q_{\phi\phi}.$$

(6.44)

Thus T_ϕ constructs the field on the concave side of the base slip line, whilst T_ϕ^{-1} constructs the field on the convex side. Note that the intrinsic direction in both cases is directed toward the base slip line.

(vi)   Straight Rough Boundary Operator, G

The purpose of this operator is to construct a field between a slip line and a straight rough boundary on which the shear stress over the length of the rough boundary is constant and equal to some fraction m of the shear yield stress of the material, k. The slip line OA is shown in Fig. 6.17(b) and intersects the rough boundary OB at some angle η where $\eta = (\cos^{-1} m)/2$. To find the column vector χ_{BA} of the slip line BA which intersects the rough boundary at an angle of $((\pi/2) - \eta)$ requires that the operator, G, be defined such that $\chi_{BA} = G\chi_{OA}$.

Since $\eta \neq \pi/4$, as a result of the rough boundary OB, OA' is not a reflection of OA as was the case for a frictionless boundary. If $\chi_{OA'}$ can be derived, then χ_{BA} can be directly obtained from (6.38) where

$$\chi_{BA} = Q_{\phi\phi} \, \chi_{OA} + P_{\phi\phi} \, \chi_{OA'} . \tag{6.45}$$

Dewhurst and Collins[13] and Collins[1] have shown that the column vector $\chi_{OA'}$ is given by

$$\chi_{OA'} = (I \cos \eta - J \sin \eta)^{-1} . (J \cos \eta - I \sin \eta) . \chi_{OA} , \tag{6.46}$$

where I is a unit matrix and J is referred to as an integration operator and is given by

$$J = \begin{bmatrix} 0 & 0 & 0 & 0 & 0 & 0 \\ 1 & 0 & 0 & 0 & 0 & 0 \\ 0 & 1 & 0 & 0 & 0 & 0 \\ 0 & 0 & 1 & 0 & 0 & 0 \\ 0 & 0 & 0 & 1 & 0 & 0 \\ 0 & 0 & 0 & 0 & 1 & 0 \end{bmatrix} .$$

Substituting for $\chi_{OA'}$ in (6.45)

$$\chi_{BA} = [Q_{\phi\phi} + P_{\phi\phi} (I \cos \eta - J \sin \eta)^{-1} (J \cos \eta - I \sin \eta)] \chi_{OA}$$

so that

$$G_\eta = [Q_{\phi\phi} + P_{\phi\phi} (I \cos \eta - J \sin \eta)^{-1} (J \cos \eta - I \sin \eta)]$$

For a frictionless boundary $m = 0$ and $\eta = \pi/4$, so that G reduces to

$$G_{\pi/4} = Q_{\phi\phi} - P_{\phi\phi} = T_\phi^{-1}, \tag{6.47}$$

which is the same result as that given in (6.44).

Similarly for a perfectly rough boundary $m = 1$ and $\eta = 0$ so that

$$G_O = Q_{\phi\phi} + P_{\phi\phi} J. \tag{6.48}$$

(vii)   Stress-Free Surface Boundary Operator, F

The function of the F operator is to develop a contour OB, from a
given slip line OA as shown in Fig. 6.17(c), on which the normal and
shear stresses are zero. Such a contour would, as a result of these
conditions, represent a stress-free surface so that all slip lines
must intersect this stress-free surface at 45°. These conditions,
as shown in references 1 and 13, enable the column vector $\chi_{OA'}$ to be
determined from which the column vector χ_{BA} can be defined as has
been done in determining the T and G operators. Hence,

$$\chi_{OA'} = (D + I)^{-1} \cdot (D - I) \cdot \chi_{OA} \tag{6.49}$$

where I is a unit matrix and D is referred to as a differentiation
operator and is given by

$$D = \begin{bmatrix} 0 & 1 & 0 & 0 & \cdot & \cdot \\ 0 & 0 & 1 & 0 & \cdot & \cdot \\ 0 & 0 & 0 & 1 & \cdot & \cdot \\ \cdot & \cdot & \cdot & \cdot & \cdot & \cdot \\ \cdot & \cdot & \cdot & \cdot & \cdot & \cdot \\ \cdot & \cdot & \cdot & \cdot & \cdot & \cdot \end{bmatrix} \cdot$$

From (6.39) the slip line $\chi_{A' O}$ can be obtained directly, where

$$\chi_{A' O} = P_{\phi\phi} \; \chi_{AB} - Q_{\phi\phi} \; \chi_{AO}. \tag{6.50}$$

The intrinsic directions of each of these column vectors can be reversed by pre-multiplication with R_ϕ, so that equations (6.49) and (6.50) can be equated to yield the following result:

$$P_{\phi\phi} \; R_\phi \; \chi_{BA} = R_\phi (D + I)^{-1}. \; (D - I). \chi_{OA} + Q_{\phi\phi} \; R_\phi \; \chi_{OA}. \tag{6.51}$$

It follows that if the function of the F operator is to develop a slip-line field from the slip line χ_{OA} such that a stress-free surface is required, then

$$\chi_{BA} = F\chi_{OA} \tag{6.52}$$

and

$$F = R_\phi^{-1}. \; P_{\phi\phi}^{-1} \; [R_\phi (D + I)^{-1}. \; (D - I) + Q_{\phi\phi} \; R_\phi]. \tag{6.53}$$

(viii)   Matrix Operator Identities

It follows from each of these matrix operators that a number of properties associated with each operator can be deduced. These are briefly summarized below, but for further details the reader is referred to reference 1.

(i) $S_\theta S_\psi \; \equiv \; S_\psi S_\theta \; \equiv \; S_{\theta+\psi}$,

(ii) $R_\theta R_\psi \; \equiv \; S_{\psi-\theta}$,

(iii) $R_\theta^2 \; = \; I$,

(iv) $R_\psi S_\theta \; \equiv \; S_\psi R_\theta \; \equiv \; R_{\theta+\psi}$,

(v) $P_\theta^* P_\psi^* \; \equiv \; P_{\theta+\psi}^*$,

(vi) $P_\theta^{*-1} \; = \; P_{-\theta}^*$,

(vii) $Q_\psi^* P_\theta^* \; \equiv \; S_\theta Q_\psi^*$,

(viii) $Q_\theta^* S_\psi + P_\theta^* Q_\psi^* \; \equiv \; Q_\psi^* S_\theta + P_\psi^* Q_\theta^* \; \equiv \; Q_{\theta+\psi}^*$,

(ix) $P_{\theta\psi} Q_{\psi\theta} \; \equiv \; Q_{\psi\theta} P_{\psi\theta}$,

190

(x) $\quad P^2_{\theta\psi} - Q_{\psi\theta}Q_{\theta\psi} \equiv I$,

(xi) $\quad P_\theta {}^* R_\psi Q_\theta {}^* \equiv Q_\theta {}^* R_\theta P_\psi {}^*$,

(xii) $\quad P_\psi {}^* R_\theta P_\psi {}^* - Q_\psi {}^* R_\psi Q_\theta {}^* \equiv R_\theta$,

(xiii) $\quad DJ \equiv I$.

(ix)   ## Matrix Operator Subroutines

All matrix operators defined in this section have been documented as computer subroutines in Appendix 1. To use any operator therefore simply requires that the subroutine be called. All subroutines are written in the Fortran language and are not dissimilar from the series of subroutines presented by Dewhurst and Collins.[13]

DETERMINATION OF THE COORDINATES OF SLIP LINES

Given that the radius of curvature of a particular slip line is known, the coordinates at any point along this slip line can be found. A slip line having a positive radius of curvature is represented in Fig. 6.18 in which the base point O is located at the origin of the Cartesian coordinates (x,y), and the x-axis is tangential to the slip line at point O.

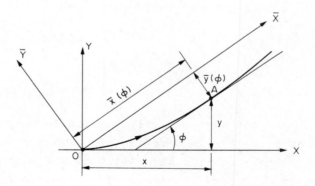

Fig. 6.18.   Definition of Mikhlin coordinates $(\bar{x},\bar{y})$.

To evaluate the (x,y) coordinates at any point A, which corresponds to a rotation ϕ, it is convenient to first calculate the Mikhlin coordinates $(\bar{x}, \bar{y})$ from which the Cartesian coordinates (x, y) can be derived directly from Fig. 6.18; they are given by[3]

$$x = \bar{x} \cos \phi - \bar{y} \sin \phi$$

and

$$y = \bar{x} \sin \phi + \bar{y} \cos \phi.$$

(6.54)

The Mikhlin coordinates can be conveniently obtained since, as demonstrated by Ewing,[11] there exists a simple relationship between the coefficients of the power series expansion of the radius of curvature and the coefficients of an equivalent power series expansion. Expressed mathematically, if

$$R(\phi) = \sum_{n=0}^{\infty} r_n \frac{\phi^n}{n!}$$

and

$$\bar{x}(\phi) = \sum_{n=0}^{\infty} t_n \frac{\phi^n}{n!} ,$$

(6.55)

then

$$\bar{y}(\phi) = - \sum_{n=0}^{\infty} t_n \frac{\phi^{n+1}}{(n+1)!} ,$$

where the t_n and r_n coefficients are related by the following recurrence relationships:

$$t_{-1} = 0,$$
$$t_0 = 0,$$
$$t_1 = r_0,$$

and
$$t_{n+1} = - t_{n-1} + r_n.$$

(6.56)

Equations (6.54) and (6.55) are directly applicable when the radius of curvature of the slip line is positive, i.e. when ϕ increases in an anti-clockwise manner from the base point of the slip line. For a negative radius of curvature these equations are modified, as given below, so as to yield the correct Mikhlin and Cartesian coordinates directly. Hence,

$$x = \bar{x} \cos \phi + \bar{y} \sin \phi$$

and
$$y = - \bar{x} \sin \phi + \bar{y} \cos \phi$$

where

$$\bar{x} = - \sum_{n=0}^{\infty} t_n \frac{\phi^n}{n!}$$

and

$$\bar{y} = + \sum_{n=0}^{\infty} t_n \frac{\phi^{n+1}}{(n+1)!} \ .$$

(6.57)

Subroutines MIKLIN and CORDXY which serve to evaluate the Mikhlin and and Cartesian coordinates respectively are listed in Appendix 2. These subroutines have been structured such that slip lines with either negative or positive radii of curvature can be handled directly.

Example 1.

Consider a slip line OA which coincides with the circumference of a circular arc of radius a as shown in Fig. 6.19. The Cartesian and

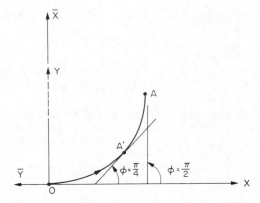

Fig. 6.19. Determination of Mikhlin and Cartesian
coordinates along the circular slip
line OA of radius a at point A.

and Mikhlin coordinates at point A are immediately known and are given by (a,a) and $(a,-a)$ respectively. From the above, these coordinates can be evaluated as follows. The slip line is represented by the column vector χ_{OA}

where

$$\chi_{OA} = \begin{bmatrix} r_0 \\ r_1 \\ r_2 \\ r_3 \\ . \\ . \end{bmatrix} = \begin{bmatrix} a \\ 0 \\ 0 \\ 0 \\ 0 \\ 0 \end{bmatrix} \ .$$

From (6.56) the coefficients of the power series expansion for the Mikhlin coordinates can be calculated. All coefficients are listed below for the column vector representation χ_{OA}:

$$r_0 = a \quad t_{-1} = t_0 = 0,$$
$$r_1 = 0 \qquad t_1 = a,$$
$$r_2 = 0 \qquad t_2 = 0,$$
$$r_3 = 0 \qquad t_3 = -a,$$
$$r_4 = 0 \qquad t_4 = 0,$$
$$r_5 = 0 \qquad t_5 = a,$$
$$r_n = 0 \qquad t_{n+1} = -t_{n-1} + r_n.$$

For $n = 5$ and $\phi = \pi/2$, the Mikhlin coordinates can be determined from (6.55) as

$$\bar{x} = \sum_{n=0}^{5} t_n \frac{\phi^n}{n!} = \phi - \frac{\phi^3}{3!} + \frac{\phi^5}{5!} = 1.00452a$$

and

$$\bar{y} = -\sum_{n=0}^{5} t_{n-1} \frac{\phi^n}{n!} = -\left(\frac{\phi^2}{2!} - \frac{\phi^4}{4!} \right) = -0.98003a.$$

To assess the influence of an increasing number of terms within the expansions, $\bar{x}$ and $\bar{y}$ have been evaluated for $n = 5$ to 9. The Cartesian coordinates have also been evaluated for these conditions from (6.54). The results are tabulated below:

n	5	6	7	8	9	Actual value
$\bar{x}$	$1.00452a$	$1.00452a$	$0.99984a$	$0.99984a$	$1.00000a$	$1.00000a$
$\bar{y}$	$-0.98003a$	$-1.00089a$	$-1.00089a$	$-0.99997a$	$-0.99997a$	$-1.00000a$
x	$0.98003a$	$1.00089a$	$1.00089a$	$0.99997a$	$0.99997a$	$1.00000a$
y	$1.00452a$	$1.00452a$	$0.99984a$	$0.99984a$	$1.00000a$	$1.00000a$

An additional set of values corresponding to $\phi = \pi/4$, i.e. point A' as shown in Fig. 6.19, is listed below:

n	5	6	7	8	9	Actual value
$\bar{x}$	$0.70714a$	$0.70714a$	$0.70710a$	$0.70710a$	$0.70710a$	$0.70710a$
$\bar{y}$	$-0.29257a$	$-0.29289a$	$-0.29289a$	$-0.29289a$	$-0.29289a$	$-0.29289a$
x	$0.70694a$	$0.70713a$	$0.70710a$	$0.70710a$	$0.70710a$	$0.70710a$
y	$0.29314a$	$0.29291a$	$0.29289a$	$0.29289a$	$0.29289a$	$0.29289a$

<u>Example 2.</u> Consider the indentation of a slab of finite thickness by a smooth flat punch of half width a. An approximate slip-line field for this problem is shown in Fig. 6.20(a), in which the circular arcs each extend through an angle of $\pi/3$.

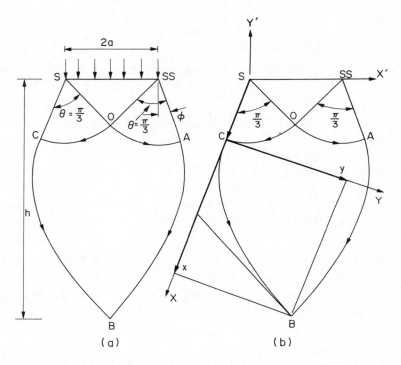

Fig. 6.20. Simple indentation representation.

Coordinate positions of S, SS, O, A, B, and C are

	S	SS	O	A	B	C	
x'	0.000	2.000	1.000	2.366	1.000	-0.366	h/a ratio = 5.429
y'	0.000	0.000	-1.000	-1.366	-5.429	-1.366	$P/2h$ = 2.06

Using the notation of Fig. 6.20(a), the column vectors of the coefficients in the series expansion of the radius of curvature of each slip line can be evaluated thus. Defining the base slip lines as OA and OC, then using the sign convention given previously, χ_{OA} is positive since the inclination of the local tangent increases in an anti-clockwise sense in moving with the intrinsic direction from O to A. Similarly χ_{OC} is negative. Thus χ_{OA} and χ_{OC} can be written

195

$$\chi_{OA} = \begin{bmatrix} a\sqrt{2} \\ 0 \\ 0 \\ 0 \\ 0 \\ 0 \end{bmatrix} \quad \text{and} \quad \chi_{OC} = \begin{bmatrix} -a\sqrt{2} \\ 0 \\ 0 \\ 0 \\ 0 \\ 0 \end{bmatrix}.$$

χ_{CB} and χ_{AB} can now be expressed directly in terms of χ_{OA} and χ_{OC} with the aid of the P^* and Q^* operators, and are given by (6.29) and (6.30). Hence,

$$\chi_{CB} = P^*_\theta \ \chi_{OA} + Q^*_\theta \ \chi_{OC}$$

and

$$\chi_{AB} = P^*_\theta \ \chi_{OC} + Q^*_\theta \ \chi_{OA},$$

where $\theta = \psi = \pi/3$. The operations $P^*\chi$ and $Q^*\chi$ are performed with the aid of the sub-routines PMULT and QMULT which are listed in Appendix 1.

If the origin of the Cartesian axes (x',y') is made to coincide with the point S as illustrated in Fig. 6.20(b), the coordinates of points SS, O, A and C can be evaluated by simple geometry. Point B can be derived from χ_{CB} and the knowledge that the angular range of the slip line from the base point C to point B spans a range of $\theta = \pi/3$ (or 60^0). This is directly performed by resorting to the sub-routines MIKLIN and CORDXY in which point C is the reference origin for the local Cartesian coordinates (X,Y). The vectorial addition of the vectors SC, Cx and Cy enables the coordinates of point B to be found. The coordinates (x',y') of all boundary points are tabulated in Fig. 6.20. Any other pair of coordinate values along the slip line CB corresponding to a range $\theta_i < \theta$, can be evaluated with the approach given above.

A computer listing for this indentation problem is provided in Appendix 3. The evaluation of the coordinates of point B are contained within the sub-routine SLCP. The Mikhlin and Cartesian coordinates associated with the slip line are evaluated in this routine by the MIKLIN and CORDXY sub-routines and vectorially added to the coordinates of point C to yield the coordinates of point B corresponding to the origin, S.

DETERMINATION OF FORCES ACTING ON A SLIP LINE

The total force acting upon a given slip line can be evaluated by
summing the elemental components of force on each elemental length,
ds, of the slip line. It is convenient to sum these forces in the
directions defined by the Mikhlin coordinates $(\bar{x}, \bar{y})$ and subsequently to
transform the total force to directions which coincide with the Cartesian axes. In deriving expressions for the total force, consideration
must be given as to whether the slip line is an α- or a β-line; Fig.
6.21(a) illustrates the directions of the normal and shear stresses
acting upon an orthogonal network of slip lines. With reference to
Fig. 6.21(b), the normal and shear stress components acting over the
range φ of the slip line OA with base point O can be summed to evaluate the resultant forces $F_{\bar{x}}$ and $F_{\bar{y}}$.

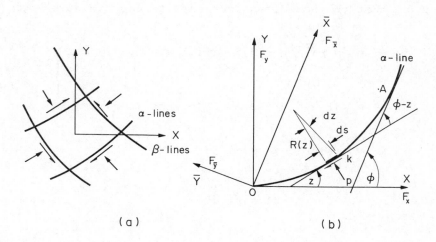

(a)   (b)

Fig. 6.21.   Normal and shear stresses acting on
slip lines.

For the elemental length ds of the α-line OA

$$dF_{\bar{x}} = - k \cos (\phi - z) \, ds + p \sin (\phi - z) \, ds$$

and

$$dF_{\bar{y}} = k \sin (\phi - z) \, ds + p \cos (\phi - z) \, ds.$$

(6.58)

The normal pressure p acting on the element ds can be evaluated in
terms of the hydrostatic pressure, p_0 , at the base point, O. For an

α-line, $p + 2k\alpha$ = constant, so that the normal pressure on the element ds is given by

$$p = p_0 - 2kz. \tag{6.59}$$

Additionally, $ds = R(z).dz$, so that the equations are reduced to

$$dF_{\bar{x}} = - k \cos (\phi-z) R(z) dz + p_0 \sin (\phi-z) R(z) dz$$

$$- 2kz \sin (\phi-z) R(z) dz$$

and

$$dF_{\bar{y}} = k \sin (\phi-z) R(z) dz + p_0 \cos (\phi-z) R(z) dz$$

$$- 2kz \cos (\phi-z) R(z) dz. \tag{6.60}$$

Integration over the range ϕ enables the total forces $F_{\bar{x}}$ and $F_{\bar{y}}$ to be evaluated so that the non-dimensionalized forces are given by

$$\frac{F_{\bar{x}}}{k} = -\bar{x} + \frac{p_0}{k} \bar{y} - 2\int_0^\phi zR(z) \sin (\phi-z) dz$$

and

$$\frac{F_{\bar{y}}}{k} = \bar{y} + \frac{p_0}{k} \bar{x} - 2\int_0^\phi zR(z) \cos (\phi-z) dz, \tag{6.61}$$

where

$$\bar{y} = \int_0^\phi \sin (\phi-z) R(z) dz$$

and

$$\bar{x} = \int_0^\phi \cos (\phi-z) R(z) dz.$$

The convolution integrals can be evaluated by expressing each of these integrals as a power series expansion.

It can be shown that if

$$\int_0^\phi z \cos (\phi-z) R(z) dz = \sum_{n=0}^\infty c_n \frac{\phi^n}{n!}$$

then

$$\int_0^\phi z \sin (\phi-z) R(z) dz = \sum_{n=0}^\infty c_{n-1} \frac{\phi^n}{n!}, \tag{6.62}$$

where the coefficients c_n are given by the recurrence relations

$$c_{n+1} + c_{n-1} = nr_{n-1}; \quad c_0 = c_{-1} = 0.$$

From (6.61) the non-dimensional forces F_x/k and F_y/k in the x and y directions, shown in Fig. 6.21(b), are given by

and

$$\left.\begin{array}{c} \dfrac{F_x}{k} = \dfrac{F_{\bar{x}}}{k} \cos \phi - \dfrac{F_{\bar{y}}}{k} \sin \phi \\[3mm] \dfrac{F_y}{k} = \dfrac{F_{\bar{y}}}{k} \cos \phi + \dfrac{F_{\bar{x}}}{k} \sin \phi. \end{array}\right\} \qquad (6.63)$$

For convenience, a sub-routine SLFORC has been developed to evaluate the magnitude of the forces $F_{\bar{x}}/k$, $F_{\bar{y}}/k$, F_x/k and F_y/k as given by (6.61) and (6.63). The sub-routine is detailed in Appendix 4, and is sufficiently general to permit the evaluation of the forces associated with each of the following cases:

(i)   an α-line with positive curvature (ϕ increases in an anti-clockwise sense from the base point). This case is represented in Fig. 6.21(b);

(ii)   an α-line with negative curvature;

(iii) a β-line with positive curvature; and

(iv)   a β-line with negative curvature.

Furthermore, as will be illustrated in the following section, the hydrostatic pressure, p_0, at the base point of the slip line is chosen to be equal to zero for numerical convenience. Using this zero value for the hydrostatic component implies that the forces acting on the slip line and calculated with the sub-routine SLFORC relate to the $2k\phi$ normal component and the shear component of stress only. It is considerably simpler to approach the solution of problems in this latter manner since the hydrostatic component at the base point can be included at some later stage in the evaluation of the total force requirements for a particular problem.

199

Example 3. To illustrate the application of sub-routine SLFORC,
Example 2 of the previous section which refers to the indentation of
a slab of finite thickness by a smooth flat punch of half width a,
will be considered. In the previous example the complete geometry
and column vectors of the coefficients in the series expansions of
the different radii of curvature of each slip line were evaluated.
With this information the indentation pressure can be directly evaluated for the slip-line field shown in Fig. 6.22. For the slip line

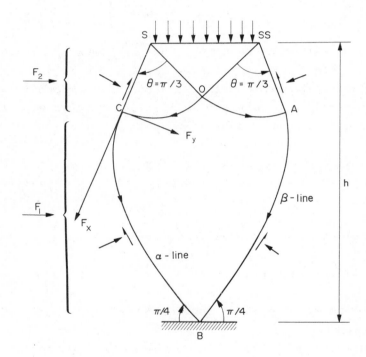

Fig. 6.22. Simple slip-line-field representation
for indentation of a slab of finite
thickness by a smooth flat punch.

X_{CB}, the forces F_x and F_y acting on this α-line can be evaluated from
sub-routine SLFORC in which $\phi = \theta = \pi/3$, SIGN1 = 1.0 since the slip
line CB is an α-line, and SIGN = 1.0 since the slip line has a positive
radius of curvature. The hydrostatic pressure at the base point C is
not known at this time so that this value will be assumed to be equal
to zero when using SLFORC. With this latter assumption, the forces
F_x and F_y can be obtained from SLFORC. The horizontal force acting on

200

the material to the right of CB due to these forces is therefore given by

$$F_1 = -kF_x \sin\left(\theta - \frac{\pi}{4}\right) + kF_y \cos\left(\theta - \frac{\pi}{4}\right). \tag{6.64}$$

The shear stress acting on CS also produces a force to the right, which is given by

$$F_2 = ka \sqrt{2} \sin\left(\theta - \frac{\pi}{4}\right). \tag{6.65}$$

The hydrostatic component of stress along CS is constant since CS is a straight line, and by setting it equal to zero at C, the hydrostatic stress component along CB has effectively been reduced by a constant amount p_c. Thus the total force to the right of SCB with all forces summed is given by

$$F_T = -kF_x \sin\left(\theta - \frac{\pi}{4}\right) + kF_y \cos\left(\theta - \frac{\pi}{4}\right) + ka \sqrt{2} \sin\left(\theta - \frac{\pi}{4}\right) + p_c h. \tag{6.66}$$

Since, from equilibrium considerations, the net force on the material in the horizontal direction is equal to zero, equation (6.66) is equal to zero so that p_c can be evaluated thus,

$$p_c = \left[kF_x \sin\left(\theta - \frac{\pi}{4}\right) - kF_y \cos\left(\theta - \frac{\pi}{4}\right) - ka \sqrt{2} \sin\left(\theta - \frac{\pi}{4}\right)\right]/h. \tag{6.67}$$

Then, using the Hencky equations, it is clear that

$$p_0 = p_c + 2k\theta$$

and the indentation pressure can be evaluated so that

$$\frac{p}{2k} = \frac{p_0}{k} + \frac{1}{2}. \tag{6.68}$$

A computerized solution and listing to this problem is given in Appendix 3.

METHOD OF SOLUTION

In the preceding sections the basic matrix-operator method used in the construction of slip-line fields and the evaluation of load requirements associated with these slip-line fields has been presented.

201

While all vectors and matrix operators referred to are of infinite dimension, a reasonable degree of accuracy can be obtained by truncating the square matrix operators to a 6 X 6 dimension. The method therefore reduces to a series of algebraic matrix manipulations and their operation on column vectors which represent the radii of curvature of the slip lines within the field considered. A library of Fortran sub-routines has been developed[13] to perform each operator function as well as to assist in the evaluation of the coordinates and the forces associated with a given slip line. For each problem it is therefore only necessary to obtain expressions for the radii of curvature of each slip line and to write a small program which incorporates the required functions of the various sub-routines. A solution sequence is presented below.

(i)   Draw an approximate slip-line field for the problem.

(ii)   Evaluate the column vector for each boundary slip line in the field. This can be accomplished with the aid of the matrix operators such that the intrinsic directions are simultaneously defined.

(iii) From these intrinsic directions, the radii of curvature of each slip line can be defined as either positive or negative. The coordinates of all points within the field can therefore be evaluated using the appropriate sub-routines.

(iv)   Noting which slip lines are α-lines and which are β-lines, the forces acting on any slip line within the field can be evaluated with the appropriate sub-routines.

(v)   Evaluation of load requirements, e.g. indentation pressure or extrusion pressure as required in a specific problem.

This basic procedure is applicable to all slip-line field solutions. The degree of complexity required, particularly in the algebraic manipulation of the matrix operators to determine the column vector representation of each slip line, will in large measure depend upon whether or·not sufficient information about the proposed field is available. Solutions can, however, as previously remarked, be broadly categorized and formulated as either direct- or indirect-type solutions.

(i)   Direct-Type Solutions

When the shape of a sufficient number of the slip lines of the proposed slip line field are known, e.g. circular arcs, etc., then these slip lines can be expressed as column vectors and similarly all associated slip lines can be individually determined by the direct application of selected matrix operators. This approach, referred to in the literature as a direct-type solution, can be systematically repeated to arrive at the column vector representation of the entire slip-line field. Slip-line fields of this type could also be systematically constructed using the straight-line approximations and numerical techniques or the "marching in" procedures discussed by Hill[3]. However, this latter method can be tedious and its accuracy is dependent on the choice of mesh size.

(ii)   Indirect-Type Solutions

When the number of slip lines of known shape is limited such that the step-by-step procedure used in the direct-type solutions will not

suffice to construct the complete slip-line field, an initial slip
line represented by the column vector, χ, can be defined from which
all slip lines can be expressed in terms of this unknown column vector,
χ. To solve for χ in this case will usually require some other constraining condition, derived either from the corresponding hodograph or
some other geometric property of the field. This type of formulation,
which is referred to as an indirect-type solution, yields a number
of algebraic expressions which can be manipulated and reduced to an
inhomogeneous matrix equation of the form

$$A\chi = \nu , \qquad (6.69)$$

where the square matrix A and vector ν are deduced from combinations
of the basic matrix operators. The initial slip line χ can be solved
from (6.69) by a simple matrix inversion and the column vectors of
all other slip lines determined. The physical significance of the
vector ν, as will be observed later, is that this vector is directly
proportional to the magnitude of the tangential velocity discontinuities in the proposed slip-line field solution. With continuous velocity fields, the manipulation of the equations resulting from the
matrix operator method can lead to an homogeneous equation for the
initial or unknown base slip line of the form

$$(A^* - \lambda I)\chi = 0 \qquad (6.70)$$

The column vector χ is therefore defined as the eigen-vector of matrix
A^* corresponding to the eigen-value λ. Further details about the
method to determine these eigen-vector slip-line solutions have been
discussed by Dewhurst[2] with particular reference to the formulations
which arise in the compression between flat frictionless dies[12] and
indentation on frictionless and rough anvils.[19]

In the following sections the application of the matrix operator
method to both direct- and indirect-type solutions associated with a
range of metal-forming processes will be presented. The main aim
will be to establish the procedure to be used in each case; for
further details the reader is referred to the published literature.

APPLICATION OF THE MATRIX-OPERATOR METHOD TO THE SOLUTION OF DIRECT-TYPE PROBLEMS

(i) Extrusion/Drawing through a Frictionless Wedge-Shaped Die

Consider the slip-line field shown in Fig. 6.23 for the extrusion or
drawing of material through a frictionless wedge-shaped die of angle
α which is valid for a reduction $r \leqslant 2 \sin \alpha/(1+2 \sin \alpha)$. The solution
proceeds as follows:

Determination of radius vectors. Let the die length OA be 2 units.
Then, since OA is a frictionless boundary, $OC = AC = \sqrt{2}$ units. Take
C as the base point and CB and CD as the base slip lines. Their
intrinsic directions will be as shown. The radius of curvature of
CB is negative since it rotates in a clockwise direction when proceeding in the intrinsic direction, and the radius of curvature of CD is
positive since it rotates in an anti-clockwise sense. Since AC and OC
are straight lines, CB and CD are circular arcs of radius OC, and

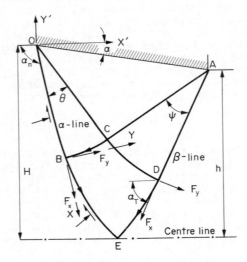

Fig. 6.23. Slip line field for extrusion/drawing through a frictionless wedge-shaped die.
Note: (i) orientation of X, Y axes at origin B
(ii) orientation of forces F_X and F_Y.

therefore the radius vectors of CB and CD are given by

$$
X_{CB} = \begin{vmatrix} -\sqrt{2} \\ 0 \\ 0 \\ 0 \\ 0 \\ 0 \end{vmatrix} \quad \text{and} \quad X_{CD} = \begin{vmatrix} \sqrt{2} \\ 0 \\ 0 \\ 0 \\ 0 \\ 0 \end{vmatrix}.
$$

Then using (6.29) and (6.30), X_{BE} and X_{DE} can be expressed in terms of X_{CB} and X_{CD} as

$$
X_{BE} = P_\theta{}^* \; X_{CD} + Q_\theta{}^* \; X_{CB}
$$

and

$$
X_{DE} = P_\psi{}^* \; X_{CB} + Q_\psi{}^* \; X_{CD}.
$$

The angles α, θ and ψ are related by the expression

$$\psi = \theta + \alpha$$

Thus for a given die angle α, values of ψ and θ can be selected which correspond to different reduction ratios. For defined values of θ and ψ it is therefore possible to obtain numerical values for the radius vectors χ_{BE} and χ_{DE}. These can be directly determined with the P^* (PSTAR) and Q^* (QSTAR) operator sub-routines. To further facilitate these analytical manipulations two further sub-routines PMULT and QMULT have been developed. These sub-routines are detailed and listed in Appendix 1, and basically perform the matrix multiplication $P^*\chi$ in the PMULT sub-routine and $Q^*\chi$ in the QMULT sub-routine respectively. The column vectors of all slip lines can therefore be directly evaluated.

<u>Calculation of coordinates.</u> Since the lengths OA, OB, OC and OD are known, together with the angles α, θ and ψ, the coordinates of A, B, C and D can be obtained relative to the origin O by simple geometry. The coordinates of E can be found relative to B by means of the sub-routine CORDXY (N, V, XBAR, YBAR, X, Y, ANG, SIGN), where X and Y are the Cartesian coordinates of a point whose angular position relative to the base point, B, is ANG and SIGN is +1 for the slip line BE which has a positive radius of curvature. Thus for the coordinates of E relative to B, V is χ_{BE}, ANG is ψ and SIGN is +1, whilst the X and Y directions are parallel and perpendicular respectively to the slip line at B.

The coordinates of E relative to O can then be found by simple geometry. For a die angle $\alpha = 10^\circ$, a leading angle $\theta = 20^\circ$ and a trailing angle ψ of 30°, the coordinates of C, D and E with $OA = 2$, in terms of the X' and Y' directions shown in Fig. 6.23 are

$\quad$ C $\quad$ (0.8112, -1.1585),
$\quad$ D $\quad$ (1.3720, -1.6290)
and $\quad$ E $\quad$ (0.9065, -2.2877).

<u>Calculation of forces.</u> The forces acting on any slip line in directions parallel and perpendicular to the slip line at its base point can be obtained as FX and FY using the sub-routine SLFORC (N, V, XBAR, YBAR

FX, *FY*, ANG, *PO*, SIGN 1, SIGN) where *PO* is the hydrostatic pressure
at the base point, SIGN 1 is +1 for an α-line and -1 for a β-line and
other parameters are as defined for CORDXY.

To calculate the forces of the slip line *BE*, i.e. the forces exerted
on material to the right of *BE*, the following arguments are used:

$$\text{SIGN 1} = +1: \quad BE \text{ is an } \alpha\text{-line,}$$
$$\text{SIGN} \quad = +1: \quad BE \text{ has a positive radius,}$$
$$V \quad = x_{BE} \quad \text{and}$$
$$\text{ANG} \quad = \psi.$$

Since the hydrostatic pressure, p_0, is unknown at this point, but is
constant in the material to the left of *OBE*, it is convenient to
assume its value as zero when calculating *FX* and *FY* and to include it
later when evaluating the total force. This will be demonstrated
in the next section.

Similarly, the forces on the material to the left of slip line *DE*
can be evaluated using SLFORC. The directions of *FX* and *FY* for *BE*
and *DE* are shown in Fig. 6.23.

The forces on the straight slip lines *OB* and *AD* cannot be evaluated
using SLFORC because of obvious singularities, but they consist only
of the hydrostatic component of the stress perpendicular to the slip
line and a shear force equal numerically to the shear stress of the
material along the slip line.

Extrusion and drawing force. To find the total extrusion force, all
forces in the horizontal direction across *OBE* can be summed as follows:

$$\Sigma F_{OBE} = kFY_{BE} \cos\left(\frac{\pi}{2} - \alpha_n\right) - kFX_{BE} \sin\left(\frac{\pi}{2} - \alpha_n\right) + k\sqrt{2}\,\cos\alpha_n + p_B H,$$

where α_n and H are as shown in Fig. 6.24. The first two terms are the
forces obtained from SLFORC resolved horizontally; the third term
corresponds to the shear stress on the straight section *OB* whilst the
last term represents the hydrostatic component at point *B* which acts
across the thickness *H*.

The hydrostatic pressure can be considered in this way since it is

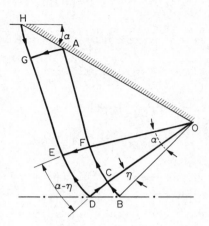

Fig. 6.24.   Slip-line field for reduction
ratios $> 2\sin\alpha/(1+2\sin\alpha)$.

constant along OB as this is a straight slip line, and by setting it
to zero at point B in SLFORC, it effectively reduces the hydrostatic
stress component along BE by a constant p_B.

Similarly, the total force acting on material to the left of ADE can
be written

$$\Sigma F_{ADE} = kFX_{DE} \cos \alpha_T - kFY_{DE} \sin \alpha_T - k \sqrt{2} \cos \alpha_T + p_D h,$$

where p_D is the hydrostatic component at D and α_T and h are as shown
in Fig. 6.23.

The hydrostatic stresses at D and B are still unknown; p_D can be
evaluated by equating ΣF_{ADE} to zero since there is no net force on
the extruded product. p_B as well as p_E can then be directly determined
from the Hencky equations.   Thus along DE which is a β-line,

$$p - 2k\phi = \text{constant},$$

where ϕ increases in the anti-clockwise direction.   Hence

$$p_E = p_D - 2k\theta$$

and

$$p_B = p_E + 2k\psi,$$

or
$$p_B = p_D + 2k(\psi-\theta).$$

For the example described previously the following values were obtained:

$$p_B/k = 0.6644; \quad p_E/k = -0.0337; \quad \text{and} \quad p_B/k = 1.0135.$$

The extrusion pressure when evaluated is

$$\Sigma F_{OBE}/H = 0.4117k.$$

Similarly, the drawing stress for the geometry of the previous example can be obtained by first equating the force across OBE to zero to determine p_B, then using the Hencky equations to find p_D and finally summing the forces across ADE. The drawing stress so calculated has the value given above.

(ii) Extrusion at High Reduction

The slip-line field shown in Fig. 6.24 is applicable to frictionless extrusion reductions $> 2 \sin \alpha/(1+2 \sin \alpha)$. If $OB = OC = OF$ is taken as 1 unit, then the radius vectors BC and CF are given by

$$\chi_{BC} = \chi_{CF} = \begin{bmatrix} -1 \\ 0 \\ 0 \\ 0 \\ 0 \\ 0 \end{bmatrix}.$$

Referring to Fig. 6.17(a) and using (6.44) with BC as the base slip line, χ_{DC} is given by

$$\chi_{DC} = T_\eta^{-1} \chi_{BC},$$

so that

$$\chi_{CD} = R_\eta T_\eta^{-1} \chi_{BC}.$$

Now taking C as the base point with CD and CF as the base slip lines, χ_{DE} and χ_{FE} can be obtained from (6.29) and (6.30), so that

$$\chi_{DE} = P_\eta^* \ \chi_{CF} + Q_\eta^* \ \chi_{CD}$$

and

$$\chi_{FE} = P^*_{\alpha-\eta} \ \chi_{CD} + Q^*_{\alpha-\eta} \ \chi_{CF}.$$

Then since $AF = OF = 1$, and AG and FE are parallel curves, it follows that

$$\chi_{AG} = \chi_{FE} + c,$$

where

$$c = \begin{bmatrix} 1 \\ 0 \\ 0 \\ 0 \\ 0 \\ 0 \end{bmatrix}.$$

Finally, referring to Fig. 6.24 and using the smooth boundary operator given by (6.44) with AG as the base slip line,

$$\chi_{HG} = T_\eta^{-1} \ \chi_{AG}.$$

By knowing the angles, it is now possible to calculate all the radius vectors and thus the coordinates of all points together with the extrusion pressure, etc., as in the previous example.

(iii)   Symmetrical and Asymmetrical Piercing Examples

Two kinds of slip-line fields for the symmetrical piercing by a rough flat punch of a block of material contained in a frictionless container have been proposed by Hill[3][20] and these are shown as Fig. 6.25 (a) and (b); they are for symmetric piercing with percentage reductions greater and less than 50%: For asymmetric piercing for reductions > 50%, see Fig. 6.25(c), the fractional reduction is defined by $[2d/(b + c + 2d)]$, where b and c are the sections of the surface of the block not covered by the punch and $2d$ is the punch width. Farah-bakhsh[21] has employed the matrix-operator technique to develop slip-

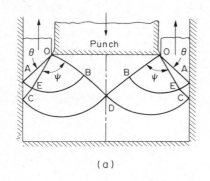

(a)

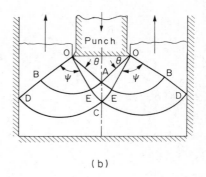

(b)

Fig. 6.25(a). Symmetrical piercing reduction > 50%.

Fig. 6.25(b). Symmetrical piercing reduction < 50%.

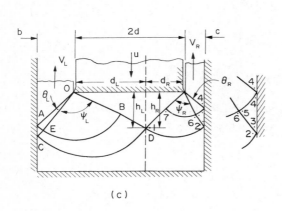

(c)

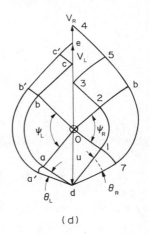

(d)

Fig. 6.25(c). Asymmetrical piercing reduction > 50%. Field valid for $bf < d$ and/or $2d > b + c$.

Fig. 6.25(d). Hodograph for asymmetrical piercing. Lettering serves to identify column vectors used in the text.

line-field solutions for a range of piercing problems.[†] An asymmetrical piercing slip-line field and its associated hodograph are shown in Fig. 6.25 (c) and (d) respectively; these represent the asymmetric analogue of the Hill solution and have been selected to provide a further example of the direct solution type of problem.

Since the slip line OA is assumed to be a straight line, AEB is a circular arc and the column vector representation of AEB is given by

---

[†]Frictionless punch indentation slip-line fields (which do not require any false heads) are easily proposed. This piercing problem has much in common with multi-hole extrusion. See pages 60 to 64 of ref. 22: *The Mechanics of Metal Extrusion*, W. Johnson and H. Kudo, Manchester University Press (1962).

$$\chi_{AE} = \chi_{EB} = \begin{vmatrix} OA \\ 0 \\ 0 \\ 0 \\ 0 \\ 0 \end{vmatrix}.$$

Using the frictionless boundary operator, χ_{CE} on the convex side of EB is given by,

$$\chi_{CE} = T_{\theta_L}^{-1} \chi_{EB} \, ,$$

so that applying the reversion operator

$$\chi_{EC} = R_{\theta_L} T_{\theta_L}^{-1} \chi_{EB} \, .$$

With base lines EB and EC, the remaining slip lines which comprise the regular net $EBDC$ can be defined from (6.29) and (6.30)

where
$$\chi_{BD} = P_{\psi_L}^* \chi_{EC} + Q_{\psi_L}^* \chi_{EB}$$

and
$$\chi_{CD} = P_{\theta_L}^* \chi_{EB} + Q_{\theta_L}^* \chi_{EC}.$$

A similar development can be carried out for the right-hand side of the slip line field. However, for the complete slip-line field to be valid three conditions are required to be satisfied, namely

(i)   point D which is common to both the left- and right-hand slip-line field solutions is required to have the same coordinates on the physical plane, i.e. $h_L = h_R$;

(ii)   the slip lines which intersect at point D must form a consistent orthogonal net, so that

$$\psi_L + \psi_R = \pi$$

and

(iii)   the hydrostatic pressure at point D, whether evaluated from either side of the field (frictionless boundary conditions) must yield identical values. This condition requires that

$$2\theta_L + \psi_L = 2\theta_R + \psi_R.$$

To analyse the field for any given values of b, c and d requires that the angles θ_L and ψ_L be selected and θ_R and ψ_R determined from the expressions which represent conditions (ii) and (iii) above. To satisfy condition (i) requires that a search technique be employed to sucessfully iterate the selected values of θ_L and ψ_L towards an acceptable solution. The geometrical performance of this process was described for the formally identical situation of multi-hole end extrusion by Johnson and Kudo (see Appendix VII of Ref. 22).

The associated hodograph can also be constructed using the matrix-operator method; the approach is analogous to the development of the slip-line field with due consideration being given to the imposed velocity boundary conditions. Once the hodograph has been constructed, the validity of the proposed slip-line field can be verified by determining the exit velocities (and directions) to ensure the conservation of volume in the forming operation.

To construct the hodograph, the downward velocity of the punch is assumed to be equal to some arbitrary value, u, which is represented by the vector od as shown in Fig. 6.25(d). If the angle between the slip line BD and the vertical line at point D in Fig. 6.25(c) is denoted by η, $ad = u \cos \eta$, and aa' is a circular arc which can be represented by a column vector such that

$$
\chi_{aa'} = \begin{vmatrix} u \cos \eta \\ 0 \\ 0 \\ 0 \\ 0 \\ 0 \end{vmatrix} . \quad \text{Similarly} \quad \chi_{ab} = \begin{vmatrix} -u \sin \eta \\ 0 \\ 0 \\ 0 \\ 0 \\ 0 \end{vmatrix} .
$$

From (6.29) and (6.30), $\chi_{a'b'}$ and $\chi_{bb'}$ are given by

$$
\chi_{a'b'} = P_{\theta_L}^* \chi_{ab} + Q_{\theta_L}^* \chi_{aa'}
$$

and

$$
\chi_{bb'} = P_{\psi_L}^* \chi_{aa'} + Q_{\psi_L}^* \chi_{ab} .
$$

Since bc is a straight line and $bc = ob = oa$,

$$\chi_{cc'} = \chi_{bb'} + u(\sin \eta)c,$$

where

$$c = \begin{vmatrix} 1 \\ 0 \\ 0 \\ 0 \\ 0 \\ 0 \end{vmatrix},$$

so that

$$\chi_{cc'} = \chi_{bb'} - \chi_{ab}.$$

Also the column vector representation of the radius of curvature of the line ec' on the convex side of the line cc' is given by

$$\chi_{ec'} = T_{\theta_L}^{-1} \chi_{cc'}.$$

The coordinates of all points within the hodograph can therefore be evaluated, and the exit velocity V_L determined, which is represented by the vector oe.

A similar approach can be used to construct the right-hand side of the hodograph from which V_R can be determined. To maintain the constancy of volume condition requires that the following relation be satisfied for the slip-line field to be valid:

$$u.2d = V_L b + V_R c.$$

Results obtained by Farahbakhsh[21] are presented in Figs. 6.26 (a) and (b) for a range of reductions. Figure 6.26(a) illustrates the variation of the average punch pressure with the degree of eccentricity for asymmetrical piercing. Figure 6.26(b) provides a comparison of the difference in the average punch pressure between symmetric and asymmetric piercing.

(iv)   Slip-Line Fields for Drawing and Wall-Ironing

Considerable research effort[8,23-27] has been devoted to the development and understanding of the two centred-fan slip-line fields first developed by Hill and Tupper.[8] More recently Dodd and Scivier[28] have

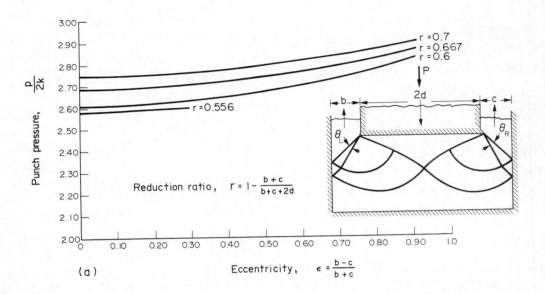

(a)

Fig. 6.26(a). Variation of the average punch
pressure with eccentricity for
asymmetrical piercing.

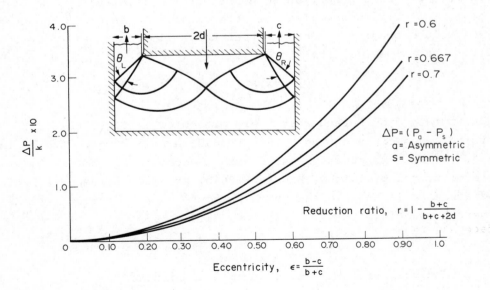

Fig. 6.26(b). Variation of the difference in average
pressure between symmetrical and
asymmetrical piercing with eccentricity.

examined in detail the general admissibility of these fields and defined the range of admissible solutions which extend from frictionless conditions to that of sticking friction. From the results for frictionless drawing evaluated by Dodd et al.[28] it was shown that a considerable number of these fields are in fact inadmissible as a result of overstressing[29] at the die exit. This particular limit on admissible solutions also coincided, for dies having a semi-die angle greater than 25°, with a mid-plane hydrostatic stress value, $p/2k$, equal to -0.5. For semi-die angles below this value $p/2k$ increased to approximately -0.7. This latter result is significant, since the probability of structural damage occuring during the deformation process is increased when large hydrostatic tensile stresses prevail at the mid-plane, i.e. point E on Fig. 6.23. For those conditions where $p_E \leqslant -k$, mid-plane cracking can be expected. See also the work of Rogers and Coffin.[24,25]

To investigate the admissibility conditions for slip-line fields in which mid-plane cracking could occur, Dodd and Kudo[30] have analysed the slip-line field, proposed by Johnson, and shown in Fig 6.27(a), which presupposes exit splitting along the line of symmetry. The method of solution[31] and results are presented in Ref. 30 for the drawing of material through frictionless dies; valid results are only obtained for semi-die angles less than 20° which correspond to an actual reduction of approximately 0.14. The range of results is severely restricted by overstressing of the material at points A and B.

When the same field is applied to the equivalent ironing[†] problem in which a frictionless mandrel is positioned parallel to the line of symmetry, the overstressing restrictions prevent any admissible solution from being derived. To investigate the ironing problem therefore required further modifications to the slip-line field shown in Fig. 6.27(a). Dodd et al.[30] have proposed the alternative slip-line field shown in Fig. 6.27(b) where the boundary MGI is now a stress-free surface and must be determined such that the normal and tangential components of stress are equal to zero everywhere along this line.

The development of the boundary slip lines and the stress-free boundary

---

†See Ref. 49, page 306, for a description of cup-ironing situations.

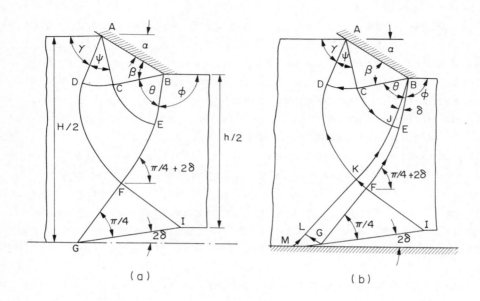

(a)   (b)

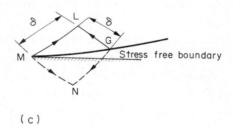

(c)

Fig. 6.27. (a) Slip-line field which provides for
mid-plane splitting in sheet
drawing.
           (b) Slip-line field which provides for
mandrel thinning in wall ironing.
           (c) Detail of curvilinear triangle
LGM in (b).

for the field shown in Fig. 6.27(b) can be conveniently developed by
the matrix-operator method.

From Hencky's first theorem for this field,

$$2\delta = \beta + \theta - \alpha - \psi - \frac{\pi}{4},$$

so that for given values of β, θ, α and ψ, δ can be evaluated directly.
Furthermore, since the slip-line field comprises two centred-fans,
χ_{CE} and χ_{CD} can be expressed in terms of the circular column vector

216

with magnitudes equal to the radii BC and AC respectively.

From (6.38), for the regular net $CJKD$, χ_{KD} and χ_{KJ} are given by

$$\chi_{KD} = P_{(\theta-\delta)\psi} \chi_{CE} + Q_{\psi(\theta-\delta)} \chi_{CD}$$

and

$$\chi_{KJ} = P_{\psi(\theta-\delta)} \chi_{CD} + Q_{(\theta-\delta)\psi} \chi_{CE}.$$

Similarly for the regular net $CEFD$ with base lines CD and CE,

$$\chi_{FD} = \chi_{FK} = P_{\theta\psi} \chi_{CE} + Q_{\psi\theta} \chi_{CD}$$

and

$$\chi_{FE} = P_{\psi\theta} \chi_{CD} + Q_{\theta\psi} \chi_{CE}.$$

Since KL and FG are straight lines,

$$\chi_{GL} = \chi_{FK} + \rho c$$

where ρ is the length KL.

The only unknown slip-line boundary is χ_{ML}. Consider the curvilinear triangle LGM extended to complete the regular net $LGMN$ as shown in Fig. 6.27(c). Since GM is a stress-free boundary χ_{GN} and χ_{GL} are related by (6.49) so that

$$\chi_{GL} = (D+I)^{-1} (D-I) \chi_{GN}$$

and from (6.52),

$$\chi_{MN} = F \chi_{GN}.$$

For the regular net $LGMN$, χ_{LM} can be obtained from (6.39), as

$$\chi_{LM} = R_\delta \chi_{ML} = P_{\delta\delta} R_\delta \chi_{GN} - Q_{\delta\delta} R_\delta \chi_{MN}.$$

The entire field can now be constructed in terms of the variables ψ, β, θ, α, ρ and the die length AB. The reductions and die pressures can be determined and the validity of each case assessed.

For further details on the formulation of stress-free boundary operators the reader is referred to reference 32 in which additional stress-

free surface operators are identified which transforms the hodograph
characteristics in accordance with velocity requirements at the free
surface boundary. Specifically, these operators have been developed
for both steady state and self-similar† problems in which the stress-
free boundary coincides with a stream line. Petryk[32] has demonstrated
the applicability of these matrix operators by developing new slip
line field solutions for (i) the steady-state problem of rolling
a rigid cylinder on a plastic half space and (ii) the steady-state
problem of machining as well as the self-similar problem of cutting
with a rigid wedge-shaped tool.

APPLICATION OF THE MATRIX-OPERATOR METHOD
TO THE SOLUTION OF INDIRECT-TYPE PROBLEMS

In recent years the matrix-operator method has been successfully
employed to analyse a range of previously unsolved or qualitatively
understood plane-strain plasticity problems which are of the indirect
type. Significant contributions include the symmetric and asymmetric
rolling of hot strip,[33-35] the indentation of a strip on a rough
anvil,[19] asymmetric extrusion,[18] machining with curly chip formation,[36]
compression studies between parallel rotating dies[37] and parallel dies
with slipping friction[38] and numerous other investigations[39-42][44] to
which the reader is referred. An excellent overview of the scope of
this method is provided by Collins.[1]

In all these solutions, the matrix operators are systematically introduced such that an inhomogeneous matrix equation, as given by (6.69),
can be formulated from which the initial or unknown base slip line,
represented by the column vector χ, can be found by a simple matrix
inversion. The column vectors of all other boundary slip lines within
the field can subsequently be evaluated from the expressions which were
initially derived to formulate the inhomogeneous equation given by
(6.69), so that the entire slip-line field and hodograph can be
constructed.

To solve for the initial slip line therefore requires that the matrices
A and ν be known. These matrices are derived from the physical and
velocity planes of the proposed slip-line solution and are represented
as combinations of the different matrix operators; the magnitude of
ν is directly proportional to the magnitude of the tangential velocity
discontinuity. Consequently, if all the slip-line angles and velocity
parameters which define the field are known, the proposed slip-line
field and hodograph can be constructed.

For problems which are relatively straightforward A and ν can be completely defined in terms of a set of prescribed slip-line angles and
velocity parameters, which by necessity, conform to the conditions of
Hencky's first theorem for the proposed field. The initial slip line
can therefore be evaluated and the entire slip-line field and hodograph
constructed. With this approach the geometry and physical boundary
conditions, etc., pertaining to, say, the reduction associated with
the deformation process are not specified *a priori*, but are in fact
determined from the solution to the problem. Using this procedure a

---

†These are problems of non-steady motion in which geometric similarity
of the entire configuration is maintained during deformation.

complete range of solutions can be easily generated by allowing each of the defining parameters of the field to vary within pre-defined limits. However, once the number of these parameters exceeds three or four - depending of course on the particular problem under investigation - the complexity and number of conditions which must be satisfied increases, and other more direct means must be sought to establish the range of the defining parameters of the field.

In the asymmetric hot rolling of strip Collins and Dewhurst[35] have identified as many as fourteen parameters which are required to compute the physical and velocity planes and the associated stress field. Of these fourteen parameters which comprise eight slip-line angles, five velocity parameters and one hydrostatic stress value at a point in the field, two velocity parameters can be classified as scaling factors, one additional velocity parameter can be specified as a result of the known roll speeds and the hydrostatic pressure can be directly evaluated if a zero horizontal force at the exit is assumed - so that only ten parameters are required to be evaluated.

In preference to the method of solution given above, the ten parameters can be obtained by resorting to an equivalent number of conditions which constrain or bound the solution. These conditions can relate to the geometry of the deformation process, compatibility within the velocity field or confirmation that the force components and moments at particular locations will independently sum to zero. The mathematical interpretation of each condition gives rise to a simultaneous system of complex non-linear algebraic equations for these unknown parameters. The solution to these equations can be accomplished by non-linear optimization techniques in which the sum of the squares of the residuals of each equation is minimized. The particular search technique which has been used by Das *et al.*[18] Dewhurst[19] and Collins and Dewhurst[35] is that due to Powell.[43] Das *et al.*[18] reported that for the solution to the asymmetric extrusion problem it was possible by "*judicious selection*" of the starting values to satisfactorily minimize these residuals within fifty to sixty iterations when using a maximum of six conditions. For the asymmetric hot-rolling solution[35] some 2000 iterations were necessary to obtain satisfactory accuracy. Other techniques may well be better suited, but as yet have not been explored.

(i)   Range of Slip-Line-Field Solutions for Extrusion/
      Drawing through Frictionless Wedged-Shaped-Dies

Four slip-line-field configurations associated with the extrusion/ drawing of material through a frictionless wedged-shape die are considered.[44] These have been designated as types I, II, III and IV and are illustrated in Fig. 6.28 (a), (b), (e) and (h) respectively. Each of these four fields, which extends over a definite range of reduction for a given die angle, has been developed by means of the matrix-operator method such that the geometric and load requirements for different values of α, η, ψ and θ have been established, where α, η, ψ and θ are as defined in Fig. 6.28. The detailed slip-line field development of type I as well as the bounding slip-line field between types II and III have already been presented in this chapter and can be considered as direct-type solutions. Type III is detailed in Refs. 13 and 17, and type IV will be presented later in this section. The four types are particularly interesting in that each subsequent case is basically an extension of the former case such that the

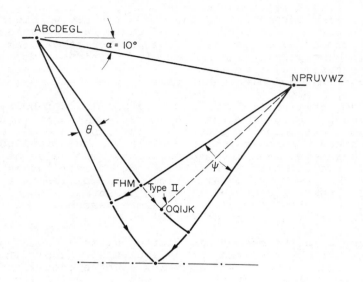

Fig. 6.28(a). Slip-line field for type I,
$r \leq 2\alpha \sin /(1 + 2 \sin \alpha)$.

bounding solution between two types can be developed from either
solution type by the appropriate choice of variables ψ, θ or η for a
given die angle α. To demonstrate the change from one case to the next
a series of nine slip-line-field solutions are presented in Fig. 6.28
(a) through to (h) for $\alpha = 10^{\circ}$. The length of the tapered die face
has been normalized to a standard length on each illustration to
provide a direct comparison of the increased reduction for each subsequent solution. Additionally, the coordinates of some of the points,
as seen in Fig. 6.28(a), are also designated by more than one alphabetic
character since additional slip-line segments will develop from these
points in subsequent fields.

Solution types. Figure 6.28(a) illustrates the standard field for
$r \leq 2 \sin \alpha/(1 + 2 \sin \alpha)$, where the semi-die angle $\alpha = 10^{\circ}$ requires
that ψ and θ are continuously reduced to the limiting case when $\psi =$
α and $\theta = 0$, i.e. the start of type II shown dotted in Fig. 6.28(a),
which corresponds to the particular solution of $r = 2 \sin \alpha/(1 + 2$
$\sin \alpha)$. With a further increase in the reduction the angle η, which
has a range $0 \leqslant \eta \leqslant \alpha$, increases, resulting in the coordinates designated $(ABCDEGL)$, (FHM) and $(OQIJK)$ shifting to the locations shown in
Fig. 6.28(b) for $\eta = 5^{\circ}$. The limiting case, when $\eta = \psi = \alpha = 10^{\circ}$ is
shown in Fig. 6.28(c) where points (FH) and (IJK) and M and Q now
represent the same respective locations. Figure 6.28(c) also provides
the limiting solution for type III which develops with a further
increase in the reduction as shown in Fig. 6.28(d) to the more familiar
geometry provided in Fig. 6.28(e). This occurs with a gradual increase
in ψ and θ such that the relation, $\psi - \theta = \alpha$, is maintained. As
these values increase the radius of curvature defined by the radius
vector $\chi_{(ABCD)G}$ is continuously increased such that the boundary

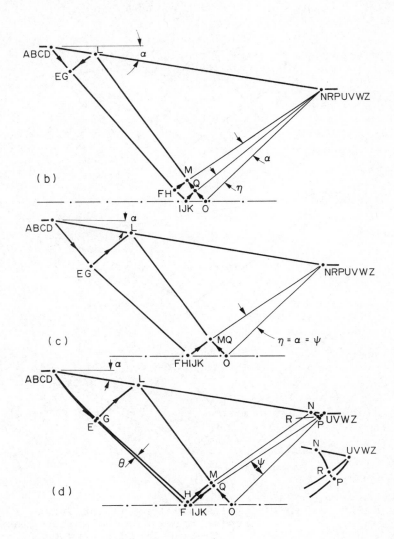

Fig. 6.28. Slip-line field development for drawing/
extrusion through wedge-shaped dies.
(b) Slip-line field for type II with
η = 5⁰.
(c) Bounding slip-line field for types
II and III.
(d) Development of the slip-line field
for type III.

conditions are satisfied to a level where the radius of curvature
approaches infinity, and point G moves towards point H as shown in
Fig. 6.28(f) where $\psi = 25^0$ and $\theta = 15^0$, ($\psi - \theta = \alpha$). This is the
limiting condition for type III. Further increase in the reduction

221

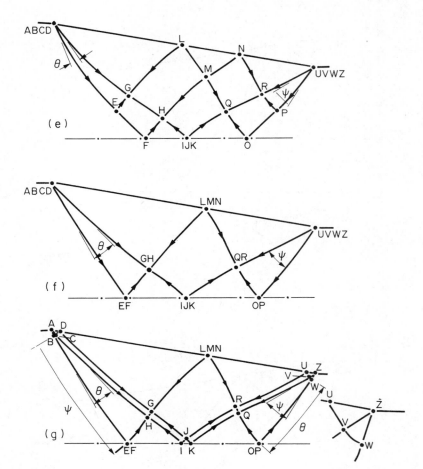

Fig. 6.28. Slip-line development for drawing/
extrusion through wedge-shaped dies.
(e) Slip-line field for type III,
$\psi = 20°$, $\theta = 10°$.
(f) Limiting slip-line field for
type III, $\psi = 25°$, $\theta = 15°$.
(g) Development of slip-line field
for type IV.

requires the points $(ABCD)$ and $(UVWZ)$ to be extended into centred
fans (BAC) and (WZV) respectively as shown in Fig. 6.28(g) with a
reduction in ψ and θ giving rise to type IV. Figures 6.28 (h) and
(i) serve to illustrate the growth of type IV as the angles ψ and θ
are further reduced.

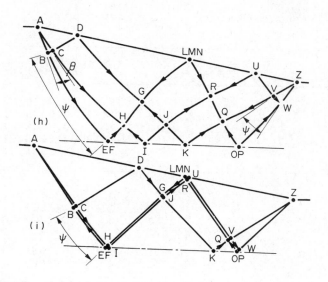

Fig. 6.28.   Slip-line field development for drawing/
extrusion through wedge-shaped dies.
(h)   Slip line for type IV, $\psi = 20^0$,
$\theta = 10^0$.
(i)   Increased reduction for type IV,
$\psi = 10.5^0$, $\theta = 0.5^0$.

The left side of Table 6.1 lists the values of the angles η, θ and ψ
and the corresponding values of reduction for the different cases
illustrated when $\alpha = 10^0$.

Extrusion and drawing pressure.   The extrusion/drawing pressures,
expressed in non-dimensional form as $p/2k$ have been evaluated for the
frictionless dies over a range of die semi-angles α.   These values
have been tabulated in Table 6.1 for types I to IV for $\alpha = 10^0$
together with the work done necessary for the homogeneous deformation
associated with the corresponding reduction, r, which is given by
$\ln(1/(1 - r))$.   Taking the ratio of $p/2k \ \ln(1/(1 - r))$ yields an
interesting result as evidenced by the appropriate column in Table
6.1.   The redundant work oscillates as a function of the reduction,
r, having a minimum value within the type II solution when η is
approximately equal to 5^0, and increases through type III to a
second maximum at the limiting condition between types III and IV.
The extent by which this ratio exceeds unity is thus a measure of
the relative amount of redundant work dissipated as inhomogeneous
distortion during the work operation.

TABLE 6.1. Extrusion/drawing results for types I to IV with $\alpha = 10°$.

Type	η	θ	ψ	r	p/2k	ℓn(1/(1-r))	p/2k ℓn(1/(1-r))	c/d
I		80.0	90.0	0.0320	0.0912	0.0325	2.8025	10.7244
		50.0	60.0	0.0709	0.1414	0.0735	1.9217	4.7477
		20.0	30.0	0.1518	0.2058	0.1646	1.2501	2.1249
Fig.6.28(a)		10.0	20.0	0.1965	0.2413	0.2188	1.1028	1.6016
		0.0	10.0	0.2578	0.3028	0.2981	1.0156	1.1796
II	0.5	—	10.0	0.2614	0.3070	0.3030	1.0134	1.1608
	3.0	—	10.0	0.2795	0.3299	0.3279	1.0061	1.0742
	4.0	—	10.0	0.2868	0.3396	0.3380	1.0048	1.0426
Fig.6.28(b)	5.0	—	10.0	0.2940	0.3497	0.3482	1.0043	1.0126
	6.0	—	10.0	0.3013	0.3601	0.3585	1.0045	0.9841
	7.0	—	10.0	0.3085	0.3709	0.3689	1.0054	0.9568
Fig.6.28(c)	10.0	—	10.0	0.3303	0.4055	0.4009	1.0116	0.8824
III	—	0.0	10.0	0.3033	0.4055	0.4009	1.0116	0.8824
Fig.6.28(d)	—	1.0	11.0	0.3373	0.4175	0.4115	1.0146	0.8603
	—	5.0	15.0	0.3618	0.4615	0.4491	1.0275	0.7903
Fig.6.28(e)	—	10.0	20.0	0.3822	0.5001	0.4816	1.0384	0.7387
Fig.6.28(f)	—	15.0	25.0	0.3895	0.5135	0.4934	1.0407	0.7217
IV		15.0	25.0	0.3895	0.5135	0.4934	1.0407	0.7217
Fig.6.28(g)	—	14.0	24.0	0.3898	9.5141	0.4938	1.0407	0.7210
Fig.6.28(h)	—	10.0	20.0	0.3968	0.5249	0.5055	1.0383	0.7051
	—	5.0	15.0	0.4188	0.5574	0.5427	1.0271	0.6589
Fig.6.28(i)	—	0.5	10.5	0.4521	0.6090	0.6017	1.0122	0.5976

This oscillatory variation of $p/2k \, \ell n \, (1/(1 - r))$ as a function of r is illustrated in Fig. 6.29 for α equal to $1°$, $10°$, $30°$ and $50°$ respectively. The minimum value increases as the die semi-angle, α, increases; however, as α tends to zero, which represents the Green solution of compression between frictionless parallel platens,[45] the redundant work component tends to zero.

This variation of $p/2k \, \ell n(1/(1 - r))$ has also been plotted as shown in Fig. 6.30 as a function of the parameter c/d used by Hill and Green,[23] where c is the length of the circular arc which has its centre at the virtual apex of the channel and joins the midpoints of the two zones of contact and d is the length of contact with each die

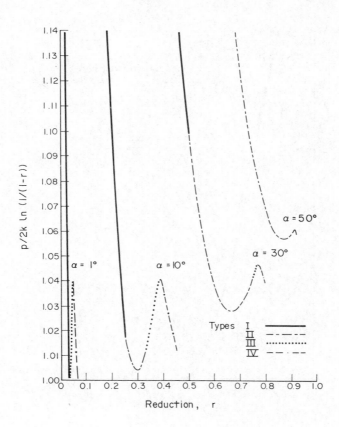

Fig. 6.29. Oscillatory behaviour of $p/2k$ $\ln(1/$
$(1 - r))$ as a function of the reduction
for selected die semi-angles extending
through types I to IV.

so that $c/d = (2 - r)\alpha/r$. The oscillatory behaviour of $p/2k$ $\ln(1/(1-r))$
is again evident as a function of the ratio c/d; as α is decreased
the curves tend towards Green's indentation solution[45] having a minimum value at unity and a maximum value corresponding to a d/c value of
$\sqrt{2}$. Both Figs. 6.29 and 6.30 have been drawn so that the relative
contribution provided by each of types I through to IV is clearly
evident; the minimum value is contained within type II, whereas the
maximum value occurs at the limiting conditions between types III
and IV.

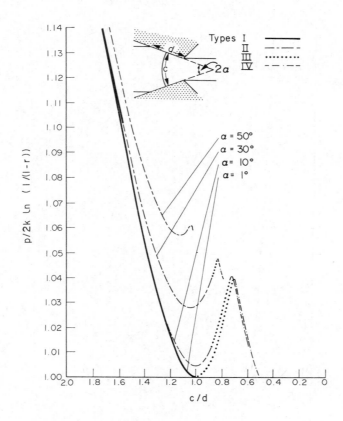

Fig. 6.30. Oscillatory behaviour of $p/2k \; \ln(1/(1 - r))$ as a function of the geometric ratio c/d for selected die semi-angles extending through types I to IV.

Figure 6.31 provides an insight into the variation of the extrusion/ drawing pressures through frictionless wedge-shaped dies as a function of the reduction for selected die semi-angles. The boundary limits provided by homogeneous compression as well as the geometric limits and the bulge limit for drawing conditions have been superimposed on these results to provide further clarification of the results presented in Fig. 6.29. Further details on the bounding limits are given in Refs. 3, 23 and 45; the reader is also referred to the work of Dodd and Scivier[28] on the static inadmissibility of some slip-line fields for sheet drawing. For $\alpha = 10^0$ the oscillatory behaviour of $p/2k$, when compared to the work done during homogeneous deformation, is

226

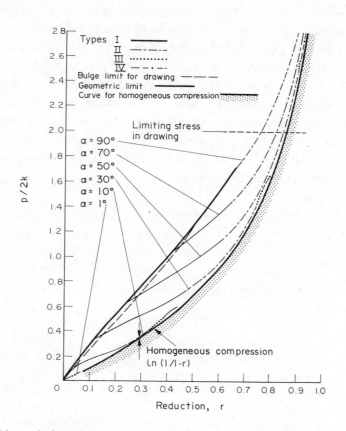

Fig. 6.31. Variation in the pressure for extrusion/
drawing through frictionless wedge-shaped
dies as a function of reduction for
selected die semi-angles.

again evidenced by the perturbation in the curve adjacent to the
$\ln(1/(1 - r))$ limit corresponding to the minimum and maximum values
observed in the $p/2k$ $\ln(1/(1 - r))$ plot.[†]

Matrix-operator formulation. The formulation of the types III and IV
slip-line field solutions using the matrix-operator method will be
presented below. The development for type III is detailed in references

---

[†]See the arrowed minimum on Fig. 6.31 for $\alpha = 10°$.

13 and 17; the approach is to identify an initial or base slip line which is represented by a column vector such that all other slip lines can be expressed in accordance with the defined function of the matrix operators. Algebraic manipulation of these column vectors can be carried out to evaluate the base slip-line column vector, consistent with the imposed boundary conditions. For the drawing/extrusion problems designated as types III and IV the base slip line can be determined from the physical plane alone; for other indirect-type solutions such as the hot rolling of strip, which is described later, the evaluation of the base slip line requires that both the physical and velocity planes be considered.

The formulation for type III is briefly summarized below. Using the notation of Fig. 6.28(e), it is convenient to denote $\chi_{(ABCD)G}$ and $\chi_{(UVWZ)R}$ as the base slip lines and to designate these column vectors, for simplicity, as χ and χ' respectively. With $ABCD$ as the base point and $(ABCD)G$ as the base line, (6.37) gives

$$\chi_{EG} = Q_{\psi\theta}\chi.$$

Since EG and FH are parallel curves (EF, GH and LM are straight lines)

$$\chi_{FH} = Q_{\psi\theta}\chi + \rho c$$

where ρ defines the length EF and c is the vector representation of a unit circular arc.

Again, with $(ABCD)G$ as the base slip line, it follows from (6.42) that

$$\chi_{LG} = T_{\psi}\chi$$

and

$$\chi_{MH} = T_{\psi}\chi - \rho c.$$

Now taking FH as a base line and using (6.44),

$$\chi_{(IJK)H} = T_{\theta}^{-1}\,\chi_{FH}$$

$$= T_{\theta}^{-1}\,(Q_{\psi\theta}\chi + \rho c). \tag{6.71}$$

Similarly, progressing from the right-hand side from the base line

MATRIX-OPERATOR METHODS FOR SOLVING PLANE-STRAIN S.L.F. PROBLEMS

$(UVWZ)R$, it can be shown that

$$\chi_{(IJK)Q} = T_\psi^{-1} \; (Q_{\theta\psi}\chi' - \rho c) \tag{6.72}$$

and

$$\chi_{MQ} = T_\theta \chi' + \rho c.$$

However, using M as the base point with MH and MQ as the base slip lines, $\chi_{(IJK)H}$ and $\chi_{(IJK)Q}$ can be obtained from (6.39),

$$\chi_{(IJK)H} = P_{\theta\psi} \; \chi_{MQ} - Q_{\psi\theta} \; \chi_{MH}$$

or

$$\chi_{(IJK)H} = P_{\theta\psi} \; (T_\theta\chi' + \rho c) - Q_{\psi\theta}(T_\psi\chi - \rho c), \tag{6.73}$$

and

$$\chi_{(IJK)Q} = P_{\psi\theta} \; \chi_{MH} - Q_{\theta\psi} \; \chi_{MQ}$$

or

$$\chi_{(IJK)Q} = P_{\psi\theta} \; (T_\psi\chi - \rho c) - Q_{\theta\psi} \; (T_\theta\chi' + \rho c). \tag{6.74}$$

Combining (6.71) to (6.74) and eliminating χ' , the following inhomogeneous equation in χ is obtained:

$$(-P_{\psi\theta}T_\psi + A_{\psi\theta} \; T_\theta^{-1} \; P_{\theta\psi}^{-1} \; A_{\theta\psi})\chi = (B_{\psi\theta} - A_{\psi\theta} \; T_\theta^{-1} \; P_{\theta\psi}^{-1} \; B_{\theta\psi})\rho c,$$

where

$$A_{\theta\psi} = T_\theta^{-1} \; Q_{\psi\theta} + Q_{\psi\theta} \; T_\psi \tag{6.75}$$

and

$$B_{\theta\psi} = T_\theta^{-1} - P_{\theta\psi} - Q_{\psi\theta}.$$

The problem of finding the initial slip-line radius vector χ thus reduces to a single matrix inversion, and from there the problem can be solved as before.

The matrix operator formulation for the type IV, slip-line-field solution shown in Fig. 6.28(h) is directly comparable with that given above for type III. In type IV the slip lines DG and UR, represented by the column vectors χ_{DG} and χ_{UR} respectively, are considered as the base or unknown slip lines. By suitable application of selected matrix operators it is possible to evaluate these column vectors such that all slip lines can subsequently be defined. Using the notation given in Fig. 6.28(h) this can be accomplished as follows:

From (6.42),
$$\chi_{(LMN)G} = T_\psi \; \chi_{DG}. \tag{6.76}$$

Since DG and CH are parallel curves, DC and GH are straight lines, also $CD = AB = AC = \rho$, so that

$$\chi_{CB} = -\rho c$$

and

$$\chi_{CH} = \chi_{DG} + \rho c.$$

For the regular net $CH(EF)B$, $\chi_{(EF)H}$ and $\chi_{(EF)B}$ are given by (6.38), so that

$$\chi_{(EF)H} = P_{\theta\psi}\,\chi_{CB} + Q_{\psi\theta}\,\chi_{CH} = -P_{\theta\psi}\,\rho c + Q_{\psi\theta}(\chi_{DG} + \rho c)$$

and

$$\chi_{(EF)B} = P_{\psi\theta}\,\chi_{CH} + Q_{\theta\psi}\,\chi_{CB} = P_{\psi\theta}\,(\chi_{DG} + \rho c) + Q_{\theta\psi}(-\rho c).$$

Once $\chi_{(EF)H}$ is known, χ_{IH} can be evaluated from (6.44), as

$$\chi_{IH} = T_{\theta}^{-1}\,\chi_{(EF)H} = T_{\theta}^{-1}\,(-P_{\theta\psi}\,\rho c + Q_{\psi\theta}\,(\chi_{DG} + \rho c)),$$

so that

$$\chi_{JG} = \chi_{IH} + \rho c. \qquad (6.77)$$

The remaining slip lines are more conveniently expressed in terms of the second unknown slip line χ_{UR}.

From (6.42),

$$\chi_{(LMN)R} = T_{\theta}\,\chi_{UR}. \qquad (6.78)$$

Since JR and KQ are parallel curves and $CD = UV = VZ = \rho$,

$$\chi_{VW} = \rho c$$

and

$$\chi_{VQ} = \chi_{UR} - \rho c.$$

For the regular net $VW(OP)Q$, $\chi_{(OP)Q}$ can be evaluated from (6.38),

$$\chi_{(OP)Q} = P_{\psi\theta}\,\chi_{VW} + Q_{\theta\psi}\,\chi_{VQ} = P_{\psi\theta}\,\rho c + Q_{\theta\psi}\,(\chi_{UR} - \rho c).$$

With $K(OP)$ as a line of symmetry, we have from (6.44),

$$\chi_{KQ} = T^{-1}_{\psi} \; \chi_{(OP)Q} = T^{-1}_{\psi} \; [P_{\psi\theta} \; \rho c + Q_{\theta\psi} \; (\chi_{UR} - \rho c)],$$

so that

$$\chi_{JR} = \chi_{KQ} - \rho c. \tag{6.79}$$

Equations (6.76) to (6.79) define the column vectors of each of the four sides of the regular net $G(LMN)RJ$ in terms of χ_{DG} and χ_{UR}. Using J as the base point with JR and JG as the base lines, $\chi_{(LMN)R}$ and $\chi_{(LMN)G}$ can also be obtained from (6.38), as

$$\chi_{(LMN)G} = P_{\psi\theta} \; \chi_{JR} + Q_{\theta\psi} \; \chi_{JG} \tag{6.80}$$

and

$$\chi_{(LMN)R} = P_{\theta\psi} \; \chi_{JG} + Q_{\psi\theta} \; \chi_{JR}. \tag{6.81}$$

Combining (6.76) to (6.81), χ_{UR} can be eliminated, and an expression for χ_{DG} obtained which is similar to that given by (6.75) for the type III solution.

(ii)   Drawing through Rough Wedged-Shaped Dies

It is also possible to utilize the matrix inversion method to evaluate the pressure required for drawing a material through rough wedge-shaped dies provided a constant friction factor is assumed rather than a constant coefficient of friction. The acute angle β between the die face and β-line is given by cos 2β = m where m is the friction factor; typical types I and II slip-line fields as related to the previous section are illustrated in Fig. 6.32.

A plot of the drawing pressure versus the reduction through rough dies is shown in Fig. 6.33(a) for types I and II. This figure clearly illustrates that there is an optimum die angle for a given reduction, die angle and frictional condition. It would be difficult to directly utilize these results in practice, however, not only because a constant friction factor is not the best assumption for cold drawing, but also because the friction tends to change with both reduction and die angle.

The variation of $p/2k$ ℓn $(1/(1 - r))$ as a function of the reduction has also been evaluated for the rough wedged-shaped die when $m = 0.25$.

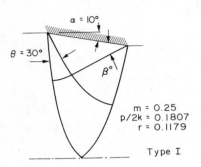

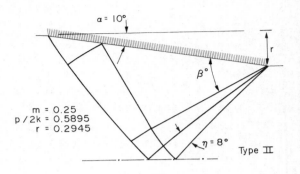

Fig. 6.32. Slip-line fields for types I and II for drawing through a rough wedged-shaped die.

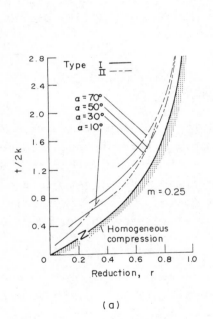

(a)

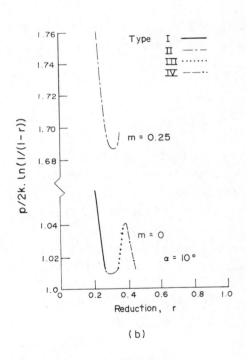

(b)

Fig. 6.33(a). Variation in the drawing pressure for rough wedge-shaped dies as a function of the reduction for selected die semi-angles.

Fig. 6.33(b). Oscillatory behaviour of $p/2k \, \ln(1/(1-r))$ as a function of the reduction.

The oscillatory behaviour, exhibited by the frictionless cases as shown in Fig. 6.29, is again evident for the solutions when the friction condition is included. The results for types I and II are illustrated in Fig. 6.33(b).

(iii) Slip-Line Field Solutions for the Hot Rolling of Strip

A general slip-line field and the corresponding hodograph for the hot rolling of strip between medium and small diameter rolls are illustrated in Fig. 6.34 (a) and (b) respectively[33]. The field is completely

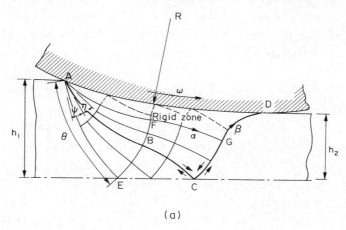

(a)

(a)   slip-line field.

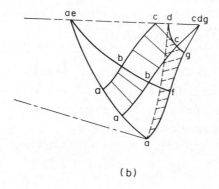

(b)

(b)   hodograph.

Fig. 6.34.   Rolling solution for small to medium diameter rolls : velocity discontinuity along *ABCGD*.

defined by the slip line angles ψ, θ and η and reduces to the particular fields given by Druyanov[46] for $\psi = 0$ and Chitkara and Johnson[47] for $\eta = 0$.

Dewhurst, Collins and Johnson[33] have analysed this slip-line field using the matrix-operator method to evaluate the overall geometry, roll torque requirements and separating forces for a range of reductions. Their approach was to identify the slip-line angles θ, ψ and η with the fundamental parameters R/h_1, h_2/h_1 and the back tension and to analyse the slip-line field in accordance with the following procedures and constraints

(i)   For hot rolling, sticking conditions are assumed to exist between the material and the roll surface, i.e. the tangential stress, τ, must be less than the shear stress of the material k. This condition is automatically satisfied by assuming a rotating rigid zone over the full arc of contact.

(ii)   Normal contact stress between the rolls and the material interface must be compressive, i.e. the mean normal pressure at point D, p_D, is required to be greater than or equal to zero.

(iii)   Selection of mean normal pressure, p, at G is such that zero front tension is attained.

(iv)   For a given value of ψ, θ and η are evaluated using linear interpolation methods such that a zero back tension results for the required reduction.

Dewhurst *et al.*[33] have evaluated a set of results pertaining to the roll-force and roll-torque requirements for a range of reductions. The results of the roll-force coefficient, P/kh_1, versus the fundamental parameter R/h_1 is presented in Fig. 6.35. Limit A represents the Chitkara and Johnson field for $\eta = 0$ whereas limit B defines the conditions at which $p_D = 0$.

For the 20% reduction, p_D, is approximately equal to $1.38k$ (limit A) when $\eta = 0$ which corresponds to the largest roll size. As η increases from zero, θ also increases, and ψ and the roll radius decrease. For $R/h_1 \approx 7.8$, $p_D = 0$. It is interesting to further examine the slip-line fields which result for R/h_1 values below this critical limit.

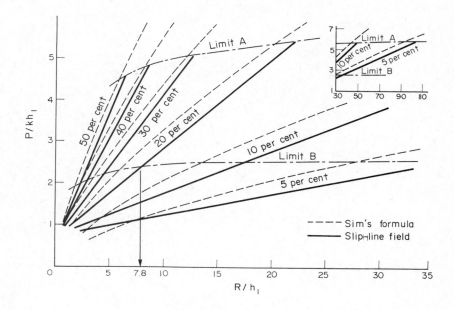

Fig. 6.35. Comparison of roll force P/kh_1, evaluated
from Sim's formula and the slip-line field
for different reductions. (P is the roll
force per unit width for each roll, and h_1
is the entry thickness).

As the roll radius is reduced the radius of curvature of the exit
slip line GD decreases and eventually degenerates into a single point
when G and D are coincident at the roll/material interface. This
limiting slip-line field solution and its associated hodograph are
illustrated in Fig. 6.36 (a) and (b) respectively. For R/h_1 values
less than this limiting case the form of the slip-line and hodograph
are shown in Fig. 6.37 in which plastic recovery of the strip occurs.
A comparison of the three slip line fields and the hodographs shown
in Figs. 6.34, 6.36 and 6.37 indicates considerable variation in the
flow pattern of the material through the rolls. In Fig. 6.34 the
velocity discontinuity $ABCGD$ crosses the centre-line of symmetry and
in Fig. 6.36 the velocity field is continuous, but in Fig. 6.37
the velocity discontinuity AFG is almost adjacent to the roll which
permits the small degree of plastic recovery downstream of the mimimum
roll gap. These differences will become more evident in the formulation of the solution of the problem using the matrix-operator method.

235

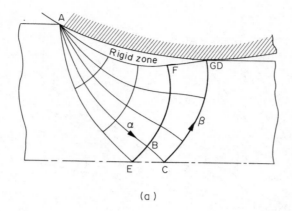

(a)

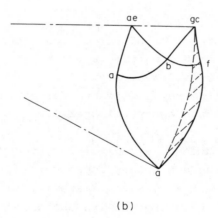

(b)

Fig. 6.36. Rolling solution with continuous velocity
          field.

The importance of the magnitude of the velocity discontinuity, particularly for the valid rolling solutions obtained with the slip-line
field shown in Fig. 6.34 where $p_D \geqslant 0$, on the resulting metallurgical
properties are discussed in Ref. 33. The reader is also referred
to reference 33 for a more complete discussion of the variation in
p_D which, under certain conditions, gives rise to "negative pressure
effects" such as that encountered in forging and indentation solutions.

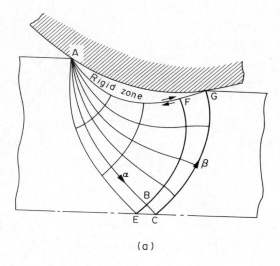

(a)

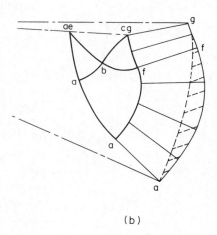

(b)

Fig. 6.37. Rolling solution with plastic recovery
of the strip: velocity discontinuity
along *AFG*.

Matrix-operator formulation. Details of the matrix-operator formulation for these slip-line fields applicable to the hot rolling of strip
are developed below.

With reference to Fig. 6.38(a), for rolling with small to medium

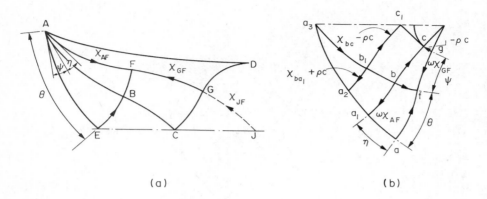

(a)   (b)

Fig. 6.38.   Vector representation of slip lines and
hodograph corresponding to Fig. 6.34.

diameter rolls, the slip line AF is represented by the column vector
χ_{AF}. From (6.37) and (6.44), the respective column vectors χ_{EF} and
χ_{JF} are given by

$$\chi_{EF} = Q_{\theta(\psi+\eta)} \ \chi_{AF} \tag{6.82}$$

and

$$\chi_{JF} = T^{-1}_{(\psi+\eta)} \ \chi_{EF} = T^{-1}_{(\psi+\eta)} \ Q_{\theta(\psi+\eta)} \ \chi_{AF}. \tag{6.83}$$

χ_{GF} can be evaluated directly from χ_{JF} by using the shift operator to
displace the base point from point J to G which corresponds to an
angular shift of η. From (6.41),

$$\chi_{GF} = S_{\eta} \ \chi_{JF} = S_{\eta} \ T^{-1}_{(\psi+\eta)} \ Q_{\theta(\psi+\eta)} \ \chi_{AF}. \tag{6.84}$$

To develop a second equation between χ_{GF} and χ_{AF} so that χ_{AF} can be
evaluated requires that the hodograph associated with this slip-line
field be considered. The images of the slip lines GF and AF represented
in the hodograph shown in Fig. 6.38(b) are geometrically similar to
the curves in the physical plane and are given by $\omega\chi_{GF}$ and $\omega\chi_{AF}$ respectively, where ω is the angular speed of the rolls. If ρ is the magnitude of the velocity discontinuity, the column vector of the circular
arc cg, χ_{cg}, is given by $-\rho c$. From (6.38) for the regular net $cgfb$,
χ_{bc} and χ_{bf} can be defined by

238

$$\chi_{bc} = P_{\psi\eta} \, \omega\chi_{GF} - Q_{\eta\psi} \, \rho c \tag{6.85}$$

and

$$\chi_{bf} = -P_{\eta\psi} \, \rho c + Q_{\psi\eta} \, \omega\chi_{GF}. \tag{6.86}$$

Similarly, for the regular net $bfaa_1$ with b as the base point,

$$\omega\chi_{AF} = P_{\theta\eta} \, \chi_{ba_1} + Q_{\eta\theta} \, \chi_{bf} \tag{6.87}$$

so that

$$\chi_{ba_1} = P_{\theta\eta}^{-1} \, \omega\chi_{AF} - P_{\theta\eta}^{-1} \, Q_{\eta\theta} \, \chi_{bf}. \tag{6.88}$$

$\chi_{b_1 a_2}$ and $\chi_{b_1 c_1}$ can be found directly from χ_{ba_1} and χ_{bc} respectively. Since the intrinsic direction describes a clockwise rotation of the tangent to the curve ba_1, the radius of curvature associated with χ_{ba_1} is negative. $\chi_{b_1 a_2}$ which has a smaller radius of curvature than χ_{ba_1} is therefore given by

$$\chi_{b_1 a_2} = \chi_{ba_1} + \rho c. \tag{6.89}$$

Similarly,

$$\chi_{b_1 c_1} = \chi_{bc} - \rho c. \tag{6.90}$$

From (6.27), (6.35) and (6.42) both $\chi_{b_1 a_2}$ and $\chi_{b_1 c_1}$ can be expressed in terms of $\chi_{a_3 b_1}$, where

$$\chi_{b_1 a_2} = Q_\psi^* \, \chi_{a_3 b_1} \tag{6.91}$$

and

$$\chi_{b_1 c_1} = R_\psi \, T_\psi \, \chi_{a_3 b_1}. \tag{6.92}$$

By the elimination of $\chi_{a_3 b_1}$ from (6.91) and (6.92), (6.90), (6.89), (6.88), (6.86), (6.85) can be used in turn to substitute for column vectors $\chi_{b_1 c_1}$, $\chi_{b_1 a_2}$, χ_{ba_1}, χ_{bf} and χ_{bc} respectively such that the second equation relating χ_{AF} to χ_{GF} results. This equation is given by[33]

$$\chi_{AF} - (Q_{\eta\theta} \, Q_{\psi\eta} + P_{\theta\eta} \, Q_\psi^* \, T_\psi^{-1} \, P_\eta^*) \, \chi_{GF}$$

$$= -(\rho/\omega) \, (P_{\theta\eta} + Q_{\eta\theta} \, P_{\eta\psi} + P_{\theta\eta} \, Q_\psi^* \, T_\psi^{-1} \, R_\psi \, (I + Q_{\eta\psi})) c. \tag{6.93}$$

From (6.84) and (6.93), χ_{GF} can be eliminated so that a basic inhomogeneous equation for the unknown slip line, χ_{AF}, as given by (6.69), results.

Hence,

$$A\chi_{AF} = B(\rho/\omega)\ c,\tag{6.94}$$

where

$$A \equiv I - \left[(Q_{\eta\theta}\ Q_{\psi\eta} + P_{\theta\eta}\ Q_{\psi}^{*}\ T_{\psi}^{-1}\ P_{\eta}^{*})(S_{\eta}\ T_{(\psi+\eta)}^{-1}\ Q_{\theta(\psi+\eta)}) \right]\tag{6.95}$$

and

$$B \equiv -(P_{\theta\eta}\ (I + Q_{\psi}^{*}\ T_{\psi}^{-1}\ R_{\psi}\ (I + Q_{\eta\psi})) + Q_{\eta\theta}\ P_{\eta\psi}).\tag{6.96}$$

Equation (6.94) reduces to the equivalent expression first derived by Dewhurst and Collins[13] for the particular case in which $\eta = 0$, i.e. the Chitkara and Johnson[47] slip-line field for the hot rolling of strip.

The manipulation of the matrix operators to evaluate χ_{AP} as given by (6.94) confirms, as previously indicated by (6.69), that the vector ν is directly proportional to the velocity discontinuity. As the roll radius is reduced, the magnitude of the velocity discontinuity is reduced. For the limiting case when this velocity discontinuity along $ABCGD$ vanishes and the slip-line field is as shown in Fig. 36(a), (6.94) reduces to

$$A\chi_{AF} = [I - A^{*}]\chi_{AF} = 0,\tag{6.97}$$

so that χ_{AF} is the eigen-vector of the matrix A^{*} corresponding to an eigen-value of unity.

For the rolling solution with plastic recovery shown in Fig. 6.39, two expressions relating χ_{AF} and χ_{GF} can again be developed from the slip-line field and the hodograph. From the physical plane the first relation is identical to that given by (6.84). The second relationship derived from the hodograph, where ρ is the velocity discontinuity along AFG, is given by[33]

$$\omega\chi_{AF} - \rho c = P_{\theta\eta}\ Q_{\psi}^{*}\ T_{\psi}^{-1}\ P_{\eta}^{*}\ (\omega\chi_{GF} + \rho c) + Q_{\eta\theta}\ Q_{\psi\eta}\ (\omega\chi_{GF} + \rho c).\tag{6.98}$$

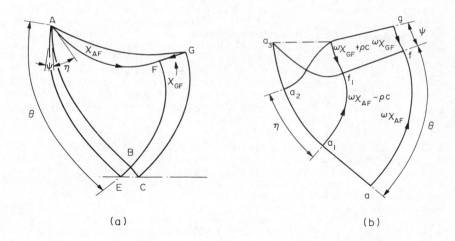

(a)   (b)

Fig. 6.39. Vector representation of slip lines and
hodograph corresponding to Fig. 6.37.

From (6.84) and (6.98), χ_{GF} can be eliminated to provide the inhomogeneous expression from which χ_{AF} can be evaluated.
Hence,

$$A\chi_{AF} = D(\rho/\omega)\ c, \qquad\qquad (6.99)$$

where A is again given by (6.95) and D is given by[33]

$$D \equiv P_{\theta\eta}\ Q^{\star}_{\psi}\ T^{-1}_{\psi}\ P^{\star}_{\eta} + Q_{\eta\theta}\ Q_{\psi\eta} + I.$$

When the velocity discontinuity vanishes, as the roll radius is increased, (6.99) again reduces to the homogeneous equation given by (6.97).

Asymmetric rolling. Asymmetries in strip rolling can arise as a result
of differences in the roll radii, speeds, surface roughness, torques
or where an initially straight strip enters the roll gap at some angle
to the line of symmetry. As a consequence of asymmetric rolling,
attributed to say the pair of rolls having different peripheral speeds,
the rolled strip can curve towards either of the two rolls. Any arguments that this curvature would necessarily be away from the roll having
the higher peripheral velocity must be assessed with due consideration
given to the highly inhomogeneous nature of the deformation process
which occurs during rolling.

Slip-line field analyses of the asymmetric hot rolling of strip have been developed by Dewhurst, Collins and Johnson[34] and Collins and Dewhurst[35] to investigate the preferred directional curvature of the rolled strip as a function of selected geometric variables and the angular velocities of the rolls. In these analyses the matrix-operator method has been used to full advantage to formulate the "indirect" type solutions. With reference to Fig. 6.34, Dewhurst *et al.*[34] have based their investigation on a generalized form of the symmetrical rolling slip-line field given by Chitkara and Johnson[47] in which $\eta = 0$, while Collins *et al.*[35] have computed their results for the asymmetric analogue of the Druyanov solution.[46]

References 34 and 35 provide a detailed description of these solutions which have been developed subject to selected stress boundary conditions at the exit and entry planes, roll geometries and roll speeds. The effectiveness of the matrix-operator method to assist in the understanding of the mechanics of asymmetrical rolling and indeed to predict the sign and magnitude of the curvature of the rolled strip is clearly demonstrated in both articles. One such computed result,[35] showing the variation in the curvature of the rolled strip as a function of the ratio of the roll radii, is illustrated in Fig. 6.40.

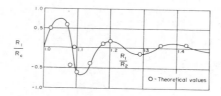

Fig. 6.40. Oscillatory behaviour of the strip
curvature, R_c, as a function of the
ratio of the roll radii, R_1/R_2 (angular
speeds of both rolls are equal, reduction
= 20%, and $R_1/H = 10$, where H is the
thickness of the strip at the entry).

This oscillatory behaviour is also exihibited by the individual roll torques when plotted as a function of the roll radius ratio.

Collins and Dewhurst[35] have compared their results with the experimental observations reported by Chekmarev and Nefedov[48] and conclude that "qualitative agreement" is indicated.

SUMMARY

As a result of the linearity of the governing partial differential equations (see equation (6.10)) in which the characteristic coordinates α and β are used as the independent variables, slip-line fields can be superimposed. Hill[16] has presented the geometric formulation of this superposition principle and demonstrated that a field can be constructed by the vectorial addition of position vectors of points having the same characteristic coordinates. The matrix operator method provides an alternative formulation to this superposition principle in the context of linear algebra. The procedures are again dependent upon the linearity of the problem, such that a series of linear operators can be defined which permit the construction of slip-line fields to be carried out by the simple manipulation of these linear operators. The matrix-operator method is particularly useful in the more complex statically indeterminate or indirect-type problem where the need to satisfy conditions in both the velocity and physical planes leads to a linear integral equation. With the matrix-operator formulation the solution to this integral equation is equivalent to inverting a matrix, which then enables the unknown base slip line or initial slip line to be determined.

The use of the matrix operator is limited to problems with boundary conditions which lead to linear integral equations. A boundary condition such as a straight boundary on which Coulomb type friction is assumed, or a curved boundary, will result in a non-linear integral equation which cannot be handled by the presently formulated method. The reader is, however, referred to the numerical methods proposed by Bachrach and Samanta[50] in which optimization techniques are employed to solve this type of non-linear integral equation.

The development of computerized packages for the matrix-operator method can be conveniently handled by small digital computer systems since core storage requirements are minimal. These computer systems can be easily interfaced with a graphic display terminal so that once the initial slip-line field has been evaluated (for indirect-type problems) the slip-line field and hodograph can be rapidly constructed on the screen for a visual assessment of the results. This visual aid could also be of considerable value to direct the iterative estimates onto the correct solution for those problems in which the solutions are severely constrained by a system of non-linear algebraic equations.[18,19,35] Problems of this type can present some numerical difficulty when the number of non-linear algebraic equations is excessive, i.e. greater than ten.[35]

The usefulness of the matrix-operator method has been clearly demonstrated in the literature. Results of particular interest relate to, (i) whether or not the rolled strip in asymmetric rolling will curve away or towards the roll with the larger peripheral speed,[35] (ii) determination of the chip deformation in orthogonal machining[36] and (iii), assessment of mid-plane cracking conditions in sheet drawing.[30] These results and others should not be viewed solely as an exercise in metal-forming analyses: identification of velocity discontinuities and mid-plane hydrostatic tension, etc., which occur in these forming operations all influence the mechanical and material properties of formed (rolled, extruded, drawn, etc.) material, and could significantly alter the probability of structural damage within these manufactured components. One might therefore expect that these methods of analyses will in the future be effectively developed to provide useful information on manufacturing variables and probable material defects and for correlating this knowledge with the fracture behaviour of these materials in defined applications.

SUMMARY OF MATRIX OPERATORS

	Type	Operation	Matrix operator
	Shift	$XY \rightarrow YZ$	S_θ
	Reversion	$XY \rightarrow YX$	R_θ
	Centre fan Convex side	$XY \rightarrow XZ$ $XZ \rightarrow XY$ $XY \rightarrow YZ$ $XY \rightarrow ZX$ $XY \rightarrow ZY$	P^*_ψ $P^{*-1}_\psi \equiv P^*_{-\psi}$ Q^*_θ $P_{\theta\psi} \equiv R_\theta \, P^*_\psi$ $Q_{\theta\psi} = R_\psi \, Q^*_\theta$
	Regular net Convex side	$\rightarrow WZ$ $\rightarrow ZW$ $\rightarrow YZ$ $\rightarrow ZY$	$P^*_\psi \chi_{XY} + Q^*_\psi \chi_{XW}$ $P_{\theta\psi} \chi_{XY} + Q_{\psi\theta} \chi_{VW}$ $P^*_\theta \chi_{VW} + Q^*_\theta \chi_{XY}$ $P_{\psi\theta} \chi_{VW} + Q_{\theta\psi} \chi_{XY}$
	Regular net Concave side	$\rightarrow ZW$ $\rightarrow ZY$	$P_{\theta\psi} \chi_{XY} - Q_{\psi\theta} \chi_{VW}$ $P_{\psi\theta} \chi_{VW} - Q_{\theta\psi} \chi_{XY}$
	Frictionless boundary	$XY \rightarrow ZY$ $ZY \rightarrow XY$ $XY \rightarrow WY$	$T_\theta = - (P_{\theta\theta} + Q_{\theta\theta})$ $T^{-1}_\theta = - P_{\theta\theta} + Q_{\theta\theta}$ $T^{-1}_\theta = - P_{\theta\theta} + Q_{\theta\theta}$

244

MATRIX-OPERATOR METHODS FOR SOLVING PLANE-STRAIN S.L.F. PROBLEMS

Type	Operation	Matrix operator

Straight rough boundary

$XY \rightarrow ZY$

$G_\eta = Q_{\psi\psi} + P_{\psi\psi}(I \cos \eta - J \sin \eta)^{-1}(J \cos \eta - I \sin \eta)$

Perfectly rough boundary ($\eta = 0$)

$XY \rightarrow ZY$

$G_o = Q_{\psi\psi} + P_{\psi\psi}J$

Stress-free surface

$XY \rightarrow ZY$

$F = R_\psi P_{\psi\psi}^{-1}[R_\psi(D + I)^{-1}(D-1) + Q_{\phi\phi}R_\phi]$

REFERENCES

1.   Collins, I. F., "Integral equation formulation of slip-line field problems". *Applications of Numerical Methods to Forming Processes*, A.S.M.E., **28**, 129 (1978).

2.   Dewhurst, P., "Eigenvector slip-line field solutions". *Applications of Numerical Methods to Forming Processes*, A.S.M.E., **28**, 121 (1978).

3.   Hill, R., *The Mathematical Theory of Plasticity*. Oxford University Press, London (1967).

4.   Green, A. P., "A theoretical investigation of the compression of a ductile material between smooth flat dies". *Phil. Mag.* **42**, 900 (1951).

5.   Alexander, J. M., "A slip-line field for the hot rolling process". *Proc. Inst. Mech. Engs.*, **169**, 1021 (1955).

6.   Prager, W. and Hodge, P. G., *Theory of Perfectly Plastic Solids*. Wiley, New York (1951).

7.   Prager, W., *An Introduction to Plasticity*. Addison-Wesley, Reading, Mass. (1959).

8.   Hill, R. and Tupper, S. J., "A new theory of the plastic deformation in wire-drawing". *Iron Steel Inst.*, **159**, 353 (1948).

9.   Sokolovskii, V. V., "Complete plane problems of plastic flow". *J. Mech. Phys. Solids*, **10**, 353 (1962).

10.   Johnson, W., Sowerby, R. and Haddow, J. B., *Plane-Strain Slip-Line Fields*. Arnold, London (1970). pp. 176.

11.   Ewing, D. J. F., "A series method for constructing slip-line fields". *J. Mech. Phys. Solids*, **15**, 105 (1967).

12.   Collins, I. F., "The algebraic-geometry of slip-line fields with applications to boundary value problems". *Proc. R. Soc.*, A, **303**, 317 (1968).

13.   Dewhurst, P. and Collins, I. F., "A matrix technique for constructing slip-line field solutions to a class of plane strain plasticity problems". *Int. J. Num. Methods Engng.*, **7**, 357 (1973).

14.   Collins, I. F., "Compression of a rigid-perfectly plastic strip between parallel rotating smooth dies". *Quart. J. Mech. Appl. Math.*, **23**, 329 (1970).

15.   Collins, I. F., "Geometric properties of some slip-line fields for compression and extrusion". *J. Mech. Phys. Solids*, **16**, 137 (1968).

16.   Hill, R., "On the vectorial superposition of Hencky-Prandtl nets". *J. Mech. Phys. Solids*, **15**, 255 (1967).

17.   Venter, R. D., Hewitt, R. L. and Johnson, W., "An engineering approach to the matrix operator technique for slip-line field construction". *Sixth North American Metalworking Research Conference Proceedings, April 16th-18th, University of Florida, Gainsville, Florida, U.S.A.*, pp. 111-118 (1978).

18.   Das, N. S., Chitkara, N. R. and Collins, I. F., "The computation of some slip-line field solutions for asymmetric extrusion". *Int. J. Num. Methods Engng.*, **11**, 1379 (1977).

19.   Dewhurst, P., "Plane strain indentation on a smooth foundation: a range of solutions for rigid perfectly plastic strip". *Int. J. Mech. Sci.*, **16**, 923 (1974).

20.   Hill, R., "A theoretical analysis of the stresses and strains in extrusion piercing". *J. Iron Steel Inst.*, **158**, 177 (1948).

21.   Farahbakhsh, B., "Application of matrix method to construct slip-line fields and associated hodographs, with computer simulation, to some plane plastic flow problems in piercing, extrusion and drawing". M.Sc. Dissertation, Mechanical Engineering Department,

University of Manchester, Institute of Science and Technology, May 1979.

22. Johnson, W. and Kudo, H., *The Mechanics of Metal Extrusion*. Manchester University Press (1962).

23. Green, A. P. and Hill, R., "Calculations on the influence of friction and die geometry in sheet drawing". *J. Mech. Phys. Solids*, 1, 31 (1952).

24. Rogers, H. C. and Coffin, L. F., "Influence of pressure on the structural damage in metal forming processes". *Trans. Am. Soc. Metals*, 60, 672 (1967).

25. Rogers, H. C. and Coffin, L. F., "An analysis of the effect of friction on sheet drawing". *Int. J. Mech. Sci.*, 13, 141 (1971).

26. Johnson, W., "Extrusion through wedged-shaped dies, Part 1". *J. Mech. Phys. Solids*, 3, 218 (1955).

27. Johnson, W., "Extrusion through wedged-shaped dies, Part 2". *J. Mech. Phys. Solids*, 3, 224 (1955).

28. Dodd, B. and Scivier, D. A., "On the static inadmissibility of some slip-line fields for sheet drawing". *Int. J. Mech Sci.*, 17, 663 (1975).

29. Hill, R., "On the limits set by plastic yielding to the intensity of singularities of stress". *J. Mech. Phys. Solids*, 2, 278 (1954).

30. Dodd, B. and Kudo, H., "A slip-line field for mid-plane cracking or splitting in sheet drawing". *Int. J. Mech. Sci.*, 22, 67 (1980).

31. Dodd, B. and Scivier, D. A., Oxford University Engineering Laboratory, Report No. 1117/75.

32. Petryk, H., "On slip-line field solutions for steady-state and self similar problems with stress free boundaries". *Archives of Mechanics (Archiwum Mechaniki Stosowanej)*, 31, 861 (1979).

33. Dewhurst, P., Collins, I. F. and Johnson, W., "A class of slip-line field solutions for the hot rolling of strip". *J. Mech. Eng. Sci.*, 15, 439 (1973).

34. Dewhurst, P., Collins, I. F. and Johnson, W., "A theoretical and experimental investigation into asymmetrical hot rolling". *Int. J. Mech. Sci.*, 16, 389 (1974).

35. Collins, I. F. and Dewhurst, P., "A slip-line field analysis of asymmetrical hot rolling". *Int. J. Mech. Sci.*, 17, 643 (1975).

36. Dewhurst, P., "On the non-uniqueness of the machining process". *Proc. R. Soc.*, A, 360 587 (1978).

37. Collins, I. F., "Compression of a rigid perfectly smooth plastic strip between parallel rotating smooth dies". *Quart. J. Mech. Appl. Math.*, 23, 329 (1970).

38. Das, N. S., Bannerjee, J. and Collins, I. F., Plane strain compression of rigid-perfectly plastic strip between parallel dies with slipping friction". *J. Appl. Mech.* 46, 317 (1979).

39. Collins, I. F., "Slip-line field solutions for compression and rolling with slipping friction". *Int. J. Mech. Sci.*, 11, 971 (1969).

40. Collins, I. F., "On the rolling of a rigid cylinder on a rigid/perfectly plastic half space". *J. de Mecanique Applique*, 2, 431 (1978).

41. Collins, I. F., "Geometric properties of some slip-line fields for compression and extrusion". *J. Mech. Phys. Solids*, 16, 137 (1968).

42. Venter, R. D. and Hewitt, R. L., "An introduction to the matrix inversion technique for solving plate strain metal forming problems". *4th Symposium on Engineering Applications of Solid Mechanics,* Ontario Research Foundation (1978).

43. Powell, M. J. D., "A Fortran subroutine for solving systems of non-linear algebraic equations". Harwell Report AERE-R-5947 (1968). Reprinted in *Numerical Methods for Non-linear Algebraic Equations* (edited by P. Rabinowitz), Gordon & Breach, New York (1970).

44. Venter, R. D., Hewitt, R. L. and Johnson, W., "Application of the matrix inversion technique to extrusion and drawing problems". *Applications of Numerical Methods to Forming Processes*, A.S.M.E., Winter Conference, San Francisco, AMD-Vol. 28, 143 (1978).

45. Green, A. P., "A theoretical investigation of the compression of a ductile material between smooth flat dies". *Phil. Mag.*, 42, No. 331, 900 (1951).

46. Druyanov, B. A., "Sheet rolling under maximum friction conditions". *Plastic Flow of Metals*, 1, 80 (1971). (Translated from the Russian, Plenum Publishing Corp., New York.)

47. Chitkara, N. R. and Johnson, W., "Some results for rolling with circular and polygonal rolls". *Proc. 5th M.T.D.R. Conf.*, 391 (1965). (Pergamon Press, Oxford.)

48. Chekmarev, A. P. and Nefedov, A. A., *Obrabotka Metallov Davleniem*, 4, 2 (1956). (In Russian.) (British Lending Library Translation R.T.S. 8939.)

49. Johnson, W. and Mellor, P. B., *Engineering Plasticity*. Van Nostrand Reinhold London (1973).

50. Bachrach, B. I. and Samanta, S. K., "A numerical method for computing plane plastic slip-line fields". *J. Appl. Mech.*, 43, 97 (1976).

Appendix 1

Matrix Operators

Each of the matrix operators P_ϕ^*, Q_ϕ^*, R_ϕ, S_ϕ, $P_{\theta\psi}$, $Q_{\theta\psi}$, T_ϕ and T_ϕ^{-1} which have been defined can be represented as a square matrix. When using these operators in the computerized construction of slip-line fields it is convenient to contain the development of each of these operators in an independent subroutine. Each subroutine serves only to evaluate the elements which comprise the particular matrix operator. The subroutines are listed below and each matrix operator has been defined as an NxN matrix where N is equal to six.

A. SUBROUTINE PSTAR

$$P_\phi^* = \begin{bmatrix} \phi_0 & 0 & 0 & 0 & 0 & \cdot \\ \phi_1 & \phi_0 & 0 & 0 & 0 & \cdot \\ \phi_2 & \phi_1 & \phi_0 & 0 & 0 & \cdot \\ \cdot & \cdot & \cdot & \cdot & \cdot & \cdot \\ \cdot & \cdot & \cdot & \cdot & \cdot & \cdot \\ \cdot & \cdot & \cdot & \cdot & \cdot & \cdot \end{bmatrix}$$

where $\phi_m = \dfrac{\phi^m}{m!}$.

```
    SUBROUTINE PSTAR (N,ANG,P)
    DIMENSION P(N,N), A(N)
    A(1) = 1.0
    DO10 I = 2,N
 10 A(I) = A(I-1)* ANG/FLOAT (I-1)
    DO20 I = 1,N
    DO20 J = 1,N
 20 P(I,J) = 0.0
    DO30 J = 1,N
    DO30 I = J,N
    K = 1 + I - J
 30 P(I,J) = A(K)
    RETURN
    END
```

Subroutine PSTAR evaluates the coefficients in the square matrix P^*_ϕ. The angle ϕ is represented by ANG and each element is designated, $P_{i,j}$, where $i,j = 1,N$.

SUBROUTINE PSTAR (N, ANG, P)

SUBROUTINE PSTAR (6, 1.0, P^*_ϕ) for ϕ = 1 radian

P^*_ϕ is given by

$$
P^*_\phi =
\begin{bmatrix}
1.0000 & 0.0000 & 0.0000 & 0.0000 & 0.0000 & 0.0000 \\
1.0000 & 1.0000 & 0.0000 & 0.0000 & 0.0000 & 0.0000 \\
0.5000 & 1.0000 & 1.0000 & 0.0000 & 0.0000 & 0.0000 \\
0.1667 & 0.5000 & 1.0000 & 1.0000 & 0.0000 & 0.0000 \\
0.0417 & 0.1667 & 0.5000 & 1.0000 & 1.0000 & 0.0000 \\
0.0083 & 0.0417 & 0.1667 & 0.5000 & 1.0000 & 1.0000
\end{bmatrix}
$$

B.   SUBROUTINE QSTAR

$$
Q^*_\phi = -
\begin{bmatrix}
\phi_1 & \phi_2 & \phi_3 & \cdot & \cdot & \cdot \\
\phi_2 & \phi_3 & \phi_4 & \cdot & \cdot & \cdot \\
\phi_3 & \phi_4 & \phi_5 & \cdot & \cdot & \cdot \\
\phi_4 & \cdot & \cdot & \cdot & \cdot & \cdot \\
\cdot & \cdot & \cdot & \cdot & \cdot & \cdot \\
\cdot & \cdot & \cdot & \cdot & \cdot & \cdot
\end{bmatrix}
$$

where $\phi_m = \dfrac{\phi^m}{m!}$.

```
SUBROUTINE QSTAR (N,ANG,Q)
DIMENSION P(N,N), A(2N-1)
N2 = 2N-1
A(1) = 1.0
DO10 I = 2, N2
10 A(I) = A(J-1)* ANG/FLOAT (I-1)
DO20 J = 1,N
DO20 I = 1,N
20 Q(I,J) = - A(I+J)
RETURN
END
```

Subroutine QSTAR evaluates the coefficients in the square matrix Q^*_ϕ. The angle ϕ is represented by ANG and each element is designated, Q_{ij}, where $i,j = 1,N$.

SUBROUTINE QSTAR (N, ANG, Q)

SUBROUTINE QSTAR (6, 1.0, Q^*_ϕ) for ϕ = 1 radian, Q^*_ϕ is given by

$$
Q^*_\phi =
\begin{bmatrix}
-1.0000 & -0.5000 & -0.1667 & -0.0417 & -0.0083 & -0.0014 \\
-0.5000 & -0.1667 & -0.0417 & -0.0083 & -0.0014 & -0.0002 \\
-0.1667 & -0.0417 & -0.0083 & -0.0014 & -0.0002 & -0.0000 \\
-0.0417 & -0.0083 & -0.0014 & -0.0002 & -0.0000 & -0.0000 \\
-0.0083 & -0.0014 & -0.0002 & -0.0000 & -0.0000 & -0.0000 \\
-0.0014 & -0.0002 & -0.0000 & -0.0000 & -0.0000 & -0.0000
\end{bmatrix}
$$

C. SUBROUTINE RMAT

$$R_\phi = - \begin{bmatrix} \phi_0 & \phi_1 & \phi_2 & \phi_3 & \cdot & \cdot \\ 0 & -\phi_0 & -\phi_1 & -\phi_2 & \cdot & \cdot \\ 0 & 0 & \phi_0 & \phi_1 & \cdot & \cdot \\ 0 & 0 & 0 & -\phi_0 & \cdot & \cdot \\ 0 & 0 & 0 & 0 & \cdot & \cdot \\ 0 & 0 & 0 & 0 & \cdot & \cdot \end{bmatrix}$$

```
      SUBROUTINE RMAT (N,ANG,R)
      DIMENSION R(6,6), A(6)
      A(1) = 1.0
      DO10 I = 2,N
   10 A(I) = A(I-1)* ANG/FLOAT (I-1)
      DO20 J = 1,N
      DO20 I = 1,N
   20 R(I,J) = 0.0
      DO30 I = 1,N
      DO30 J = 1,N
      K = 1 + J - I
   30 R(I,J) = - A(K)* (-1.0)** I
      RETURN
      END
```

where $\phi_m = \dfrac{\phi^m}{m!}$.

Subroutine RMAT evaluates the coefficients in the square matrix R_ϕ.
The angle ϕ is represented by ANG and each element is designated,
R_{ij}, where $i,j = 1,N$.
SUBROUTINE RMAT (N, ANG, R)
SUBROUTINE RMAT (6, 1.0, R) for $\phi = 1$ radian, R_ϕ is given by

$$R_\phi = - \begin{bmatrix} 1.0000 & 1.0000 & 0.5000 & 0.1667 & 0.0417 & 0.0083 \\ 0.0000 & -1.0000 & -1.0000 & -0.5000 & -0.1667 & -0.0417 \\ 0.0000 & 0.0000 & 1.0000 & 1.0000 & 0.5000 & 0.1667 \\ 0.0000 & 0.0000 & 0.0000 & -1.0000 & -1.0000 & -0.5000 \\ 0.0000 & 0.0000 & 0.0000 & 0.0000 & 1.0000 & 1.0000 \\ 0.0000 & 0.0000 & 0.0000 & 0.0000 & 0.0000 & -1.0000 \end{bmatrix}$$

D. SUBROUTINE SMAT

$$S_\phi = \begin{bmatrix} \phi_0 & \phi_1 & \phi_2 & \phi_3 & \cdot & \cdot \\ 0 & \phi_0 & \phi_1 & \phi_2 & \cdot & \cdot \\ 0 & 0 & \phi_0 & \phi_1 & \cdot & \cdot \\ 0 & 0 & 0 & \phi_0 & \cdot & \cdot \\ 0 & 0 & 0 & 0 & \cdot & \cdot \\ 0 & 0 & 0 & 0 & \cdot & \cdot \end{bmatrix}$$

```
      SUBROUTINE SMAT (N,ANG,S)
      DIMENSION S(6,6), A(6)
      A(1) = 1.0
      DO10 I = 2,N
   10 A(I) = A(I-1)* ANG/FLOAT (I-1)
      DO20 J = 1,N
      DO20 I = 1,N
   20 S(I,J) = 0.0
      DO30 I = 1,N
      DO30 J = 1,N
      K = 1 + J - I
   30 S(I,J) = A(K)
      RETURN
      END
```

where $\phi_m = \dfrac{\phi^m}{m!}$.

251

Subroutine SMAT evaluates the coefficients in the square matrix S_ϕ. The angle ϕ is represented by ANG and each element is designated, $S_{i,j}$, where $i,j = 1,N$.

SUBROUTINE SMAT (N, ANG, S)

SUBROUTINE SMAT (6, 1.0, S_ϕ) for ϕ = 1 radian, S_ϕ is given by

$$
S_\phi = \begin{bmatrix}
1.0000 & 1.0000 & 0.5000 & 0.1667 & 0.0417 & 0.0083 \\
0.0000 & 1.0000 & 1.0000 & 0.5000 & 0.1667 & 0.0417 \\
0.0000 & 0.0000 & 1.0000 & 1.0000 & 0.5000 & 0.1667 \\
0.0000 & 0.0000 & 0.0000 & 1.0000 & 1.0000 & 0.5000 \\
0.0000 & 0.0000 & 0.0000 & 0.0000 & 1.0000 & 1.0000 \\
0.0000 & 0.0000 & 0.0000 & 0.0000 & 0.0000 & 1.0000
\end{bmatrix}
$$

E.   SUBROUTINE QMAT

$Q_{\theta\phi} = R_\phi\, Q_\theta^\star$

```
SUBROUTINE QMAT (N, THETA, PSI, QA)
DIMENSION QA(6,6), R(6,6), Q(6,6)
CALL   RMAT   (N, PSI, R)
CALL PSTAR (N, THETA, Q)
DO10 I = 1,N
DO10 J = 1,N
QA(I,J) = 0.0
DO10 K = 1,N
QA(I,J) = QA(I,J) + R(I,K)* Q(K,J)
10 CONTINUE
RETURN
END
```

Subroutine QMAT performs the matrix multiplication of R_ψ by $Q_\theta^\star$ to yield the coefficients of the square matrix $Q_{\theta\psi}$. Subroutines PSTAR and RMAT are called directly. The angles θ and ψ are represented by THETA and PSI respectively and each element of the matrix $Q_{\theta\psi}$ by $(QA)_{i,j}$ where $i,j = 1,N$.

SUBROUTINE QMAT (N, THETA, PSI, QA)

SUBROUTINE QMAT (6, 1.0, 1.0, $Q_{\theta\phi}$) for $\theta = \phi = 1.0$,

$$
Q_{\theta\psi} = \begin{bmatrix}
-1.5906 & -0.6889 & -0.2127 & 0.0507 & -0.0098 & -0.0016 \\
0.6889 & 0.2127 & 0.0507 & 0.0098 & 0.0016 & 0.0002 \\
-0.2127 & -0.0507 & -0.0098 & -0.0016 & -0.0002 & -0.0000 \\
0.0507 & 0.0098 & 0.0016 & 0.0002 & 0.0000 & 0.0000 \\
-0.0097 & -0.0016 & -0.0002 & -0.0000 & -0.0000 & -0.0000 \\
0.0014 & 0.0002 & 0.0000 & 0.0000 & 0.0000 & 0.0000
\end{bmatrix}.
$$

F. SUBROUTINE PMAT

$$P_{\theta\phi} = R_\theta \, P_\phi$$

```
SUBROUTINES PMAT (N, THETA, PSI, PA)
DIMENSION PA(6,6) R(6,6), P(6,6)
CALL   RMAT   (N, THETA, R)
CALL PSTAR (N, PSI, P)
DO10 I = 1,N
DO10 J = 1,N
PA(I,J) = 0.0
DO10 K = 1,N
PA(I,J) = PA(I,J) + R(I,K)* P(K,J)
10 CONTINUE
RETURN
END
```

Subroutine PMAT simply performs the matrix multiplication of R_θ by P_ψ to yield the coefficients of the square matrix $P_{\theta\psi}$. Subroutines PSTAR and RMAT are called directly. The angles θ and ψ are represented by THETA and PSI respectively and each element of the matrix $P_{\theta\psi}$ by $(PA)_{ij}$ where $i,j = 1,N$.

SUBROUTINE PMAT (N, THETA, PSI, PA)

SUBROUTINE PMAT (6, 1.0, 1.0, $P_{\theta\psi}$) for $\theta = \phi = 1.0$, $P_{\theta\psi}$ is given by

$$P_{\theta\psi} = \begin{bmatrix} 2.2796 & 1.5906 & 0.6889 & 0.2125 & 0.0500 & 0.0083 \\ -1.5906 & -2.2795 & -1.5903 & -0.6875 & -0.2083 & -0.0417 \\ 0.6889 & 1.5903 & 2.2778 & 1.5833 & 0.6667 & 0.1667 \\ -0.2125 & -0.6875 & -1.5833 & -2.2500 & -1.5000 & -0.5000 \\ 0.0500 & 0.2083 & 0.6667 & 1.5000 & 2.0000 & 1.0000 \\ -0.0083 & -0.0417 & -0.1667 & -0.5000 & -1.0000 & -1.0000 \end{bmatrix}.$$

G. SUBROUTINE TMAT

$$T_\phi = - P_{\phi\phi} - Q_{\phi\phi}$$

$$T_\phi^{-1} = - P_{\phi\phi} + Q_{\phi\phi}$$

```
SUBROUTINE TMAT (N, ANG, TA, TB)
DIMENSION TA(6,6), TB(6,6) QA(6.0) PA(6,6)
CALL QMAT (N, ANG, ANG, QA)
CALL PMAT (N, ANG, ANG, PA)
DO10 I = 1,N
DO10 J = 1,N
TA(I,J) = - PA(I,J) - QA(I,J)
TB(I,J) = - PA(I,J) + QA(I,J)
RETURN
END
```

Subroutine TMAT performs the matrix additions as shown above. The coefficients of the square matrices T_ϕ and T_ϕ^{-1} are presented by TA and TB respectively, i.e. $(TA)_{ij}$ and $(TB)_{ij}$, where $i, j = 1, N$.

SUBROUTINE TMAT (N, ANG, TA, TB)

SUBROUTINE TMAT (6, 1.0, T_ϕ, T_ϕ^{-1}) for $\phi = 1.0$

T_ϕ and T_ϕ^{-1} are given by

$$
T_\phi = \begin{bmatrix}
-0.6889 & -0.9017 & -0.4761 & -0.1618 & -0.0402 & -0.0067 \\
0.9017 & 2.0668 & 1.5395 & 0.6777 & 0.2067 & 0.0414 \\
-0.4762 & -1.5395 & -2.2680 & -1.5817 & -0.6664 & -0.1666 \\
0.1618 & 0.6777 & 1.5817 & 2.2498 & 1.5000 & 0.5000 \\
-0.0403 & -0.2067 & -0.6664 & -1.5000 & -2.0000 & -1.0000 \\
0.0069 & 0.0415 & 0.1666 & 0.5000 & 1.0000 & 1.0000
\end{bmatrix}
$$

$$
T_\phi^{-1} = \begin{bmatrix}
-3.8702 & -2.2796 & -0.9016 & -0.2632 & -0.0598 & -0.0099 \\
2.2796 & 2.4923 & 1.6410 & 0.6973 & 0.2099 & 0.0419 \\
-0.9016 & -1.6410 & -2.2876 & -1.5849 & -0.6669 & -0.1667 \\
0.2632 & 0.6973 & 1.5849 & 2.2502 & 1.5000 & 0.5000 \\
-0.0597 & -0.2099 & -0.6669 & -1.5000 & -2.0000 & -1.0000 \\
0.0097 & 0.0419 & 0.1667 & 0.5000 & 1.0000 & 1.0000
\end{bmatrix}
$$

H.   SUBROUTINE PMULT

$$X_{IJ} = P_\phi^* \, X_{MN}$$

```
SUBROUTINE PMULT(N,ANG,V,PV)
DIMENSION V(6),PV(6),A(6)
A(1)=1.0
DO 10 I=2,N
10   A(I)=A(I-1)+ANG/FLOAT(I-1)
DO 30 I=1,N
PV(I)=0.0
DO 20 J=1,I
20   PV(I)=PV(I)+A(I-J+1)*V(J)
30   CONTINUE
RETURN
END
```

Subroutine PMULT directly carries out the matrix multiplication of P_ϕ^* and X_{MN} where X is the column vector of the coefficients in the series expansion of the radius of curvature. For convenience of manipulation the elements of the square matrix are evaluated within this subroutine.

SUBROUTINE PMULT (N, ANG, V, PV)

SUBROUTINE PMULT (6, ϕ, X_{MN}, X_{IJ})

I.   SUBROUTINE QMULT

$$X_{IJ} = Q^*_\phi \ X_{MN}$$

```
SUBROUTINE QMULT(N,ANG,V,QV)
DIMENSION V(6),QV(6),A(20)
M=2*N
A(1)=ANG
DO 10 I=2,M
10   A(I)=A(I-1)*ANG/FLOAT(I)
DO 30 I=1,N
QV(I)=0.0
DO 20 J=1,N
20   QV(I)=QV(I)-A(J+I-1)*V(J)
30   CONTINUE
RETURN
END
```

Subroutine QMULT is equivalent to subroutine PMULT; only the operators
P^*_ϕ and Q^*_ϕ are interchanged.

SUBROUTINE QMULT (N, ANG, V, QV)

SUBROUTINE QMULT (6, ϕ, X_{MN}, X_{IJ})

Appendix 2

The Mikhlin and Cartesian Coordinates of a Slip Line

For positive radius of curvature,

$$x = \bar{x} \cos \phi - \bar{y} \sin \phi \text{ and } y = \bar{x} \sin \phi + \bar{y} \cos \phi$$

where

$$\bar{x} = \sum_{n=0}^{\infty} t_n \frac{\phi^n}{n!} \qquad \text{and } \bar{y} = - \sum_{n=0}^{\infty} t_n \frac{\phi^{n+1}}{(n+1)!} \; .$$

For negative radius of curvature,

$$x = \bar{x} \cos \phi + \bar{y} \sin \phi \text{ and } y = - \bar{x} \sin \phi + \bar{y} \cos \phi$$

where

$$\bar{x} = - \sum_{n=0}^{\infty} t_n \frac{\phi^n}{n!} \qquad \text{and } \bar{y} = \sum_{n=0}^{\infty} t_n \frac{\phi^{n+1}}{(n+1)!} \; ;$$

also,

$$t_{n+1} = - t_{n-1} + r_n, \qquad t_1 = r_0, \; t_0 = 0 \text{ and } t_{-1} = 0.$$

256

```
      SUBROUTINE MIKLIN (N, V, XBAR, YBAR, ANG, SIGN)
      DIMENSION V(6), A(6), XT(6), YT(6)
      XT(1) = 0.0
      YT(1) = 0.0
      A(1) = 1.0
      XT(2) = SIGN* V(1)
      YT(2) = 0.0
      A(2) = ANG
      DO10 I = 3,N
      XT(I) = SIGN* V(I-1) - XT(I-2)
      YT(I) = - SIGN* XT (I-1)
   10 A(I) = A(I-1)* ANG/FLOAT(I-1)
      XBAR = 0.0
      YBAR = 0.0
      DO20 I=2,N
      XBAR = XBAR + XT(I)* A(I)
   20 YBAR = YBAR + YT(I)* A(I)
      RETURN
      END


      SUBROUTINE CORDXY (N,V, XBAR, YBAR, X, Y, ANG, SIGN)
      DIMENSION V(6)
      CALL MIKLIN (N, V, XBAR, YBAR, ANG, SIGN)
      X = XBAR* COS(ANG) - SIGN* YBAR *SIN(ANG)
      Y = SIGN* XBAR* SIN(ANG) + YBAR* COS(ANG)
      RETURN
      END
```

Subroutine MIKLIN evaluates the Mikhlin coordinates $(\bar{x},\bar{y})$ along a
slip line at some angle ϕ. The angle ϕ is represented by ANG, the
radius vector χ by the N-dimensional column vector V, and SIGN is
assigned a positive unit value if the radius of curvature is positive
and a negative unit value if the radius of curvatire is negative.

SUBROUTINE MIKLIN (N, V, XBAR, YBAR, ANG, SIGN)
SUBROUTINE MIKLIN (N, χ, $\bar{x}$, $\bar{y}$, ϕ, ± 1.0)

Subroutine CORDXY evaluates the Cartesian coordinates at a point along
the slip line once the Mikhlin coordinates are known.

SUBROUTINE CORDXY (N, V, XBAR, YBAR, X, Y, ANG, SIGN)
SUBROUTINE CORDXY (N, χ, $\bar{x}$, $\bar{y}$, x, y, ϕ, ± 1.0)

The Determination of Expressions for the Mikhlin Coordinates

With reference to Fig. A.1, the expressions for the Mikhlin coordinates
can be derived as shown below.

The length $O'A'$ of the slip line OA is given by $R(z)dz$. The components
of $O'A'$ which contribute to the Mikhlin coordinates $\bar{x}$ and $\bar{y}$ are therefore given by

$$O'B' = R(z).\, dz \cos (\phi-z)$$

and

$$A'B' = R(z).\, dz \sin (\phi-z).$$

Integrating over all elements, $O'A'$, of the slip line OA enables the

257

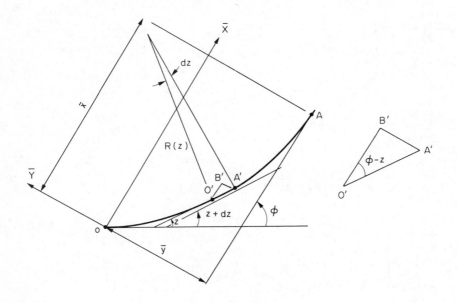

Fig.   A.1.

Mikhlin coordinates to be evaluated.   These are given by

$$\bar{x}(\phi) = \int_0^\phi R(z) \cos(\phi-z) \, dz$$

and

$$\bar{y}(\phi) = \int_0^\phi R(z) \sin(\phi-z) \, dz.$$

Since $R(z)$ has a known power series expansion given by

$$R(z) = \sum_{n=0}^{\infty} r_n \frac{z^n}{n!} \, ,$$

the following relationships can be obtained for the general convolution integrals for $\bar{x}(\phi)$ and $\bar{y}(\phi)$ given above.[13]

$$\bar{x}'(\phi) = R(\phi) - \bar{y}(\phi) \text{ and } \bar{y}'(\phi) = \bar{x}(\phi),$$

so that

$$\bar{x}(\phi) = \sum_{n=0}^{\infty} t_n \frac{\phi^n}{n!} \text{ and } \bar{y}(\phi) = \sum_{n=0}^{\infty} t_n \frac{\phi^{n+1}}{(n+1)!} \, ;$$

also

$$t_{n+1} + t_{n-1} = r_n \text{ and } t_0 = 0 = t_{-1}.$$

Appendix 3

Computer Listing for Indentation Problem

A listing for the programme to generate the slip-line field for the
indentation of a rigid plastic medium of finite depth by a flat smooth
punch is provided below. The reader is referred to Fig. 6.20.

```
        C        PROGRAM FOR THE GENERATION OF SLIP LINE FIELDS
        C        INDENTATION BY A SMOOTH FLAT PUNCH
1                DIMENSION  XOA(6),XOC(6),XCB(6),PSX(6),QSX(6)
2                N=6
        C        READ IN HALF WIDTH OF PUNCH,A,AND ANGLE THETA
3                WRITE(6,99)
4          99    FORMAT(2X,'SLIP LINE FIELD SOLUTION FOR INDENTING'///)
5                READ(5,101)A,THETA
6         101    FORMAT(2F10.0)
        C        SET VALUE OF PI AND CONVERT TO RADIANS
7                PI=3.14159265
8                THETAR=THETA*PI/180.0
        C        CALCULATE LENGTH OF OS, RADIUS OF ARC
9                RHO=A*SQRT(2.0)
        C        SET SLIP LINE VECTORS FOR OA AND OC
10               XOA(1)=RHO
11               XOC(1)=-RHO
12               DO 10 I=2,N
13               XOA(I)=0.0
14         10    XOC(I)=0.0
        C        CALCULATE CHI-CB
15               CALL PMULT(N,THETAR,XOA,PSX)
16               CALL QMULT(N,THETAR,XOC,QSX)
17               DO 20 I=1,N
18         20    XCB(I)=PSX(I)+QSX(I)
19               WRITE(6,22)(PSX(K),K=1,N)
20               WRITE(6,22)(QSX(K),K=1,N)
21               WRITE(6,22)(XCB(K),K=1,N)
22         22    FORMAT(6(2X,F10.3))
        C        CALCULATE COORDINATES WITH ORIGIN AT S
23               XS=0.0
24               YS=0.0
25               XSS=2.0*A
26               YSS=0.0
27               XO=A
28               YO=-A
29               PSI=THETAR-PI/4.
30               XC=-RHO*SIN(PSI)
31               YC=-RHO*COS(PSI)
32               XA=2.0*A+RHO*SIN(PSI)
33               YA=YC
34               GAMMA=3.0*PI/2.-PSI
35               CALL SLCF(N,XCB,XC,YC,XB,YB,GAMMA,THETAR,+1.0,+1.0)
36               WRITE(6,200)
```

259

```
37      200     FORMAT(1HL,2X,'CO-ORDINATE POSITIONS OF S,SS,O,A,B AND
                C'.//.10X. 1'X',12X,'Y',/)
38              WRITE(6,201) XS,YS,XSS,YSS,XO,YO,XA,YA,XB,YB,XC,YC
39      201     FORMAT(2X,2F12.4)
        C               CALCULATE FORCES ON SLIP LINE CB AND RESOLVE HORIZONTALLY
        C               ASSUME INITIALLY THAT HYDROSTATIC COMPONENT AT C IS ZERO
40              CALL SLFORC(N,XCB,XBAR,YBAR,FX,FY,THETAR,0.0,1.0,1.0)
41              FH=-FX*SIN(PSI)+FY*COS(PSI)
        C               ADD ON CONTRIBUTION FROM SHEAR FORCE ALONG CS
42              FH=FH+RHO*SIN(PSI)
        C               THIS IS EQUAL TO PC* HEIGHT OF SLAB FROM ZERO TO HORIZONTAL
        C               1FORCE.HENCE
43              PC=FH/(YB-YS)
        C               THEN FROM HENCKY
44              PO=PC+2.*THETAR
        C               CALCULATE NON-DIMENSIONAL TOTAL PRESSURE ON PUNCH,P/2K
45              PTOT=PO/2.+0.5
        C               CALCULATE H/B RATIO
46              HB=(YS-YB)/A
47              WRITE(6,202)HB,PTOT
48      202     FORMAT(////,2X,'H/B RATIO =',F4.2,10X,'P/2K =',F4.2,////)
49              STOP
50              END

51              SUBROUTINE SLCP(N,XSL,XO,YO,XF,YF,THETA,PHI,SIGN2,SIGN3)
        C               SUBROUTINE TO CALCULATE THE COORDINATES OF ONE END OF A SLIP
        C               LINE IN ANY CARTESIAN COORDINATE SYSTEM GIVEN THE COORDINATE
        C               OF THE OTHER END
        C               N-DIMENSION OF VECTORS
        C               XSL=SLIP LINE CONSIDERED
        C               XO,YO.   COORDINATES OF S OR L (GIVEN)
        C               XF,YF    COORDINATES OF S OR L (TO BE FOUND)
        C               THETA=ANGLE BETWEEN TANGENT TO SLIP LINE AT S AND X-AXIS
        C               MEASURED +VE IN ANTICLOCKWISE SENSE
        C               PHI=ANGULAR SPAN OF SLIP LINE
        C               SIGN2=+1.0 FOR A +VE SLIP LINE AND -1.0 FOR A -VE SLIP LINE
        C               SIGN3= +1.0 IF COORDINATES OF S ARE GIVEN,-1.0 IF COORDINATES
        C               OF L ARE GIVEN
52              DIMENSION XSL(6)
53              CALL CORDXY(N,XSL,XX,YY,X,Y,PHI,SIGN2)
54              XF=XO+SIGN3*(X*COS(THETA)-Y*SIN(THETA))
55              YF=YO+SIGN3*(X*SIN(THETA)+Y*COS(THETA))
56              RETURN
57              END

58              SUBROUTINE QMULT(N,ANG,V,QV)
59              DIMENSION V(6),QV(6),A(20)
60              M=2*N
61              A(1)=ANG
62              DO 10 I=2,M
63      10      A(I)=A(I-1)*ANG/FLOAT(I)
64              DO 30 I=1,N
65              QV(I)=0.0
66              DO 20 J=1,N
67      20      QV(I)=QV(I)-A(J+I-1)*V(J)
68      30      CONTINUE
69              RETURN
70              END

71              SUBROUTINE PMULT(N,ANG,V,PV)
72              DIMENSION V(6),PV(6),A(6)
73              A(1)=1.0
74              DO 10 I=2,N
75      10      A(I)=A(I-1)*ANG/FLOAT(I-1)
76              DO 30 I=1,N
77              PV(I)=0.0
78              DO 20 J=1,I
79      20      PV(I)=PV(I)+A(I-J+1)*V(J)
80      30      CONTINUE
81              RETURN
82              END

83              SUBROUTINE SLFORC(N,V,XBAR,YBAR,FX,FY,ANG,PO,SIGN1,SIGN)
84              DIMENSION V(6),C(20)
85              C(1)=0.0
86              C(2)=0.0
87              DO 10 I=3,N
```

```
88      10      C(I)=SIGN *FLOAT(I-2)*V(I-2)-C(I-2)
89              D1=2.0
90              D2=1.0
91              DO 20 I=3,N
92              D1=D1*FLOAT(I)
93              D2=D2*FLCAT(I-1)
94              C(1)=C(1)+C(I)*ANG**I/D1
95      20      C(2)=C(2)+C(I)*ANG**(I-1)/D2
96              CALL MIKLIN(N,V,XEAR,YBAR,ANG,SIGN)
97              FXBAR=-SIGN1*SIGN*XBAR-SIGN*PO*YBAR-2.0*SIGN1*SIGN*C(1)
98              FYBAR=-SIGN1*SIGN*YBAR+SIGN*PO*XBAR-2.0*SIGN1*C(2)
99              FX=FXBAR*COS(ANG)-FYBAR*SIN(ANG)*SIGN
100             FY=FYBAR*COS(ANG)+FXBAR*SIN(ANG)*SIGN
101             RETURN
102             END
103             SUBROUTINE MIKLIN(N,V,XBAR,YBAR,ANG,SIGN)
104             DIMENSION V(6),A(6),XT(6),YT(6)
105             XT(1)=0.0
106             YT(1)=0.0
107             A(1)=1.0
108             XT(2)=SIGN*V(1)
109             YT(2)=0.0
110             A(2)=ANG
111             DO 10 I=3,N
112             XT(I)=SIGN*V(I-1)-XT(I-2)
113             YT(I)=-SIGN*XT(I-1)
114     10      A(I)=A(I-1)*ANG/FLOAT(I-1)
115             XBAR=0.0
116             YBAR=0.0
117             DO 20 I=2,N
118             XBAR=XBAR+XT(I)*A(I)
119     20      YBAR=YBAR+YT(I)*A(I)
120             RETURN
121             END
122             SUBROUTINE CORDXY(N,V,XBAR,YBAR,X,Y,ANG,SIGN)
123             DIMENSION V(6)
124             CALL MIKLIN(N,V,XEAR,YBAR,ANG,SIGN)
125             X=XBAR*COS(ANG)-SIGN*YBAR*SIN(ANG)
126             Y=SIGN*XBAR*SIN(ANG)+YBAR*CCS(ANG)
127     22      FORMAT(6(2X,F10.6))
128             WRITE(6,22)X,Y
129             WRITE(6,22)XBAR,YBAR
130             RETURN
131             END
```

```
        $DATA
SLIP LINE FIELD SCLUTICN FOR INDENTING


    1.414           1.481           0.775           0.271           0.071           0.015
    1.481           0.775           0.271           0.071           0.015           0.003
    2.895           2.256           1.046           0.342           0.086           0.017
  3.570866        2.371784
  3.839461       -1.906565
CO-ORDINATE POSITICNS OF S,SS,O,A,B AND C

        X               Y

    0.0000          0.0000
    2.0000          0.0000
    1.0000         -1.0000
    2.3660         -1.3660
    1.0007         -5.4291
   -0.3660         -1.3660



H/B RATIO =5.43          P/2K =2.06
```

Results

(a) For the column vector χ_{CB},

$$\chi_{CB} = P^*_\theta \ \chi_{OA} + Q^*_\theta \ \chi_{OC}.$$

$$\chi_{CB} = \begin{vmatrix} 1.414 \\ 1.481 \\ 0.775 \\ 0.271 \\ 0.071 \\ 0.015 \end{vmatrix} + \begin{vmatrix} 1.481 \\ 0.775 \\ 0.271 \\ 0.071 \\ 0.015 \\ 0.003 \end{vmatrix} = \begin{vmatrix} 2.895 \\ 2.256 \\ 1.046 \\ 0.342 \\ 0.086 \\ 0.017 \end{vmatrix}$$

for $\theta = 60^0 = \pi/3$ and $a = 1$ (unity).

(b) Coordinates of points S, SS, O, A, B, and C as illustrated in Fig. 6.20 (a) are listed below.

$$S(0.000, \quad 0.000), \quad A(2.366, -1.366),$$
$$SS(2.000, \quad 0.000), \quad B(1.000, -5.429),$$
$$O(1.000, -1.000), \quad C(-0.367, -1.366).$$

(c) h/a ratio = 5.429 and $p/2k$ = 2.06.

Appendix 4

Subroutine SLFORC

```
      SUBROUTINE  SLFORC (N,V,XBAR,VBAR,FX,FY,ANG,PO,SIGN1,SIGN)
      DIMENSION V(6),C(20)
      C(1) = 0.0
      C(2) = 0.0
      DO 10 I = 3,N
   10 C(I) = SIGN *FLOAT(I-2)*V(I-2)-C(I-2)
      D1 = 2.0
      D2 = 1.0
      DO 20 I = 3,N
      D1 = D1*FLOAT(I)
      D2 = D2*FLOAT(I-1)
      C(1) = C(1) + C(I)*ANG**I/D1
   20 C(2) = C(2) + C(I)*ANG**(I-1)/D2
      CALL MIKLIN (N,V,XBAR,YBAR,ANG,SIGN)
      FXBAR = - SIGN 1*SIGN*XBAR - SIGN*PO*YBAR - 2.0*SIGN1*SIGN*C(1)
      FYBAR = - SIGN 1*SIGN*YBAR + SIGN*PO*XBAR - 2.0*SIGN1*C(2)
      FX = FXBAR*COS(ANG) - FYBAR*SIN(ANG)*SIGN
      FY = FYBAR*COS(ANG) + FXBAR*SIGN(ANG)*SIGN
      RETURN
      END
```

Subroutine SLFORC evaluates the forces F_x and F_y acting on the slip line having an angular range ϕ. The angle ϕ is represented by ANG, the radius vector χ by the N-dimensional column vector V, and the hydrostatic pressure component, p_0, at the base point by PO. SIGN is assigned a positive unit value if the radius of curvature is positive and a negative unit value if the radius of curvature is negative. SIGN1 is made equal to +1.0 when the slip line is an α-line and equal to -1.0 when the slip line is a β-line. The values of $\bar{x}$ and $\bar{y}$ which are represented by XBAR and YBAR are obtained from the MIKLIN subroutine.

SUBROUTINE SLFORC (N, V, XBAR, YBAR, FX, FY, ANG, PO, SIGN1, SIGN)

(i)   For an α-line with positive curvature
        SUBROUTINE SLFORC (N, χ, $\bar{x}$, $\bar{y}$, F_x, F_y, ϕ, p_0, 1.0, 1.0)

(ii)   For an α-line with negative curvature
        SUBROUTINE SLFORC (N, χ, $\bar{x}$, $\bar{y}$, F_x, F_y, ϕ, p_0, 1.0, -1.0)

(iii)   For a β-line with positive curvature
        SUBROUTINE SLFORC (N, χ, $\bar{x}$, $\bar{y}$, F_x, F_y, ϕ, p_0, -1.0, 1.0)

(iv)   For a β-line with negative curvature
        SUBROUTINE SLFORC (N, χ, $\bar{x}$, $\bar{y}$, F_x, F_y, ϕ, p_0, -1.0, -1.0)

A set of results are presented below for each of the above cases in which a constant unit radius of curvature is used, $\phi = \pi/4$ and $p_0 = 0$.

(i) α-line, SIGN1 = 1.0
        + ve curvature, SIGN = 1.0
        $\bar{x} = 0.7071$ $\bar{y} = -0.2926$
        $F_{\bar{x}} = -0.8636$ $F_{\bar{y}} = -0.2926$
        $F_x = -0.4038$ $F_y = -0.8176$

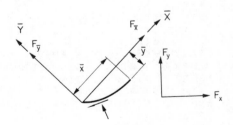

(ii) α-line, SIGN1 = 1.0

      - ve curvature, SIGN = -1.0

      $\bar{x} = 0.7071$ $y = 0.2926$

      $F_{\bar{x}} = 0.8636$ $F_{\bar{y}} = -0.2926$

      $F_x = 0.4038$ $F_y = -0.8176$

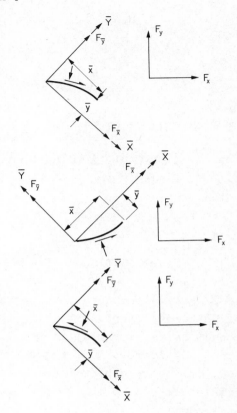

(iii) β-line, SIGN1 = -1.0

      + ve curvature, SIGN = 1.0

      $\bar{x} = 0.7071$ $\bar{y} = -0.2926$

      $F_{\bar{x}} = 0.8636$ $F_{\bar{y}} = 0.2926$

      $F_x = 0.4038$ $F_y = 0.8176$

(iv) β-line, SIGN1 = -1.0

      - ve curvature, SIGN = -1.0

      $\bar{x} = 0.7071$ $\bar{y} = 0.2926$

      $F_{\bar{x}} = -0.8636$ $F_{\bar{y}} = 0.2926$

      $F_x = -0.4038$ $F_y = 0.8176$

CHAPTER 7

Plasticity Problems for other than Plane-Strain Conditions

INTRODUCTION

The preceding chapters have considered, in some detail, the application of the theory of plasticity to the quasi-static plane-strain deformation of an isotropic rigid-perfectly plastic, rate insensitive material. Within the framework of the assumed material behaviour, slip-line-field (s.l.f.) theory can be regarded as mathematically rigorous, and for a certain class of problems provides valuable insight into deformation modes and forming loads. However, it will be apparent that by requiring plane-strain deformation the number of actual metalworking operations for which the technique is appropriate is limited and even under a plane-strain mode, s.l.f. analysis becomes unwieldly for non-steady state problems where the field has to be updated to account for changes in material boundaries. In addition, the material model may prove to be too restrictive and it may be necessary to resort to an elastic-plastic model - which is the case if the determination of residual stresses is the aim. Furthermore, the neglect of work-hardening, anisotropic behaviour, strain rate and temperature effects is inappropriate for certain types of problems. These remarks are not intended to diminish the value of s.l.f. analysis but rather to alert the reader to the consideration of more suitable constitutive equations and alternative analytical procedures, depending upon the circumstance under examination. It is outside the scope of this monograph to attempt to cover the methods of handling a wide variety of metalworking problems. A recent article by Johnson and Sowerby[1] surveys some of the more standard analytical techniques applied to the study of sheet and bulk metal-forming operations, while emphasizing the need for a reliable modelling of material behaviour, the process *per se* and tribological features. In any given process one (or more) of these aspects may dominate and it is essential to recognize the order of approximation inherent in any theoretical study if useful predictions are to be made.

In this final chapter it is our aim to provide a review of some selected topics and to supply a limited, but up-to-date bibliography which we hope can constitute a basis for further study.

THE METHOD OF CHARACTERISTICS FOR OTHER THAN PLANE-STRAIN PROCESSES

(i)   Plane Stress

A state of stress is said to be one of plane stress if a system of rectangular coordinates x, y, z can be chosen so that $\sigma_z = \tau_{yz} = \tau_{zx} = 0$. If a thin plate is loaded only in its plane, i.e. the x-y plane, the stress state is approximately plane. If, during subsequent plastic deformation, the thickness, h, does not remain uniform the state of stress may still be treated as approximately plane providing the rate of change of thickness with distance measured parallel to the surface of the plate remains small. The equations of equilibrium in the absence of body forces are[2,3]

$$\frac{\partial}{\partial x}(h\sigma_x) + \frac{\partial}{\partial y}(h\tau_{xy}) = 0 \tag{7.1}$$

and

$$\frac{\partial}{\partial x}(h\tau_{xy}) + \frac{\partial}{\partial y}(h\sigma_y) = 0, \tag{7.2}$$

where σ_x, σ_y and τ_{xy} denote the stress components averaged through the thickness.

In addition, if the material is plastic the stress components must satisfy a yield criterion which may be written in the form

$$F(\sigma_x, \sigma_y, \tau_{xy}) = f(\sigma_1, \sigma_2) = 0, \tag{7.3}$$

where σ_1 and σ_2 are principal stresses in the plane and $\sigma_3 = \sigma_z$ is zero.

The von Mises yield criterion for plane stress is

$$\sigma_1{}^2 - \sigma_1\sigma_2 + \sigma_2{}^2 = 3k^2 = Y^2, \tag{7.4}$$

and for the Tresca yield criterion is

$$(\sigma_{max} - \sigma_{min}) = 2k = Y, \tag{7.5}$$

where σ_{max} and σ_{min} are the maximum and minimum values of $(\sigma_1, \sigma_2, 0)$. The locus of each yield criterion in the (σ_1, σ_2) plane as shown in Fig. 7.1, is an ellipse for the von Mises criterion and a hexagon for the Tresca criterion; the figure shows the intersection of the von Mises yield circular cylinder and the Tresca hexagonal prism or cylinder with the plane $\sigma_3 = 0$.

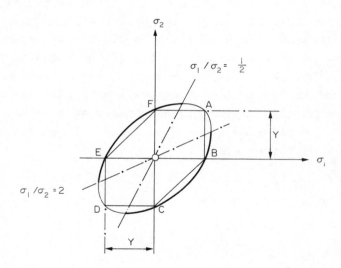

Fig. 7.1. Intersection of the Tresca and von Mises
yield surfaces by the plane $\sigma_3 = 0$.

Plane stress problems,[†] like those of plane strain, can be solved by

---

[†]When using the method of characteristics here the material is assumed to behave in a rigid-perfectly plastic manner.

the method of characteristics, but their solution is intrinsically more difficult.[2,4] When the von Mises yield criterion and Lévy-Mises flow rule are invoked, Hill[2] has demonstrated that the characteristics of stress and velocity are the same and their direction coincides with that of zero rate of extension. This parallels the situation for plane strain, but for the case of plane stress, the stress state will dictate whether directions of zero rate of extension can exist in the x-y plane. In the general development of the theory Hill, *op cit.*, showed that two such directions can occur at any point and that these are equally inclined at an angle $(\pi/4 + \psi/2)$ to the algebraically greater principal stress, say $\sigma_1 > \sigma_2$. The angle ψ is given by

$$\sin \psi = \frac{1}{3} \left(\frac{\sigma_1 + \sigma_2}{\sigma_1 - \sigma_2} \right), \qquad (7.6)$$

and therefore, providing

$$(\sigma_1 + \sigma_2) < 3 (\sigma_1 - \sigma_2), \qquad (7.7)$$

the angle ψ is real, the characteristics are distinct and the equations hyperbolic. Equality of the two sides of equation (7.7) results in the characteristics being coincident and the equations parabolic. All other stress states are elliptic and this leads to the result that no direction of zero rate of extension exists within the plane, or at a point the principal plastic strain increments (or strain rates) within the plane are of the same sign. Permissible stress states leading to the existence of characteristics are shown by the thickened arcs on the von Mises ellipse in Fig. 7.1.

The variation of the stress components along the characteristics are given in Ref. 2. These expressions are generally more complicated than the Hencky equations since they include the variation of the thickness of the material along the characteristics. In this form no general method of solution is available. If uniform thickness is assumed the expressions are greatly simplified and are more in keeping with the form of the Hencky equations. This approach is usually adopted in many unsteady state problems where calculations for yield point loads, etc., are based on incipient fields of characteristics. In domains where the thickness is deemed uniform an analogy to Hencky's First Theorem arises and in particular if a segment of a characteristic is straight, so are the corresponding segments of other members of the family. Domains where both families of characteristics are straight indicate regions of constant stress.

In Ref. 2, and in a subsequent article by Hill,[5] it was demonstrated that the principal stresses are given by

$$\frac{k(3 \sin \psi \pm 1)}{\sqrt{(1 + 3 \sin^2 \psi)}} , \qquad (7.8)$$

which are easily derived from (7.4) and (7.6). Reference 5 deals with permissible discontinuities of stress, velocity and surface slope for a rigid-plastic *thin* sheet deformed in its own plane under conditions of plane stress. It is demonstrated, *op cit.*, that one such discontinuity in velocity is the mathematical idealization of a localized neck, whose breadth is comparable to the thickness of the sheet. Furthermore, the localized neck can only coincide with a characteristic. Fracture will usually occur in this localized zone with the adjacent material moving apart in its plane with a certain relative velocity, v, inclined at an angle ψ to the neck, where ψ is defined in (7.6). The situation is shown schematically in Fig. 7.2.

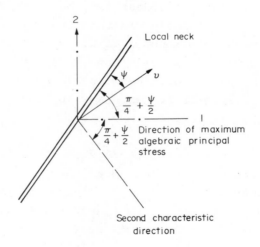

Fig. 7.2. Velocity discontinuity across
a localized neck.

One well-known physical occurence of a localized neck is that which exists under conditions of uniaxial tension,[6] particularly when the tensile strip is wide compared with its thickness. In this case the neck is inclined at 54° 44' to the axis of tension.[5] The necking angle can also be obtained from Mohr's strain circle (elastic strains ignored) for uniaxial tension, since the neck corresponds to the direction of zero rate of extension.

Depending upon the hardening behaviour of a real material, a wide strip specimen deformed in uniaxial tension may show first a diffuse necking mode[7] before finally fracturing along a localized neck.[5] Currently, there is a great deal of research interest in necking-type discontinuities and discussion about how they relate to the onset of failure, particularly in sheet-metal-forming operations. It is outside the scope of this present section to survey this area; however, Refs. 8 and 9 and their supporting bibliography should prove a suitable starting point for the interested reader. The prime intention here is to cite a number of references wherein the method of characteristics has been applied to certain plane-stress problems. As already stated the theoretical background has been laid down by Hill,[2,5] with Ref. 5 providing the basis for many practical solutions. As with plane-strain solutions, the network of characteristics can comprise zones of constant stress (both families of slip lines being straight but not orthogonal), domains analogous to centred-fan fields where the curved characteristics can be described in simple geometric terms (i.e. no longer circular arcs) and where at the same time necking-type discontinuities are permitted within the field. In many cases it is not necessary to attempt to solve the stress expressions along the characteristics in a point-to-point manner, in order to arrive at the stress distribution associated with a proposed field of characteristics. Use can be made of equation (7.6) and a relatively simple relationship which exists between the two normal stresses (along and perpendicular to a characteristic direction) and the shear stress at any point along a characteristic. These components can be readily expressed in terms of polar coordinates which becomes significant when establishing the stress field around a singularity, i.e. centred-fan fields in the plane-strain context, and in dealing with problems of axial symmetry.

In Ref. 5 fields of characteristics are presented for tensile strips symmetrically notched in the plane with either sharp V-notches or V-notches with a circular root, resulting in yield point loads and corresponding constraint factors for the different notch geometries. In a relatively recent article Ewing and Spurr[10] demonstrated how the fields of characteristics could be extended[†] for the V-notch specimens to calculate a critical half width of the test piece, i.e. below which the plastic zone is likely to spread to the free parallel sides of the strip. In a companion paper Ewing and Richards[11] evaluated plane-stress yield-point loads for single-edge notched tensile strips (typical of specimens used in fatigue crack propagation studies), based on a simple pattern of localized necks.

In 1954 Gaydon and McCrum[13] derived the yield-point load for a thin square plate of rigid-plastic material with a central circular hole, loaded by uniform normal stresses along the outside edges and in the plane of the plate. The upper-bound solutions consisted of either (i) a network of characteristics radiating from the periphery of the hole and extending to the mid-point of each edge (analogous to a network of logarithmic spirals in the plane strain sloution[14]) or (ii) a series of straight localized necks connecting the hole and the outside edges of the plate. Somewhat later, Sheppard and Gaydon[15] evaluated the end couples necessary to produce plastic flow in a thin plate in the form of a ring sector. Characteristics were established for both the von Mises and Tresca yield criteria. Green[16,17] presented fields of characteristics (of both plane stress and plane strain) for the plastic yielding in bending and shear of both cantilever and fixed-ended beams. In Ref. 16 plane-stress solutions were given for strongly supported cantilever beams with a uniform taper, when yielding under a uniform shear stress applied over the end face of the beam. The collapse stress found was always slightly lower than that derived for a plane-strain solution of similar geometry. The most general field of plane stress is reproduced in Fig. 7.3 with deformation occurring by rotation of the rigid cantilever about point O; along the curve DJE there is a necking-type discontinuity. Additional plane-stress solutions are to be found in Ref. 17, which treats of either built-in and simply-supported beams, uniformly or centrally point-loaded, the beams possessing either a rectangular or an 'I' cross-section. In the latter case it was assumed that the flanges yielded in either pure tension or compression over a certain length adjacent

---

†The construction is analogous to that given by Bishop[12] in the plane strain context.

to the regions of tension and compression in the web, with the plane
stress solution applying for the web.

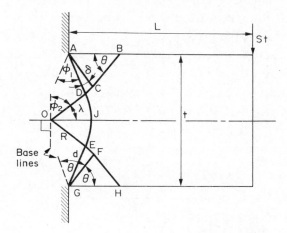

Fig. 7.3. Plane-stress slip-line field solution
for a uniform cantilever beam under
end shear loading.

Petricone and Salerno[18] employed the plane stress solutions given by
Green[16,17] to study the collapse of I-section haunched beams under
uniform loading, see Fig. 7.4. Since the bending moment of a built-in,

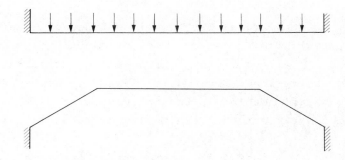

Fig. 7.4. A uniformly loaded Haunched beam.

uniformly loaded, uniform beam is twice as large at the ends as at the
mid-section, the haunched beam serves to reduce the amount of material
in the beam structure. When the design criterion is the minimization
of the weight of the beam, i.e. the weight is taken as the objective
function, this becomes a formidable task in optimization because of
the number of parameters involved. The latter authors pre-selected
certain beam dimensions and calculated others in terms of these, which

lead to a classification by weight of acceptable beam designs. More
recently Johnson and his co-workers[19-22] have provided a detailed
study of plane-stress solutions for cantilever beams under shear and
axial loading, using the procedures of the aforementioned articles.
By allowing for axial loading Ref. 19 extends the earlier work of
Green[16] on cantilever beams of rectangular cross-section. Similar
results are presented in Ref. 20 for tapered cantilevers of rectangular
cross-section loaded as shown in Fig. 7.5. It is often a common construction practice to include holes in beams to facilitate the passage

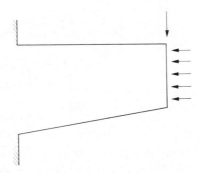

Fig. 7.5. Tapered cantilever beam under shear
and axial loads.

of utility components. This situation is addressed in Ref. 21 by
Ranshi *et al.*, dealing with the collapse of cantilever beams under
shear-type loading, with a rectangular hole located at various positions
along the beam centre-line. A study of I-section cantilever beams
under shear and axial loading is to be found in Ref. 22, which general-
izes some of the work performed previously by Green.[17]

The theory of characteristics for plane-stress problems is also to be
found treated in a recent text by Szczepinski.[23] Stress and velocity
expressions along the characteristics are derived from the von Mises
yield criterion and associated flow rule, and as mentioned earlier
these are greatly simplified if the material thickness is regarded as
constant. In addition, some derivations are provided for the Tresca
yield condition and associated flow rule. In the particular case where
the principal stresses are of opposite sign it is demonstrated that
the characteristics are orthogonal and the expressions for stress and
velocity along them are identical to the Hencky and Geiringer equations.

PLASTICITY PROBLEMS FOR OTHER THAN PLANE STRAIN CONDITIONS

The basic theory of plane plastic stress when axial symmetry prevails is treated in its own right by Szczepinski;[23] the geometric condition results in a simplification of the equations *vis-a-vis* the more general plane-stress case. Solution procedures are outlined by him for thin annular rings loaded in their plane at either the inner or outer rim, and yielding according to the von Mises criterion and associated flow rule. Szczepinski, *op cit.*, also devotes a chapter to the method of characteristics applied to thin-walled shells of arbitrary double curvature, appropriate for certain stretch-formed and drawn components. Coincident characteristics for stress and velocity are established based on the von Mises yield criterion and associated flow rule. By accounting for the curvature of the shell these expressions along the characteristics generalize the standard plane-stress case.

(ii) Axial Symmetry

In axial symmetry the non-vanishing components of stress referred to cylindrical polar coordinates (r, θ, z) are $\sigma_r, \sigma_z, \sigma_\theta$ and τ_{rz}, regarding Oz as the axis of symmetry. The non-vanishing components of velocity are u and w referred to the r and z directions respectively. The component of velocity in the hoop (or circumferential) direction is necessarily zero since flow is confined to meridian planes.

The equations of equilibrium, the yield criterion and the associated flow rule are compatible in the number of unknowns. If the Mises yield criterion and associated flow rule are used the equations governing the stresses and velocities are not hyperbolic[2,24,25] and considerable difficulties arise in their solution. When, however, the Tresca yield criterion and associated flow rule[26,27] are employed, dependent upon the position of the stress point on the yield locus, the governing equations are kinematically or statically determinate in character, as illustrated by Shield.[25] The statically determinate case arises when the heuristic hypothesis of Haar and von Karman[†] is satisfied. The stress and velocity fields are then hyperbolic with identical

---

†The hypothesis is that the circumferential stress is equal to one of the principal stresses in the meridional planes during plastic deformation.

families of characteristics. Shield, *op cit.*, has given expressions
for pressure and velocity along the slip lines; these differ from the
Hencky and Geiringer equations only in extra terms in r, the radial
coordinate. When r becomes very large the equations reduce to those
of the theory of plane strain.[†] Although the equations are analogous
to those derived for plane strain they are much more difficult to
handle and are generally employed in their finite difference form, as
illustrated by Shield.

The equations derived by Shield[25] and Hill[2] for axi-symmetric flow
can be applied directly to the problem of expanding a thick-walled
sphere. The Haar - von Karman hypothesis obviously applies in this
particular case, and on any meridian plane the slip lines are logarithmic spirals. In a manner similar to that of the expansion of a
thick-walled cylinder under conditions of plane strain, Chapter 5,
Section 2, the yield-point pressure can be determined when the sphere
is just fully plastic. Although this problem can be solved by much
simpler methods, the implications of the technique are significant.
It was demonstrated in Chapter 5, Section 6, that consideration of
the radially inward flow of a thick-walled cylinder could lead to an
ideal die profile in plane-strain drawing. Analogously, the radial-
flow field can form the basis of the construction of an ideal die
profile for the axi-symmetric case. The deformation mode in such
ideal forming operations is one where the streamlines are tangential
to the principal stress directions and therefore bisect the slip-line
directions. Thus, at any point along a streamline the velocity along
the intersecting α- and β-lines is the same. Streamlined flow has
been discussed by Hill[28] in the context of plane-strain deformation
and by Richmond and Morrison[29] for axi-symmetric plastic flow. These
latter authors used the Tresca yield criterion and associated flow
rule and the hypothesis of Haar and von Karman, in order to establish
a frictionless ideal die profile for drawing or extrusion by the method
of characteristics. They did not proceed, as suggested above, by
considering a radial flow field of logarithmic spirals and building
a die profile around this. As discussed in Refs. 28 and 29, many
streamlined profiles can be designed for a given reduction, and

---

[†]See also the book by Hill, Ref. 2.

Richmond and Morrison, *op cit.*, proposed that the shortest axial length die could be realized by having a centred-fan field emanating from the exit point of the die. In the case of axi-symmetric flow, Hencky's First Theorem does not hold and even though the exit bounding slip line is straight other members of the family within the fan are not. The die profile was constructed on a trial-and-error basis; the stress relationships along the slip lines were cast into a finite difference form, as proposed by Shield,[25] and solved on a digital computer. The die profiles are generally concave in shape with zero entrance angle and a finite exit angle. The shortest die should be chosen because it is likely to minimize the frictional force which must always be present in practice because of interface die-workpiece friction. In addition to minimizing the forming loads streamlined flow should reduce the internal damage incurred by the material and an increase in the fatigue life of the drawn or extruded product might be anticipated. This has been reported for specimens deformed in plane strain through ideal dies,[30,31] as well as for aluminium rod extruded through ideal, axi-symmetric dies[31] manufactured in accordance with the calculations of Ref. 29.

The rather complex shape of streamlined die profiles should not be regarded wholly as a deterrent to their manufacture since this can be achieved quite easily on a numerically controlled machine tool. In discussing streamlined dies an interesting parallel was raised in Ref. 29 with regard to the design of ideal nozzles in supersonic compressible gas flow.[32] In this case the field equations are also hyperbolic and can be solved by the method of characterisitcs.†

Sortais and Kobayashi[33] have also constructed an optimum die profile for axi-symmetric extrusion (or drawing) where the starting point was a radial-flow field of logarithmic spirals, as discussed earlier. Their construction does not lead to a minimum axial length die. Nevertheless, the paper is of interest since the authors employed the von Mises yield criterion and associated flow rule, along with the Haar and von Karman hypothesis, and demonstrated that the characteristics for stress and velocity were the same.

---

†The nozzles are of course expansion nozzles, with the gas accelerating in the divergent section. Note also that, in general, the character-istics are not orthogonal.

The theory due to Shield[25] has formed the basis of the solution method
to a number of axi-symmetric problems on indentation and the like.
To recapitulate, the material is assumed rigid-perfectly plastic, to
obey the Tresca yield condition and associated flow rule and the
hypothesis of Haar and von Karman is adopted. Shield, *op cit.*, determined the pressure to indent a semi-infinite body with a smooth,
circular, flat-ended rigid punch. Similarly, Eason and Shield[34]
calculated the indentation pressure for a rough, circular, flat-ended
punch. In both of these papers an attempt was made to provide a
statically admissible extension of the slip-line-field net into the
non-deforming zone in the manner of Bishop.[12] Lockett[35] has considered
the indentation of a semi-infinite body by a rigid frictionless conical
indentor, appropriate for the analysis of the Rockwell hardness test.
Calculations were performed for a number of semi-cone angles between
approximately 50 and 90 degrees; pressure distributions and certain
dimensions of the field(s) of characteristics were reported. The
plastic collapse of axi-symmetric V-notched bars has been studied by
Szczepinski *et al.*[36] The calculated constraint factors were very
similar to those derived under plane strain conditions. It will be
apparent that one-half of the field of characteristics developed in
Ref. 36 also comprises the incipient field for the frictionless compression of a truncated solid cone, i.e. a frustum, see Suh *et al.*[37]
These latter authors also provided stress and velocity solutions for
increasing interfacial frictional conditions. As the coefficient of
friction increased between the compression platen and the material,
a rigid "dead-metal" cone of material started to develop under the
platen as the complete or shearing friction condition was approached.

(iii)   Soils

The yield criteria of Tresca and von Mises are adequate for most metals,
since their yielding behaviour in not generally influenced by the hydrostatic part of the stress tensor. On the other hand, the yielding of
materials such as clay, ice, soils, compacted snow and certain plastics
is dependent upon the hydrostatic stress. Such materials can possess
complex mechanical properties and modelling their yield behaviour and
associated deformation mode is generally more complicated than with
an ideal metal. The equations which determine the velocity fields in

many of these materials have not been completely resolved. The analytical models tend to fall into two main groups, according to whether or not coincidence of the principal axes of stress with the principal axes of strain rate (or strain increment) is deemed to occur. Drescher[38] has recently conducted an experimental investigation aimed at assessing the operative *flow rule* for granular materials, and his results indicate that, in general, the principal axes of stress and strain rate are not coaxial.

Some thirty years ago Hill[2] proposed a yield criterion for pressure-sensitive materials deforming under plane-strain conditions. If σ_1 and σ_2 are the principal stresses in the plane of deformation, then the yield criterion for an isotropic solid can be expressed as

$$F(p, \tau_m) = 0. \tag{7.9}$$

In the above equation $p = -(1/2)(\sigma_1 + \sigma_2)$ and $\tau_m = (1/2)(\sigma_2 - \sigma_1)$, and these quantities are the mean compressive stress in the plane and the algebraic maximum shear stress respectively. The yield criterion (7.9) can be represented by a locus referred to the pair of coordinate axes $(\sigma_1 + \sigma_2)/2$ and $(\sigma_2 - \sigma_1)/2$. If the locus is closed on one side the material yields at a certain level of pure hydrostatic tension only.[†] Hill, *op cit.*, suggested plotting on the same diagram a number of stress circles (in accordance with Mohr's construction) each representing a plastic state, and then determining the envelope to the stress circles. He showed that under certain stress states it was possible for circles to lie wholly within the envelope, and that the stress equations were hyperbolic (with two, non-orthogonal, characteristic directions) only if contact with the envelope was real.[††] This point is also discussed by Kingston and Spencer.[39] Hill also demonstrated

---

[†] When yielding is independent of p, as for an ideal metal, $\tau_m = \pm k$ and the locus degenerates into a pair of parallel lines $2k$ apart.
[††]Hill developed the theory of plane plastic stress (discussed at the beginning of this chapter) for the yielding of pressure-sensitive materials under plane-strain conditions. The yield criterion for plane stress is formally a special case of (7.9) and the investigation of the existence of characteristics is mathematically analogous.

that if the material was assumed incompressible and that the principal
axes of stress and strain rate were coaxial, then the velocity characteristics coincided with the slip lines, i.e. they are orthogonal, and
hence are distinct from the stress characteristics. The yield function
(7.9) is not the plastic potential in this instance, and whilst this
is physically acceptable many uniqueness proofs in the theory of
plasticity demand their coincidence. In addition, distinct stress and
velocity characteristics are not in accord with certain experimental
data.

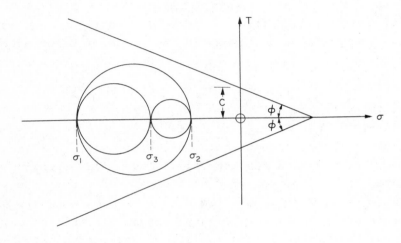

Fig. 7.6. Coulomb yield envelope.

In soil mechanics Coulomb's[40] yield criterion is often applied with
the yield locus represented by a pair of oblique straight lines, as
shown in Fig. 7.6. Coulomb's criterion states that the shear stress
τ acting on any section through the soil depends linearly on the
cohesion stress, c, and the normal stress, σ, on the section at that
point, i.e.

$$\tau < c - \sigma \tan \phi, \tag{7.10}$$

where ϕ is the angle of friction of the soil. Tensile stresses are
considered positive and therefore $\sigma < c \cot \phi$. Failure of the soil
is deemed to occur when the largest of the stress circles, in Fig.
7.6, touches the yield envelope. Contact of the circles with the
envelope is always real in this instance. Taking σ_3 to be the intermediate principal stress the yield condition of (7.9) can be expressed

as

$$(\sigma_2 - \sigma_1) = 2c \cos \phi - (\sigma_2 + \sigma_1) \sin \phi. \qquad (7.11)$$

If general stress components are employed an equally acceptable way of writing (7.11) is

$$f = (\frac{\sigma_x + \sigma_y}{2}) \sin \phi + \sqrt{\frac{1}{4}(\sigma_x - \sigma_y)^2 + \tau_{xy}^2} - c \cos \phi = 0. \qquad (7.12)$$

Equation (7.12) is also applicable to plane strain deformation ($e_3 = e_z$ = 0), and for the two dimensional problem the equilibrium equations (neglecting the weight of the soil) and (7.12) are hyperbolic. Shield[41] has provided expressions for the stress along the characteristics (see also Ref. 39), which are equally inclined at an angle ($\pi/4$ + $\phi/2$) to the direction of the algebraically greater principal stress. It transpires that in this case the characteristics for stress and velocity are identical, and Ref. 41 provides the variation of the velocities along the characteristics, whose directions coincide with those of zero rate of extension. Note that (7.12) is taken as the plastic potential and hence the strain-rate components are derivable in the usual manner. As shown by Shield, *op cit.*, the soil is not incompressible, and plastic deformation must be accompanied by an increase in volume if $\phi \neq 0$. In practice the degree of dilatancy is limited, and indeed certain soils and other granular media can show a decrease in volume (also limited in its extent) with deformation. The assumption of constant volume may well be more suited to problems of continued plastic flow. However, the majority of solutions to problems of non-steady state deal only with incipient fields of characterisitics at the onset of flow. Incipient fields of characteristics have been given by Shield[41] for the indentation of a semi-infinite mass of soil by both a rigid flat-bottomed punch and a wedge-shaped indenter. The fields are similar is appearance to those proposed when indenting an ideal metal. When using this type of formulation the velocity solutions should be carefully checked to establish whether the predicted volume changes are at all reasonable. In the context of the indentation problem just referred to, there is good reason to believe they are not.[42]

The yield criterion of (7.11) holds for other than plane flow. As shown by Shield[43] it is most simply represented by a surface drawn in three-dimensional principal stress space. It is a right hexagonal pyramid equally inclined to the $\sigma_1, \sigma_2, \sigma_3$ coordinate axes, with its vertex at the point

$$\sigma_1 = \sigma_2 = \sigma_3 = c \cot \phi. \qquad (7.13)$$

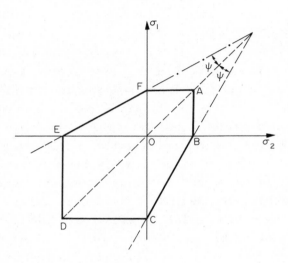

Fig. 7.7. Intersection of the Coulomb yield surface with the plane $\sigma_3 = 0$

$$CB = 2c \tan (\pi/4 - \phi/2),$$
$$OC = 2c \tan (\pi/4 + \phi/2),$$
$$\tan \psi = \sin \phi.$$

Figure 7.7 shows a section of the yield surface made by the plane $\sigma_3 = 0$; sections formed by other planes $\sigma_3 = $ constant differ in size but possess the same shape. The associated flow rule still predicts that plastic flow is accompanied by dilatation. Cox, Eason and Hopkins[44] have applied the Coulomb yield criterion and associated flow rule to the problem of axially symmetric plastic deformations of rigid-perfectly plastic soils. In particular, a solution was obtained for the incipient plastic flow of a semi-infinite region of soil indented by a flat-ended, smooth, rigid, circular cylinder, where the plastic régimes subscribe to the Haar-von Karman hypothesis. In this particular case the characteristics for stress and velocity are identical.

As already mentioned the degree of dilatancy predicted by the flow rule associated with the Coulomb yield criterion is questionable, see also Ref. 45. To overcome this problem Spencer[42] proposed a model for the plane deformation of a soil which requires the Coulomb yield criterion but not the associated flow rule. He assumed the material to be incompressible and the deformation to be comprised of the resultant of two simple shears directed along the stress charact-eristics.[†] Spencer, *op cit.*, applied the theory to the indentation of a semi-infinite mass of soil by a frictionless, flat-bottomed, rigid punch. The stress field is identical to that proposed earlier by Shield,[41] but the resulting velocity field is of course different due to the assumed material incompressibility in Spencer's model. Zero volume change is more in keeping with experimental data cited by Spencer in the same article. In passing it is worthwhile noting that in the study of the practical handling of granular materials, e.g. the flow in hoppers and chutes, the weight and acceleration of the material should at least be considered initially in any analytical model of the process. The field equations developed by Shield have been extended by Morrison and Richmond[46] to include such terms, and although more complex the equations still remain hyperbolic.

It is not possible within the framework of the present section to do more than highlight certain aspects of a vast and complex subject. The review articles of Refs. 48 and 49 will provide the reader with a more comprehensive coverage of the earlier literature on soil mech-anics, whilst the texts by Sokolovskii[50] and Salencon[51] give a more detailed account of the theoretical fundamentals of the subject, as founded on the theory of plasticity.

ANISOTROPY

Most metallic solids after forming are substantially anisotropic in that they exhibit differences in material properties in different directions.

[†]An important feature of the theory is the dependence of strain rate on both stress and stress rate, with the consequence that for isotropic materials the principal axes of stress and strain rate need not be coaxial.

Anisotropy is of two main kinds, namely,

(a) crystallographic anisotropy, arising from a preferred orientation of the crystal grains in a polycrystalline aggregate;
and

(b) microstructural anisotropy, governed by the variation in
the morphology of the grain structure and the non-random
distribution of metallic, intermetallic and non-metallic
phases, referred to as mechanical fibring.

Both sources of anisotropy have an effect on the material properties.
In general, with mechanical fibring, the distribution of the microstructural constituents conforms approximately to the deformation of the
material as a whole. Thus in rolled plate or sheet the inclusions,
etc., are elongated in the rolling direction and this can result in
inferior tensile and impact properties in the transverse direction.
Crystallographic anisotropy (texture) usually develops during the
thermal/mechanical processing stages of production, and more often is
the prime source of anisotropy. It is now well known that texture
can exert an influence on the electrical, magnetic and mechanical
properties of a material. Therefore, it is important to be able to
identify those textures which are likely to bring about some improvement in material performance and then to establish processing techniques which will give rise to the desired texture. This latter aspect
has been covered in detail in the review article by Dillamore and
Roberts.[52]

Theoretical attempts at describing anisotropic behaviour can be divided
into two main categories. One is the mathematical theory of plasticity
(a macroscopic approach), and the other is the physical theory of
plasticity (a crystallographic approach). As stated by Lin,[53] the
latter theory attempts to explain why things happen the way they do,
while the former theory is generally founded on hypotheses and assumptions of a phenomenological character based on experimental observations.
Two recent texts by Backofen[54] and Reid[55] cover certain aspects of each
theory and provide a good introduction to the subject of anisotropy
and the deformation of single crystal and polycrystalline materials.

(i)   Crystallographic Approach

In the single crystals of many metals it is well known that the main mechanism of plastic deformation, on a microscopic scale, is a simple shear parallel to certain crystallographic planes and in a particular direction.   In general the primary systems are those crystallographic planes of widest spacing and slip occurs on these planes in the direction of closest atomic packing.   For face-centred cubic (f.c.c.) crystals the systems likely to be activated are {111}<110>, while the equivalent set in body-centred cubic (b.c.c.) crystals is {110}< 111>. [†]

According to Schmid's law for yielding in a single crystal, slip will first occur on that system which first attains the critical value of resolved shear stress, τ^*.   In a rod-shaped crystal under uniaxial tension σ, by stress transformation

$$\tau = \sigma \cos \phi \cos \lambda, \tag{7.14}$$

where ϕ and λ are the angles made by the slip plane normal and the slip direction to the rod axis respectively.   Hence, σ has to be increased (up to some yield value σ_y) until the critical stress, τ^*, is achieved on the active system according to (7.14).   The ratio σ_y/τ^* is known as the Schmid factor and clearly the quantity will depend upon the orientation of the tensile axis with respect to the crystal structure.   It is not difficult, as least in principle, to envisage how strengthening can be obtained through preferred orientation; useful strengthening (texture hardening[57]) is achieved when the orientation of the crystal structure makes slip and hence yielding more difficult under the applied stress system.

For f.c.c. crystals, the Schmid factor when averaged for all orientations of the tensile axis within the unit stereographic triangle is

---

[†]In b.c.c. crystals slip is less restricted and can occur on planes containing the <111> direction - termed "pencil glide". Note that the Miller system for identifying crystallographic planes and directions is used in this section. The following brackets,( ) and [ ], around the indices identify a plane and direction respectively. Due to symmetry many planes and directions are deemed equivalent and brackets { } and < > respectively, define equivalent sets. See Ref. 56 for a more detailed discussion.

$\simeq 2.24$, see Ref. 55 or the article by Calnan and Clews.[58] In general
a single slip system will be activated but depending upon the orientation, e.g. pulling along [100], as many as eight could be operative
each having attained the critical shear stress τ^*.

Under more complex loading conditions the same rules persist. The
applied stresses are transformed to the possible slip systems, resulting in a generalization of the Schmid law and forming the basis for
the construction of crystallographic yield loci. The simplest of
these is the case of biaxial stressing, where principal stresses are
applied in the longitudinal and transverse directions of a sheet.
The sheet is assumed to possess an ideal sheet texture $\{hk\ell\}<uvw>$,
i.e. the crystallographic planes $\{hk\ell\}$ lie in the plane of the sheet
with the direction $<uvw>$ aligned with the longitudinal or rolling
direction. Piehler and Backofen[59] have constructed plane-stress
crystallographic yield loci for a number of ideal sheet textures based
on $\{111\}<110>$ slip in f.c.c. crystals or equivalently $\{110\}<111>$ slip
in b.c.c. crystals. A detailed account of the method of construction
is also available in Refs. 54, 60 and 61. A further generalization
is to be found in the work of Kocks[62] where stress states other than
biaxial are discussed. In all cases the yield loci are convex outward,
but they possess corners. Fig. 7.8 shows the yield loci calculated
for an ideal "cube on face" texture, i.e. (001) planes in the plane
of the sheet, for the case of biaxial stressing. The three loci, (a)
to (c) of Fig. 7.8, have been obtained by rotatiog the ideal component
about the sheet normal 0, 22.5 and 45 degrees respectively to the x,
or rolling direction.

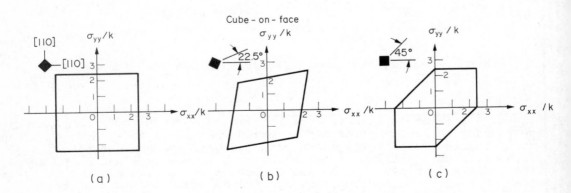

Fig. 7.8. Crystallographically derived yield loci
for a "cube-on-face" texture.

PLASTICITY PROBLEMS FOR OTHER THAN PLANE STRAIN CONDITIONS

It is beyond the scope of the present text to review studies concerned
with the work-hardening behaviour of metals. As pointed out by Cottrell,[63] work-hardening involves the group behaviour of a large number
of dislocations. There are numerous ways in which the dislocations
can arrange themselves and interact with each other, and herein lies
the major difficulty of elucidating the finer details of the mechanisms
of hardening. Much work has gone into investigating the stress-strain
behaviour of single crystals of metal - usually pure metals.[64-67] The
use of optical, electron optics and X-ray techniques have facilitated
the identification of structures arising from plastic deformation.
Such information has led to theories regarding the formation of both
the structure and the observed hardening curves, in terms of these.[64]
In spite of the progress that has been made there still remains to be
given a definitive account of the hardening behaviour, particularly
in the later stages of deformation, i.e. in the so-called stage III
or "parabolic hardening" domain.

It will be appreciated that problems are compounded when attempting
to explain the work-hardening behaviour of polycrystalline metals.
In general, the microstructures are much more complex because of the
presence of inclusions, etc.. Furthermore, the precise nature of the
influence of grain boundaries and the constraints imposed on individual
grains by its neighbours are unknown. Certain aspects of polycrystal
deformation and single-crystal deformation have been presented by
Kocks.[62]

To take a broad view, the theories of polycrystalline deformation fall
into two main classes, those which assume equal straining of each
crystal and hence preserve continuity of the aggregate and those which
are based on equal stressing of each crystal. The former can be regarded as being the more realistic and providing an upper bound for the
yield stress,[62] whilst the latter approach provides a lower bound.[†]

Much of the work on the yield strength of plastically constrained
crystals stems from the original study by Taylor[68] of f.c.c. metals.
Taylor assumed that plastic deformation (elastic strains were ignored)

---

†The crystallographic yield loci constructed on the basis of the
generalized Schmid law are often referred to as lower bounds.

was effected by slip on the {111}<110> system. The assumption of the uniform straining of each crystal ensures cohesion of the aggregate but ignores stress continuity across the grain boundaries. For incompressible deformation an arbitrary imposed shape change requires, in general, the operation of five independent shears from all the possible slip systems. At first sight this would appear to be the selection of a combination of five from the equivalent twelve {111}<110> systems, i.e. $^{12}C_5$ or 792 choices. It transpires, however, that not all of the systems are independent and it can be shown that the choice has to be made from 384 possibilities. Taylor introduced the hypothesis that among all combinations of slip systems capable of accommodating the imposed strain the actual set of active glide shears is that in which their absolute sum is a minimum. Selection can be a lengthy procedure without recourse to electronic computers; programming techniques have been developed[69-72] to ascertain the active slip systems. Taylor considered {111}<110> slip only, but the programming procedures permit other slip systems to be taken into account (in particular for b.c.c. metals), as well as allowing for deformation by twinning; see Refs. 71 and 72 and the article by Chin[73] which surveys some of the work in this area.

In his original article Taylor[68] considered the case of uniaxial deformation under axial symmetric flow, i.e. where the longitudinal and transverse strains are related in the ratio 1: $-\frac{1}{2}$: $-\frac{1}{2}$. For a given crystal orientation he then proceded to compute the glide shear, γ, on all possible slip systems, and proposed that the actual set capable of satisfying the imposed strain was the one where the quantity was

$$\sum_{j=1}^{5} |\gamma_j|,$$

minimized. If more than one set has the same minimum value then these are equally likely to operate. With the further assumption that the critical shear stress τ_c is attained on each system, the work done in an increment of plastic strain is

$$dW = \tau_c \sum_{j=1}^{5} |\gamma_j|. \tag{7.15}$$

The same work is done in uniaxial tension and therefore

$$\sigma_{xx} \cdot d\varepsilon_{xx} = \tau_c \sum_{j=1}^{5} |\gamma_j| ,$$

or

$$M = \frac{\sigma_{xx}}{\tau_c} = \frac{\sum\limits_{j=1}^{5} |\gamma_j|}{d\varepsilon_{xx}} , \qquad (7.16)$$

where M is referred to as the Taylor factor. Since the γ_j are related to the imposed strain through the transformation rule, the summation of the shears is expressible in terms of $d\varepsilon_{xx}$ and the right-hand side of (7.16) is evaluated as a numerical quantity.

The M factor can be determined for all orientations of the tensile axis with respect to the cube axes of the crystal, within the unit stereographic triangle.[54,55] The average value $\bar{M}$ over all orientations is found to be

$$\bar{M} = \sigma_y/\tau_c \simeq 3.06 .$$

The result is to be interpreted as defining the yield strength, σ_y (in terms of the critical shear stress), of a randomly orientated polycrystal. The result is insensitive to grain size.

A later analysis by Bishop and Hill (B-H),[74,75] based on the principle of maximum work, reinforced some of the assumptions made by Taylor by illustrating that the yield criterion is satisfied on the active systems selected by Taylor without exceeding it on the inactive ones. B-H[74,75] also proved the hypothesis made by Taylor, namely that the absolute sum of the active shears is a minimum. Notwithstanding the more rigorous treatment by B-H, their approach possesses certain computational advantages over the method of Taylor. The B-H procedure identifies the yield stress state(s) which maximizes the work done on the material, for an arbitrary imposed strain and not merely uniaxial deformation. Only fifty-six stress states[†] need to be inspected,[75,76] and these correspond to the vertices of the polyhedral surface in stress space representing the yield criterion of the crystal. Each

---

†Actually twenty-eight states, which with their negatives, makes fifty-six in total.

of these stress states can activate either six or eight slip systems
and therefore, in general, provides a choice for the operative set of
five.

The B-H analysis can be employed to plot crystallographic yield loci,
with the starting point a statement of the imposed strain. The easiest
way of proceeding is to assume an ideal sheet texture, as was discussed
for loci bssed on the generalized Schmid law, and impose principal
strains in the rolling and transverse directions of the sheet material.
The third strain is then determined from the incompressibility condition. These strains are then transformed to the cube axes of the
crystal and the B-H criterion is imposed to determine the maximum
work done and the associated stress state. This procedure was followed
by Piehler and Backofen,[59] who at this stage then transformed the
stresses back to the specimen axes. By taking the stress normal to
the sheet at zero, the two in-plane stresses (not necessarily principal
stresses) can be determined. It is possibly more direct to proceed
in the manner indicated in Fig. 7.9. The coordinate axes in the figure
are the normal stresses in the plane of the sheet, and the construction
of the locus is based on the principle of the Equivalence of Plastic
Work. The imposed strain is known and in particular the ratio, $d\varepsilon_{xx}/$
$d\varepsilon_{yy}$, where x and y correspond to the rolling and transverse directions
of the sheet. A line Σ is then drawn in the plane of Fig. 7.9 perpendicular to a direction ($d\varepsilon$ in the figure) which is the *vector* sum of
$d\varepsilon_{xx}$ and $d\varepsilon_{yy}$. The perpendicular distance to Σ from the origin of
the locus is the maximum work quantity (expressed as a function of
critical shear stress) computed from the B-H analysis. Computer
routines can facilitate the plotting and the boundary of the locus
is formed by the inner envelope of the intersecting Σ lines constructed
for a full range of strain ratios, $d\varepsilon_{xx}/d\varepsilon_{yy}$.[77]

Hosford and Backofen[78] applied the B-H analysis to ideal sheet textures
deforming under uniaxial tension. They relaxed the conditions of axially symmetric flow and imposed different ratios of width strain to
thickness strain, the so-called r-value. They varied r over a wide
range and at each selected value computed the work done in an increment
of axial strain. The lowest value corresponds to the expected behaviour
and hence the most probable value of r for the selected texture. In
turn, they could compute the yield stress of the material expressed

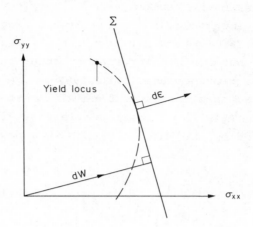

Fig. 7.9.   Schematic representation of the derivation
of an upper-bound yield locus.

in units of the Taylor factor M.   Note the difference in the Hosford
and Backofen approach in respect of some of the calculations referred
to earlier, through the imposition of different r-values.   Some of
this work has been re-examined by Bassani,[79] who also discussed the
plotting of crystallographic yield loci using the B-H analysis.

For further discussion of the behaviour of polycrystalline solids the
interested reader is referred to the articles by Hutchinson[80] and
Lin,[53] where elastic-plastic deformation is also considered.

With rare exception the description of textures in terms of one or
more ideal orientations is an oversimplification.   X-ray texture
goniometry[81] is a common method of studying the crystallite orientation
through the determination of a pole figure.   This is a stereographic
projection which shows the variation in density of a plane normal (or
pole) with orientation, for a selected set of crystal planes.   Intens-
ities are plotted as multiples of the intensity expected from a randomly
orientated specimen.   When the pole figure of a single coupon of material, cut from the plane of a sheet, is determined by the Schulz reflection method[82] information is obtained up to only about 70 degrees from
the centre of the pole figure.   The cause of the limitation is the
defocusing of the Bragg reflection and this has been analysed in Ref.
83.   Pole figures obtained in this manner are usually referred to as

incomplete pole figures. To obtain a complete pole figure either a combined transmission-reflection method[52,81] is necessary or some form of composite specimen is used.[84] One disadvantage of the pole figure is that it gives information only about the distribution of plane normals and does not contain information about rotation around these normals. It will be clear that three angles are required to describe fully the orientation of a crystallite with respect to a physical reference frame. This is demonstrated in Fig. 7.10, where the orientation is specified by the Euler angles ψ, θ (=$\cos^{-1}\xi$), ϕ with respect

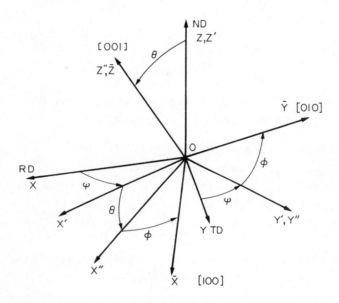

Fig. 7.10. The three successive rotations through the Euler angles (ψ,θ,ϕ), which relate the crystal axes [100], etc., to the sheet reference axes *ND*, etc..

to the specimen axes. In a sheet the most obvious choice of specimen axes is the normal, transverse and rolling directions. The intuitive determination of the (three angle) crystallite orientation distribution, i.e. the probability of a crystallite having a particular orientation, from a number of pole figure distributions would, in general, be difficult. For the case of cubic crystals Roe[85] and Bunge[86] independently proposed a general analytical method for obtaining the crystallite orientation distribution function (CODF) from a limited number of pole figure distributions. The CODF is given by a series of generalized spherical harmonics and the original papers of Roe and Bunge, along with Refs. 87 and 88, illustrate how this is achieved. The results can be represented graphically by plotting the probability of a crystallite having a given orientation in Euler space and taking constant sections of one of the Euler angles, most usually constant ϕ sections. Ideal orientations $(hk\ell)$ $[uvw]$ are represented as single points in each of these sections and charts can be prepared to facilitate the interpretation of the resulting CODFs.[89]

The CODF permits a more rigorous means of correlating texture and mechanical properties. In those cases where a physical or mechanical property of a single crystal shows anisotropy, a solution for the bulk anisotropy of polycrystals becomes possible[90,91] providing the orientation dependence can also be expanded as a series of generalized spherical harmonics. These analytical techniques have been developed by Davies *et al.*[92-94] (and others[88,95]) to determine the variation in tensile yield strength with orientation in the plane of a rolled sheet for a number of metals. The angular variation in yield stress can be determined on the basis of,

(a) the Schmid law and

(b) the B-H technique for the determination of the Taylor M-factor, but modified to incorporate the Hosford and Backofen[78] criterion of non-axisymmetric flow. Hence, the expected plastic strain ratio can also be evaluated.

Plane-stress crystallographic yield loci can also be determined from either the generalized Schmid law or the B-H analysis. In Ref. 77 predictions for a number of sheet metals are given. The actual textures in processed sheets have the effect of smoothing the predicted yield surfaces *vis-à-vis* those constructed for ideal sheet textures, i.e. the corners on the yield surface are removed. However, depending upon the texture severity very rapid changes in curvature of the yield surface can occur.

The CODF in conjunction with a selected crystallographic slip system, e.g. {111} <110> in f.c.c. crystals, can be utilized to predict the change in textures under an imposed straining mode. Kallend and Davies[96] and Van Houtte[97] have given details of the technique in their analytical treatment of the development of rolling textures. Since, in general, there is some latitude in the choice of the active system this may have a marked effect upon the predicted crystal rotations. In Ref. 96 an attempt was made to identify the operative set of shears on the basis of the stacking fault energy of the material,[98,99] but this did not appear to have a marked effect on the predicted textures. Both Refs. 96 and 97 considered the effect of deformation twinning on the resulting texture; in the latter reference the ratio of twinning to slip deformation was varied from zero to 100% to demonstrate the influence.

The use of CODF analysis also permits the modelling of textures arising from phase transformations. Certain aspects of the theoretical treatment have been given by Sargent[100] and applications are to be found in the work of Davies *et al.*[101,102]

In spite of the rigour that can be brought to certain aspects of texture analysis through the use of CODF, it is unlikely that they will find general usage as the texture parameter in analyses of metal-forming processes. It would be altogether too demanding to try to assess in this way the overall texture changes arising during the forming of a metal part. At the present time crystallographic yield loci, etc., can be established on the basis of the initial texture of the undeformed sheet. Even allowing that texture changes can be calculated following some simple straining mode (see earlier discussion and also Ref. 103), the predicted subsequent yield surfaces are normalized with respect to a critical shear stress. The texture and hardening behaviour are not linked in the analysis, and furthermore the subsequent yield surfaces are symmetrical so that Bauschinger effects are excluded. No consideration is paid to other structural features such as second phases, inclusions and the like.

(ii) Macroscopic Theories of Anisotropy

Any yield criterion for an anisotropic metal is usually founded on the assumptions made for an isotropic metal, namely, that yielding is independent of moderate hydrostatic pressures and that the resulting yield locus is convex. Furthermore, by identifying the yield function with the plastic potential, the ratio of the components of the plastic-strain increments can be established and the increment itself found to be normal to the yield locus.

One of the simplest functions capable of describing initial anisotropy is the quadratic form,

$$f = \frac{1}{2} C_{ijk\ell} \, \sigma_{ij} \sigma_{k\ell} - \bar{\sigma}^2 = 0 \qquad (7.17)$$

or

$$F = \frac{1}{2} D_{ijk\ell} \, S_{ij} S_{k\ell} - \bar{\sigma}^2 = 0, \qquad (7.18)$$

where $S_{ij} = \sigma_{ij} - \delta_{ij} \, \sigma_{ii}/3$, is the deviatoric stress, δ_{ij} the Kronecker delta and $\bar{\sigma}$ the yield stress.

If, for example, $C_{ijk\ell}$ is expressed as the following fourth-order isotropic tensor,

$$C_{ijk\ell} = \frac{3}{2} \, (\delta_{ik}\delta_{j\ell} + \delta_{i\ell} \, \delta_{jk}) - \delta_{ij} \, \delta_{k\ell}, \qquad (7.19)$$

then (7.17) reduces to the von Mises yield criterion.

By considering the symmetry of the stress and plastic-strain increment tensor and since the increment of plastic work is a scalar quantity, then the eighty-one independent coefficients, $C_{ijk\ell}$, can be reduced to twenty-one. If it is now assumed that there exists three orthogonal principal axes of anisotropy such that:

(i)   the direct strain increments are independent of shear stresses,

(ii) the shear strain increments are independent of direct stresses and

(iii) the shear strain increments depend only on the corresponding shear stresses,

then by invoking the plastic incompressibility assumption the number of independent coefficients are reduced to six.

If the coefficients remain in strict proportion to each other as plastic deformation occurs the material will harden isotropically and the initial yield surface merely expands in size. The quadratic form of the yield function excludes any Bauschinger effect.

295

With six independent coefficients the yield condition can be expressed in the following form, due to Hill:[2,104]

$$2f(\sigma_{ij}) \equiv F(\sigma_{yy}-\sigma_{zz})^2 + G(\sigma_{zz}-\sigma_{xx})^2 + H(\sigma_{xx}-\sigma_{yy})^2 +$$

$$+ 2L\sigma_{zx}^2 + 2M\sigma_{zx}^2 + 2N\sigma_{xy}^2 = 1. \tag{7.20}$$

The coefficients F, G, H, etc., characterize the current state of anisotropy. When

$$L = M = N = 3F = 3G = 3H,$$

the expression (7.20) reduces to the von Mises yield criterion if F is equated to $1/2Y^2$ with Y the yield stress in uniaxial tension. It is important to note that the stresses in (7.20) are referred to the principal axes of anisotropy, characterized by the Cartesian coordinates x, y and z. This orthotropic symmetry may or may not exist in a real material. In rolled plate and sheet the principal axes of anisotropy are intuitively associated with the rolling, transverse and through-thickness directions. The coefficients F, G, H and L, M, N can be obtained, in principle, by applying a uniaxial stress and a shear stress respectively, relative to the principal axes of anisotropy until yielding occurs.

If f in (7.20) is taken as the plastic potential then the plastic strain increments, referred to the principal axes of anisotropy, are

$$
\begin{aligned}
d\varepsilon_{xx} &= \lambda \left[H(\sigma_{xx}-\sigma_{yy}) + G(\sigma_{xx}-\sigma_{zz}) \right], \\
d\varepsilon_{yy} &= \lambda \left[F(\sigma_{yy}-\sigma_{zz}) + H(\sigma_{yy}-\sigma_{xx}) \right], \\
d\varepsilon_{zz} &= \lambda \left[G(\sigma_{zz}-\sigma_{xx}) + F(\sigma_{zz}-\sigma_{yy}) \right], \\
d\varepsilon_{yz} &= \lambda L \, \sigma_{yz}, \\
d\varepsilon_{zx} &= \lambda M \, \sigma_{zx}, \\
\text{and} \qquad d\varepsilon_{xy} &= \lambda N \, \sigma_{xy},
\end{aligned}
\tag{7.21}
$$

where λ is a non-negative scalar factor of proportionality, as discussed in Chapter 2.

More will be said about the above anisotropic model since it has been the most widely applied, particularly in investigations into sheet metal forming. However, the lack of generality in the model is evident,

296

and Refs. 105 to 110 provide some alternative ones. The references just cited are by no means exhaustive and should be taken as being representative only of the many investigations in this area. The article by Edelman and Drucker[105] published in 1951 still provides a good survey of different yield functions, ranging from that due to von Mises and the isotropic hardening class to initial anisotropy and more complex hardening rules. The more sophisticated models attempt to account for developing anisotropy and the Bauschinger effect by permitting translation, rotation and distortion of the yield surface in stress space. Such a yield function can be expressed as

$$f = \tfrac{1}{2} D_{ijk\ell} \, (s_{ij} - \alpha_{ij}) \, (s_{ij} - \alpha_{ij}) - k^2 = 0. \qquad (7.22)$$

The quantity α_{ij} is a translation tensor, usually taken as a function (often linear) of the plastic strain, and k is a yield stress quantity which is regarded as a scalar function of the plastic strain. Equation (7.22) is of the form obtained by Baltov and Sawczuk[107] and Svensson,[108] although the respective authors place different interpretations on the moduli $D_{ijk\ell}$. Shrivastava et $al.$[110] have attempted a general mathematical description of yielding and the subsequent hardening rule, and they demonstrate that many of the more significant models (including (7.22)) can be derived from their more general formulation. The second-order effect, related to axial strain accumulation in cyclic torsion,[111-113] can also be accounted for with their model.

It is not an easy task to devise loading systems which permit the evaluation of several stress components simultaneously. For this reason the experimental determination of initial and subsequent yield surfaces is somewhat restricted, and much of the work that has been performed has been carried out on thin-walled tubes under combined axial and torsional loading or axial loading coupled with internal pressure. References 114 to 117 provide the results of investigations performed along the lines just indicated. It is evident that, in general, the operative hardening rule is very complex. Translation and distortion of the yield surface can occur in different combinations with or without the existence of cross-effect,[114,115,118] e.g. influencing the axial strength of a tube by overstraining in torsion. It is also clear that depending upon the definition of yielding, i.e. whether it be the limit of purely elastic behaviour or some permitted amount of permanent strain, a different form of yield surface can be obtained from the same set of experimental results.[117]

In view of the preceding comments it is not surprising to find that in general the macroscopic models of yielding and work-hardening are not *a priori* predictive since there is no attempt to delineate the physical events which control the observed behaviour. In addition, many of the hardening models are quite complex mathematically, and for this reason less sophisticated models of anisotropy and the Bauschinger effect have usually been incorporated into analyses of metal-forming processes.

The role of plastic anisotropy in deep drawing was first brought into focus by Lankford *et al.*[119] through their study of the press formability of automobile fenders from a variety of sheet steels. They correlated successful draws with the product of the strain-hardening index n, in the Ludwik expression[†]

$$\sigma = A \varepsilon^n, \tag{7.23}$$

and the plastic strain ratio, r.

As is now well known the r-value can be described in terms of some of the anisotropic coefficients of (7.20) and (7.21). It has been remarked that the principal axes of anisotropy in rolled plate and sheet are usually associated with the rolling, transverse and through-thickness directions, say x, y and z respectively. A tensile test conducted on a specimen cut from the plane of a sheet in the rolling direction would reveal, using (7.21), the following ratios between the strain increments:

$$d\varepsilon_{xx} : d\varepsilon_{yy} : d\varepsilon_{zz} = H + G : -H : -G. \tag{7.24}$$

The plastic strain ratio, (width strain to thickness strain), is therefore

$$r_x = d\varepsilon_{yy}/d\varepsilon_{zz} = H/G.$$

[†]An empirical expression relating the uniaxial flow stress with the axial (natural) strain via the material constants A and n. This may or may not provide an adequate fit to observed σ-e behaviour over a large range.

PLASTICITY PROBLEMS FOR OTHER THAN PLANE STRAIN CONDITIONS

Similarly for a specimen pulled in the transverse direction, the plastic strain ratio is

$$r_y = d\epsilon_{xx}/d\epsilon_{zz} = H/F.$$

Planar isotropy, i.e. where properties are independent of orientation within the plane of the sheet, occurs when $F=G$ and $2N=F+G+4H$. Assuming planar isotropy, and for the particular case of plane stress where principal stresses only are applied in the x and y directions, the yield criterion (7.20) can be expressed as

$$(1+r)\ (\sigma_{xx}^2 + \sigma_{yy}^2) - 2r\ \sigma_{xx}\sigma_{yy} = (1+r)\ \sigma_u^2,$$

or

$$(\sigma_{xx} + \sigma_{yy})^2 + (1+2r)\ (\sigma_{xx} - \sigma_{yy})^2 = 2(1+r)\sigma_u^2. \qquad (7.25)$$

In the above equations σ_u is the uniaxial yield strength in the plane of the sheet and r the plastic-strain ratio. The yield locus is an ellipse when plotted with σ_{xx} and σ_{yy} as coordinate axes. For the extreme case of $r=0$ the yield locus is a circle; increasing r elongates the ellipse in the first and third quadrants. With $r=1$, complete isotropy prevails and the yield criterion reduces to that of von Mises.

Whitely[120] applied the Hill model to the drawing of cylindrical cups from circular blanks and concluded that the limiting drawing ratio (LDR), i.e. the ratio of blank diameter to punch diameter, should increase with the r-value. For the case of planar isotropy he deduced that the

$$\mathrm{LDR}\ \alpha\ \left[\frac{(1+r)}{2}\right]^{\frac{1}{2}}. \qquad (7.26)$$

There is experimental evidence[121] to suggest that the LDR does indeed increase with increasing average r-value; however, as discussed in Refs. 122 and 123, the effect is not as great as is implied by equation (7.26).

A certain amount of empiricism has led to expressions which purport to indicate the degree of planar anisotropy by

$$\Delta r = \frac{r_0 + r_{90} - 2r_{45}}{2} \qquad (7.27)$$

299

and of normal anisotropy by

$$\bar{r} = \frac{r_0 + r_{90} + 2r_{45}}{4} \,. \tag{7.28}$$

The r_0, r_{45} and r_{90} refer to experimentally determined plastic-strain
ratios for specimens cut from the plane of the sheet at 0, 45 and 90
degrees respectively, to the rolling direction. It is desirable also
to quote the magnitude of uniaxial strain at which the r-value is
determined, since in practice the quantity could vary with strain.
Since it is exceptional to find sheet material that is planar isotropic,
the use of (7.28) in (7.26) permits r to be replaced by $\bar{r}$, without
altering the predicted trend of the LDR. A practice that has developed
for sheet steels has been to use the expression for Δr to ascertain
the magnitude and location of the ears in the commonly observed four-
fold earing behaviour. When Δr is positive earing occurs in the 0-
and 90-degree directions, and in the 45-degree directions when Δr is
negative. When the quantity is close to zero the earing is minimized.

There is a limit to the r-values that can be realized in real metals,
particularly those of cubic structure. In steels the r-values can
vary widely and an upper limit of about 3 can be obtained with inter-
stitial free steels.[123] For rimming steels typical average, $\bar{r}$, values
lie between 1 and 1.4, while for aluminium killed drawing quality
(A.K.D.Q.) grades $\bar{r}$ ranges between 1.4 and 2.0. A word of caution
should be injected at this point, not to refute the general observation
about equating improved drawability with higher $\bar{r}$ values but to the
effect that it depends on the drawing process and on whether or not
the texture is a dominant parameter. Reference 124 reports the results
of drawing both cylindrical and square cups from a variety of aluminium
alloy sheets. The $\bar{r}$ values for these materials were all less than
unity and not very dissimilar; however, the observed trend for the
LDR when drawing circular cups was consistent with (7.26). No correlation with $\bar{r}$ was observed when drawing square cups and in certain
cases very little cup depth could be obtained before fracture occurred.
The process appears to be controlled through the fracture strains
developed in the alloys by different straining modes. No suggestion
is made that equation (7.26) is applicable equally to the drawing of
square and cylindrical cups, but rather to avoid any indiscriminate
association of $\bar{r}$ with drawability.

The anisotropic coefficients in (7.20) are usually determined from r-value measurements, but they can be assessed from the measurement of yield stress; this immediately provides a check on the Hill model. To determine the r-values a certain amount of plastic deformation has to occur, and it is appropriate to calculate a current r-value from the ratio of the strain increments, i.e. at some predetermined strain level a given increment in axial strain is imposed and the width and thickness strain increments are evaluated. The instantaneous flow stress can also be measured at this level of strain and this would ensure that the anisotropic coefficients, determined from either stress or strain measurements, are obtained on the same material structure. Whatever method is adopted it often transpires that there is a much wider variation in measured r-values with orientation than there is with flow stress and in a manner not consistent with theory.

Notwithstanding the above remarks, the most widely used verification of the Hill model has been made by comparing the uniaxial stress-strain behaviour of specimens cut from the plane of the sheet with that obtained from equal biaxial stressing, usually by means of the bulge test.[125] With the assumption of planar isotropy equation (7.25) relates the current yield stress in uniaxial tension, σ_u to that in biaxial tension ($\sigma_{xx} = \sigma_{yy} = \sigma_b$) as follows:

$$\sigma_b = \left[\frac{1+r}{2}\right]^{\frac{1}{2}} \sigma_u. \tag{7.29}$$

In the absence of planar isotropy an averaging procedure is adopted for r in the manner of (7.28), or some variant of this theme. Likewise $\bar{\sigma}_u$ would represent the average of the current yield (flow) stresses.

It can also be demonstrated that the equivalent strain in uniaxial and biaxial tension can be related through the longitudinal strain, ε_u, and thickness strain, ε_t, respectively, in the following manner:

$$\varepsilon_u = \left[\frac{1+r}{2}\right]^{\frac{1}{2}} \cdot \varepsilon_t. \tag{7.30}$$

Thus from (7.29) and (7.30) the behaviour in biaxial tension can be predicted from uniaxial data or vice-versa. The procedure was employed by Bramley *et al.*[126] who demonstrated that the degree of correspondence between theory and experiment was quite good for a number of stabilized steels with $\bar{r}>1$.

It will be noted from (7.29) that σ_b/σ_u is greater or less than unity as r (or $\bar{r}$) is greater or less than unity. Woodthorpe and Pearce[127] found conflicting experimental evidence for this predicted trend for a number of materials where $\bar{r}<1$. Hill[128] has recently proposed a modification to his original anisotropic yield criterion, which for the particular case of biaxial stressing can be expressed as

$$|\sigma_{xx}+\sigma_{yy}|^n + (1+2r)\ |\sigma_{xx}-\sigma_{yy}|^n = 2\ (1+r)\ \sigma_u^{\ n}, \qquad (7.31)$$

so that the ratio σ_b/σ_u becomes

$$\frac{\sigma_b}{\sigma_u} = \frac{1}{2}\ [\ 2(1+r)]^{1/n}. \qquad (7.32)$$

Equation (7.32) can now resolve the discrepancy observed by Woodthorpe and Pearce, *op cit.*, by selecting,[†] $1<n<2$. For $n=2$ then, (7.31) and (7.32) are identical to (7.25) and (7.29) respectively.

In a similar vein, Bassani[79] has suggested the following yield function:

$$|\sigma_{xx}+\sigma_{yy}|^n + \frac{n}{m}\ (1+2r)\ \sigma_u^{(n-m)}\ |\sigma_{xx}-\sigma_{yy}|^m = \left[1+\frac{n}{m}(1+2r)\right]\sigma_u, \qquad (7.33)$$

and for convexity of the yield surface n and $m > 1$. The ratio σ_b/σ_u is

$$\frac{\sigma_b}{\sigma_u} = \frac{1}{2}\ \left[1+\frac{n}{m}(1+2r)\right]^{1/n}. \qquad (7.34)$$

For $n=m$ (7.33) reduces to (7.31), and Hill's original model is recovered when $n=m=2$.

The introduction of three- and four-parameter phenomenological yield functions can be justified to the extent that they may provide better correspondence with experimental data than the quadratic yield function. Other attempts at modifying the quadratic form are to be found in the articles by Hosford[129] and Gotoh.[130]

---

†The yield loci defined by (7.31) are ovals, and in particular become ellipses when $n=2$. For $1<n<2$ the ovals are elongated in the first and third quadrants *vis-à-vis* the elliptic loci.

As stated earlier much of the interest in anisotropy and its influence on material formability has stemmed from observations made during deep drawing processes. It is not at all clear what the benefits are that might be realized through texture control when dealing with stretch-forming operations, i.e. the situation where the principal surface strains in a sheet-metal component are both positive. Much of the theoretical work in this area has dealt with the prediction of forming limit diagrams (FLDs)[131,132] based on an original model by Marciniak and Kuczynski[†] (M-K);[133] subsequent computational procedures are given in Refs. 134 and 135. A FLD is shown schematically in Fig. 7.11, the coordinate axes representing the principal surface strains and the curve defining the extent of the useful limits of straining, i.e. the limit strains, prior to rupture of the material. When attempting to calculate a curve similar to that in Fig. 7.11, it is customary

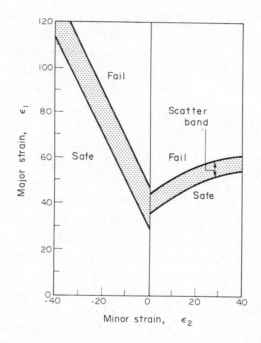

Fig. 7.11. Schematic representation of a forming limit diagram.

[†]The model assumes a material inhomogeneity characterized by a local thickness variation, i.e. a trough or groove, and the simultaneous straining of the groove and adjacent sheet material. The end point in the process is usually defined as the attainment of a plane-strain condition or of some critical thickness strain in the groove.

to assume that the sheet component is undergoing a proportional straining
process within its plane. The straining ratio ρ can then be altered
from plane strain ($\rho=0$) to balanced biaxial tension ($\rho=1$). Ghosh[9]
has reviewed some of the theoretical work associated with FLDs. Some
of the contemporary trends have been to

(i)   allow for void growth in the model,[8,136]

(ii)   modify the classical flow theory of plasticity by permitting
        corners to develop on the yield surface (vertex theory),[8,137]
        and

(iii)   to incorporate strain-rate effects.[138]

All of these trends serve simply to modify to some extent the original
M-K model. The influence of anisotropy predicted by most of these
models is for a low r-value (<1) to enhance the useful limits of formability, particularly in processes approaching balanced biaxial tension.
The experimental evidence on this point has not been unequivocal, and
objections to the M-K model and to those analyses employing a quadratic
yield function have been raised. The latter issue has been addressed
by Parmar and Mellor,[139] who employed the three-parameter yield function
(7.31), along with the M-K model, to predict the FLD. They demonstrated
that the shape of the yield surface will influence the calculated limit
strains, in particular decreasing n below 2 reduces the limit strains
for all straining ratios away from plane strain. The calculations
were presented for a constant value of r. Bassani et al.[140] have
performed similar calculations using the yield function given by (7.33).
Here again the shape of the yield surface affected the predicted FLDs,
in a manner not dissimilar to the findings of Ref. 139. They also
demonstrated that a lowering of the r-value should enhance the limit
strains. The most significant change in the shape and magnitude of
the FLD came about when the calculations were performed on the basis
of the deformation theory of plasticity as opposed to the classical
flow (or incremental) theory. This opens up another area of investigation, namely the choice of the appropriate constitutive equation;
however, this is outside the limits of the present discussion. What
can be said is that at the present time there is no direct evidence
linking anisotropy, as characterized through the r-value, to improved
formability in stretch-forming processes. Nonetheless, before closing
the discussion on this topic the reader may benefit from the following
interpretation of some of the preceding statements, which in turn may
serve as an assessment of some of the scattered literature on the

subject.

If the yield function (7.25) is embodied in the M-K analysis, then it can be rationalized how low r-values would be predicted to enhance limit strains in the region of balanced biaxial tension. With this type of material the stress states between balanced biaxial tension and plane strain are much wider apart than with high r-value material; see Fig. 7.12. Thus, when the end point in the process is the attainment of *plane strain in a groove*, a much larger proportion of the

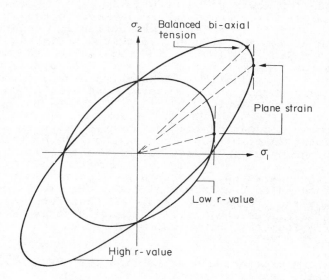

Fig. 7.12. Yield loci for a high and low r-value material according to equation (7.25).

yield surface has to be transversed (for low r-value materials) when changing the straining mode in the groove from one of balanced biaxial stress to plane strain. As already mentioned, the same trend in general is exhibited when functions (7.31) or (7.33) are incorporated in the M-K model. It is recognized that these latter yield loci can modify the shape of the forming limit curves drastically, such that the maximum surface strain is no longer achieved at balanced biaxial tension. Nevertheless low, as compared to high, r-values tend to enhance the limit strain in all regions away from plane strain.[134,140] It is to be noted that the loci defined by (7.31) or (7.33), with appropriate choice of parameters, e.g. $n=1$ in (7.31), can develop flats and corners similar to the crystallographic loci predicted for ideal textures. These latter loci can lead to some interesting interpretations regarding formability and one aspect is developed briefly here.

Firstly, it has to be recognized that forming limit diagrams are usually constructed theoretically on the basis of some proportional straining path imposed on an element, and this defines just one point on the curve. Actual forming processes involve individual elements of a component undergoing distinct straining histories while maintaining the integrity of the part and thus leading to the development of strain gradients. Consider, for example, the hydrostatic bulging of a circular diaphragm where the straining of elements varies from plane strain at the clamped edge to balanced biaxial tension at the pole. For high r-value materials ($r>>1$), when the yield function is given by (7.25), little distinction exists between the plane strain and balanced biaxial stress states. Therefore, this type of material should have the ability to readily distribute the strain between the clamped edge and the pole, producing a more spherical bulge. The reverse would be true for low r-value materials. The M-K model, by considering individual material elements, may well lead to the same conclusion regarding the spread in strain distribution for each type of material. However, the attainment of high limit strains in the vicinity of the dome (achieved with the low r-value material in the M-K model) does not provide the complete story. If materials did behave in accordance with the above reasoning it is likely the high r-value material would produce a component of improved dome height because the material is being better utilized.

The same conclusion can be reached about ability to distribute strain if the starting material possessed an ideal "cube texture", (001)[100]. The crystallographic yield loci for such a material has been shown in Fig. 7.8. As first pointed out by Dillamore *et al*.[141] in the context of the bulging operation, with this particular texture a balanced biaxial stress state can impose all straining modes between plane strain and balanced biaxial tension and therefore the textured sheet will form into a spherical cap. Evidence of this is to be found in the work of Wilson,[121] who bulged very heavily cubed-textured copper sheets, see also Ref. 103.

The suggestions made about distributing the strain in textured sheet of high r-value material appear plausible, and the experimental evidence of Ref. 121 cannot be refuted. It would be misleading, however, to deduce an r-value for the textured sheet on the basis of (7.28), (since it would be less than unity,) and then to try and interpret it according to the yield function (7.25). This latter criterion is simply not appropriate for cube-textured material.

The two conditions of either maximizing the limit strain or developing uniformity of straining are unlikely to be mutually exclusive. The end point when biaxially stretching ductile materials is usually signified by the development of a localized neck. This may well occur in regions which have experienced some form of diffuse instability, i.e. zones which are undergoing accelerated thinning but whose presence in biaxially stretched components are not as readily detected as is the onset of diffuse necking in a tensile bar. Here again there is no direct evidence which relates the r-value with improved instability strains computed on the basis of pressure or load attaining a maximum value in the manner of Considère; see the discussion by Sowerby and Johnson[142] which expands on this theme. While the presence of a localized neck can certainly be regarded as some form of heterogeneity, the detailed mechanisms leading to its existence have not yet been clearly elucidated. Internal voiding has often been proposed as a significant factor with the initiation and growth of voids being attributed to unfavourable stress states, compounded by the presence of relatively undeformable second phases which initially give rise to inhomogeneous straining on a microscopic level. However, the examination of microstructures during the course of tensile testing invariably fails to reveal evidence of where a neck will form. The volume fraction of voids tends to be small, and void coalescence on a large scale is not usually detected even in the presence of very acute necks just prior to rupture. Expressions such as "saturation in local hardening rate" are often very evident when discussing strain localization. The hardening rate will be influenced by such features as the presence of second phases and developing substructure and texture, but in a manner that is not readily predictable. Texture *per se* is not likely to be the controlling factor in the fracture process. For the present satisfaction must be had with imperfect models relating texture and formability.

SLIP-LINE FIELDS FOR ANISOTROPIC MATERIALS

In 1949 Hill[143] applied the analysis in Ref. 104 to establishing the existence of characteristics for the plane flow of non-hardening anisotropic metals, see also Ref. 2. Under plane-strain conditions the yield locus is an ellipse in Mohr's stress space, with coordinate axes defined as in Fig. 7.13. For isotropic materials the locus is a circle whose radius is the yield shear stress of the material, k. It was demonstrated that the characteristics for the stresses and velocities are the same. The characteristics are orthogonal and they lie in the directions of maxumum shear strain rate, i.e. the slip lines, but they do not, in general, coincide with the maximum shear-stress directions.

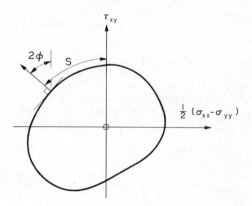

Fig. 7.13. Yield locus for an arbitrary state of anisotropy, plotted in Mohr's stress space.

In a manner analogous to the development of the Hencky equations for an isotropic material the following expressions are established along the slip lines:

$$p + 2Tg.(\phi) = C_1 \text{ along an } \alpha\text{-line}$$

and

$$p - 2Tg(\phi) = C_2 \text{ along a } \beta\text{-line.}$$

(7.35)

The quantity T is the yield shear stress with respect to the principal axes of anisotropy in the plane of deformation, and $g(\phi)$ is given in terms of an elliptic integral. Solutions using the above expressions and the construction of slip-line fields is less straightforward than for the isotropic case and recourse is usually made to numerical quadratures. However, a geometrical relationship analogous to Hencky's First Theorem still carries over to the anisotropic case. In addition, the velocity equations along the slip lines are unchanged from the isotropic case (the Geiringer equations), as are the procedures for constructing the hodograph from the slip-line field.

Johnson and Sowerby[144] applied the above theory to study the incipient earing behaviour in a flange during the drawing of cylindrical cups. By assuming plane-strain deformation of the flange, and a particular state of anisotropy, a slip-line-field net (and corresponding hodograph) was developed in the flange. The case of symmetric four-fold earing was established which, as remarked earlier, is often seen to occur in cups drawn from sheet steels. Note that the anisotropic model itself would not permit the prediction of more than four ears. Johnson and his co-workers[145,146] have used the same slip-line-field model to study the bulk forming of anisotropic metals. Reference 145 deals with plane strain indentation and Ref. 146 with incipient plane-strain extrusion through wedge-shaped dies. In both these articles the variation in forming load and deformation mode is compared with that of the isotropic case. The greatest shortcoming of all of these studies is that they apply only to the onset of flow. Immediately flow is started material elements begin to rotate, especially when velocity discontinuities are crossed, and new directions for the principal axes of anisotropy (even supposing the anisotropic coefficients are unchanged) are established.

In 1972 Booker and Davis[47] and Rice[147] independently proposed a further generalization of the Hill model for the plane-strain deformation of anisotropic metals. These authors allowed for an arbitrary state of anisotropy such that the yield function is of arbitrary convex shape when plotted in Mohr's stress space, see Fig. 7.13. The generalized Hencky equations take the following form:†

$$p + s = c_1 \text{ along an } \alpha\text{-line}$$

and

$$p - s = c_2 \text{ along a } \beta\text{-line,}$$

(7.36)

where p is the hydrostatic stress and s the arc length measured around the yield locus in an anti-clockwise sense, as illustrated in Fig. 7.13. Obviously, (7.36) should reduce to (7.35) for the particular case of anisotropy considered by Hill, i.e. the ellipsoidal yield criterion in Mohr's stress space. Rice, *op cit.*, has pointed to the fact that the $2Tg(\phi)$ term in (7.35) corresponds to an expression for the arc length around an elliptical yield locus. It also transpires that for the case of arbitrary anisotropy the Geiringer equations and the construction of the hodograph are unchanged from the isotropic case.

---

† Booker and Davies[47] obtained this form as a special case in a more general formulation for pressure sensitive anisotropic materials.

PLASTICITY PROBLEMS FOR OTHER THAN PLANE STRAIN CONDITIONS

In spite of the apparently simple form of (7.36) the construction of specific fields is complicated, and as yet no general numerical procedure appears to have been found. Chitkara and Collins[148] have demonstrated a completely graphical procedure for constructing slip-line fields for anisotropic materials defined by an arbitrary convex yield locus. They considered the incipient deformation of a finite slab compressed between parallel, perfectly rough, overhanging platens. The graphical technique was presented in a clear and concise form and could serve as a starting point for other investigators wishing to apply the method. In the original paper whilst only elliptical loci were considered, thus permitting the principal axes of anisotropy to be inclined at any arbitrary angle to the axes of symmetry of the strip, yet it was claimed that the technique could be applied with equal facility to any arbitrary convex locus.

ANALOGIES WITH METAL-WORKING OPERATIONS

(i)   Minimum-weight Frames

In Chapter 4 a distinction was drawn between a slip-line-field solution and an upper-bound approach. In this monograph the name "upper bound" has been given to any arbitrary kinematically admissible, velocity field where the deforming region is assumed to consist of a number of discrete rigid zones separated by lines of tangential velocity discontinuity, (t.v.d.). Figures 4.8 (b) and (c) illustrate how the hodograph can be derived from the physical plane in a way exactly analogous to the construction of a force (or Maxwell) diagram for a plane statically determinate pin-jointed structure using Bow's notation. All the energy dissipated in the deformation process occurs in crossing the lines of velocity discontinuity, since the material between the discontinuities is assumed rigid in the upper-bound method. Figure 7.14 shows a simple pattern of t.v.d.s somewhat simpler than that given in Fig. 4.8(b), for the plane-strain extrusion of a rigid, perfectly plastic material through a wedge-shaped die of semi-angle α, along which shearing occurs. The corresponding hodograph is given in Fig. 7.15. The energy dissipated at the discontinuities, per unit width of material, is

$$kV_1 BC + kV_2 AB + kV_3 AC, \qquad (7.37)$$

where $kV_3 AC$ is the energy dissipated in shearing along the die wall. The rate at which work is done by the mean pressure, $\bar{p}$, on the ram is

$$\bar{p}.1.1. \qquad (7.38)$$

Equating (7.37) to (7.38) determines $\bar{p}$. Note that this will necessarily be an overestimate, as shown by equation (4.4).

Now all equations of the type in (7.37) can be written as

$$k \sum_{i=1} l_i V_i, \qquad (7.39)$$

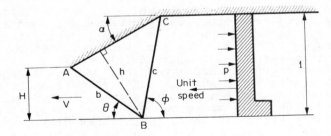

Fig. 7.14. Pattern of t.v.d.s for extrusion through a rough wedge-shaped die.

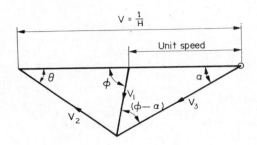

Fig. 7.15. Hodograph to Fig. 7.14.

where l_i is the length of the ith discontinuity and V_i the magnitude of the tangential velocity discontinuity across it, as obtained from the physical plane and hodograph respectively. Examples using patterns of many more lines will be found in Refs. 149 and 150. If we require the energy dissipation to be minimized then clearly $\Sigma_{i=1}^{N} l_i V_i$ has to be minimized.

Now consider a two-dimensional pin-jointed framework, the total weight of which is W, i.e.

$$W = \sum_{i=1}^{N} w_i S_i A_i, \tag{7.40}$$

where w_i is the weight per unit volume of the material of the ith member of the frame, A_i its cross-sectional area and S_i its length. If bending and buckling are negligible, then (7.40) can be rewritten as

$$W = \sum_{i=1}^{N} \frac{w_i}{\sigma_i} \cdot S_i \cdot F_i,$$ (7.41)

where F_i is the force in the ith member. Suppose that w_i/σ_i is the
same for all bars and equal to K, then if we require W to be a minimum,
then $\sum_{i=1}^{N} S_i F_i$ must be a minimum. For any framework, S_i is found
from the space diagram and F_i from the force diagram, obtained by
applying Bow's notation in conjunction with the space frame diagram.
(The following discussion has in mind that all members of a frame are
of the same material and therefore stressed to the same level, but
this is just a particular case of $w_i/\sigma_i = K$.)

Figure 7.16 shows a two-dimensional frame drawn to the same geometric
proportions as Fig. 7.14. The force diagram to Fig. 7.16 is shown in
Fig. 7.17; its correspondence with the hodograph shown in Fig. 7.15
is obvious. Therefore, providing (7.37) is minimized (7.41) will also
be minimized and thus we have developed a good upper bound for the
weight of the frame required to carry loads disposed as shown in Fig.
7.16.

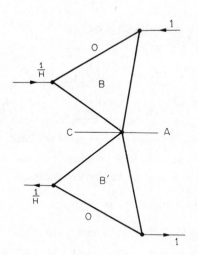

Fig. 7.16. Two-dimensional space frame.

Johnson and Sowerby[168] have optimized upper bounds of the type shown
in Fig. 7.14 for various frictional conditions over the die wall.
Although the minimum-weight frame has been developed by considering

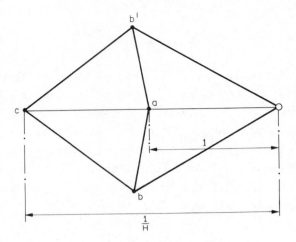

Fig. 7.17.   Force diagram obtained from Fig. 7.16
using Bow's method.

shearing friction the analogy would still hold if the space frame was
slightly modified as follows.   For frictionless extrusion the term
kV_3AC in (7.37) would be omitted and consequently if the member in
the space frame corresponding to the die wall was replaced by a rigid
foundation (or the like) to which the space frame was attached, then
the analogy would still be valid.

It is essential to appreciate that the upper bound of Fig. 7.14 does
not provide an absolute minimum value for the energy dissipation.
Alternative solutions, albeit more complex, can be obtained which will
yield smaller values for energy dissipation and thus the associated
geometrically similar space frame will also be reduced in weight.   The
upper bound can be continuously improved until the slip-line-field
solution is approached.

If the space frame is constructed with the same geometric proportions
as the slip-line field, the energy dissipation can be calculated
either via equations of the type (7.37) or (4.4) (see p. 451 of Ref.
149) or by the more complete expression (2.13).

Two further examples of frames composed of many straight bars (closely
approximating obvious slip-line-field patterns) are shown in Figs.

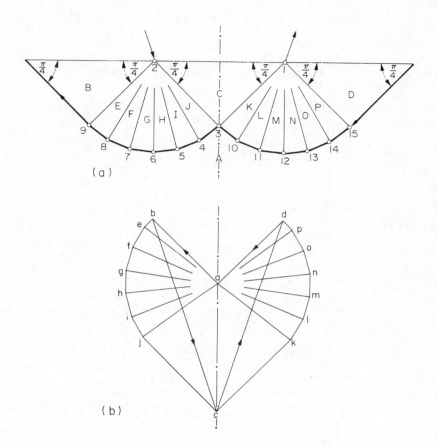

Fig. 7.18. (a) Two-dimensional space frame.
          (b) Force diagram obtained from (a).

7.18(a) and 7.19(a). The corresponding force or Maxwell diagrams are shown in Figs. 7.18(b) and 7.19(b). For sustaining externally applied forces at the specified points, the bar lengths and dispositions are such that a nearly minimum weight frame - the criterion of minimum weight being that of an infinite array of "bars" arranged to follow the limiting pattern that is a slip-line field - is obtained.[170]

If the displacement or deflection diagram for each of the joints of the frames in Fig. 7.18(a) and Fig. 7.19(a) is drawnout systematically using the well-known method of Williot, then Figs. 7.18(c) and 7.19 (c) are obtained. One end of every bar approaches (compression) or recedes from (tension) the other end; since the stress is the same

313

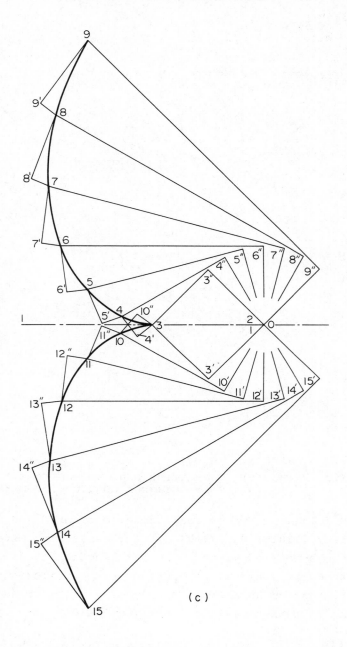

Fig. 7.18.   (c)   Displacement diagram associated
              with (a), obtained using Williot's
              method.

in every bar, so is the strain. Besides axial strain, one end of a
bar is generally displaced transversely with respect to the other;
thus the bars rotate. All this follows simply from requiring joints
not to separate.

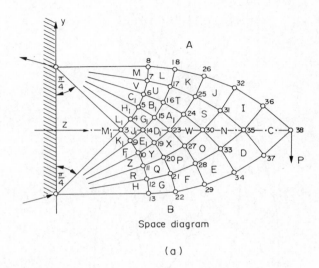

Space diagram

(a)

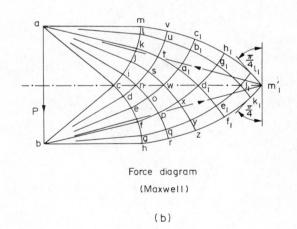

Force diagram

(Maxwell)

(b)

Fig. 7.19. (a) Two dimensional space frame.
(b) Force diagram obtained from (a).

Noteworthy is the analogy of (i) a space frame and a metal working
physical plane diagram, (ii) the corresponding force diagram and hodograph and (iii) the respective displacement diagram and a force-plane

315

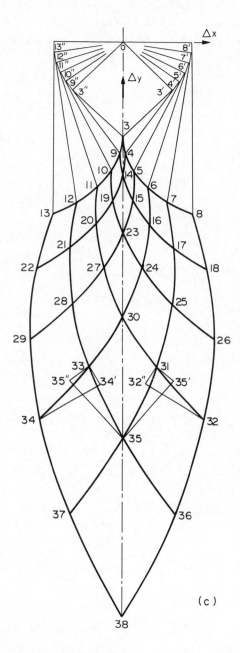

Fig. 7.19. (c) Displacement diagram associated
with (a), obtained using Williot's
method.

diagram.

Michell[151] appears to have been the first author to formulate the problem of the design of minimum-weight frames. Hemp has given great impetus and brought rigour to this area of work, especially through his book[171] and associates A. S. L. Chan[155] and H. S. Y. Chan.[162] (A doctoral thesis by E. W. Johnson[169] is interesting as being the only experimental work known to the authors in this field. Photoelasticity was used to ascertain the effect of joints.) Hegemier and Prager[167] also developed a rigorous analogy between the slip-line field and minimum-weight frame by showing that the equations of displacement of an optimized framework are formally identical with the basic equations of the slip-line field, i.e. equation (3.4) or (3.5) with (3.8). These authors, *op cit.*, also demonstrate that the optimized framework loaded in stationary creep cannot be less stiff than any other framework which uses the same amount of material and permits the same allowable range of axial stress.

In the bibliography (Refs. 151 to 173) will be found other closely connected work on minimum-weight frames; the articles by Wasiutynski and Brandt[159] and Sheu and Prager[166] should be useful since these authors have reviewed some of the published work on the subject up to 1963 and 1968 respectively.

(ii) The Transverse Plastic Bending of Rigid-perfectly Plastic Plates

The essence of this analogy is the identification of velocity in a typical plane-strain upper-bound deformation mode with angular velocity in the corresponding mode for an isotropic uniformly thin plate. Trajectories of maximum stress/strain rate (or slip lines) in plane strain correspond to trajectories of principal curvature, or yield lines, in the analogous plate problem. Two examples will suffice to explain the analogy. Note that as well as using slip-line fields, all that pertains to any metal-working upper-bound mode is analogously applicable to plastic plate bending.

Figure 7.20(a) shows, in plan, a rectangular plate carrying a concentrated load P at its centre, O. The collapse load causes the four portions of the plate shown, incipiently, to rotate about a supported plate side; the arrows in the diagram are angular velocity vectors (following the right-hand screw rule). There are discontinuities in angular velocity parallel to the diagonals of magnitude $\omega*$; Fig. 7.20 (b) is the angular velocity plane diagram for Fig. 7.20(a). It is easily verified that

$$P.a.\omega_{AB} = 4.OB.\omega*.M_p$$

or
(7.42)

$$P/4.M_p = (a/b + b/a).$$

$M_p = \sigma_o t^2/4$ and this is the bending moment per unit length of line for a plate of thickness t and plane-strain yield stress σ_o.

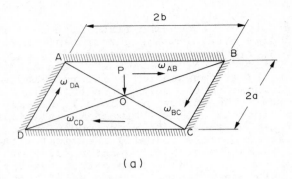

(a)

(b)

Fig. 7.20. (a) Rectangular plate clamped at its
edges and carrying a concentrated
load at its centre.
(b) Hodograph to (a).

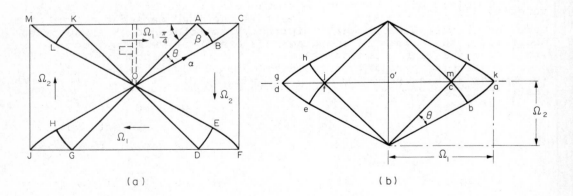

(a)   (b)

Fig. 7.21. (a) Similar to 7.20(a), but showing
a more complex deformation mode.
(b) Hodograph to (a).

Figure 7.21(a) shows a more complex mode of deformation, to which the angular velocity hodograph of Fig. 7.21(b) belongs. It may easily be shown that the non-dimensionalized concentrated transverse load $P/4M_p$ to cause plastic collapse of the plate is equal to $\bar{p}/2k$, the mean pressure to cause extrusion (or indentation, see dotted punch or indenter in Fig. 21(a)) when the shape and size of the orthogonal net (or slip-line field) is the same for the two different physical systems.

Many examples of this analogy have been given in Ref. 174.

Collins[175,176] has presented the underlying theory of this analogy and extended it to provide lower bounds and to identify complete solutions.

(iii) The Force-plane Diagram for Plane-strain Slip-line Fields

Force-plane diagrams (f.p.d.) can be drawn for fictitious velocity fields from force equilibrium considerations only and enable both,
   (i)   the force to cause an operation to take place, and
   (ii)   the force on a given plane segment in the physical plane, to be found directly.

The diagram has special value when the validity of the fictitious velocity field is immediately obvious by inspection or can be established by drawing a hodograph, because
   (i)   it is straightforward to build-up on a basis of assembling equilibrium force polygons for several individual blocks in a manner familiar to engineers; and
   (ii)   the force on a plane segment can be obtained directly without recourse to the Hencky equations; this is not usually quickly carried out in the ordinary way via the use of a slip-line field;
   (iii) results can be obtained without calling upon all the theory necessary to establish the foundations of slip-line-field theory and this recommends the approach to engineers and technologists.

The notions and methods which use the force plane approach and the results obtainable are best illustrated with examples.

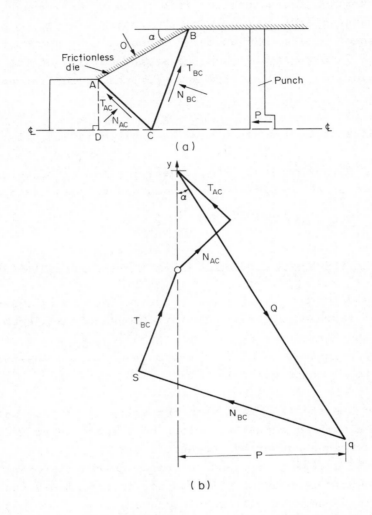

Fig. 7.22.   (a)   Pattern of t.v.d.s or force planes
                   for small reduction extrusion through
                   a frictionless wedge-shaped die of
                   semi-angle α.
             (b)   Force plane diagram to (a).

In Fig. 7.22(a) AC and BC are two lines of t.v.d. selected to account for the plane-strain frictionless extrusion shown. To calculate the punch force P, to cause extrusion, the force polygon for material in triangle ABC is drawn; the normal force and shear force on AC are here

320

designated N_{AC} and T_{AC} and those on BC by N_{BC} and T_{BC}. The two shear forces are assumed to be k times the line length. Note that the actual or true forces along these lines cannot exceed $k.AC$ and $k.BC$, since k is the greatest shear stress the material can support. Material to the left of AC sustains no horizontal force but since it must be plastic the vertical force on the centre-line below AC, exerted from AC, is $2k.DC = 2k.AC \cos \theta$. Starting from an origin O, see Fig. 7.22 (b), N_{AC} and $T_{AC} = kAC$ may be drawn; the end of vector T_{AC}, y, joined to O is perpendicular to the centre-line DC. From y a line is drawn perpendicular to the die face AB and its length yq determines the die force, Q. In Fig. 7.22(b), vector $T_{BC} = k.BC$, ends at O and from its start, s, a perpendicular line N_{BC} is drawn to intersect the line representing force Q at q. The horizontal component of Q is the punch force, P; the normal forces of all the three planes are found in the five-sided force polygon. In effect two unknown normal forces N_{AC} and N_{BC} have been found by satisfying two force (plane) equilibrium requirements, i.e. those for the vertical and horizontal directions.

Solving a problem similar to that in Fig. 7.22(a), by using the more elaborate pattern of four t.v.d.s as shown in Fig. 7.23(a) (i.e. for fractional reduction $r = 2 \sin \alpha/(1 + 2 \sin \alpha)$) the f.p.d. of Fig. 7.23(b) is arrived at; essentially two force polygons - one for each of triangles ADC and ACB - have been joined together.

The strategy in choosing the t.v.d. pattern of Fig. 7.23(a), obviously derives from a prior acquaintanceship with slip-line-field theory. It is easily argued, however, that certain chosen lines must be at 45^0 to the centre-line and the die face AB. It is easy to show that the punch or die force found by this method is the same as that given after calculating the usual total plastic work dissipation rate by shearing across the discontinuity lines and equating it to the work rate done by the punch.

In Fig. 7.24(a), for a fractional reduction of 0.5, the same procedure has been followed for a wedge-shaped frictionless die of semi-angle 30^0, with a 30^0 circular arc substituted for line DC of Fig. 7.23(a). The resulting force-plane diagram is that of Fig. 7.24(b); clearly the latter figure is also a f.p.d. for the slip-line field appropriate to the die geometry defined.

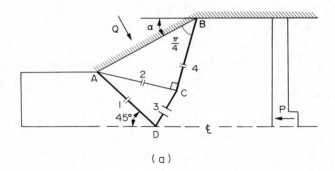

(a)

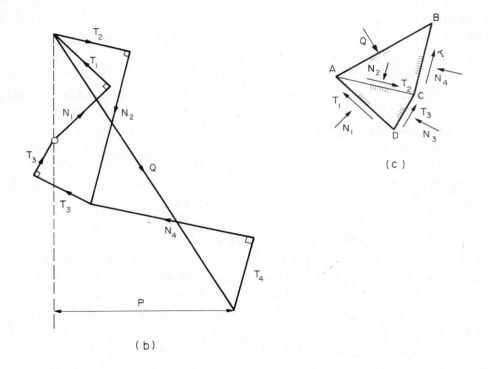

(b)

(c)

Fig. 7.23.   (a)   Pattern of t.v.d.s for end extrusion
through a frictionless wedge-shaped
die of semi-amgle α: fractional
reduction $r = 2 \sin \alpha / (1 + 2 \sin \alpha)$.

(b)   Force plane diagram for (a).

(c)   Force system on blocks.

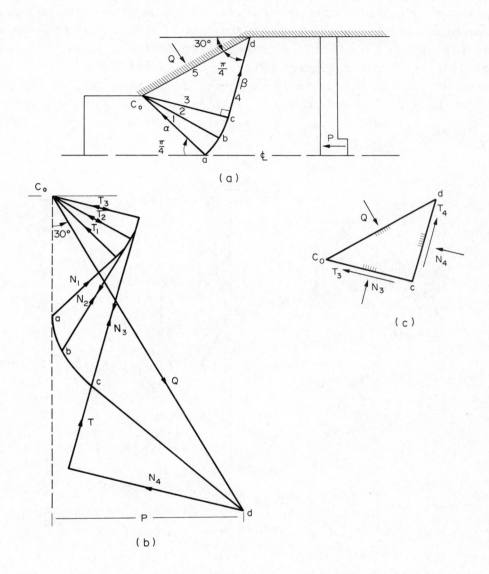

Fig. 7.24. (a) Slip-line field for extrusion through
a frictionless wedge-shaped die of
semi-angle $30°$ and reduction $r =$
0.50.
(b) Force plane diagram for (a).
(c) Force system on blocks.

Three further obvious examples of f.p.ds. for s.l.f.s are given in Figs. 7.25-7.27. Points in the physical plane of metal-working possess corresponding points in the force-plane field so that the force on any plane joining two points in the former is given (to a certain scale) by the line joining the corresponding points in the force plane. Ram force to effect extrusion for large ranges of geometry are easily read off from the f.p.ds.,e.g. in Fig. 7.26(b) p_{10}, p_8, p_5, are the forces necessary to extrude through the orifice given from chambers of depth $N-10$, $N-8$ and $N-5$ in Fig. 7.26(a).

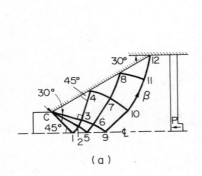

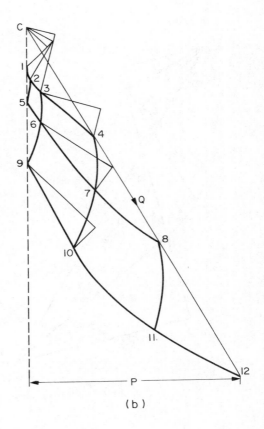

Fig. 7.25. (a) Slip-line field for extrusion through a frictionless wedge-shaped die of semi-angle $30°$, reduction $r > 0.50$.

(b) Force plane diagram for (a).

The force-plane diagram and method applied either to finding upper bounds by the sliding-block method or slip-line fields has much to commend it for engineers by way of simplicity and directness.

The approach can be seen as a sophisticated development of that used to find the normal and frictional forces on a flat-face oblique tool in orthogonal machining, beginning from a supposed knowledge of the magnitude of the force on the shear plane in the material which lies between the tool tip and the free surface; see Ref. 177.

The development of force-plane diagrams and the systematic treatment to include slip-line fields as above is discussed in Refs. 177 and 178. However, **f.p.d.** approaches were first publicized by Green and Wallace[179] and later further developed by Green, Sparling and Wallace.[180] The technique was also discovered independently by Halling and Mitchell[181] and extended by them to include load calculation for axisymmetric rod extrusion.

The force plane method is only simple to apply when the forces on a given straight line are prescribable: this is the case in the examples presented above, e.g. *CI* in each of Figs. 7.25-7.27. If this is not so, e.g. as in *drawing* through a die, see Fig. 7.24 - then a trial-and-error method is required to find the drawing force, if this is to be

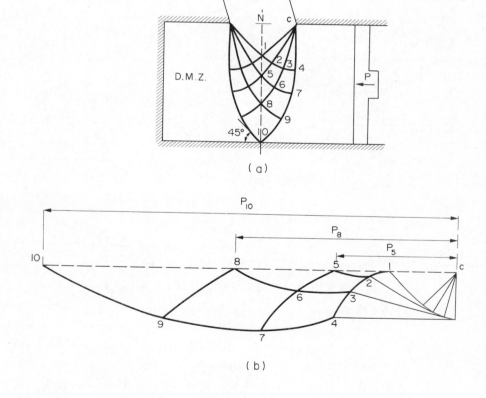

(a)

(b)

Fig. 7.26.   (a). Slip-line field for steady state
                   side-extrusion of moderate reduction
                   from a frictionless container.
            (b). Force plane diagram for (a).

found graphically. Solutions involving curved boundaries and starting lines often appear to require solution by taking moments about certain carefully selected points but see Ref. 182.

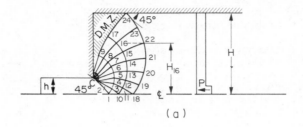

(a)

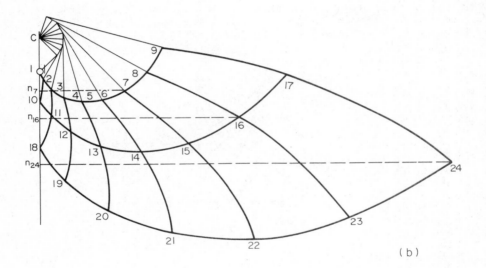

(b)

Fig. 7.27. (a) Slip-line field for steady state end extrusion from a frictionless container in which a dead-metal zone (d.m.z.) is deposited on the die face: the fractional reduction $r > 0.5$.

(b) Force plane diagram for (a).

PLASTICITY PROBLEMS FOR OTHER THAN PLANE STRAIN CONDITIONS

REFERENCES

1. Johnson, W. and Sowerby, R., in "Application of numerical methods to forming processes" (edited by H. Armen and R. F. Jones), p. 1. A.S.M.E. Winter Annual Meeting, San Francisco. A.S.M.E. (1978).
2. Hill, R., *Mathematical Theory of Plasticity*. Oxford University Press (1950).
3. Hodge, P. G., Jr., "Yield conditions in plane plastic stress". *J. Math. Phys.* **29**, 38 (1951).
4. Hodge, P. G., Jr., "The method of characteristics applied to problems of steady motion in plane plastic stress". *Q. Appl. Math.* **8**, 381 (1950).
5. Hill, R., "On discontinuous plastic states with special reference to localized necking in thin sheets". *J. Mech. Phys. Solids*, **1**, 19 (1952).
6. Nadai, A., *Theory of Flow and Fracture of Solids*, Vol. 1. McGraw-Hill (1950).
7. Swift, H. W., "Plastic instability under tension". *J. Mech. Phys. Solids*, **1**, 1 (1952).
8. Needleman, A. and Rice, J. R., in *Mechanics of Sheet Metal Forming Material Behaviour and Deformation Analysis* (edited by D. P. Koistrinen and N. M. Wang), p. 237. Symposium held at G.M. Research Labs. Plenum Press (1978).
9. Ghosh, A. K., *Ibid.*, p. 287.
10. Ewing, D. J. F. and Spurr, R. J. D., "The yield point loads of symmetrically notched metal strips". *J. Mech. Phys. Solids*, **22**, 37 (1974).
11. Ewing, D. J. F. and Richards, C. E., "The yield point loads of singly-notched pin-loaded tensile strips". *J. Mech. Phys. Solids*, **22**, 27 (1974).
12. Bishop, J. F. W., "On the complete solution to problems of deformation of a rigid-plastic solid". *J. Mech. Phys. Solids*, **2**, 43 (1953).
13. Gaydon, F. A. and McCrum, A. W., "A theoretical investigation of the yield point loading of a square plate with a central circular hole". *J. Mech. Phys. Solids*, **2**, 156 (1954).
14. Sowerby, R. and Johnson, W., "Use of slip-line-field theory for the plastic design of press vessels". *Fourth Int. Conf. on Stress Analysis and its Influence on Design*, p. 303. Inst. Mech. Engrs. (1971).
15. Sheppard, W. H. and Gaydon, F. A., "Plastic bending of a ring sector with end couples". *J. Mech. Phys. Solids*, **5**, 296 (1955).
16. Green, A. P., "A theory of plastic yielding due to the bending of cantilever and fix-ended beams - Part I". *J. Mech. Phys. Solids*, **3**, 1 (1954).
17. Green, A. P., "A theory of plastic yielding due to the bending of cantilevers and beams - Part II". *J. Mech. Phys. Solids*, **3**, 143 (1954).
18. Petricone, R. and Salerno, V. L., "Plastic analysis and design of a haunched beam". *Trans. New York Acad. Sci.* **178**, 657 (1970).
19. Johnson, W., Chitkara, N. R. and Ranshi, A. S., "Plane stress yielding of cantilevers in bending due to combined shear and axial load". *J. Strain Analysis*, **9**, 67 (1974).
20. Ranshi, A. S., Chitkara, N. R. and Johnson, W., "Plane stress-plastic collapse loads for tapered cantilevers and haunched beams". *Int. J. Mech. Sci.* **16**, 867 (1974).
21. Ranshi, A. S., Johnson, W. and Chitkara, N. R., "Collapse loads

for thin cantilevers with rectangular holes along the centre-line". *J. Strain Analysis*, 11, 84 (1976).

22. Ranshi, A. S., Chitkara, N. R. and Johnson, W., "Plastic yielding of I-beams under shear, and shear and axial loading". *Int. J. Mech Sci.* 18, 375 (1976).

23. Szczepinski, W., *Introduction to the Mechanics of Plastic Forming of Metals*. Sijthoff & Noordhoff, The Netherlands (1979).

24. Symonds, P. S., "On the general equations of problems of axial symmetry in the theory of plasticity". *Q. Appl. Math.* 6, 448 (1948).

25. Shield, R. T., "On the plastic flow of metals under conditions of axial symmetry". *Proc. R. Soc.*, A, 233, 267 (1955).

26. Koiter, W. T., "On partially plastic thick-walled tubes". *Biezano Ann. Vol.*, *Haarlem*, 232 (1953).

27. Prager, W., "On the use of singular yield conditions and associated flow rules". *J. Appl. Mech.* 20, 317 (1953).

28. Hill, R., "A remark on diagonal streaming in plane plastic strain". *J. Mech. Phys. Solids*, 14, 245 (1966).

29. Richmond, O. and Morrison, H. L., "Streamlined wire drawing dies of minimum length". *J. Mech. Phys. Solids*, 15, 195 (1967).

30. Devenpeck, M. L. and Richmond, O., "Strip drawing experiments with a sigmoidal die profile". *Trans. ASME, J. Eng. Ind.* 87B, 425 (1965).

31. Sowerby, R., Sambasivan, B. and Caddell, R. M., "The influence of the die profile on the properties of extruded aluminium". *Proc. Third Symposium on Eng. Application of Solid Mechs.*, Vol. 2, p. 27. Univ. Toronto, Canada (1976).

32. Liepmann, H. W. and Roshko, A., *Elements of Gas Dynamics*. John Wiley (1958).

33. Sortais, H. C. and Kobayashi, S., "An optimum die profile for axisymmetric extrusion". *Int. J. Machine Tool Design and Research*, 8, 61 (1968).

34. Eason, G. and Shield, R. T., "The plastic indentation of a semi-infinite solid by a rough circular punch". *Zeit. ang. Math. Phys. (ZAMP)*, 11, 33 (1960).

35. Lockett, F. J., "Indentation of a rigid/plastic material by a conical indentor". *J. Mech. Phys. Solids*, 11, 345 (1963).

36. Szczepinski, W., Dietrich, L., Drescher, E. and Miastkowski, J., "Plastic flow of axial-dymmetric notched bars pulled in tension". *Int. J. Solids Structures*, 2, 543 (1966).

37. Suh, N. P., Lee, R. S. and Rogers, C. R., "The yielding of truncated solid cones under quasi static and dynamic loading". *J. Mech. Phys. Solids*, 16, 357 (1968).

38. Drescher, A., "An experimental investigation of flow rules for granular materials using optically sensitive glass particles". *Geotechnique*, 26, 591 (1976).

39. Kingston, M. R. and Spencer, A. J. M., "General yield conditions in plane deformations of granular media". *J. Mech. Phys. Solids*, 18, 233 (1970).

40. Coulomb, C. A., "Test on the applications of the rules of maxima and minima to some problems of the statics relating to architecture". *Mem. Math. Phys.* 7, 343 (1773).

41. Shield, R. T., "Mixed boundary value problems in soil mechanics". *Q. Appl. Math.* 11, 61 (1953).

42. Spencer, A. J. M., "A theory of the kinematics of ideal soils under plane strain conditions". *J. Mech. Phys. Solids*, 12, 337 (1964).

43. Shield, R. T., "On Coulomb's law of failure in soils". *J. Mech. Phys. Solids*, 4, 10 (1955).

44. Cox, A. D., Eason, G. and Hopkins, H. G., "Axially symmetric plastic deformations in soils". *Phil. Trans. R. Soc.*, A, **254**, 1 (1961).

45. Mandl, G. and Fernández Luque, R., "Fully developed plastic shear flow of granular materials". *Geotechnique*, **20**, 277 (1970). Also discussion to that paper by Spencer, A. J. M., *Ibid* **21**, 190 (1971).

46. Morrison, H. L. and Richmond, O., "Application of Spencer's ideal soil model to granular materials flow". *Trans. ASME.*, J. *Appl. Mech.*, **43E**, 49 (1976).

47. Brooker, J. R. and Davis, E. H., "A general treatment of plastic anisotropy under conditions of plane strain". *J. Mech. Phys. Solids*, **20**, 239 (1972).

48. Keldi, A., "Soil mechanics". *Appl. Mech. Rev.* **8**, 357 (1955).

49. Sobotka, Z., "Slip lines and slip surfaces in the theory of plasticity and soil mechanics". *Appl. Mech. Rev.* **14**, 753 (1961).

50. Sokolovskii, V. V., *Statics of Granular Media*. Pergamon Press, Oxford (1965).

51. Salencon, J., *Applications of the Theory of Plasticity in Soil Mechanics*. John Wiley & Sons (1977).

52. Dillamore, I. L. and Roberts, W. T., "Textures in wrought and annealed materials". *Metall. Rev.* **10**, 329 (1965).

53. Lin, T. H., "Physical theory of plasticity". In *Adv. Appl. Mech.*, **11**, 255 (1971).

54. Backofen, W. A., *Deformation Processing*. Addison-Wesley, Reading, Mass. (1972).

55. Reid, C. N., *Deformation Geometry for Materials Scientists. International Series on Materials Science and Technology*, Vol. II. Pergaomon Press, Oxford (1973).

56. Barrett, C. S. and Massalski, T. B., *Structure of Metals*, 3rd edition. McGraw-Hill, New York (1966).

57. Backofen, W. A., Hosford, W. F. and Burke, J. J., "Texture hardening". *ASM Trans. Qrt.* **55**, 264 (1962).

58. Calnan, E. A. and Clews, C. J. B., "The development of deformation textures in metals - Part II. Body centred cubic metals". *Phil. Mag.* **42**, 616(1951).

59. Piehler, H. R. and Backofen, W. A., "The prediction of anisotropic yield surfaces for textured sheet", in *Textures in Research and Practice* (edited by J. Grewen and G. Wasserman), p. 436. Springer, Vienna (1969).

60. Piehler, H. R., Doctor of Science Thesis, Department of Metallurgy, M.I.T. (1967).

61. da C. Viana, C. S., Ph.D. Thesis, Department of Metallurgy and Materials Science, University of Cambridge (1978).

62. Kocks, U. F., "The relation between polycrystal deformation and single-crystal deformation". *Met. Trans.* **1**, 1121 (1970).

63. Cottrell, A. H., *Dislocations and Plastic Flow in Crystals*. Clarendon Press, Oxford (1953).

64. Clarebrough, L. M. and Hargreaves, M. E., "Working hardening of metals". *Prog. Metal Phys.* **8**, 1 (1959).

65. Hirth, J. P. and Weertman, J., *Work Hardening*. Metallurgical Society Conf., Vol. 46. Gordon & Breach (1968).

66. Le Hazif, R. and Poirer, J-P., "Cross slip on {110} planes in aluminium single crystals compressed along <100> axis". *Acta Met.* **23**, 865 (1975).

67. Saeki, Y. and Miura, S., "Plastic deformation and prominent cross slip of <100> orientated aluminium single crystals". *Trans. Jap. Inst. Met.* **18**, 843 (1977).

68. Taylor, G. I., "Plastic strain in metals". *J. Inst. Metals*, **62**, 307 (1938).

69. Chin, G. Y. and Mammel, W. L., "Computer solutions to the Taylor analysis for axisymmetric flow". *Trans. AIME*, **239**, 1400 (1967).

70. Chin, G. Y., Mammel, W. L. and Dolan, M. T., "Taylor's theory of texture for axisymmetric flow in body-centred cubic metals". *Trans. AIME*, **239**, 1854 (1967).

71. Chin, G. Y., Hosford, W. F. and Mendorf, D. R., "Accommodation of constrained deformation in f.c.c. metals by slip and twinning". *Proc. R. Soc.*, A 309, 433 (1969).

72. Chin, G. Y., Mammel, W. L. and Dolan, M. T., "Taylor analysis for {111} <112> twinning and {111} <110> slip under conditions of axisymmetric flow". *Trans. AIME*, **245**, 383 (1969).

73. Chin, G. Y., "Tension and compression textures", in *Textures in Research and Practice* (edited by J. Grewen and G, Wasserman), p. 51. Springer, Vienna (1969).

74. Bishop, J. F. W. and Hill, R., "A theory of the plastic distortion of a polycrystalline aggregate under combined stresses". *Phil. Mag.* **42**, 414 (1951).

75. Bishop, J. F. W. and Hill, R., "A theoretical derivation of the plastic properties of polycrystalline face centred metals". *Phil. Mag.* **42**, 1298 (1951).

76. Bishop, J. F. W., "A theoretical examination of the plastic deformation of crystals by glide". *Phil. Mag.* **44**, 51 (1953).

77. da C. Viana, C. S., Kallend, J. S. and Davies, G. J., "The use of texture data to predict the yield locus of metal sheets". *Int. J. Mech. Sci.* **21**, 355 (1979).

78. Hosford, W. F. and Backofen, W. A., "Strength and plasticity of textured metals" in *Fundamentals of Deformation Processing*, p. 259. Syracuse Univ. Press (1964).

79. Bassani, J. L., "Yield characteristics of metals with transversely isotropic properties". *Int. J. Mech. Sci.* **19**, 651 (1977).

80. Hutchinson, J. W., "Elastic-plastic behaviour of polycrystalline metals and composites". *Proc. R. Soc.* A 319, 247 (1970).

81. Cullity, B. D., *Elements of X-ray Diffraction*. Addison-Wesley, New York (1956).

82. Schulz, L. G., "A direct method of determining preferred orientation of flat reflection samples using a geiger counter X-ray spectrometer". *J. Appl. Phys.* **20**, 1030 (1949).

83. Chernock, W. P. and Beck, P. A., "Analysis of certain errors in X-ray reflection method for the quantitive determination of preferred orientations". *J. Appl. Phys.* **23**, 341 (1952).

84. Elias, J. A. and Heckler, A. J., "Complete pole figure determination by composite sampling techniques". *Trans. AIME*, **239**, 1237 (1967).

85. Roe, R. J., "Description of crystallite orientation of polycrystalline materials; III. General solution of pole figure inversion". *J. Appl. Phys.* **36**, 2024 (1965).

86. Bunge, H. J., "Zur darstellung allgemeinen Texturon". *Zeit Metallk.* **52**, 872 (1965).

87. Kallend, J. S., Ph.D. Thesis, Department of Metallurgy and Materials Science, University of Cambridge, England (1970).

88. Morris, P. R. and Heckler, A. J., "Crystallite orientation analysis for rolled cubic materials", in *Advances in X-ray Analysis*, II, 454 (1968).

89. Davies, G. J., Goodwill, D. J. and Kallend, J. D., "Charts for analysing crystallite distribution function plots for cubic materials". *J. Appl. Cryst.* **4**, 67 (1971).

90. Pursey, H. and Cox, H. L., "The correction of elastic measurements on slightly anisotropic materials". *Phil. Mag.* **45**, 295 (1954).

91. Bunge, H. J. and Roberts, W. T., "Orientation distribution,elastic and plastic anisotropy in stabilized sheet steel". *J. Appl. Cryst.* **2**, 116 (1969).

92. Kallend, J. S. and Davies, G. J., "The prediction of plastic anisotropy in annealed sheets of copper and α-brass". *J. Inst. Metals*, **98**, 242 (1970).

93. Kallend, J. S. and Davies, G. J., "The elastic and plastic anisotropy of cold rolled sheets of copper, gilding metal and α-brass". *J. Inst. Metals*, **99**, 257 (1971).

94. Davies, G. J., Goodwill, D. J., Kallend, J. S. and Ruberg, T., "The correlation of structure and texture with formability". *J. Inst. Metals*, **101**, 270 (1973).

95. Bunge, H. J. "Uber die elastischen Konstanten Kubischer Materialien mit beliebiger textur". *Kristall und Technik*, **3**, 431 (1968).

96. Kallend, J. S. and Davies, G. J., "A simulation of texture development in f.c.c. metals". *Phil. Mag.* **25**, 471 (1972).

97. Van Houtte, P., "Simulation of the rolling and shear textures of brass by the Taylor theory adapted for mechanical twinning". *Acta Met.* **26**, 591 (1978).

98. Dillamore, I. L. and Stoloff, N. S., "Texture development under conditions of imposed strain; influence of stacking fault energy and degree of order", in *Textures in Research and Practice* (edited by J. Grewen and G. Wasserman), p. 110. Springer, Vienna (1969).

99. Dillamore, I. L., "The stacking fault energy dependence of the mechanisms of deformation in f.c.c. metals". *Met. Trans.* **1**, 2463 (1970).

100. Sargent, C. M., "Texture transformations". *Scripta Met.* **8**, 821 (1974).

101. Davies, G. J., Kallend, J. S. and Morris, P. P., "The quantitative prediction of transformation textures". *Acta Met.* **24**, 159 (1976).

102. Kallend, J. S., Morris, P. P. and Davies, G. J., "Texture transformations - the misorientation distribution function". *Acta Met.* **24**, 361 (1976).

103. Sowerby, R. da C. Viana, C. S. and Davies, G. J., "The influence of texture on the mechanical response of commercial purity copper sheets in some simple forming processes". *Mats. Sci. Engng.* to be published).

104. Hill, R., "The theory of the yielding and flow of anisotropic metals". *Proc. R. Soc.*, A, **198**, 281 (1948).

105. Edelman, F. and Drucker, D. C., "Some extensions of elementary plasticity theory". *J. Franklin Inst.* **251**, 581 (1951).

106. Ziegler, H., "A modification of Prager's hardening rule". *Q. Appl. Math.* **17**, 55 (1959).

107. Sawczuk, A. and Baltov, N., "A rule of anisotropic hardening". *Acta Mech.* **1**, 81 (1965).

108. Svennson, N. L., "Anisotropy and the Bauschinger effect in cold rolled aluminium". *J. Mech. Engng. Sci.* **8**, 162 (1965).

109. Eisenberg, M. A. and Phillips, A., "On non-linear kinematic hardening". *Acta Mech.* **5**, 1 (1968).

110. Shrivastava, H. P., Mroz, Z. and Dubey, R. N., "Yield criterion and the hardening rule for a plastic solid". *Zeit. ang. Math. Mech.* **53**, 625 (1973).

111. Swift, H. W., "Length changes in metal due to torsional overstrain". *Engineering*, **163**, 253 (1947).

112. Ronay, M., "On second-order strain accumulation in aluminium in reversed cyclic torsion at elevated temperatures". *Int. J. Solids Struct.* **3**, 167 (1967).

113. Freudenthal, A. M. and Gou, P. F., "Second-order effects in the theory of plasticity". *Acta Mech.* **8**, 34 (1969).
114. Ivey, H. J., "Plastic stress-strain relations and yield surfaces for aluminium alloys". *J. Mech. Engng. Sci.* **3**, 15 (1961).
115. Michno, M. J. and Findley, W. N., "Subsequent yield surfaces for annealed mild steel under servo controlled strain and load histories: Aging, normality, convexity, corners, Bauschinger and cross effects". *Trans. ASME, J. Eng. Mat. Tech.* **97H**, 25 (1975).
116. Michno, M. J. and Findley, W. N., "An historical perspective of yield surface investigations for metals". *Int. J. Non-linear Mech.* **11**, 59 (1976).
117. Phillips, A. and Lee, C.W., "Yield surfaces and loading surfaces. Experiments and recommendations". *Int. J. Solids Structs.* **15**, 715 (1979).
118. Phillips, A. and Weng, G. J., "An analytical study of an experimentally verified hardening low". *Trans. ASME, J. Appl. Mech.* **42E**, 375 (1975).
119. Lankford, W. T., Snyder, S. C. and Bauscher, J. A., "New criterion for predicting the press performance of deep drawing quality steels". *Trans. Am. Soc. Metals*, **42**, 1197 (1950).
120. Whitely, R. L., "The importance of directionality in deep drawing quality sheet steel". *Trans. Am. Soc. Metals*, **52**, 154 (1960).
121. Wilson, D. V., "Plastic anisotropy in sheet metals". *J. Inst. Metals*, **94**, 84 (1966).
122. Hosford, W. F. and Kim, C., "The dependence of deep drawability on normal anisotropy; crystallographic analysis". *Met. Trans.* **7A**, 468 (1976).
123. Dillamore, I. L., "Material properties for sheet formability". Brit. Steel Corp. Report No. MG/16/72 (1972).
124. Sowerby, R. and Sareen, B. K. in *Formability Topics - Metallic Materials*, p. 49. A.S.T.M., STP 647 (1978).
125. Johnson, W. and Duncan, J. L., "The use of the biaxial test extensometer". *Sheet Metal Ind.* **42**, 271 (1965).
126. Bramley, A. N. and Mellor, P. B., "Plastic flow in stabilized sheet steel". *Int. J. Mech. Sci.* **8**, 101 (1966).
127. Woodthorpe, J. and Pearce, R., "The anomalous behaviour of aluminium sheet under balanced biaxial tension". *Int. J. Mech. Sci.* **12**, 341 (1970).
128. Hill, R., "Theoretical plasticity of textured aggregates". *Math. Proc. Camb. Phil. Soc.* **85**, 179 (1979).
129. Hosford, W. F., "On yield loci of anisotropic cubic metals". *Proc. 7th N. American Metalworking Res. Conf.*, p. 191. Univ. Michigan, Ann Arbor. S.M.E. (1979).
130. Gotoh, M., "A theory of plastic anisotropy based on a yield function of fourth order (plane stress state)". *Int. J. Mech. Sci.* **19**, 505 (1977).
131. Keeler, S. P., "Determination of forming limits in automative stampings". *Sheet Metal Ind.* **42**, 683 (1965).
132. Hecker, S. S., "A simple forming limit curve and results on aluminium alloys". *Proc. 7th Biennial Cong. IDDRG*, p. 5.1. Amsterdam, Netherlands (1972).
133. Marciniak, K. and Kuczynski, K., "Limit strains in the process of stretch forming sheet metal". *Int. J. Mech. Sci.* **9**, 609 (1967).
134. Sowerby, R. and Duncan, J. L., "Failure of sheet metal in biaxial tension". *Int. J. Mech. Sci.* **13**, 217 (1971).
135. Azrin, M. and Backofen, W. A., "The deformation and failure of biaxially stretched sheet". *Met. Trans.* **1**, 2857 (1970).

136. Needleman, A. and Triantafyllidis, N., "Void growth and local necking in biaxially stretched sheets". *Trans. ASME, J. Eng. Mat. Tech.* **100H**, 164 (1978).

137. Storen, S. and Rice, J. R., "Localized necking in thin sheets". *J. Mech. Phys. Solids,* **23**, 421 (1975).

138. Ghosh, A. K., "The influence of strain hardening and strain rate sensitivity on sheet metal forming". *Trans. ASME, J. Eng. Mat. Tech.* **99H**, 264 (1977).

139. Parmar, A. and Mellor, P. B., "Predictions of limit strains in sheet metal using a more general yield criterion". *Int. J. Mech. Sci.* **20**, 385 (1978).

140. Bassani, J. L., Hutchinson, J. W. and Neale, K. W., "On the prediction of necking in anisotropic sheets", in *Metal Forming Plasticity* (edited by H. Lippmann), p. 1. IUTAM Symp., Tutzing, Germany, 1978. Springer-Verlag (1979).

141. Dillamore, I. F., Mella, P. and Hazel, R. J., "Preferred orientation of the plastic behaviour of sheet metal". *J. Inst. Metals,* **100**, 50 (1972).

142. Sowerby, R. and Johnson, W., "A review of texture and anisotropy in relation to metal forming". *Mats. Sci. Engng.* **20**, 101 (1975).

143. Hill, R., "The theory of plane plastic strain for anisotropic metals". *Proc. R. Soc.* **A 198**, 428 (1949).

144. Johnson, W. and Sowerby, R., "The prediction of earing in cups drawn from anisotropic sheet using slip line field theory". *J. Strain Analysis,* **9**, 102 (1974).

145. Venter, R., Johnson, W. and deMalherbe, M. C., "The plane strain indentation of anisotropic aluminium using a frictionless flat rectangular punch". *J. Mech. Engng. Sci.* **13**, 416 (1971).

146. Johnson, W., de Malherbe, M. C. and Venter, R., "Some slip line field results for the plane strain extrusion of anisotropic material through frictionless wedge shaped dies". *Int. J. Mech. Sci.* **15**, 109 (1973).

147. Rice, J. R., "Plane strain slip line field theory for anisotropic rigid/plastic materials". *J. Mech. Phys. Solids,* **21**, 63 (1973).

148. Chitkara, N. R. and Collins, I. F., "A graphical technique for constructing graphical technique for constructing anisotropic slip-line fields". *Int. J. Mech. Sci.* **16**, 241 (1974).

149. Johnson, W. and Mellor, P. B., *Engineering Plasticity.* von Nostrand-Reinhold (1973).

150. Johnson, W. and Mamalis, A. G., in *Engineering Plasticity: Theory of Metal Forming Processes,* Vol. 2 (edited by H. Lippmann), 1. C.I.S.M. Courses and Lectures No. 139. Springer Verlag (1977).

151. Michell, A. G., "The limits of economy in frame-structures". *Phil. Mag.* **8**, 589 (1904).

152. Drucker, D. C. and Shield, R. T., "Design for minimum weight". *Proc. Ninth Int. Congr. Appl. Mechs.,* Part 5, 212. Brussels, 1956. University of Brussels (1957).

153. Prager, W., in *Non Homogeneity in Elasticity and Plasticity* (edited by W. Olzak), 125. Proc. I.U.T.A.M. Symposium, Warsaw, 1958. Pergamon Press (1959).

154. Shield, R. T., in *Plasticity* (edited by E. H. Lee and P. S. Symonds), 580. Proc. Second Symposium on Naval Struct. Mechanics. Pergamon Press (1960).

155. Chan, A. S. L., "The design of Michell Optimum Structures". Rep. Coll. Aeronautics Cranfield, No. 142 (1960).

156. Johnson, W., "An analogy between upper bound solutions for plane strain metal working and minimum weight two-dimensional frames".

Int. J. Mech. Sci. 3, 239 (1961).

157. Johnson, W., "Extrusion, forging, machining, indenting, minimum weight frames and high rate sheet metal forming". *Proc. Int. Prod. Eng. Res. Conf.* 342. Pittsburg, September (1963).

158. Prager, W., in *Mathematical Optimization Techniques* (edited by R. Bellman), 279. University of California Press (1963).

159. Wasiutynski, E. and Brandt, A., "The present state of knowledge in the field of optimum design of structures". *Appl. Mech. Rev.* 16, 341 (1963).

160. Cox, H. L., *The Design of Structures of Least Weight*. Pergamon Press (1965).

161. Hemp, W. S., "Studies in the theory of Michell structures". *Proc. Eleventh Int. Congr. Appl. Mechs.* 621. Munich, 1964. Springer-Verlag (1966).

162. Chan, H. S. Y., "Half-plane slip line fields and Michell structures". *Q. J. Mech.* 34E, 486 (1967).

163. Taylor, J. E., "The strongest column: an energy approach". *Trans. ASME, J. Appl. Mech.* 34E, 486 (1967).

164. Prager, W. and Taylor, J. E., "Problems of optimal structural design". *Trans. ASME, J. Appl. Mech.* 35E, 102 (1968).

165. Prager, W., "Optimal structural design for given stiffness in stationary creep". *Zeit. ang. Math. Phys.*

166. Sheu, C. Y. and Prager, W., "Recent developments in optimal structural design". *Appl. Mech. Revs.* 21, 985 (1968).

167. Hegemier, G. A. and Prager, W., "On Michell trusses". *Int. J. Mech. Sci.* 11, 209 (1969).

168. Johnson, W. and Sowerby, R., "Upper bound techniques applied to plane strain extrusion, minimum weight two-dimensional frames and rotationally symmetric flat plates". *Bull. Mech. Engng. Educ.* 8, 269 (1969).

169. Johnson, E. W. Ph.D. Thesis, Department of Mechanical Engineering, University of British Columbia, Canada (1970).

170. Johnson, W., Chitkara, N. R., Reid, S. R. and Collins, I. F., "The displacement field and minimum weight two-dimensional frames". *Int. J. Mech. Sci.* 13, 547 (1971).

171. Hemp, W. S., *Optimum Structures*. Clarendon Press, Oxford (1973).

172. Sawczuk, A. and Mroz, Z. (Eds.), *Optimization in Structural Design*. Proc. I.U.T.A.M. Symposium, Warsaw, Poland, 1973. Springer Verlag (1975).

173. Prager, W., "Optimal layout of trusses with finite numbers of joints". *J. Mech. Phys. Solids*, 26, 241 (1978).

174. Johnson, W., "Upper bounds to the load for the transverse bending of flat rigid-perfectly plastic plates". *Int. J. Mech. Sci.* 11, 913 (1969).

175. Collins, I. F., "On an analogy between plane strain and plate bending solutions in rigid/perfect plasticity theory". *Int. J. Solids Structures*, 7, 1057 (1971).

176. Collins, I. F., "On the theory of rigid/perfectly plastic plates under uniformly distributed loads". *Acta Mech.* 18, 233 (1973).

177. Johnson, W. and Mamalis, A. G., "Force polygons to determine upper bounds and force distribution in plane strain metal forming processes". *Proc. 18th M.T.D.R. Conf.* 11. London, 1977. MacMillan Press, London (1978).

178. Johnson, W. and Mamalis, A. G., "Some force plane diagrams for plane strain slip line fields". *Int. J. Mech. Sci.* 20, 47 (1978).

179. Green, J. W. and Wallace, J. F., "Estimation of load and torque in the hot rolling process". *J. Mech. Engng. Sci.* 4, 136 (1962).

180. Green, J. W., Sparling, L. G. M. and Wallace, J. F., "Shear plane theories of hot and cold flat rolling". *J. Mech. Engng. Sci.* 6, 219 (1964).
181. Halling, J. and Mitchell, L. A., "The solution of axi-symmetric plastic deformation problems for equilibrium force diagram consideration and the application of the method to the extrusion process". *Int. J. Prod. Res.* 4, 141 (1965).
182. Sparling, L. G. M. and Willows, R. A. L., "A study of the hot rolling of thick flat slabs". *Inst. Mech. Engrs., Proc. 1970-71,* Vol. 185. 82/71.

Appendices

5. SUFFIX NOTATION AND THE SUMMATION CONVENTION

Suffix notation

In this appendix right-handed rectangular Cartesian coordinate systems
are considered and the axes denoted by Ox_1, Ox_2, Ox_3 rather than the
more usual Ox, Oy, Oz. A right-handed system is such that if the Ox_1
axis is rotated through $90°$ to the Ox_2 axis a right-handed screw fixed
to the axes would advance in the Ox_3 direction. The convention that
a lower case letter suffix takes the values 1, 2, 3 is adopted and
consequently the coordinates (x_1, x_2, x_3) of a point P may be written
concisely as x_i. Similarly, the components A_1, A_2, A_3 of a vector **A**
may be written as A_i, where i takes the values 1, 2, 3, that is the
symbol A_i represents the three components.

Suffix convention

The scalar product of two vectors **A** and **B** is given in terms of the
components of the vectors by

$$\mathbf{A.B} = A_1 B_1 + A_2 B_2 + A_3 B_3$$

$$= \sum_{i=1}^{3} A_i B_i.$$

It is convenient to use a summation convention for repeated letter
suffixes. According to this convention, if a letter suffix occurs
twice in the same term it is summed from 1 to 3. Consequently, the
scalar product of **A** and **B** is written as

$$A.B = A_i B_i,$$

that is, the summation sign is omitted. Repeated suffixes are often called dummy suffixes since any letter that does not appear elsewhere in the expression may be used, for example

$$A_i B_i = A_j B_j.$$

Other examples of the use of the summation convention are

$$C_{ii} = C_{11} + C_{22} + C_{33},$$

$$C_{ij} B_j = C_{i1} B_1 + C_{i2} B_2 + C_{i3} B_3,$$

and $\quad C_{ij} C_{ij} = C_{11} C_{11} + C_{12} C_{12} + C_{13} C_{13} + C_{21} C_{21} + C_{22} C_{22}$

$$+ C_{23} C_{23} + C_{31} C_{31} + C_{32} C_{32} + C_{33} C_{33}.$$

A suffix which appears once in a term is known as a free suffix and is understood to take in turn the values 1, 2, 3. If a free suffix appears in any term of an equation or expression it must appear in all the terms.

Unit base vectors and the Kronecker delta

If i_1, i_2 and i_3 are three unit base vectors in the directions Ox_1, Ox_2 and Ox_2, respectively, the position vector **r** of a point P with coordinates x_i is

$$\mathbf{r} = x_1 \mathbf{i}_1 + x_2 \mathbf{i}_2 + x_3 \mathbf{i}_3$$

$$= x_i \mathbf{i}_i.$$

Similarly the vector **A** may be written in terms of its components as

$$\mathbf{A} = A_i \mathbf{i}_i.$$

The scalar products of the base vectors are given by

$$\mathbf{i}_i . \mathbf{i}_j = \delta_{ij}, \tag{1}$$

where δ_{ij} is known as the Kronecker delta and

$$\delta_{ij} = 1 \text{ for } i = j,$$

and

$$\delta_{ij} = 0 \text{ for } i \neq j.$$

The Kronecker delta is sometimes known as the substitution operator since

$$A_i = \delta_{ij} A_j. \tag{2}$$

Also $\delta_{ii} = 3$.

Orthogonal transformations

Consider a right-handed rectangular Cartesian coordinate system Ox_i^* with the same origin as Ox_i. The coordinates of a point P with respect to Ox_i are x_i and with respect to Ox_i^* are x_i^*. Consequently,

$$x_i \mathbf{i}_i = x_j^* \mathbf{i}_j^*, \tag{3}$$

where $\mathbf{i}_i^*$ are the unit base vectors for the axes Ox_i^*. By forming the scalar product of each side of (3) and $\mathbf{i}_k^*$, using (1) and the substitution operator property (2) gives

$$x_k^* = a_{ki} x_i, \tag{4}$$

where

$$a_{ki} = \mathbf{i}_k^* \cdot \mathbf{i}_i = \cos(x_k^* \hat{O} x_i).$$

Similarly,

$$x_i = a_{ki} x_k^*. \tag{5}$$

The nine coefficients a_{ki} are not all independent and in general

$$a_{ki} \neq a_{ik}.$$

Since the magnitude of the position vector $\mathbf{r}$ of the point P is independent of the orientation of the coordinate system, that is, is an invariant,

$$x_i x_i = x_k^* x_k^*,$$

338

and using (4) this becomes

$$x_i x_i = a_{ki} a_{kj} x_i x_j.$$

Consequently,

$$a_{ki} a_{kj} = \delta_{ij}. \qquad (6)$$

Similarly it may be shown that

$$a_{ik} a_{jk} = \delta_{ij}. \qquad (7)$$

From (6) or (7) it follows that

$$|a_{ik}|^2 = 1, \qquad (8)$$

where $|a_{ik}|$ denotes the determinant of a_{ik}. The negative root of (8) is not considered since, for the identity transformation $x_i = x_i^*$ it follows that $a_{ik} = \delta_{ik}$ and $|\delta_{ik}| = 1$ and consequently, $|a_{ik}| = 1$ provided the transformations involve only right-handed systems. The transformations (4) and (5) subject to (6) or (7) are known as orthogonal transformations. Three scalar quantities A_i are the components of a vector if under orthogonal transformation they transform according to the rule

$$A_i^* = a_{ik} A_k,$$

and

$$A_k = a_{ik} A_i^*,$$

where the A_i are defined with respect to Ox_1 and A_k^* with respect to Ox_k^*. This may be taken as a definition of a vector. A vector is a first-order tensor. An invariant scalar, that is a single quantity that remains unchanged under coordinate transformation, is a zeroth-order tensor. An example of an invariant scalar is the scalar product A.B of two vectors A and B, since it is easy to show that

$$A_i B_i = A_k^* B_k^*.$$

Higher-order tensors

If the components A_i of a vector A are linear functions of the components B_i of a vector B then

$$A_i = C_{ik}B_k. \tag{9}$$

In order that this relationship be preserved under rotation of the coodinate system it is necessary that

$$A_p{}^* = C_{pq}{}^*B_q{}^*.$$

Consequently,

$$a_{pl}A_l = C_{pq}{}^*a_{qk}B_k,$$

and multiplying each side by a_{pi} and summing over the suffix p gives

$$a_{pi}a_{pl}A_l = C_{pq}{}^*a_{pi}a_{qk}B_k,$$

By then using (6) and (2) this becomes

$$A_i = C_{pq}{}^*a_{pi}a_{qk}B_k. \tag{10}$$

A comparison of (9) and (10) shows that

$$C_{ik} = a_{pi}a_{qk}C_{pq}{}^*. \tag{11}$$

Similarly it may be shown that

$$C_{pq}{}^* = a_{pi}a_{qk}C_{ik}. \tag{12}$$

The 9 quantities C_{ik} are the components of a second order tensor under orthogonal transformation of coordinates given by (4) and (5) if they transform according to (11) and (12). Higher order tensors may be introduced in a similar manner. For example, the 27 quantities D_{ijk} are the components of a third order tensor if under orthogonal transformation of coordinates given by (4) and (5) they transform according to

$$D^*_{lmn} = a_{li}a_{mj}a_{nk}D_{ijk}$$

and

$$D_{ijk} = a_{li}a_{mj}a_{nk}D_{lmn}.$$

It may be shown that only three independent scalar invariants can be formed from a second order tensor. The simplest independent invariants of a second order tensor are sometimes known as the moments and are given by

$$c_{ii}, \quad c_{ik}c_{kj}, \quad \text{and} \quad c_{ik}c_{kj}c_{ji},$$

where C_{ij} are the components of the tensor.

A second order tensor can be decomposed uniquely into a symmetric and an anti-symmetric part as follows:

$$C_{ij} = \tfrac{1}{2}(C_{ij} + C_{ji}) + \tfrac{1}{2}(C_{ij} - C_{ji})$$

$$= C_{ij}^{(s)} + C_{ij}^{(a)}.$$

The symmetric part $C_{ij}^{(s)}$ has in general six independent components since $C_{ij}^{(s)} = C_{ji}^{(s)}$ and the anti-symmetric part $C_{ij}^{(a)}$ three independent components since $C_{ij}^{(a)} = -C_{ji}^{(a)}$ that is $C_{11}^{(a)} = C_{22}^{(a)} = C_{33}^{(a)} = 0$ and $C_{12}^{(a)} = -C_{21}^{(a)}$, $C_{23}^{(a)} = -C_{32}^{(a)}$, $C_{31}^{(a)} = -C_{13}^{(a)}$. It is often convenient to decompose a second/order symmetric tensor into two parts, a deviatoric part and an isotropic part, thus,

$$T_{ij} = T'_{ij} + T\delta_{ij},$$

where $T = T_{kk}/3$. The deviatoric part has the property $T'_{ii} = 0$ since $\delta_{ii} = 3$ and the isotropic part $T\delta_{ij}$ has the same components in all coordinate systems. This follows since the Kronecker delta is what is known as a second order isotropic tensor, that is it has the same components in all rectangular Cartesian coordinate systems, since

$$\delta_{ij}{}^* = a_{ik}a_{j_1}\delta_{k_1}$$

$$= a_{ik}a_{jk}$$

$$= \delta_{ij}.$$

REFERENCES

1. Jeffreys, H., *Cartesian Tensors*. Cambridge University Press (1931).
2. Temple, G., *Cartesian Tensors*. Methuen (1960).
3. Stratton, J. A., *Electro-Magnetic Theory*. McGraw-Hill (1941).
4. Pearson, C. E., *Theoretical Elasticity*. Harvard University Press (1959).

6. CHARACTERISTICS OF PARTIAL DIFFERENTIAL EQUATIONS

A linear partial differential equation is linear in the dependent variables and their partial derivatives, that is the coefficients are constants or functions of the independent variables. A quasi-linear p.d.e. is linear in the highest order derivatives but the coefficients may be functions of the independent variables and the dependent variables and their derivatives up to the second highest orders occurring in the equation. For example, the second order p.d.e.,

$$A\frac{\partial^2 z}{\partial x^2} + 2B\frac{\partial^2 z}{\partial x \partial y} + C\frac{\partial^2 z}{\partial y^2} + D = 0, \tag{1}$$

is linear if A, B, C and D are constants or functions of x and/or y and quasi-linear if they are also functions of any one or more of z, $\partial z/\partial x$ and $\partial z/\partial y$.

In plane plasticity theory, systems of two simultaneous first-order linear or quasi-linear p.d.es. with two dependent and two independent variables occur. Such systems can sometimes be reduced to a single second order p.d.e. by eliminating one of the dependent variables and its derivatives* but in plane plasticity theory it is usually more convenient to consider the two first order p.d.es. even if a reduction to a single second order p.d.e. is possible.

---

*A system of n first order p.d.es. with n dependent and p independent variables can be reduced to a single p.d.e. with one dependent variable if it is possible to eliminate $n - 1$ dependent variables and their first derivatives. If each equation is differentiated once with respect to each of the p independent variables, np new equations and in general $(1/2)p(p + 1)(n- 1)$ new unknowns, which are the second derivatives of the $(n - 1)$ variables to be eliminated are created. When $(1/2)p(p +1)(n - 1) > np$, the increase in the number of functions to be eliminated is greater than the number of new equations created. In general it is not possible to reduce a system of two first order p.d.es. with two dependent and two independent variables to a single second order p.d.e.

The concept of characterisitics is now introduced by considering equation (1) which may be linear or quasi-linear. Suppose z, $\partial z/\partial x$ and $\partial z/\partial y$ are prescribed† at all points on a curve C defined by $x = x(s)$ and $y = y(s)$ and it is desired to extend the solution to the neighbourhood of C by using a Taylor series approach. To do this the second derivatives $\partial^2 z/\partial x^2$, $\partial^2 z/\partial y \, \partial x$ and $\partial^2 z/\partial y^2$ must be determined at all points on C from equation (1) and

$$\frac{d}{ds}\left(\frac{\partial z}{\partial x}\right) = \frac{\partial^2 z}{\partial x^2}\frac{dx}{ds} + \frac{\partial^2 z}{\partial x \, \partial y}\frac{dy}{ds} \tag{2}$$

and

$$\frac{d}{ds}\left(\frac{\partial z}{\partial y}\right) = \frac{\partial^2 z}{\partial x \, \partial y}\frac{dx}{ds} + \frac{\partial^2 z}{\partial y^2}\frac{dy}{ds}. \tag{3}$$

This is possible unless,

$$\begin{vmatrix} A & 2B & C \\[2mm] \dfrac{dx}{ds} & \dfrac{dy}{ds} & 0 \\[2mm] 0 & \dfrac{dx}{ds} & \dfrac{dy}{ds} \end{vmatrix} = 0,$$

that is, unless

$$A\left(\frac{dy}{dx}\right)^2 - 2B\frac{dy}{dx} + C = 0. \tag{4}$$

A curve in the (x,y) plane such that equation (4) holds for all points on the curve is called a characteristic curve and when z, $\partial z/\partial x$ and $\partial z/\partial y$ are prescribed on the curve, the second derivatives of z are indeterminate on it.

If $B^2 - AC > 0$, the roots λ_1 and λ_2 of equation (4) are real and there are two characteristic curves passing through every point in the (x,y) plane. The characteristic curves are given by the solutions of the ordinary differential equations, $dy/dx - \lambda_1(x,y) = 0$ and $dy/dx + \lambda_2(x,y) = 0$. Equation (1) is then classified as hyperbolic. An example is the wave equation,

$$\frac{\partial^2 z}{\partial x^2} - \frac{\partial^2 z}{\partial y^2} = 0.$$

If $B^2 - AC = 0$, there is one characteristic curve passing through every point in the (x,y) plane. Equation (1) is then classified as parabolic.

---

†The prescribed values on the curve must satisfy the relationship

$$\frac{dz}{ds} = \frac{\partial z}{\partial x}\frac{dx}{ds} + \frac{\partial z}{\partial y}\frac{dy}{ds}.$$

An example is the heat-flow equation,

$$\frac{\partial^2 z}{\partial x^2} = \frac{\partial z}{\partial y} \; .$$

If $B^2 - AC < 0$, there are no real characteristic curves and equation (1) is classified as elliptic. An example is Laplace's equation,

$$\frac{\partial^2 z}{\partial x^2} + \frac{\partial^2 z}{\partial y^2} = 0 .$$

If the equation is quasi-linear, the particular solution considered may determine the class of the equation. For example the p.d.e.

$$\frac{\partial^2 z}{\partial x^2} + z\frac{\partial^2 z}{\partial y^2} = 0 ,$$

is elliptic in any domain in which z is positive and hyperbolic in any domain in which the solution is negative.

If equation (4) is satisfied at all points on a curve this does not mean that in general the second derivatives of z are infinite. For a solution to be possible the following three equations, which are equivalent if equation (4) holds, must be satisfied on the curve.

$$\begin{vmatrix} A & 2B & D \\[2mm] \dfrac{dx}{ds} & \dfrac{dy}{ds} & \dfrac{d}{ds}\left(\dfrac{\partial z}{\partial x}\right) \\[3mm] 0 & \dfrac{dx}{ds} & \dfrac{d}{ds}\left(\dfrac{\partial z}{\partial y}\right) \end{vmatrix} = 0 , \tag{5a}$$

$$\begin{vmatrix} A & D & C \\[2mm] \dfrac{dx}{ds} & \dfrac{d}{ds}\left(\dfrac{\partial z}{\partial x}\right) & 0 \\[3mm] 0 & \dfrac{d}{ds}\left(\dfrac{\partial z}{\partial y}\right) & \dfrac{dy}{ds} \end{vmatrix} = 0 , \tag{5b}$$

and

$$\begin{vmatrix} D & 2B & C \\[2mm] \dfrac{d}{ds}\left(\dfrac{\partial z}{\partial x}\right) & \dfrac{dy}{ds} & 0 \\[3mm] \dfrac{d}{ds}\left(\dfrac{\partial z}{\partial y}\right) & \dfrac{dx}{ds} & \dfrac{dy}{ds} \end{vmatrix} = 0 . \tag{5c}$$

In plasticity theory the most important class of p.d.e. is the hyperbolic. For any problem involving a hyperbolic p.d.e. such as equation (1) with suitable boundary and initial conditions, the determination of the field of characteristics constitutes a solution to the problem since the variation in z along a characteristic can be found from any one of equations (5). If the equation is linear, that is if A, B, C and D are functions of x and y only, the field of characteristic curves can be found directly without determining z but if the equation is quasi-linear, which is more usual in applications, the determination of the characteristic curves and z must proceed simultaneously.

Discontinuities of the second derivatives of z are possible across characteristic curves but not across any other curves. The value of z cannot be prescribed arbitrarily on a curve which cuts any characteristic more than once. It follows, that in general no solution exists for a hyperbolic p.d.e. such as equation (1) in the interior of a closed curve in the (x,y) plane if z is prescribed at all points on the curve. For example, the Dirichlet problem for the equation

$$\frac{\partial^2 z}{\partial x^2} - \frac{\partial^2 z}{\partial y^2} = 0,$$

is in general without solution.

The terms elliptic, hyperbolic and parabolic arise because of the analogy with the quadratic form,

$$ax^2 + 2bxy + cy^2 + dx + gy + f = 0. \tag{6}$$

Equation (6) is the equation of an ellipse if, $(b^2 - ac) < 0$, a hyperbola if $(b^2 - ac) > 0$ and a parabola if $(b^2 - ac) = 0$.

Two simultaneous linear or quasi-linear first-order p.d.es.

$$P\frac{\partial u}{\partial x} + Q\frac{\partial u}{\partial y} + R\frac{\partial v}{\partial x} + S\frac{\partial v}{\partial y} = T \tag{7}$$

and

$$P'\frac{\partial u}{\partial x} + Q'\frac{\partial u}{\partial y} + R'\frac{\partial v}{\partial x} + S'\frac{\partial v}{\partial y} = T'; \tag{8}$$

are now considered. Suppose u and v are prescribed on a curve C defined by $x = x(s)$ and $y = y(s)$ and it is desired to extend the solution to the neighbourhood of C. This can be done if $\partial u/\partial x$, $\partial u/\partial y$, $\partial v/\partial x$ and $\partial v/\partial y$ can be determined from equations (7) and (8) and

$$\frac{du}{ds} = \frac{\partial u}{\partial x}\frac{dx}{ds} + \frac{\partial u}{\partial y}\frac{dy}{ds} \tag{9}$$

and

$$\frac{dv}{ds} = \frac{\partial v}{\partial x}\frac{dx}{ds} + \frac{\partial v}{\partial y}\frac{dy}{ds}. \tag{10}$$

The partial derivatives are determinate unless

$$\begin{vmatrix} \dfrac{dx}{ds} & \dfrac{dy}{ds} & 0 & 0 \\[2mm] 0 & 0 & \dfrac{dx}{ds} & \dfrac{dy}{ds} \\[2mm] P & Q & R & S \\[1mm] P' & Q' & R' & S' \end{vmatrix} = 0 \qquad (11)$$

and

$$\begin{vmatrix} dx & dy & 0 & dv \\[1mm] 0 & 0 & dx & dv \\[1mm] P & Q & R & T \\[1mm] P' & Q' & R' & T' \end{vmatrix} = 0. \qquad (12)$$

There are three other equations which are equivalent to equation (12). Equation (11) is of the form

$$A(dx)^2 - 2B\,dx\,dy + C(dy)^2 = 0, \qquad (13)$$

which is a quadratic in dy/dx and is identical to equation (4). If A, B and C are single valued, equation (13) will give two values for dy/dx. If $(B^2 - AC) > 0$ these values will be real, i.e. there are two real curves through each point along which the partial derivatives are not determinate. These curves are the characteristics.

If $(B^2 - AC) = 0$, there is one real value of dy/dx and there is one characteristic through each point. If $(B^2 - AC) < 0$ there are no real characteristics.

Equations (7) and (8) are known as hyperbolic if $(B^2 - AC) > 0$, parabolic if $(B^2 - AC) = 0$ and elliptic if $(B^2 - AC) < 0$.

Equation (12) gives the variation of u or v along the characteristics.

7.   CENTRED-FAN FIELDS: NODAL POINTS

Boundary values: coordinates of points on the circular arc of a
centred-fan field

M	N	X	Y	M	N	X	Y
		Radius 0.0				*Radius* 0.4	
	3				3	-0.01363	0.10353
	6				6	-0.05359	0.20000
	9				9	-0.11716	0.28284
	12				12	-0.20000	0.34641
	15				15	-0.29647	0.38637
	18				18	-0.40000	0.40000
		Radius 0.1				*Radius* 0.5	
	3	-0.00341	0.02588		3	-0.01704	0.12941
	6	-0.01340	0.05000		6	-0.06699	0.25000
	9	-0.02929	0.07071		9	-0.14645	0.35355
	12	-0.05000	0.08660		12	-0.25000	0.43301
	15	-0.07412	0.09659		15	-0.37059	0.48296
	18	-0.10000	0.10000		18	-0.50000	0.50000
		Radius 0.2				*Radius* 0.6	
	3	-0.00681	0.05176		3	-0.02044	0.15529
	6	-0.02679	0.10000		6	-0.08038	0.30000
	9	-0.05858	0.14142		9	-0.17574	0.42426
	12	-0.10000	0.17321		12	-0.30000	0.51962
	15	-0.14824	0.19319		15	-0.44471	0.57956
	18	-0.20000	0.20000		18	-0.60000	0.60000
		Radius 0.3				*Radius* 0.7	
	3	-0.01022	0.07765		3	-0.02385	0.18117
	6	-0.04019	0.15000		6	-0.09378	0.35000
	9	-0.08787	0.21213		9	-0.20503	0.49497
	12	-0.15000	0.25981		12	-0.35000	0.60622
	15	-0.22235	0.28978		15	-0.51883	0.67615
	18	-0.30000	0.30000		18	-0.70000	0.70000

M	N	X	Y		M	N	X	Y
		Radius 0.8					*Radius* 0.9	
	3	-0.02726	0.20706			3	-0.03067	0.23294
	6	-0.10718	0.40000			6	-0.12058	0.45000
	9	-0.23431	0.56569			9	-0.26360	0.63640
	12	-0.40000	0.69282;			12	-0.45000	0.77942
	15	-0.59294	0.77274			15	-0.66706	0.86933
	18	-0.80000	0.80000			18	-0.90000	0.90000
		Radius 1.0					*Radius* 1.0	
	3	-0.03407	0.25882		3		0.25882	-0.03407
	6	-0.13397	0.50000		6		0.50000	-0.03397
	9	-0.29289	0.70711		9		0.70711	-0.29289
	12	-0.50000	0.86603		12		0.86603	-0.50000
	15	-0.74118	0.96593		15		0.96593	-0.74118
	18	-1.00000	1.00000		18		1.00000	-1.00000

Extension of centred-fan field: nodal points for an equiangular 5-degree net

ratio r/p = 0.0

M	N	X	Y		M	N	X	Y
3	3	0.26784	0.03486		12	3	1.09762	-0.32118
3	6	0.25840	0.10616		12	6	1.30001	-0.05585
3	9	0.22989	0.17485		12	9	1.44391	0.29426
3	12	0.18304	0.23581		12	12	1.49857	0.71815
3	15	0.11998	0.28412		12	15	1.43462	1.19449
3	18	0.04414	0.31547		12	18	1.22733	1.69143
6	3	0.55392	-0.00323		15	3	1.30906	-0.59754
6	6	0.57344	0.14675		15	6	1.65535	-0.32989
6	9	0.55213	0.30684		15	9	1.96496	0.07642
6	12	0.48600	0.46586		15	12	2.18985	0.62432
6	15	0.37413	0.61123		15	15	2.27685	1.30138
6	18	0.21917	0.72980		15	18	2.17237	2.07708
9	3	0.83807	-0.12142		18	3	1.44983	-0.93874
9	6	0.92881	0.09901		18	6	1.95773	-0.72589
9	9	0.96252	0.35933		18	9	2.48034	-0.32160
9	12	0.92431	0.64505		18	12	2.95625	0.30346
9	15	0.80289	0.93652		18	15	3.30788	1.16106
9	18	0.59231	1.20986		18	18	3.44593	2.23841

ratio r/p = 0.1

M	N	X	Y		M	N	X	Y
3	3	0.27133	0.06164		12	3	1.12120	-0.30287
3	6	0.25808	0.16155		12	6	1.34660	-0.00725
3	9	0.21775	0.25865		12	9	1.50841	0.38669
3	12	0.15092	0.34557		12	12	1.57039	0.86801
3	15	0.06023	0.41503		12	15	1.49705	1.41347
3	18	-0.04974	0.46046		12	18	1.25767	1.98705

6	3	0.56454	0.02261	15	3	1.33747	-0.58555
6	6	0.58812	0.20409	15	6	1.71647	-0.29248
6	9	0.56203	0.39972	15	9	2.05862	0.15671
6	12	0.48041	0.59586	15	12	2.30930	0.76778
6	15	0.34114	0.77676	15	15	2.40699	1.52907
6	18	0.14658	0.92557	15	18	2.28848	2.40787
9	3	0.85555	-0.09843	18	3	1.48138	-0.93433
9	6	0.95949	0.15422	18	6	2.03071	-0.70397
9	9	0.99845	0.45559	18	9	2.60133	-0.26237
9	12	0.95373	0.78944	18	12	3.12539	0.42620
9	15	0.81054	1.13302	18	15	3.51558	1.37830
9	18	0.56015	1.45789	18	18	3.66977	2.58300

ratio r/p = 0.2

M	N	X	Y	M	N	X	Y
3	3	0.27481	0.08843	12	3	1.14478	-0.28457
3	6	0.25775	0.21694	12	6	1.39319	0.04135
3	9	0.20560	0.34246	12	9	1.57292	0.47912
3	12	0.11881	0.45533	12	12	1.64220	1.01787
3	15	0.00047	0.54593	12	15	1.55948	1.63246
3	18	-0.14361	0.60544	12	18	1.28802	2.28268
6	3	0.57515	0.04845	15	3	1.36589	-0.57355
6	6	0.60279	0.26144	15	6	1.77760	-0.25506
6	9	0.57193	0.49260	15	9	2.15227	0.23700
6	12	0.47483	0.72586	15	12	2.42875	0.91125
6	15	0.30815	0.94230	15	15	2.53713	1.75675
6	18	0.07399	1.12135	15	18	2.40459	2.73866
9	3	0.87304	-0.07544	18	3	1.51239	-0.92991
9	6	0.99018	0.20944	18	6	2.10369	-0.68205
9	9	1.03439	0.55184	18	9	2.72231	-0.20314
9	12	0.98316	0.93383	18	12	3.29454	0.54893
9	15	0.81818	1.32952	18	15	3.72329	1.59553
9	18	0.52799	1.70593	18	18	3.89361	2.92759

ratio r/p = 0.3

M	N	X	Y	M	N	X	Y
3	3	0.27830	0.11521	12	3	1.16836	-0.26627
3	6	0.25743	0.27233	12	6	1.43977	0.08995
3	9	0.19346	0.42627	12	9	1.63742	0.57155
3	12	0.08669	0.56509	12	12	1.71402	1.16773
3	15	-0.05928	0.67684	12	15	1.62191	1.85144
3	18	-0.23748	0.75042	12	18	1.31837	2.57830
6	3	0.58577	0.07429	15	3	1.39430	-0.46673
6	6	0.61747	0.31878	15	6	1.83872	-0.21765
6	9	0.58183	0.58548	15	9	2.24592	0.31729
6	12	0.46924	0.85586	15	12	2.54820	1.05471
6	15	0.27517	1.10783	15	15	2.66727	1.98444
6	18	0.00140	1.31712	15	18	2.52069	3.06945

9	3	0.89052	-0.05245	18	3	1.54447	-0.92550
9	6	1.02086	0.26465	18	6	2.17667	-0.66014
9	9	1.07032	0.64809	18	9	2.84330	-0.14391
9	12	1.01259	1.07822	18	12	3.46368	0.67166
9	15	0.82582	1.52601	18	15	3.93110	1.81277
9	18	0.49583	1.95396	18	18	4.11745	3.27219

ratio r/p = 0.4

M	N	X	Y	M	N	X	Y
3	3	0.28178	0.14199	12	3	1.19195	-0.24796
3	6	0.25711	0.32773	12	6	1.48636	0.13855
3	9	0.18132	0.51007	12	9	1.70193	0.66398
3	12	0.05457	0.67485	12	12	1.78583	1.31758
3	15	-0.11904	0.80775	12	15	1.68434	2.07043
3	18	-0.33136	0.89540	12	18	1.34871	2.87393
6	3	0.59638	0.10013	15	3	1.42271	-0.54955
6	6	0.63214	0.37613	15	6	1.89984	-0.18024
6	9	0.59173	0.67836	15	9	2.33957	0.39758
6	12	0.46366	0.98587	15	12	2.66764	1.19817
6	15	0.24218	1.27337	15	15	2.79741	2.21212
6	18	-0.07119	1.51290	15	18	2.63680	3.40023
9	3	0.90801	-0.02946	18	3	1.57602	-0.92109
9	6	1.05154	0.31986	18	6	2.24966	-0.63822
9	9	1.10625	0.74434	18	9	2.96428	-0.08468
9	12	1.04201	1.22261	18	12	3.63282	0.79439
9	15	0.83346	1.72251	18	15	4.13871	2.03001
9	18	0.46367	2.20200	18	18	4.34129	3.61678

ratio r/p = 0.5

M	N	X	Y	M	N	X	Y
3	3	0.28527	0.16878	12	3	1.21553	-0.22966
3	6	0.25678	0.38312	12	6	1.53294	0.18715
3	9	0.16918	0.59388	12	9	1.76643	0.75641
3	12	0.02245	0.78462	12	12	1.85765	1.46744
3	15	-0.17879	0.93865	12	15	1.74678	2.28941
3	18	-0.42523	1.04039	12	18	1.37906	3.16955
6	3	0.60700	0.12597	15	3	1.45112	-0.53755
6	6	0.64682	0.43347	15	6	1.96096	-0.14282
6	9	0.60163	0.77124	15	9	2.43323	0.47787
6	12	0.45807	1.11587	15	12	2.78709	1.34163
6	15	0.20919	1.43890	15	15	2.92755	2.43981
6	18	-0.14378	1.70867	15	18	2.75290	3.73102
9	3	0.92549	-0.00647	18	3	1.60757	-0.91667
9	6	1.08223	0.37508	18	6	2.32264	-0.61630
9	9	1.14219	0.84059	18	9	3.08527	-0.02545
9	12	1.07144	1.36700	18	12	3.80197	0.91713
9	15	0.84111	1.91901	18	15	4.34642	2.24724
9	18	0.43151	2.45003	18	18	4.56513	3.96137

ratio r/p = 0.6

M	N	X	Y	M	N	X	Y
3	3	0.28876	0.19556	12	3	1.23911	-0.21135
3	6	0.25646	0.43851	12	6	1.57953	0.23575
3	9	0.15704	0.67769	12	9	1.83094	0.84885
3	12	⁻0.00967	0.89438	12	12	1.92946	1.61730
3	15	⁻0.23855	1.06956	12	15	1.80921	2.50840
3	18	-0.51911	1.18537	12	18	1.40941	3.46518
6	3	0.61762	0.15181	15	3	1.47953	-0.52556
6	6	0.66149	0.49081	15	6	2.02209	-0.10541
6	9	0.61154	0.86413	15	9	2.52688	0.55816
6	12	0.45249	1.24587	15	12	2.90654	1.48509
6	15	0.17620	1.60444	15	15	3.05768	2.66749
6	18	⁻0.21637	1.90444	15	18	2.86901	4.06181
9	3	0.94297	0.01652	18	3	1.63911	-0.91226
9	6	1.11291	0.43029	18	6	2.39562	-0.59439
9	9	1.17812	0.93685	18	9	3.20626	0.03378
9	12	1.10086	1.51140	18	12	3.97111	1.03986
9	15	0.84875	2.11550	18	15	4.55413	2.46448
9	18	0.39935	2.69806	18	18	4.78898	4.30597

ratio r/p = 0.7

M	N	X	Y	M	N	X	Y
3	3	0.29224	0.22235	12	3	1.26269	-0.19305
3	6	0.25614	0.49390	12	6	1.62612	0.28435
3	9	0.14490	0.76149	12	9	1.89544	0.94128
3	12	-0.04178	1.00414	12	12	2.00128	1.76715
3	15	-0.29830	1.20046	12	15	1.87164	2.72738
3	18	-0.61298	1.33035	12	18	1.43975	3.76080
6	3	0.62823	0.17765	15	3	1.50795	-0.51356
6	6	0.67617	0.54816	15	6	2.08321	-0.06800
6	9	0.62144	0.95701	15	9	2.62053	0.63845
6	12	0.44690	1.37587	15	12	3.02599	1.62855
6	15	0.14321	1.76997	15	15	3.18782	2.89518
6	18	-0.28895	2.10022	15	18	2.98511	4.39260
9	3	0.96046	0.03950	18	3	1.67066	-0.90784
9	6	1.14360	0.48550	18	6	2.46860	-0.57247
9	9	1.21405	1.03310	18	9	3.32724	0.09302
9	12	1.13029	1.65579	18	12	4.14025	1.16259
9	15	0.85639	2.31200	18	15	4.76183	2.68172
9	18	0.36719	2.94610	18	18	5.01282	4.65056

ratio r/p = 0.8

M	N	X	Y	M	N	X	Y
3	3	0.29573	0.24913	12	3	1.28627	-0.17475
3	6	0.25581	0.54929	12	6	1.67270	0.33295
3	9	0.13275	0.84530	12	9	1.95995	1.03371
3	12	-0.07390	1.11390	12	12	2.07309	1.91701

M	N	X	Y	M	N	X	Y
3	15	-0.35806	1.33137	12	15	1.93407	2.94637
3	18	-0.70685	1.47534	12	18	1.47010	4.05643
6	3	0.63885	0.20349	15	3	1.53636	-0.50156
6	6	0.69084	0.60550	15	6	2.14433	-0.03058
6	9	0.63134	1.04989	15	9	2.71418	0.71874
6	12	0.44132	1.50587	15	12	3.14544	1.77202
6	15	0.11022	1.93551	15	15	3.31796	3.12287
6	18	-0.36154	2.29599	15	18	3.10122	4.72338
9	3	0.97794	0.06249	18	3	1.70221	-0.90343
9	6	1.17428	0.54071	18	6	2.54158	-0.55055
9	9	1.24999	1.12935	18	9	3.44823	0.15225
9	12	1.15972	1.80018	18	12	4.30939	1.28533
9	15	0.86403	2.50850	18	15	4.96954	2.89896
9	18	0.33503	3.19413	18	18	5.23666	4.99515

ratio r/p = 0.9

M	N	X	Y	M	N	X	Y
3	3	0.29921	0.27591	12	3	1.30985	-0.15644
3	6	0.25549	0.60469	12	6	1.71929	0.38155
3	9	0.12061	0.92911	12	9	2.02445	1.12614
3	12	-0.10602	1.22367	12	12	2.14491	2.06687
3	15	-0.41781	1.46228	12	15	1.99651	3.16535
3	18	-0.80073	1.62032	12	18	1.50044	4.35205
6	3	0.64946	0.22933	15	3	1.56477	-0.48956
6	6	0.70552	0.66285	15	6	2.20545	0.00683
6	9	0.64124	1.14277	15	9	2.80784	0.79903
6	12	0.43573	1.63587	15	12	3.26489	1.91548
6	15	0.07723	2.10104	15	15	3.44810	3.35055
6	18	-0.43413	2.49176	15	18	3.21733	5.05417
9	3	0.99543	0.08548	18	3	1.73376	-0.89902
9	6	1.20496	0.59593	18	6	2.61456	-0.52864
9	9	1.28592	1.22560	18	9	3.56921	0.21148
9	12	1.18914	1.94457	18	12	4.47854	1.40806
9	15	0.87168	2.70499	18	15	5.17725	3.11619
9	18	0.30287	3.44217	18	18	5.46050	5.33975

ratio r/p = 2.0

M	N	X	Y	M	N	X	Y
3	3	0.30270	0.30270	12	3	1.33343	-0.13814
3	6	0.25517	0.66008	12	6	1.76587	0.43015
3	9	0.10847	1.01291	12	9	2.08896	1.21857
3	12	-0.13814	1.33343	12	12	2.21672	2.21672
3	15	-0.47757	1.59318	12	15	2.05894	3.38434
3	18	-0.89460	1.76530	12	18	1.53079	4.64768
6	3	0.66008	0.25517	15	3	1.59318	-0.47757
6	6	0.72019	0.72019	15	6	2.26658	-0.04424
6	9	0.65114	1.23565	15	9	2.90149	0.87932
6	12	0.43015	1.76587	15	12	3.38434	2.05894
6	15	0.04424	2.26658	15	15	3.57824	3.57824
6	18	-0.50672	2.68754	15	18	3.33343	5.38496

9	3	1.01291	0.10847	18	3	1.76530	-0.89460
9	6	1.23565	0.65114	18	6	2.68754	-0.50672
9	9	1.32185	1.32185	18	9	3.69020	0.27071
9	12	1.21857	2.08896	18	12	4.64768	1.53079
9	15	0.87932	2.90149	18	15	5.38496	3.33343
9	18	0.27071	3.69020	18	18	5.68434	5.68434

Additional References

Arcisz, M. (1969) "Cutting of a bimetallic strip by smooth rigid punches", *J. Mech. Phys. Solids*, 17, 437.

Bai, Y. and Dodd, B. (1982) "A slip-line field solution for plane strain indentation by an obtuse angle wedge", *Int. J. Mech. Sci.*, 24, (in press).

Bai, Y., Johnson, W. and Dodd, B. (1982) "On tangential velocity discontinuities being coincident with stress discontinuities", *Int. J. Mech. Sci.*, 24, (in press).

Bhasin, Y. P., Oxley, P. L. B. and Roth, R. N. (1980) "An experimentally determined slip-line field for plane strain wedge indentation of a strain-hardening material", *J. Mech. Phys. Solids*, 28, 149.

Collins, I. F. (1981) "Boundary value problems in plane strain plasticity". In *Mechanics of Solids: The Rodney Hill 60th Anniversary Volume* (Ed. H. G. Hopkins and M. J. Sewell), Pergamon Press.

Laue, K. and Stenger, H. (1981) *Extrusion*. pp. 457. ASME.

Johnson, W. (1980) "A short review of metal forming mechanics", *Proc. 3rd Int. Conf. Mechanical Behaviour of Materials*, Vol. 1, p. 167.

Oxley, P. L. B. (1980) "Metallic friction under near-seizure conditions", *Wear*, 65, 227.

Sahay, C. and Dubey, R. N. (1980) "Indentation as a basis for metal cutting", *Mech. Res. Comm.* 7, 377.

Saxena, S. K., Chitkara, N. R. and Johnson, W. (to be published) "Plastic yielding of deeply notched blocks when indented by wedge-shaped rigid punches with parallel sides".

Wang, Z. R. and Ku, C. L. (1981) "A new method to prove the rule of change of normal stress along a slip-line", *Int. J. Mech. Engg. Educ.* 9, 251.

Zienkiewicz, O. C. and Godball, P. N. (1974) "Flow of plastic and visco-plastic solids with special reference to extrusion and forming processes", *Int. J. Numerical Methods in Eng.* 8, 3.

Author Index

Subject Index

SUBJECT INDEX

Wax 5
Weak solutions 41
Work hardening 25

Yield criterion: von Mises 24,
      29
  Tresca 29